PARIS DREAMS, PARIS MEMORIES

THE CITY AND ITS MYSTIQUE

Charles Rearick

Stanford University Press
Stanford, California

Stanford University Press
Stanford, California

©2011 by the Board of Trustees of the Leland Stanford Junior
University. All rights reserved.

Printed in the United States of America on acid-free,
archival-quality paper

Library of Congress Cataloging-in-Publication Data

Rearick, Charles, 1942-
Paris dreams, Paris memories : the city and its mystique / Charles
Rearick.
p. cm.
Includes bibliographical references and index.
ISBN 978-0-8047-7092-7 (cloth : alk. paper) —
ISBN 978-0-8047-7093-4 (pbk. : alk. paper)
1. Collective memory—France—Paris. 2. Paris (France)—Public
opinion. 3. Paris (France)—History—19th century. 4. Paris (France)—
History—20th century. I. Title.
DC723.R43 2011
944'.36108—dc22
2010024490

Typeset by Bruce Lundquist in 10/15 Sabon

To Anne, Deborah, Andrew, and
(grandson) Isaiah Charles Aminzadeh

This city was built at the meeting point of three elements in a place where they mingled with one another. It was constructed on the clay of memories, on the sands of dreams and on the groundwaters of oblivion, cold and black, whose flow never ceases for a moment, washing away the foundations day after day.

—MAGDALENA TULLI,
Dreams and Stones, trans. Bill Johnston
(St. Paul, Minn.: Archipelago Books, 2004)

La ville est autre chose qu'un simple objet géographique: elle est le produit d'une histoire, le produit aussi de nos représentations et de notre imagination. . . . [The city is something other than a simple geographical object; it is the product of a history, the product also of our representations and our imagination. . . .]

—MARCEL RONCAYOLO,
Lectures de Villes, formes et temps (Marseille: Éditions Parenthèses, 2002)

On vient à Paris chercher la beauté, l'intelligence, l'objet bien fait, la joie, le plaisir et les illusions. [People come to Paris seeking beauty, intellect, beautifully made things, joy, pleasure, and illusions.]

—ELSA TRIOLET
Pour que Paris soit (Paris: Éditions Cercle d'Art, 1956)

Contents

List of Illustrations   xi

Acknowledgments   xiii

Introduction   1

1. Paris—Praised, Modernized, Remembered, Staged, and Loved:
Nineteenth-Century Foundations   6

2. The Memory of a Certain Belle Époque (1914–circa 1960):
Or How the Turn-of-the-Century Lived on Beyond Its Time   44

3. Postwar Modernizing and the Resistance of Memory
(1945–circa 1980)   82

4. New Varieties of a "Nouveau Paris" (1974– . . .)   119

5. Paris in Comparison   158

6. Contemporary Paris—Images, Spirit, Soul, and Sites   186

Conclusion: To Know Paris   222

Appendix 1. Unusual and Unexpected Paris—A Sampler   229

Appendix 2. Landmark Paris Imagery   230

Appendix 3. Modern Paris Timeline   232

Notes   235

Selected Bibliography   269

Index   273

Illustrations

Map 1. Paris and its *arrondissements* (districts)   xvi

Map 2. Paris suburbs (selected communes)   xvii

Figure 1.1. The "old Paris" that the Prefect Haussmann gutted: "The Rue des Trois-Canettes" (circa 1865).   11

Figure 1.2. Destroying the old Paris (circa 1877).   12

Figure 1.3. The Avenue de l'Opéra (circa 1890).   15

Figure 1.4. The Grands Boulevards (circa 1880).   23

Figure 1.5. Old Paris—untouched by Second Empire renovations (circa 1900).   24

Figure 1.6. On the edges of the vaunted "beau Paris" (circa 1900).   33

Figure 1.7. Representations of Parisian workingwomen (1896).   36

Figure 1.8. The burned-out shell of the Hôtel de Ville (1871).   42

Figure 2.1. The memory of the Belle Époque lives on.   45

Figure 2.2. The capital suffered scattered damage in the First World War.   46

Figure 2.3. Ecstatic throngs filled the Grands Boulevards to celebrate the end of the "Great War."   47

Figure 2.4. The unscathed conquerors in the most chic cafés on the Champs-Élysées.   72

Figure 2.5. Jewish prisoners interned in the 1930s housing project of Drancy (1942).   73

Figure 3.1. Paris's international business district, La Défense.   89

Figure 3.2. The Tour Albert. Paris's first "skyscraper" apartment building.   91

Figure 3.3. The thirteenth arrondissement—before modernization (circa 1900). 95

Figure 3.4. Gentrification in the de-industrialized, massively redeveloped thirteenth arrondissement. 96

Figure 3.5. Profiles of 1970s modernity: the Olympiades. 97

Figure 4.1. Cyclists, strollers, and rollers enjoy the *Rive droite* expressway Sundays and holidays. 124

Figure 4.2. Paris-Plage. 127

Figure 4.3. The annual Fête des Vendanges de Montmartre. 130

Figure 4.4. A semblance of convivial community lives on—in the Jardin Villemin along the Canal Saint-Martin. 135

Figure 4.5. Street demonstrations, a fundamental part of the capital's political life. 452

Figure 4.6. Traces of embattled memory: the basilica Sacré-Coeur vs. the Paris Commune. 155

Figure 5.1. Traffic-choked streets—even before the automobile era. 169

Figure 5.2. Away from the celebrated "beau Paris," disparate beautiless buildings abound. 175

Figure 5.3. The Square du Vert Galant—surrounded by archetypical elements of Parisian beauty. 177

Figure 5.4. *The* most prestigious classic vista of the City of Light: the Champs-Élysées (circa 1900). 179

Figure 5.5. The Parc de Belleville. 181

Figure 6.1. Commemorative plaques on Paris elementary schools recall the more than 11,000 Parisian children deported to death camps. 192

Figure 6.2. The oldest chocolate candy shop (*confiserie chocolatier*) in Paris—À la Mère de Famille. 194

Figure 6.3. A now-rare "village" of small villas in the shadow of high-rise apartment buildings. 205

Figure 6.4. Soulful places in the contemporary city include some formerly industrial sites, such as the Canal Saint-Martin. 209

Acknowledgments

In the course of my work on this book, I have had the good fortune of finding many helpful people on both sides of the Atlantic—more than I can name here. At the University of Massachusetts and nearby, colleagues and friends lent support in many forms. I am especially grateful to those who read chapters of the manuscript and offered suggestions: Brian Bunk, Daniel Gordon, Lisa Lieberman, Dorothy McFarland, Wilhelmina Van Ness, Laura Ricard, and (at Boston University) Kyri Claflin. I have benefited from conversations about Paris with Brett Berliner and Ronald Story over the years, and more recently from quizzing Anna Taylor on the medieval background of my subject. My work on a special Paris issue of *French Historical Studies* brought me into stimulating discussions with Rosemary Wakeman (co-editor) and the journal's editors, Ted and Joby Margadant, as well as contributors Dominique Kalifa and David Jordan.

Parisian friends have helped me more than they know. Responding to my observations and questions, speaking from their different perspectives, they have enriched my understanding of Paris immeasurably during my yearly sojourns. For that and, above all, for the gift of their friendship, I thank Jacques and Nicole Theureau, Maïté Aubois, Rémi and Noëlline Coudouel, Serge Quenisset (who introduced me to La Courneuve), Bernard Turpin, Pierre-Jacques Derainne, Jacques Borgé, Jean-Claude Klein, Jean-Dominique Goffette, Marc Defradas, and Évelyne Cohen. Professor Cohen graciously hosted me when I was an "enseignant invité" at the University of Paris VII in the spring of 2005.

To the archivists and librarians who facilitated my research in Paris year after year, I owe a huge debt of gratitude. I cannot possibly list them all, but I will happily thank by name a few who were memorably helpful: Alfred Fierro, Odile Sanson, Geneviève Madore, Yves Chagniot, and Jean-Paul Avice at the Bibliothèque historique de la Ville de Paris; Raphaël Gérard, Conservateur of the Musée Montmartre; Brigitte Lainé and Isabelle Gallois at the Archives de Paris; and Françoise Gicquel at the Paris Police archives.

In Paris, while reading everything I could about Parisian life past and present, I also learned much from walking, often hours on end, in every part of the city. Those long explorations were especially enjoyable when a friend or family member was with me, sharing observations and talking over the changes we noticed (always changes) in the city. Allan Potofsky accompanied me on many a walk in quarters from Belleville to Bagnolet and out in Saint-Denis as well. Jean-Dominique Goffette (an expert on the Grands Boulevards), Scott Haine, Ronald Story, and Bernard Turpin also strolled through large stretches of the city with me. Out in the long-unfashionable thirteenth arrondissement, I was lucky enough to meet a couple of particularly well-informed residents—Jean-Claude Klein and Gérard Conte (an enthusiast of local history and published historian of the arrondissement)—who expertly guided me around and recounted their historical knowledge and memories of the district. An older resident of the thirteenth, Edemon Berthier, also cordially received me and told of his experiences from living and working there over more than half a century.

My longtime friend Bernard Turpin has discussed Parisian life and literature with me regularly for years, in addition to giving me opportunities to sample the splendors of France outside the capital. Thanks to him, too, I found apartments in historically crucial areas of Paris, which became part of my life for a month or more every year for almost twenty years. The first was near the Grands Boulevards (center of leading nineteenth-century theaters, cafés-concerts, and fashionable cafés); the second is near Montmartre, a stone's throw from the Place Blanche and the Rue Lepic (in the ninth arrondissement amid streets lined with dwellings where once lived such luminaries as Berlioz, Bizet, Turgeniev, Émile Zola, Toulouse-Lautrec, and André Breton).

Members of my family have also helped over the years in a variety of ways too numerous to detail here. My heartfelt thanks go to my wife, Mary, who has been a Paris companion many a time as well as a critical reader, and my children: Anne (who helped me with all kinds of matters photographic), Deborah, and Andrew.

Donald Sluter of the Department of Geosciences at the University of Massachusetts helped prepare the maps. Lastly, I have been fortunate to have the support and suggestions of Editor Norris Pope as well as excellent contributions of copy editor Richard Gunde, production editor Judith Hibbard, Sarah Crane Newman, and other staff members at Stanford University Press.

C. R. July 31, 2010, South Deerfield, Massachusetts.

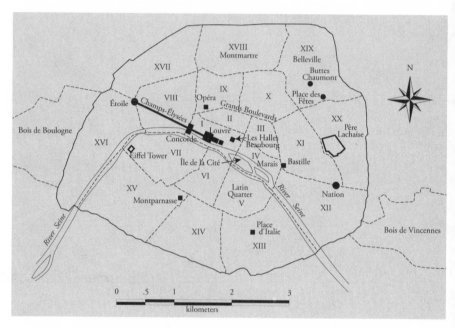

MAP 1. Paris and its *arrondissements* (districts). Created by Donald Sluter of the University of Massachusetts Geosciences Department.

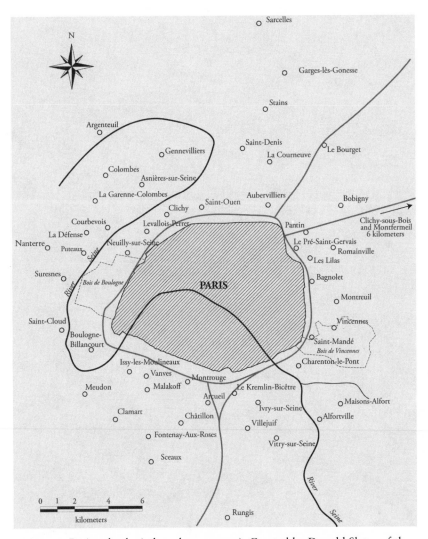

N

Sarcelles

Garges-lès-Gonesse

Stains

Argenteuil

Saint-Denis
Gennevilliers
La Courneuve   Le Bourget

Colombes
Asnières-sur-Seine

La Garenne-Colombes
Aubervilliers   Bobigny
Saint-Ouen
Courbevois   Clichy
Levallois-Perret   Pantin   Clichy-sous-Bois
and Montfermeil
6 kilometers
La Défense
Neuilly-sur-Seine
Nanterre   Le Pré-Saint-Gervais
Puteaux   Romainville
Les Lilas

Suresnes   Bagnolet
Seine   Bois de Boulogne   PARIS

River   Montreuil

Saint-Cloud   Vincennes

Boulogne-
Billancourt   Saint-Mandé
Bois de Vincennes
Issy-les-Moulineaux   Charenton-le-Pont
Vanves
Meudon   Montrouge
Malakoff   Le Kremlin-Bicêtre
Arcueil   Maisons-Alfort
Clamart   Ivry-sur-Seine   Alfortville
Châtillon   Villejuif
Fontenay-Aux-Roses   Vitry-sur-Seine

Sceaux

River

0   1   2   4   6

kilometers   Seine

Rungis

MAP 2. Paris suburbs (selected communes). Created by Donald Sluter of the
University of Massachusetts Geosciences Department.

Introduction

The Paris that inhabits imaginations around the world is a "moveable feast" of pleasure, beauty, and elegance. The Paris that most Parisians know is a workaday big city with traffic jams, supermarkets, and skyscrapers; it is also a sprawling multiethnic *agglomération* of ten million people. The Paris that the city's recent mayors have promoted is a world cultural capital—or the "new Athens." Those different versions of the city, along with a few others, are the subject of this book. We should think of Paris "in the plural," writer Julian Green has urged.[1] Taking that idea as a starting point, I have written an account of how and why those several "Parises" became important and how they have together shaped the fabled, flawed great city of our time.

Paris is not just a city, it's a "world," the Emperor Charles V remarked (reportedly) in the sixteenth century. The city's multiple facets and identities, together with its size, have made it difficult to comprehend and describe—from the Middle Ages on. In our time, the problem is even more daunting than ever: how can that great variegated "world" be captured or represented in words and images?

French phrases describing Paris over the centuries may offer us some help on that question, though they all have limitations, focusing as they do on one or another feature or role. Some writers have pictured the city as a vital organ—the heart and the brain of France, and the head (*tête*) of the world. To some it has been a "paradise," to others a "new Babylon," a hell, and a "stinking ulcer." Poetic minds have also portrayed the city as a lion, a spider, a ship, an ocean, a volcano, a furnace, a sewer, a brothel, a labyrinth, a beacon, a star, and . . . The list goes on and on.[2]

Only a few of the images have become conventions—or what scholars call social representations, widely shared by Parisians and foreigners alike. Those few play leading roles in this study of modern Paris. As widely accepted ways of perceiving and imagining the city, they can tell us much about the sources of Paris's extraordinary appeal. Of course, they are not faithful likenesses of quotidian realities—as my chapters show in detail. They have nonetheless played leading roles in the history that has produced the city we can visit today: they have been primary frames of reference for Parisian decision-making and common experience over time. To grasp their historical importance, we need to track the multiple Parises in their interplay and their relation to documented events and experience. Viewed in those ways, they can help us understand the multifarious city better than monographs focusing on a single identity or theme, such as revolution, capital of modernity, or capital of the world (excellent though the monographs may be in their own right).

Perhaps the best known of those representations is the phrase "the city of light," which has been a premier identity of Paris for more than a century, despite the persistent reign of darkness in many quarters. Others include the aesthetic "old Paris," the "capital of pleasures," the folksy hometown known in French slang as "Paname," and a stylish woman. How and why did such images come to represent Paris? And with what consequences for the city itself? My answers follow in the first four chapters of this book, period-by-period accounts of the city's history from the mid-nineteenth century to the present. The first chapter is a look back at the crucial formative period of Paris's modern identities and experience—from the Second Empire to the First World War. The next three chapters carry the story through the rest of the twentieth century and into the twenty-first. By zooming in on the last century-and-a-half, this short history can concentrate on showing how the city of our time developed its distinctive combination of identities and its mystique.

A final chapter examines another classic way of characterizing Paris, which is to describe the city's singular "atmosphere," its spirit, and its persona. Writers have regularly expatiated on Paris's charm, wit, and personality, usually with a feminine figure in mind. Others have told us about the city's spirit and soul. The personality, the spirit, and the soul of Paris? Those are subjects that I have long wanted to understand—without knowing how. How to access such ethereal matters? I still wondered after more than thirty years of annual sojourns in the French capital. Eloquent writing on such subjects, unfortunately, often ends in vagueness: the key turns out to be a je-ne-sais-quoi essence. Paris's charm, we learn, is . . . undefinable and inexplicable. Just what is that elusive something that makes the city more than the sum of its parts . . . or something other than that sum? What exactly has enchanted so many people? How did Paris get its exalted reputation, its prestige, and its romanticized imagery?

For answers to the questions about its spirit and soul, I concluded, we must listen to what Parisians themselves have said about their city, because they have been the primary exponents of those notions and presumably have intimate knowledge on which to draw. Accordingly, I have taken stock of the views of a wide range of Parisians and sources (see Chapter 6)—from writers and municipal officials to ordinary people, public opinion surveys, sociological studies, and the Parisian popular press (the métro's free weekly, for example, and the mass-circulation *Télérama*'s special issues on the capital).

For a historical perspective on the city's extraordinary fame and prestige, I have surveyed the centuries-old tradition of high praise and awestruck description of Paris. This book spotlights the modern forms of that tradition—in particular, a handful of representations that became core identities of the city from the nineteenth century to the present. French scholars, whose example I follow, call the ensemble of such representations an "imaginary." By using that term, they are not deeming it inconsequential fantasy, illusion, or "phantasmagoria." Nor am I. The Parisian imaginary highlighted in this book, I have tried to show, has guided the construction of piece after piece of the world called "Paris." Its images and scenarios, crystallized as collective memories, have structured how Paris has been viewed, described, and admired. They have also made their marks on the built city by shaping the consciousness of administrators, urban planners, and decision-makers at many levels. For example, painterly images of pre-1914 Montmartre served as models for preservationist planning half a century later (see Chapter 2). And the old popular-culture dream of warm local community (Paname) has inspired municipal programs for revitalizing social and cultural life in the *quartiers* since the 1980s.

The importance of these long-term cultural structures—representations, memories, imaginaries—tends to get lost in accounts of the tumultuous events, acts of the powerful (kings, presidents, urbanists), and grand monuments in Paris's rich history. This study, countering that tendency, highlights the Paris that has lived for centuries in hearts and minds, transcending political crises, revolutions, street battles, wars, and urban-renewal "massacres." That enduring Paris has been endlessly described and praised, painted, photographed, filmed, romanticized, dreamed, remembered, lamented, and loved—but not investigated with a focus on the perspectives and questions that drive this work.

Particularly important for that Paris—and this study—are Parisian places and times that have loomed large in popular culture dreams and memory. They include such iconic glamour spots as the Moulin Rouge and Maxim's, but also lowlife haunts, the city's "villages," and selective images from the period called the "Belle Époque." This book attempts to explain how and why such disparate set pieces became popular favorites, mainstays of collective memory, and focal points of dreams about Paris as a whole.[3]

Pieces of this story have been set out in specialized studies examining representations of Paris in one genre or another—above all, in literature, painting, cinema, and photography.[4] My aim, as far as is possible in one relatively short volume, is to show how the various strands have converged at points and together made certain kinds of images vivid in the mind's eye—even in the minds of many who have never set foot in the French capital. I have taken a wide-angle view of Paris image-making and its many sources—from the arts and state-sponsored projects to commercial entertainments and tourist guides. The goal is to understand the city's several faces *and* the multiform whole, the metropolis that is at once world capital *and* village, modern *and* old.

To that end I have drawn on the testimony of a wide variety of observers—Parisians, provincials, and foreigners. They have told us, from their different perspectives, what the city has meant, how it has rated when compared with rival cities (Chapter 5), and what has been most important over the decades.

Of all the observers considered, the admirers and aficionados of Paris (self-styled "lovers of Paris") have given us the most evocative readings of the city, and they have addressed my more difficult questions most directly. Writers who were inveterate strollers, in particular, have provided many fine-grained descriptions—of everyday sights as well as special places and moments they found most beautiful and enjoyable. They have also written about the city's soul and spirit with the most authority (see Chapter 6). Though they tell us little about demographic changes, building codes, and urbanist plans, they have given us eloquent accounts of aesthetic and affective experience. Theirs is an intimate, sentimental, and picturesque Paris. Their enthusiasms and dreams may help us see more in Paris and understand better its extraordinary mystique and appeal, if not its soul.

CHAPTER I

Paris—Praised, Modernized, Remembered, Staged, and Loved

Nineteenth-Century Foundations

PRAISED TO THE SKIES

Visitors to France first hailed Paris as a paradise back in the Middle Ages, when somewhere out of this world was the best place anyone could imagine. French and foreign writers alike made that flattering comparison, sometimes citing the similarity of the words *Parisius* and *paradisus* as etymological proof. But paradise could mean many things. When an English bishop called Paris "the paradise of the world" in the fourteenth century, he—a bibliophile—had in mind especially the city's twenty-eight bookstores. Other admirers invoked exalted *earthly* imagery: Paris as a majestic woman—"the queen" of cities and "mother" of cities—high tributes indeed, but none could match the dream potential of the celestial imagery. With its splendid churches, eminent scholars and university, beautiful houses of nobles and prelates, fine arts and crafts, and the abundance of food and wine in its many taverns, late-medieval Paris was—according to travelers and proud locals—"magnificent," "peerless," and a "place of delights." In short, an earthly paradise.[1]

It enjoyed that sky-high reputation as early as the twelfth century. Some clerics were so impressed with Paris's bounty of riches and pleasures that they denounced it as a fatal snare, best avoided: "Flee [this] Babylon, flee and save your souls," urged Saint Bernard in the mid-twelfth century. A German visitor in the following century, enjoying the delights of the place, fell back on the heaven-on-earth line, but scaled it down significantly: the city was a paradise for the rich, he wrote, . . . and a dreadful swamp for the poor. That qualifier, however, did not take hold in the emerging tradition of Paris description, a tradition shaped early on by enthusiasms fixed in the loftiest of metaphors.[2]

The accolades as well as the reproaches have echoed down through the centuries, only the palette of words and imagery changing from time to time. In the early nineteenth century, the French authors of *Paris pittoresque* hailed the city not as heaven but as the "capital of the civilized world" and "the marvel of the world." "Everything ever conceived in thought or dreamed to be beautiful, pleasing, and gigantic. . . . All that is Paris."[3]

The praise from foreigners swelled to a resounding high in the now-celebrated period around the turn of the twentieth century. Guidebooks then were instrumental in framing individual experiences with a collective memory, one that had taken shape centuries earlier in the writings of awestruck travelers and learned Parisians. Designed to interest visitors seeking the best of Paris, the guides told readers what to see and how to put it all into words and memory.

Addressing tourists from the English-speaking world, *Conty's Pocket Guide to Paris* (1898) declared it "a model city," "a wonderful city, "and "the gayest city in the world." There "business and pleasure are harmoniously combined." Visitors could be sure to find a "reception" that "fully justifies the prodigious vogue which this wonderful city enjoys throughout the entire world." The English guide *Cassell's* (1900) began by describing Paris as "the beautiful city . . . , which for ages has been recognized as the chief capital of Europe." Bouquets of superlatives appeared year after year. "The most attractive treasury of art and industry in the world," "the most cosmopolitan city in Europe," "indisputably the cradle of high culinary art"—these were not the boasts of a proud Parisian, but the remarks of the sober German-based Baedeker, passing along conventional judgments as matters of fact. The "charms of the seductive capital" are so great, Baedeker assured its readers, that "no one quits [it] without regret." Among those charms was a beauty that "French writers of all ages" and "many foreigners" have celebrated.[4]

None of the guides mentioned the city's big rats, large enough to eat cats. Nor did they quote the French writers of the time who described Paris as a "sewer" and a "hell," rife with poverty and alcoholism.[5] The guides also ignored tuberculosis-ridden slums and the new "ugliness" cropping up after the turn of the century—tall buildings spoiling historic perspectives, brazen displays of pornography, and the noisy, dangerously fast automobiles, "autobuses," and trucks that destroyed "the charm of strolling," as a French journalist lamented in 1907.[6] Strolling the Grands Boulevards meant running an obstacle course of smelly urinals that were like a "jumble of cesspools," wrote a former city council member in 1907.[7] Crossing the boulevards on foot required maneuvering through heaps of horse manure, discarded papers, and rotting meat, fish, cheeses, and vegetables thrown out by street vendors. Another lost charm of the city was good dining (already!), reported a knowledgeable man-about-town in 1900. Parisians were so busy and harried, he testified, that they ate "hastily, without taste and without pleasure." "With this fever that we bring to everything, we absorb chemical products and we don't even notice that they are bad."[8] Clearly the guidebooks and writers who described Paris as wonderful and beautiful were telling only part of the story.

But some of the city's enthusiasts found so much to love about Paris that its defects did not matter. To some, even its famed beauty was inconsequential. Parisian writer André Billy, for example, author of two volumes (1909) describing in detail "our beautiful Paris," did not count its aesthetic charms as a source of "the love of Paris." Love for the city, he maintained, sprang from an "innate temperament" and strong interests in the life of the present and past. The lovers of Paris had in common "a keen instinct of sociability with the taste for modern existence," a "curiosity for the past," and a "general preoccupation with public life." Then, complicating the matter further, Billy acknowledged that the *amoureux de Paris* were quite diverse: some relished "Parisian partying" ("'la noce' parisienne"), while others loved the artistic, historical, and intellectual life.[9] Many of them were neither born in the city nor residents of it. So by this eminent Parisian's account, the love of Paris springs not from an aesthetic sensibility or living in the city, but rather from an assortment of sympathies and dispositions, which can be identified but not wholly explained.

The topic is worth pursuing. What has made Paris so beloved? Is that love traceable to an innate temperament, or is it a miscellany of acquired tastes and penchants? And how can people love something as large and heterogeneous as a modern metropolis?

One common way is to focus on only certain parts of the city and ignore the rest. Selective vision has been the rule in guidebooks, memoirs, and most essays. Billy's books, for example, left out poor working-class neighborhoods, banal streets, and even most pleasure spots. Guidebooks long promised to inform the visitor about "everything worth seeing," but most have proceeded with very limited notions of what is worthwhile, sticking to canonical sites, omitting everything outside the center.

Yet those guides and countless writers, from the Middle Ages on, have showered praise on the whole city—its beauty, spirit, atmosphere, and people—and have expressed love for the totality. Twentieth-century guidebooks, quoting tributes from centuries past, cast the greatness of the city as timeless and transcendent, setting it in the realm of myth. A book of 1924, for example, begins with the medieval monk's hymn to the "queen of cities." Generations of travel writers reiterated the old lines about the French capital's superiority—without offering any comparative evidence. Nor did they acknowledge the exalted praise that has been heaped on other cities over the centuries. According to an oft-quoted medieval poet in England, for example, London was the "soveraign of cities, semeliest in sight."[10] Seventeenth-century books on Dutch towns commonly touted the greatness of each featured city and its attractions. "Civic bragging" was a convention from the Renaissance on.[11]

So the tributes to Paris accumulated over centuries in poems, travel accounts, and songs, well before guidebooks became an institution and before tourism promoters joined the cause. Montaigne's oft-quoted appreciation set a high standard early on: Paris was "the glory of France and one of the most noble of ornaments of the world." He went on to declare his great love for the capital, personified as a woman in the already-conventional way. The more he saw of other beautiful cities, the more the beauty of Paris won his affection. He loved "her" so tenderly that even her "warts, spots, and blemishes" (*verrues* and *taches*) were dear to him.[12] Poems, memoirs, essays, histories, and guidebooks centuries later added to the chorus of praise, but have often left the reader wondering exactly what was it that was so beautiful and lovable—or not.

Most have not been able to embrace the "warts and blemishes" in an all-encompassing love. Paris was "the dirtiest city in the world," declared Louis-Sébastien Mercier in the 1790s, referring to the clogged, narrow, filthy streets, among other things. Critics in Mercier's time decried the

city's defects more insistently than ever before, moved by hope for enlightened improvements. Sensitivity to foul odors and bad air was on the
rise, Alain Corbin has shown. "The capital is no more than a vast sewer
[*cloaque*]," wrote one observer of the mud-and-manure-covered streets
in 1789. "The air is putrid," he added, noting that people could scarcely
breathe in some quarters.[13] Popular entertainments in Paris, too, stirred
outcries of disgust. Why, asked a letter to the *Journal de Paris* (1782), do
theaters persist in giving the people vulgar jokes, the spectacle of the worst
morals, and "licentious performances"?[14]

A small group of observers, in contrast, presented a mixed picture: for
them, the intermingling of the delightful and the repulsive was the defining feature of Paris. "Clearly it is not enough to call it the first city in the
world, the capital of splendor and enchantment," concluded a Russian traveler in 1789–1790. "If you go farther you will see crowded streets, and an
outrageous confusion of wealth and poverty. Close by a glittering jewelry
shop lies a pile of rotten apples and herrings; filth is everywhere and even
blood streaming from the butchers' stalls. You must hold your nose and
close your eyes. . . . In a word, every step brings a new atmosphere, new
objects of luxury or the most loathsome filth; thus you must call Paris the
most magnificent and most vile, the most fragrant and the most fetid city."[15]

Most observers were content with giving simpler descriptions, retouch-
ing the familiar old ones. By the early twentieth century, several of those
views had crystallized into popular conventions passing as truisms. The
most widely known images and themes from the nineteenth century folded
willy-nilly into several phrases: the City of Light, Old Paris, the Capital of
Pleasures, and Paname. Each was a response to the others in some way, each
conditioned by others, in a continuing discussion. Together they formed
what can be called the classic imaginary of modern Paris. This chapter looks
back to see how those characterizations arose and what they meant—in the
culture of Parisians and in the imagination of many far from the capital.

THE CITY OF LIGHT

"Modern" Paris emerged in the 1850s and 1860s through an ambitious
urban renewal program undertaken by the Emperor Napoleon III. Or rather,
that was how the supporters of the Second Empire described it. In their

admiration for the bold projects, they made it sound as though the emperor and his prefect for Paris, Georges-Eugène Haussmann, had created a new and different city in the place of the old. In fact, only some central areas became "modern" in that period. Nonetheless, the operations carried out were massive: they included 165 kilometers of new streets, 560 kilometers of sewers, 24 squares and two large parks, and an infrastructure of new town halls, hospitals, and schools. Workers demolished 20,000 buildings and constructed 34,000.[16] All that rebuilding, along with embellishments before and afterward, generated a fresh wave of admiration of Paris as a

FIGURE 1.1. The "old Paris" that the Prefect Haussmann gutted. In this street and others on the Île de la Cité, the self-styled demolition artist had the homes of about 25,000 people demolished to clear the way for new public buildings: a new Hôtel Dieu hospital, the Tribunal of Commerce, and additions to the Palais de Justice, among others. "The Rue des Trois-Canettes," photograph by Charles Marville (cira 1865). (Bibliothèque historique de la Ville de Paris.)

FIGURE 1.2. Destroying the old Paris—slums razed and a natural mound
leveled to make way for the grand Avenue de l'Opéra (circa 1877). Charles
Marville photograph. (Bibliothèque historique de la Ville de Paris.)

showplace of modernity, epitomized by broad, straight, well-lighted new
thoroughfares.

Admirers identified the city lights as a crowning touch and propagated
the sobriquet "Ville Lumière"—"City of Light"—toward the end of the
nineteenth century. The city lights had been impressive for a couple of centuries, but not exceptional enough to warrant the title. Candle-lit lanterns
illuminated streets in the late seventeenth century; brighter lamps burning
oil replaced them in the late eighteenth century. Though weak and scattered by later standards, those early lights were doubtless remarkable to
visitors who knew only the dark lanes of small towns and villages. In the
eighteenth century Paris was already well lighted in comparison to London, but it was still far from being the "city of light." It became much
brighter when gas lamps were installed in the 1840s. Then in the second
half of the nineteenth century its lighting multiplied a hundred fold—from
350 million to 75,000 million candle hours, with the increased use of gas

plus the introduction of electric lamps.[17] Gas lighting in the late nineteenth century was generous to the point of seeming "reckless"—to the sensible American reporter Richard Harding Davis. "[The Parisian] . . . raises ten lamp-posts to every one that is put up in London or New York, and he does not plant them only to light some thing or some person, but because they are pleasing to look at in themselves." They also brightened spirits, he noted. "It is difficult to feel gloomy in a city which is so genuinely il-luminated that one can sit in the third-story window of a hotel and read a newspaper by the glare of the gas-lamps in the street below." Yet the ap-parent excess was economically shrewd, he added, "for it helps to attract people to Paris, who spend money there, so that in the end the lighting of the city may be said to pay for itself."[18]

In 1900, when Paris hosted its biggest-ever world's fair, the expression "Ville Lumière" gained currency in tourist literature and celebratory re-portage. The fifty million visitors who came to the "Exposition universelle" were met with a dazzling profusion of electric lighting—in the pavilions and the Palais de l'Électricité and all the way up the Eiffel Tower. Outside the fairgrounds the new lights illuminated the city's monuments and cen-tral boulevards. Elsewhere gas lights were still the rule. Yet overall Paris was far behind New York, whose inhabitants were less concerned with keeping down the expense. Nothing in Paris compared with the twelve-to-fourteen-story building on Broadway whose façade was a galaxy of bright bulbs in advertising signs, a veteran Parisian journalist pointed out in 1899. "When night comes, the whole gable lights up and sets the air ablaze with flaming colors." The lighting in "the vast stores" "in all the large American streets, . . . even after the closing hour," was also impres-sive in contrast to what he knew back home.[19]

Although Paris was not widely known as the "Ville Lumière" *before* 1900, it had been associated with light since the eighteenth century—in the metaphorical sense. When Victor Hugo used the phrase "Paris is the city of light"[20] in 1875, he was speaking *figuratively*, in the tradition of the Enlightenment. He was contrasting his beloved capital with the "dark cities" across Europe, the politically and intellectually less advanced ones. Paris, once again free of king and emperor, was the "edge of the future," he continued. Paris was "Progress" in its visible form. Even when Europe and the rest of France languished in dark times, Paris was not eclipsed—at least in the eyes of democrats like Hugo. Here light and progress meant the cause of liberty and democracy, the legacy of the Enlightenment and French Revolution.

The phrase "city of light" also referred to Paris's renown as a shining center of civilization—a reputation it had enjoyed since the era of Louis XIV. In the eighteenth century, nobles from all over Europe and Russia traveled to the city to learn the sophisticated manners and lifestyle of the local elite, to improve their French, to buy luxury goods, to enjoy the theater (along with the "filles" found there), to visit the cultural monuments—museums, great churches, palaces—and to learn about Europe's finest intellectual and artistic accomplishments.[21] In the nineteenth century, visitors went to Paris with the additional expectation of enjoying gastronomic pleasures, available everyday in elegant restaurants. A guidebook of 1855 assured readers that the capital would live up to its high culinary reputation: "it is, of all the towns in the world, the one where one eats the best!" That claim, endlessly reiterated by French writers and guidebooks, became a proverbial truth that fit naturally with Paris's already celebrated primacy in ideas, art, literature, and taste.[22]

To its admirers, Haussmann's "modern Paris" represented striking "progress," meaning material improvement and greater order, achieved through the effective use of state power. Haussmann's projects of demolition and rebuilding were part of a universal civilizing process, writer Théophile Gautier argued in 1855. "Civilization carves out broad avenues in the dark maze of small streets, intersections, [and] dead ends of the old city; civilization brings down [abat] the [primitive] dwellings as the pioneer of America fells [abat] the trees."[23] To the modernizers, slum clearance, letting in fresh air and sunlight, did more than improve public health. It also opened the crime-and-rebellion-prone backstreets to lawful moral order, and it facilitated mobility and commerce—hallmarks of modern civilization.

Boosters of the Bonapartist regime went so far as to dub the renovated Paris the "capital of the world," the successor to Rome as a center of far-reaching civilizing power and influence. Government officials added substance to the claim by organizing world's fairs in Paris in 1855 and 1867, *expositions universelles* on an unprecedented scale. People from all over

FIGURE 1.3. The Avenue de l'Opéra, completed (1879) well after Haussmann's downfall, opened onto to the grandiose new Opéra (Palais Garnier, completed in 1875) on one end and two older high-culture shrines at the other end: the Louvre and the Théâtre-Français. Undated (circa 1890?) photograph by Fiorillo. (Bibliothèque historique de la Ville de Paris.)

the globe came to see firsthand the fruits of progress on display in the expositions and in the renovated city—from new wide boulevards to new well-lighted (and nearly odor-free) sewers open for public tours from 1867 on.[24] At the same time, visitors came to experience the fabled pleasures of Paris as well. For each of those high tides of tourism, lovers of the city poured out fresh appreciations in essays, books, and guides.

Modernizing operations sharply divided Parisians in the nineteenth century (as in the twentieth) and stirred vehement objections on several grounds. The renovations, cried the critics, left a deadening, rigid order where lively old quarters had once been. The straight, standardized new streets were, to them, boring and monotonous. The new cityscape was inhuman and mechanistic, even militarist in inspiration—"aligned like a regiment under arms," charged the authors of a book entitled *Paris, capitale du monde*, published in 1867.[25]

To these and other critics of the Bonapartist regime, the grand title "world capital" was empty and deceptive, a glittery sham covering over terrible wrongs done to the city and its inhabitants. The social and cultural changes in Paris troubled them even more than the physical alterations. In becoming the world capital, Paris was losing its character, they believed: it was losing both its historic identity and its traditional manners and morals. The "immigration of the entire world" was overwhelming it. The "invasion" of corrupting foreigners or "Barbarians" was destroying the old familiar order of Parisian identities and social relations. The new order was marked by a "crude desire to shine, to put on a show, to make life into a theatrical scene." The women of Paris embraced the decadent new ways more readily than the men, maintained the (male) authors of *Paris, capitale du monde*, declaring flatly: "The Parisienne has disappeared." Even the French language, one of the foundations of the old civilization, was going down, as neologisms and argot flooded in. The new barbarism having conquered Paris, the rest of France was next. The provinces were losing their own distinctive life and character in their eagerness to imitate the glamorous world capital.[26]

The makeover of Paris destroyed not only particular traditions and memory sites, but also a general sense of the past—myriad webs of memory joining the dead and the living, added the conservative Catholic writer Louis Veuillot. "City without a past, minds without memories, hearts without tears, souls without love! City of uprooted multitudes, moving mass of human dust, you can grow and become the capital of the world, [but] you will never have citizens." "These big streets, these big quays, these big buildings, these big sewers . . . exude [*exhalent*] ennui." The renovations meant desolation, not progress.[27] These laments for a disappearing authentic Paris have been (and still are) a recurrent counterpoint to the fine talk of modernity and progress.

To less jaundiced observers, Paris as "world capital" meant simply that it was a home to foreigners and their varied ways from many lands. That was what Baedeker guides routinely suggested with the remark "Paris has long enjoyed the reputation of being the most cosmopolitan city in Europe." That reputation, Baedeker explained, owed much to Paris's renowned university, which had drawn professors and students from all over Europe since the late Middle Ages. "Cosmopolitan" also meant that the city's cultural offerings and entertainments were extraordinarily diverse and bountiful, so that, as Baedeker put, "the artist, the scholar, the merchant, and the votary of pleasure alike find [there] the most abundant scope for their pursuits."[28]

Acclaim for the renovated capital rose to a fortissimo in anticipation of legions of visitors coming to see the Universal Exposition of 1867. For that event, the most notable collection of Parisiana to date appeared: a two-volume *Paris-Guide*, written by 125 of the nation's leading writers and artists, with a lengthy introduction by Victor Hugo. The editor, an opponent of the Bonapartist regime, had required of all the contributors that they love Paris and serve "the cause of progress." Accordingly, they all wrote lovingly about their assigned aspects of the city, old and new. Many of them waxed nostalgic but stopped short of condemning the recent renovations. Even the author of an essay on "Old Paris," the revolutionary socialist Louis Blanc, generally approved of urban renewal—in particular, the renovations that brought sunlight and air to "unhealthy streets." Yet he also implored authorities to show mercy toward "some of the warts and blemishes that Montaigne loved."[29]

Three years later, modern Paris and "the cause of progress" suffered terrible setbacks. The bloody battles, deprivation, and destruction it suffered in 1870–1871 left nightmarish memories that shadowed the images of light and beauty for decades. Caught up in a foolish war with Prussia, France's army met with defeat at Sedan in September 1870, and the emperor was captured on the battlefield. The Second Empire then fell to revolutionary crowds in the capital. The Prussian army, meanwhile, approached Paris and laid siege. The proud "world capital" was cut off from the world—as well as the rest of France—and slowly starved over four months. In early January 1871 the Prussian artillery began a terrifying daily bombardment. Finally, on the 29th the French government yielded to the harsh terms of an armistice, surrendering the capital that had held on valiantly for months. Prussian troops paraded down the Champs-Élysées a few days later, a symbolic insult that Parisians (even in the quarter) tried not to witness.[30]

Parisians shared a common sorrow and humiliation, but they were deeply divided about the best direction for the city to take. In March 1871

those who embraced the revolutionary tradition's dreams of social democracy declared Paris an independent Commune, rejecting the authority of
the conservative national government based at Versailles. Paris became
a fiery battleground when the Versailles authorities sent in the army to
put down the Commune in May. During a final "bloody week," artillery
shells and fires set by the desperate Communards destroyed many public
buildings, including city hall, the Ministry of Finance, and the Tuileries
Palace. The old nightmare of Paris in ruins became a reality for the city
that Haussmann had just finished renovating. The army killed an estimated 20,000 men, women, and children, and it took 43,500 prisoners.
So ended the last of the capital's revolutions. The Paris that conservative
forces bludgeoned and conquered was a "stinking ulcer," wrote the poet
Rimbaud in May 1871. It was more than ever a "whore" (*putain*), yet for
all that, it had a "splendid" beauty.[31]

After the devastation of the "terrible year" (Hugo's phrase), Paris was
rebuilt with remarkable swiftness. The new Third Republic continued
the Second Empire's projects, completing the Haussmannian city without
Haussmann. Just seven years after the devastating civil war, the city showed
off its recovery by hosting another world's fair (1878). Eleven years after
that, on the centennial of the French Revolution, it hosted a much grander
"universal exposition," and then a still larger one in 1900 (drawing 51 million visitors to 1889's 32 million and 83,000 exhibitors to 1889's 61,722).
With the dictator Napoleon III long gone and a republic fully ensconced,
everyone was free to extol the greatness and the charms of Paris without
fear of lending support to an authoritarian regime. In covering fair after
fair, guidebook and travel writers sang hosannas to the city with all its new
forms of glory. No event did more than the world's fairs to put Paris in
the international limelight as "the capital of nineteenth century," as Walter Benjamin famously put it. Although he can be faulted for disregard-
ing the case for London as the capital of the century, Benjamin justifiably
highlighted Paris's importance as a showcase of technological and cultural
modernity, luxury merchandise ("commodity fetishism"), entertainment,
and utopian dream images ("phantasmagorias").[32]

The exuberant praise of Paris crystallized into a tradition of clichés—
the City of Light, the most beautiful city in the world, the most civilized

and sophisticated, and the Capital of Pleasures. In guidebooks and histories, Paris history became a triumphalist epic, a narrative of progress that
glossed over revolutions, civil war, destruction, and decay.[33] This chorus
of praise was in a full crescendo at a time when critics were deploring the
city as a hothouse for all that was ugly and alienating in modern civilization—with things only getting worse.[34] The view of Paris history as a
success story left out the "warts," the darkness, and the battles, and it
shaped the rest into a neat order.

The Second Empire had hoped to pass on a Paris tale of Cinderella-like
transformation from shabbiness to splendor, wrought by the power of a
beneficent monarch. Its successor, the Third Republic, fashioned a story
of longer-term progress, not due to kings or emperors, but to reason and
science (Enlightenment), the French Revolution, the heroic citizen nation,
and the freedom-loving people of Paris. The new Republic backed off
from heady talk of the "capital of the world" and instead saluted Paris as
a democratic and cultural leader. And it carried on the Second Empire's
practice of inviting the world to enjoy the great city in conjunction with
displays of progress at periodic "universal expositions." The spectacular
showpiece that the Third Republic commissioned for the 1889 fair, the
Eiffel Tower, surpassed all the earlier monuments to modernity. That bril-
liantly engineered iron structure (a thousand-feet high—the world's tallest
edifice until 1929) was intended to symbolize France's industrial progress
under the Republic, but it quickly became the most popular symbol of
the city—and simply a giant plaything for the masses, the most popular
attraction at the fair.[35]

Certainly the capital was France's most fitting locale for celebrations
of progress. Around the turn of the century Paris was not only the nation's economic incubator and powerhouse, but also one of Europe's
most dynamic industrial centers. Its manufacturing sector included much
more than a large garment industry and world-famous luxury products.
It was also a world leader in new technologies—bicycles, automobiles,
cinema, electrical equipment, and airplanes (the latter taking off in the
years 1906–1908 with locally made automobile motors).[36] In the cultural
realm, most famously of all, Paris was a brilliant star, a crucible of creativity in painting, sculpture, decorative arts, and architecture. Its bounty of

stellar talents and their works brought the city a worldwide reputation as the capital of the arts, even though Vienna was probably more deserving of the title at the turn of the century.[37]

Visitors spread amazing tales of the intellectual vitality of not only the cultural elite, but also the Parisian people in general. Echoing hyperbole from the likes of Victor Hugo and Theodore de Banville, the American journalist Theodore Child reported that the air of Paris imparted brilliance to all who breathed it. The washerwomen working along the Seine were telling proof. "For the lavandières, like all the Parisians, participate in the essential and permanent advantage of Paris over all the other cities of the universe; they drink in ideas with the air they breathe, and their conversation is as sparkling and full of genius as that of the wits who sit at Tortoni's [a chic café on the Grands Boulevards] and evolve clever sayings for the boulevard journals."[38]

Accounts taking a historical perspective traced the city's preeminence not to the air, but to rational decision-making and progressive leadership. They told of enlightened authorities undertaking project after project, bringing forth a new urban order of circulation, light, and air into quarters of dark, cramped disorder. Baedeker and other guides relayed that story on to foreigners, telling visitors of the "magnificent improvements" carried out in the second half of the century while dismissing the critics' complaint about the "monotony" of the resulting cityscape. The beauty of the light-filled modern capital became a dogma, endlessly recited.

At best that description fit only a part of the city—some renovated quarters in the center, the main streets and places most visible to visitors. Several other versions of the city brought out other truths and other kinds of attractions. Two of the most notable of those competing characterizations were "Old Paris" and the "capital of pleasures."

"OLD PARIS"

The spots and blemishes that held charm for Montaigne were also dear to some Parisians in the nineteenth century—and even dearer when demolition crews went to work on blemished "Old Paris," as they did periodically through the century. A couple of decades before Haussmann's works began, the city administrator Rambuteau undertook some limited urban renewal entailing demolitions. Outraged critics decried the destruction of the *picturesque*—the quirky, irregular, all-too-human relics of ages past that were a favorite of the Romantics. Victor Hugo, most resoundingly, lambasted the "vandalism" and pleaded for preservation of the city's historical fabric. Haussmann's more extensive renovations in the 1850s and 1860s, implementing a more comprehensive plan, stirred more and stronger outcries from defenders of "old stones."[39]

Demolishing the old—several thousand old houses and several small churches—also meant destroying familiar ways of life for the poor who lived there. So "Old Paris" was also the rallying cry of opposition to the prideful elites and the social consequences of slate-cleaning projects. Old Paris, viewed by its defenders, was a collection of beloved dwellings from many eras, close-knit neighborhoods, and narrow streets alive with entertainers, shops and street vendors, and common people. It was the stage for periodic fêtes, when its cobblestone streets and squares filled with crowds and performers, games and music—good times open to even the lowliest of inhabitants. Poor crowded quarters, which modernizers saw as dark, decrepit, and disease-ridden slums, were to others hallowed grounds where revered ancestors had lived and died. To the latter, dilapidated dwellings were once-noble town-houses and the residences of dignitaries and great writers. The most banal of decayed buildings were precious monuments in the eyes of those whose family memories dwelled there, and their demolition was the destruction of a precious past. "Cities have a soul, which is their past," declared Louis Blanc in his essay on "Le Vieux Paris" for the 1867 *Paris-Guide*, "and their material beauty has all its value only when it bears the visible traces of an additional beauty that is composed of memories—terrible or wrenching [*pathétique*] memories, which amuse or move, which sadden or console."[40]

In addition to beauty and memories, the old city with its narrow, crooked streets and hovels held a Romantic attraction as a shadowy setting for stories that entertained readers all over France. The "Old Paris" of popular literature and the mass-circulation press was a world of poor dark neighborhoods associated with crimes, mysteries, and police hunts. Eugène Sue's *Les Mystères de Paris* (1842) was a fountainhead of that genre: it was a runaway success as a serial novel in a newspaper (147 episodes in 1842–1843), then a book, and a play (1844), altogether making him the best-paid author in Paris. Sue's contribution to the Parisian imaginary was in part inspired by the American imaginary—the forest wilderness and Indians depicted in James Fenimore Cooper's novels. If for readers of Sue the capital's slums became an urban wilderness full of daring and dangerous "savages," for readers of Hugo's *Les Misérables* (1862) the scruffy neighborhoods were refuges of the hardworking poor and simple folks down on their luck. Zola's novel *L'Assommoir* (1877) spun more tales of lower-class heroes and antiheroes, setting them in parts of the city still untouched by renewal. Both *Les Misérables* and *L'Assommoir* went on to reach theater audiences, too: Hugo's novel was produced on stage in Paris in 1878, and Zola's one year later. Thanks to this rich literary tradition, together with the crime stories featured regularly in popular newspapers, the old Paris of the poor held out fascinating possibilities of intrigue and gritty struggle that the rebuilt and well-lighted city could not rival.[41]

"Old Paris" at its seediest was also the refuge of outcasts and the wretchedly poor—Parisians far removed from the fashions and mobility of the "world capital" pacesetters. Haussmann's efforts to rid Paris of the "horribly picturesque" slum dwellers fell far short of success, reporter Georges Grisson showed in his book *Paris horrible* (1882): the undesirables only moved to new quarters, as rats do after fleeing a demolished shack. "There's always, always the horrible Paris," Grisson argued: a large population of beggars, bums, drifters, prostitutes, and pimps always finds a place in the city. "Paris is not only the brilliant, smart, *viveur* and showy Paris of the Boulevard des Italiens, the Avenue de l'Opéra and the Champs-Élysées; it is also the desolate, hungry, despairing, frightful Paris of somber, foul, and musty quarters, where thousands of human beings vegetate, without a fire, without bread, without strength and without hope, while awaiting the end, in an atmosphere of pestilence and malediction." Yet even those "disinherited" Parisians experienced "ferocious joys" and "gross amusements" and "sometimes frightening pleasures." Grisson's account of "horrible" Paris, he assured readers, was in turns "sinister and grotesque, distressing [*navrant*] and funny . . . but . . . always picturesque and . . . always true."[42]

So Old Paris was mourned and missed, but also recalled, dreamed, and enjoyed in the late nineteenth century. Self-styled lovers of Paris, who

FIGURE 1.4. The Grands Boulevards were the fashionable center of Paris from the 1830s to the 1870s (according to some) or through the turn-of-the-century (according to others). They were the stamping ground of elegant gentlemen and stylish women, journalists, and playwrights, who frequented the chic cafés, restaurants, theaters, and shops there, particularly from Madeleine to the Boulevard des Italiens. Photograph by Hippolyte Blancard (circa 1880). (Bibliothèque historique de la Ville de Paris.)

included some of the most articulate of Parisians, were the most voluble of mourners. They wrote pleas for remembrance, but they did not block the projects of clearance and demolition. And they did not even try to get the old urban landscape reconstructed afterward. The will to stop "progress" was weak, even among lovers of the old.

The will to preserve went mostly into documenting what was being destroyed. Photographer Charles Marville took the lead in creating a visual record of streets and structures destined for demolition in the 1860s. State

FIGURE 1.5. Untouched by Second Empire renovations, Old Paris lived on in narrow streets behind the famed boulevards. There scruffy buildings from centuries past harbored a lowlife world of cheap drinking places, flophouses, dance halls, and streetwalkers. The Rue des Vertus (third arrondissement) (circa 1900). (Photo UPF/Archives de Paris—11Fi 4227.)

authorities commissioned him to photograph not out of sympathy for the old, but to have an archival reminder of the wretchedness "before." Parisian art lovers preferred seeing dilapidated old places rendered in drawings, etchings, and lithographs. "Picturesque" views of dark, narrow streets and timeworn buildings became a popular genre among collectors through the rest of the nineteenth century. Although the connoisseurs of the *pittoresque* disliked the razings, they avoided overt politics and went into antiquarian researches and the amassing of visual "documents." Some of them banded together to found local historical societies, devoted to re-searching the classical past of nobles' townhouses and churches. In 1897, with excavation work for the new métro bringing back memories of the Second Empire's demolitions, lovers of the Parisian past managed to establish a municipal institution for their cause: the Commission du Vieux Paris. Members of the commission—writers, historians, antiquarian collectors, and some local political leaders—began inventorying historically important structures and buying "photographic documentation" for the city's museum and library collections.

Professing a love of Old Paris, photographer Eugène Atget earned his living by catering to that demand, selling his pictures of "old streets, . . . the beautiful civil architecture from the sixteenth to the nineteenth century, old townhouses, historic or curious houses, beautiful facades, beautiful doorways, beautiful paneling, door knockers, old fountains, period stairways (wood and wrought iron), [and] the interiors of all the churches of Paris."[43] Lovers of Old Paris, prizing beautiful survivals, wanted Atget to show a venerable city unmarred by such modern intrusions as tall buildings and automobiles. While preserving a memory of Paris, they also wanted to forget much—the capital's revolutionary upheavals, bloody street battles, and everything built since the eighteenth century.

Though the preservationist documents did not reach many people, the memory of a certain Old Paris did take hold through other channels—works of popular literature, history, and even entertainment—in the decades following Haussmann's work. Picture postcards of timeworn streets and buildings made frozen-in-time views of the past widely familiar.[44] Alongside Zola's widely read novels evoking old working-class neighborhoods, popular histories evoked the colorful street life of olden times—celebrations, games, entertainments, and sundry peddlers through centuries past, lovingly recounted by such writers as Victor Fournel and Edouard Drumont.[45] Similar interests in the distant past brought success to the theme-park reproduction of "Le Vieux Paris" at the Paris world's fair in 1900: time-traveling sightseers walked through narrow crooked streets lined with medieval towers to see costumed craftsmen and merchants amid replicas of the old Halles, the Porte Saint-Michel, the birth house of Molière, and the Fair Saint-Laurent. It was one of the biggest-drawing attractions of the exposition.[46]

Nonetheless, real survivals of Old Paris came under almost constant attack. Authorities set up a new way of justifying destruction in 1894 when they classified the worst slums officially as public-health menaces—*îlots insalubres*—believed to be contaminating hotbeds of tuberculosis. Six areas were so identified early in the twentieth century (by 1920 twenty-seven were).[47]

But usually the reason for demolition of old buildings was commercial gain, not health concerns. In the early twentieth century, as the pick-ax crews worked at a quickened pace, lovers of the past issued cries of outrage and sorrow in a stream of books and articles about historic Paris, its beauty, and its destruction. "Unequal struggle, alas! for the vandals are legion!" lamented historian Georges Cain in a 1911 book about the death throes of old Paris. "The pearl of Europe each day tends to be Americanized further, losing its legendary cachet of good grace and great memories." Piece after piece of the city's charm and beauty disappeared, making way for big new "inane and dull" buildings on right-angled streets—"heavy and stupid," "banal architecture."[48] With every vanishing piece of the past, Old Paris looked more charming and attractive than ever—to its defenders.

CAPITAL OF PLEASURES

Urban renewal in the 1860s wiped out a flourishing popular entertainment district on and near the Boulevard du Temple, famed for its inexpensive vaudevilles, farces, mimes, and melodrama theaters (hence the nickname "boulevard of crime"). But elsewhere the capital gained an array of new places of pleasure and nightlife for better-off Parisians and visitors: theaters, racetracks, *cafés-concerts*, cabarets, wax museums, restaurants, dance halls, cafés, and restaurants.[49] With all those added to the surviving older places of entertainment and the daily spectacle of fashionable life on the boulevards, Paris was more than ever "the city of pleasure and of pleasures par excellence," as Alfred Delvau put it in 1867. "Nowhere else can people amuse themselves as much and in as many ways."[50] For Delvau that was a point of pride; for others it was cause for shame. The authors of *Paris, capitale du monde* (1867), for example, deplored Paris's becoming "the amuser of Europe." Though their title echoed a boast, they were in fact critics of the new city and its amusement "mission." The destruction of old quarters, they maintained, had destroyed "old morals, old habits, ancient traditions," opening the way to cheap pleasures and extravagant novelty, feverishly pursued. "Horse races, gambling, parades with costume or even without, easy women low and high, . . . [and] slang"—"there are the new elements of the new civilization." Pleasure-seeking "idlers" (*désœuvrés*) and "millionaires" from all over the globe were overrunning the "the city of pleasures."[51]

The city's reputation as a mecca of hedonism grew even stronger in the last decades of the century, even though the Republic's leaders preached an austere morality of work and duty. The world's fairs in 1889 and 1900 spawned ever more entertainments for the millions of visitors, and each time a new round of guidebooks trumpeted the city's earthly delights. Paris "is the very capital of the kingdom of pleasures," declared guidebook writer Camille Debans in 1889. Like Delvau two decades earlier, Debans wholeheartedly approved of the rampant pleasure-seeking. What set Paris apart from other capitals was not simply the quantity and quality of its enjoyments, he maintained, but also its open acceptance of all manner of them. Elsewhere people had to act slyly and hypocritically, but in Paris pleasure was a "social necessity" and a "normal state."[52]

Visitors wove their own tales into the city's legend, telling their country-men how enjoyable the city was for even the most modest Parisians as well as foreigners. In recounting a year-long sojourn in 1912, Englishwoman Maude Annesley recalled the everyday high spirits of Parisians in a drab quarter surrounding the Gare du Nord: "they are so unconcerned, so neat, so full of joie de vivre! A bored face is seldom, if ever, seen in this city." Men were particularly cheerful, she observed: "The man in the street is gay, childlike in his amusements, spontaneous, and delightfully happy." Parisian women, however, gave Annesley pause: most of them were "co-quettes" suffering from nervous tensions. But that observation did not stop her from generalizing further about "Parisian gaiety." Temperament was only a part of it, she opined: "there must also be something in the air, because foreigners, who take up their abode there, nearly always lose their dreary look after a few weeks, and acquire a brisk one in its place."[53]

Much of the fantasy-laced talk of pleasure was aimed at males. As an English guide to the "gayest city in the world" (1889) put it: "One comes here to feast and dance and laugh, and for the society of charming women, more hospitable here than elsewhere."[54] Guidebooks working that vein assumed that masculine visitors arrived seeking an extraordinary sexual playground, one reputed to be the best in the world. "You have finally set foot in the Promised Land for all your appetites as a bored man who wants amusement, for all your caprices of a schoolboy on the run who wants to have fun, for all your fantasies as a conjugal slave who wants to be liberated," Delvau wrote sympathetically.[55] Other travelers might come without such fantasies or frustrations, but they quickly develop "many new and unsuspected capacities for enjoyment and adventure" once in Paris, observed Richard Harding Davis.[56]

The hordes of foreigners drawn by the expositions through the second half of the century regularly renewed the city's reputation for untrammeled hedonism—or debauchery. "The Exposition of 1867 gave us renown as a European Sodom," and the subsequent fairs of 1878 and 1889 "only confirmed it," noted a disgusted French senator in 1900. While critics like the senator wanted to clean up the city's entertainments, the boosters of its pleasures noted that Paris's "loose morals" and bad reputation resulted in more tourist business. "On the slightest pretext, the 'Pharisee' [the hypocritical foreign critic] rushes back, overjoyed to be free of the censure of his small town. He doesn't fear being scandalized a little, and more often returns without being scandalized enough."[57] A stream of pleasure guides written for English and American tourists—from Captain Wray Sylvester's *Nocturnal Pleasures of Paris* (1895) to Bruce Reynolds' *Paris with the Lid Off* (1927)—reflected and encouraged the common-male fantasies about the city.

In the modernized metropolis, nighttime amusements and sexual adventure flourished as never before. With the spread of gas lights and improved policing, the boulevards of the Second Empire became more than ever a nocturnal playground for a diverse set of Parisians, ranging from the fashionable to the ragtag, joined by growing numbers of provincials and foreigners. Women for sale boldly exhibited themselves on the sidewalks and in the cafés, often using the light and shadow to their advantage. The phrase "Paris by night" became a famous siren call, shorthand for an array of pleasures linked to sexual fantasies. With the cover of darkness came the promise of a carnivalesque release from rational control—unlimited possibilities for hedonist excesses—or "a high old time," as Sylvester's guidebook put it.[58] After dark the City of Light, under the aegis of reason and work, morphed into a shadowy realm of alluring dangers and carnal pleasures. Paris by night became a legend of moveable feasts, an unending party, a riotous rebellion against the daytime order of toil and constraint.

STAGING PARIS

From the Second Empire on, savvy Parisians recognized that an embellished Paris could bring countless new opportunities for economic gain. Adopting a tradition of kings from Louis XIV on, Haussmann built with the understanding that a magnificent city would attract more foreigners and their money, which would be "a source of prosperity for the [local] population," wrote Maxime du Camp in 1875. Ordinary Parisians, too, realized that "the pleasures [of Paris] attract foreigners and that foreigners bring money." So the Parisian "joins in, multiplies the places of amusement, gets rich, and, like the dog that eats his master's dinner, he takes his part of the cake; he amuses himself as much as he can."[59] Many of the successful new "places of amusement" offered commercial spectacles of Parisian life, high and low. Many were also atmospheric sets in which customers could play in famously Parisian ways.[60]

One district of the capital above all emerged in the fin de siècle as the main stage-set for dreams of Parisian fun: Montmartre. The name itself evoked not just a poor, hilly quarter, but a distinctive popular culture and way of life. As a village outside the city limits until 1860, it was free of Paris taxes, and its drinking places flourished by providing cheaper drink. As a semi-rural area of low rents, Montmartre was home to poor working people and artists. Politically it was an enclave of radicalism. Its leading role in the Commune of 1871 remained a vivid memory for both the Right and the Left. But in the fin de siècle it became best known for its exciting dissident variant of French culture, produced by Bohemian artists and writers who lived, worked, and played there. "We have the Montmartre genre, Montmartre art, Montmartre wit"—all different from *Parisian* styles and wit, André Billy pointed out in 1907. Montmartre creations, he observed, were an "exaggeration" of strengths and deficiencies of the French as a whole.[61] Montmartre, so quintessentially Parisian in the minds of foreigners and provincials, owed much of its special character to provincials—and to foreigners as well. It was a man from the Quercy, Clavel d'Aurimont, who first drew curiosity-seekers to his Montmartre quarry with drink and song at the end of the eighteenth century.[62] The founder of the famous cabaret Chat Noir, Rodolphe Salis, was from Chatellerault, and many of his singers were also immigrants to Paris. The leading ballad-eer of the Parisian riffraff, Aristide Bruant, came from the Loiret. Joseph Oller, founder of the Moulin Rouge, was a native of Spanish Catalonia. Artists Caran d'Ache, Willette, Steinlen, and Toulouse-Lautrec also came from places far from the Montmartre they helped to define.

By the turn of the century Montmartre was center stage for commercial productions of the Paris imaginary. Montmartre's artistic and literary cafés were "now among the shows of Paris," reported the author of *The Life of Paris* in 1900. "Some of the Bohemians for the decorative part of the scheme are hired precisely like the waiters, and paid on a truck system of free drinks. The net result is the patronage of provincials and of foreign-ers, especially candid souls from overseas, who think they are looking on something peculiarly Parisian." Applause was "manufactured" by leaders of claques, and a policeman was kept visible to show that the authorities were concerned with maintaining order.[63] The much-publicized Chat Noir became a showcase Bohemia for tourists, and it spawned numerous imi-tators. So did Aristide Bruant's cabaret—already before 1900, even while the original was still in business.

Dance halls, too, were stage-managed to play to visitors' dreams. Some of the women available for dancing were actually "decoys" hired by the proprietors to pose as simple fun-loving Parisiennes, the Baedeker guides pointed out. Hinting at prostitution, the propriety-conscious Baedeker declared it obvious that "ladies cannot attend these balls." The Moulin Rouge earned mention as "perhaps the chief of these places of amusement on the right bank."[64] The same taint attached to such other well-known halls as the Moulin de la Galette, the Latin-Quarter's Bal Bullier, and the Salle Wagram near the Arc de Triomphe. After the First World War the hireling of the dance hall became known as the "professional dancer," the most prominent of whom were men profiting from the new scarcity of adult males—"gigolos" preying on well-off, older women.

Other entrepreneurs staged lowlife Paris for sightseers seeking frissons of fear and disgust. Visits to the haunts of derelicts, drunks, prostitutes, and pimps had taken on a fashionable cachet in the mid-nineteenth century when they became known as favorite nightspots of visiting dukes of Russia. Hence the thrills of "slumming" known as the "tour of the Grand Dukes." In the last decades of the century guidebooks and memoirs routinely described some of the lowlife dens as fascinating attractions to be visited. Tourists often hired a guide for a tour, and some also paid a police detective to go along, just to be safe, as guidebooks recommended. In addition, the sightseers paid for drinks in each dive (*assommoir*) visited. Two of the best-known dreadful places were the Château Rouge and Père Lunette, close together on the Left Bank in a courtyard and a back street off the Place Maubert. The reason that tourists "so particularly remember these two places," noted Davis, "is that these are the only two places any one ever sees, and . . . [the visitors] do not recall the fact that the neighboring houses were of hopeless respectability, and that they were able to pick up a cab within a hundred yards of these houses."[65]

Young Frenchmen who know all the worlds of Paris tell you mysteriously of these places, and of how they visited them disguised in blue smocks and guarded by detectives; . . . and every newspaper correspondent who visits Paris for the first time writes home of them as typical of Parisian low life. They are as typical of Parisian low life as the animals in the Zoo in Central Park are typical of the other animals we see drawing stages and horse-cars and broughams on the city streets, and you require the guardianship of a detective when you visit them as much as you would need a policeman in Mulberry Bend or at an organ recital in Carnegie Hall. They are show-places, or at least they have become so, and though they would no doubt exist without the aid of the tourist or the man about town of intrepid spirit, they count upon him, and are prepared for him with set speeches.[66]

The habitués of the dives—homeless beggars, thieves, alcoholic men and women, "heavy-eyed absinthe-drinkers [who] raise their heads to stare mistily at the visitor"—were not necessarily actors, but they were part of the show for visitors. Completing the decor were sensational wall paintings depicting bloody crimes and notorious murders—"ghastly" scenes full of "scarlet paint for blood." In the Château Rouge "a sharp-faced boy," speaking an almost unintelligible argot, gave an admiring talk about the criminals and their crimes, "and he roars forth the name of 'Antoine, who murdered the policeman Jervois,' as though he were saying 'Gambetta, the founder of the republic.'" In sum, the Château Rouge was "a miserable chamber of horrors." Nearby, just around a couple of corners, the café of Père Lunette was similar in clientele ("the lowest class of women and men") and in decor—walls "painted throughout with faces and scenes a little better in execution than those in the Château Rouge, and a little worse in subject."[67]

In the decade after 1900, a spate of sensationalist newspaper stories about brazen young delinquents depicted their lives as a drama of passionate love affairs, erotically charged dances, and deadly fights in the city's poorer parts. Dubbed *apaches*, they became the romantic antiheroes of a new popular legend. Capitalizing on the craze, some nightspots began hiring brawny porters from Les Halles and homeless men from the riverbanks to play the role of apache. But some of the unsavory characters that visitors saw in "faked apache dens" did not come from lowlife at all. "Red-aproned golden-casqued girls" danced and drank with "sinister-looking apaches with caps drawn over their eyes" . . . when tour groups entered such places. "In the course of the dancing a quarrel would break out. A duel with knives would be fought. The Grand Dukes had their money's worth of thrills; and then the girls took off their aprons and the men donned respectable hats and went quietly home to bed."[68] The real-life apaches had disappeared by the 1920s, and so had the Grand Dukes, but the tours were still a flourishing business. Guides still took provincials and foreigners to dingy accordion-music dance halls (*bals musettes*) in the Rue de Lappe and the Passage Thiéré (near Bastille), and they still dropped into shabby cafés and *caves* around Les Halles to hear singers perform Bruant's songs.[69]

The Moulin Rouge was a commercial stage-set of a different order, offering a more complex mix of Parisiana. Created in 1889, it was designed for moneyed Parisians and tourists seeking relief from Haussmann's modernity and the stale conventionality of most other chic nightspots. Its fake windmill façade linked it to the neighborhood's past—to the working windmills that had been prominent fixtures up on the slopes of the Butte Montmartre for centuries. The most famous of the authentic windmills, the Moulin de la Galette, had been converted to a dance hall early in the nineteenth century, and at century's end it lived on as an unpretentious hilltop haunt of local working-class people and impecunious artists. In contrast, the red pseudo-windmill, constructed on the boulevard below (in the Place Blanche), was much more accessible to a citywide, fashionable clientele. Its creators gave it a red exterior that signaled pleasures of the sort found in brothels and devilish dives (the Château Rouge, for example). In addition, its director immediately hired the city's most talented dancers of the cancan, that provocatively high-kicking, leg-baring performance hitherto found in low-class dance halls. In the new *bal*, where the admission price was high, the dance was a sexy simulacrum of the "popular," a lively show of erotic vulgarity staged for well-to-do spectators. The Moulin Rouge became known, too, for showcasing fun-loving models and artists. Festive evenings, featuring costumed parades and beautiful young women, were billed as special and "grand," though

FIGURE 1.6. On the edges of the vaunted "beau Paris" were the many rustic dwellings of the working poor, cut off from all that excited the capital's many admirers. This farm-like complex (in the Rue Château des Rentiers) was one of many in the peripheral thirteenth arrondissement circa 1900. (Photo UPF/ Archives de Paris—11Fi 3155.)

they were in fact routine performances every weekend. Leaving nothing to chance, the publicity-savvy management liberally distributed free passes to the press as well as to notables and celebrities to lend an aura of *Tout-Paris* glamour to the place.[70]

By 1900 Montmartre cabarets and the Moulin Rouge were world-famous attractions, whose offerings were defined by tourist expectations as much as by local inspiration. Although Montmartre, like the Capital of Pleasures generally, was becoming a prisoner of its past and reputation, it thrived in that role—at least up to the First World War. The district that seemed to some the epitome of Paris benefited from masterful promotion of its artistic Bohemia and edgy places of pleasure. Nowhere else in the city was there such a concentration of showplaces catering to the world's dreams of Paris.

PARIS AS A WOMAN

In imaginations almost everywhere, the capital was also epitomized by a human form—a feminine one, especially in the second half of the nineteenth century. Earlier, in the era of the revolutions of 1830 and 1848, Paris had been often personified as masculine, a heroic fighting figure. But in the decades following the ravages of the Commune and civil war of 1871, the face of the revolutionary was too disturbing to many. The fierce resistance of the Communards had shocked and frightened conservatives with not only male firebrands, but also the image of working women of Paris as fire-setting furies—*pétroleuses*.[71] That made a gentle woman's face more warmly welcome than ever. So late-nineteenth-century tributes to the city dwelled affectionately on Paris's politically innocent daughters, extolled for their alluring looks and charming personalities, unthreatening in every way.

Another facet of the city's feminine identity was the Seine, often described in the same terms as Parisian women. The river was "seductive" and "charming." She—*la* Seine—was languorous and curvaceous. "As it meanders and envelops like an elegant scarf, it gives Paris the attractiveness of a pretty woman," explained Paul Jarry in 1911.[72] Yet that gendered view of the river, a favorite of writers, did not become a truly popular emblem of Paris. Perhaps too many ordinary people knew an unappealing face of the Seine—its flotsam of dead fish, cats, dogs, and human cadavers (anyone fishing out a body could collect fifteen francs from the prefecture).[73]

The feminine emblems that became commonplace were rather the sexy, fun-loving young Parisienne and the elegant high-fashion woman. The former appeared in countless drawings in the light-hearted men's magazine *La Vie parisienne* and the bright posters of Jules Chéret. The ultra-stylish Parisienne became a standard image in the second half of the nineteenth century as new masters of haute couture (Worth, Doucet, Paquin, Redfern) established themselves in Paris and gained worldwide fame. To personify the "city of Paris" in an icon at the Universal Exposition of 1900, officials chose a statue of a tight-skirted, high-fashion Parisienne and placed it over the main entrance gate. Other faces of Paris that became famous were those of star actresses, dancers, demimondaines, and high-society beauties, disseminated widely as mass-produced studio photos and reproductions of paintings by artists such as Jean Béraud and Giovanni Boldini.[74]

Rhapsodic descriptions of Parisian women were staples for male journalists, who combined the admiring flâneur's gaze with the traditional praise of Paris. "If you recognize the true Parisienne and can distinguish her from all other women," declared writer Armand Silvestre in a 1900 guidebook, "you will truly know Paris. For the Parisienne is the secret and ever-singing soul [of Paris], the ever-vibrant charm, the always dazzling grace." Silvestre had in mind, as most chroniclers did, a perky young working girl, a pretty *midinette*, viewed running errands and going to and from work, catching the eye of the men she passes on the sidewalk. As Silvestre described her, she trots along like a partridge, attracts men irresistibly, and laughs at her admirers, yet she is good-hearted and sympathetic. She was the "flower that grew up among the paving stones" of the working-class quarters Montmartre and Belleville. Ignored were the many young women who were exhausted from overwork, malnourished, depressed, and ill, and those who resorted to prostitution just to survive.[75]

A specialized publishing industry fed men's fantasies about the city's women, especially about the *petites femmes de Paris*. Guidebooks for men, erotic postcards and photographs, and magazines such as *La Vie parisienne* depicted young Parisian women as a type—sexy, light-hearted, and ever ready for amorous adventure. That was exactly what a host of provincial men as well as foreigners were eager to believe and to find. Some women profited from the capital's reputation by feigning affection and sexual interest and then fleecing the out-of-towners, warned Delvau. But enough others made themselves fully available that the legend of the capital's ready-and-willing sirens waxed strong in the second half of the nineteenth century. Out in the provinces the image of the capital turned erotic from the Second Empire to the turn-of-the-century, Alain Corbin tells us. Visitors with a sexual spree in mind found, theirs for the choosing, a multitude of women working the streets and hotels as well as fantasy-serving "maisons de rendez-vous" (with *filles* dressed as brides or nuns, for example) in the "great Babylon."[76]

For critics of the big city, the women available for purchase were symptomatic of a generalized immorality: Paris itself was a whore. Some critics also vented their moral indignation on ordinary Parisiennes, negatively

FIGURE 1.7. In the turn-of-the-century imaginary (shaped by popular song and literature), Parisian workingwomen were young, light-hearted, pretty, and stylish. As a foil to that idealized image, the prostitute also figured as typically or symbolically Parisian. In Pierre Vidal's drawings (1896) for a book on the boulevards, both types were featured—three "honest" women strolling together on the boulevards in contrast to other women who lingered alone, waiting to be picked up. Drawings by Pierre Vidal, reproduced as illustrations for *La Vie des Boulevards Madeleine-Bastille* by Georges Montorgueil (1896).

stereotyped as egoistic, superficial, artificial, and destructive. Misogynist conceptions were notoriously rife in the second half of the century. Although the frightening figure of the Commune's *pétroleuses* had faded into the historical background by the century's close, along with the revolutionary identity of the city, fears of the convention-challenging "New Woman" were mounting. Yet these did not play out generally in popular characterizations of the capital. Around 1900 the feminine images most commonly representing Paris were attractive ones: images of pretty working-class coquettes (the *midinettes*), demimondaines, and haute-couture beauties.[77] They all lent support to visions of the city as a light-hearted, seductive, fashionable woman.

PANAME: PARIS OF THE LITTLE PEOPLE

While images of Paris's women, pleasures, modernity, artistic brilliance, and beautiful antiquities won over elites and visitors, a quite different imagery became the favorite of ordinary Parisians: a vision of the city as a cluster of modest neighborhoods that were like villages, full of good humble working people. The chief purveyor of that view was popular song. Many a tune depicted the life of that local everyday village Paris, affectionately nicknamed "Paname" early in the twentieth century. A living semblance of such an imagined Paris centered in the poorer *faubourgs*, districts just outside the city center, particularly beyond the Grands Boulevards on the Right Bank, and the quarters to the north and the east inhabited by worker families—Belleville, Ménilmontant, and Montmartre.[78] Ordinary folk were still numerous in the central quarters too, although many of the poorest had been displaced by Haussmann's urban renewal.

Paname was the Paris of the "little people"—the multitude of small craftsmen, unskilled workers, shopkeepers, seamstresses and shop girls, as well as a motley populace that earned a living in the streets: singers and organ grinders, sellers of hats and lampshades, pushcart vendors of fruits and vegetables, ragpickers, newspaper hawkers, and itinerants who sharpened scissors, re-caned chairs, pulled teeth, mended pots, and exhibited trained bears and parrots.

Even after the Second Empire's slum-clearings, Paris was the most densely populated city in the world—with over 2.5 million people living in its twenty arrondissements toward the end of the century.[79] The apartment buildings and houses of poor and not-so-poor families were overstuffed with inhabitants. Public spaces, too, were crowded, especially main arteries and markets, during the day. Thoroughfares in almost every quarter teemed with people buying and selling, lugging goods, and making their way to work or pleasure on foot and on bicycles, dodging an onrush of fiacres (over 15,000), horse-drawn omnibuses (766), trams, wagons, carts—and automobiles (over 2,000 as early as 1900).[80] Thousands of cafés and other drinking places were busy day and night. In the evenings they provided poor and modest Parisians with a modicum of comfort that was lacking at home—light, heat, and sociability.[81] Each night, too, the central market Les Halles was swarming with plebeians from all over the city, where they bought food at the lowest prices and drank and ate in the market-workers' cafés.

Whether they lived in the Marais or Belleville or the Faubourg Saint-Antoine, the little people of Paris spoke a common vernacular of playful slang, and they enjoyed the same simple pleasures in cafés and neighborhood dance halls. Most of them lived and worked right in their home district and rarely went outside the city, except for Sunday outings to nearby riverside resorts in spring and summer. The neighborhood they called their "quartier" was not the official administrative quarter, but a subjectively defined locality, often described as a village, centering around home, a favorite café, shops, friends, workplace, and perhaps a parish church. With that social reality as a common reference point, a more global sense of popular Parisian community developed in entertainments such as the café-concerts, where populist singers like the Second Empire star Thérésa served up songs and humor ostensibly relaying the viewpoints of the working people (as art historian T. J. Clark has explained).[82] The larger "imagined community" (Benedict Anderson's term, here applied to the city) was also nourished by populist writers, politicians, and the popular press, all of which flourished in the new era of democracy and mass literacy of the late nineteenth century.

As the songs depicted them, the people of Paname grew up poor and good-hearted, fell in love, and raised families of more good ordinary people, while coping from time to time with sickness, insolvency, and the death of loved ones. In the sadder songs called "realist," some of the good women fell into prostitution, as a means of survival or after being abandoned by deceitful men, and died young. In the moral universe of Paname, these and other hapless *faubouriens* were salt-of-the-earth Parisians whose sorrows threw into bold relief the good fortune and good times of the well off. Their stories, sentimental and melodramatic, were the subjects of some of the most widely known songs of the time—notably, those of Aristide Bruant and Eugénie Buffet.[83]

The populist image of an amiable community called Paname was not simply a paean to the good humble Parisians. It was also a dangerously distorting fiction, a false memory evoking a bygone time of few newcomers, fewer marginal people, and no divisive subcultures of significance. At best it simply ignored the large population of provincials and foreigners living in Paris (foreigners made up 7 percent of the population before 1914—three times more than in London, Vienna, or Berlin).[84] But in times of economic downturns and heightened political antagonisms, a dark side of the Paname fable surfaced: a populist hostility toward groups seen as different from "true" Parisians—foreigners, Jews, and the rich. In that version, the "little people" figured as the antithesis of the city's "cosmopolitans," the "others" whose privileged experience and loyalties reached far beyond the neighborhoods of humble Parisians. Such resentments surfaced and even erupted into acts of violence most notably during the Dreyfus affair in the late 1890s, as they did later in the 1920s, '30s, and '40s.[85] In better times, for most Parisians as for Paris aficionados living abroad, the appeal of Paname has been its gentle, sentimental side—evocations of friendly, face-to-face community life enjoyed by Paris's plebeians, especially those in the neighborhoods untouched by the demolition crews that made the modern City of Light.

The nickname "Paname" became widely popular during the First World War when its use spread from homesick Parisian soldiers in the trenches to the home front. And it has remained familiar to Parisians right up to the present. Foreigners may not know the slangy term, but many around the world know well the classic Paname imagery: they know it from Piaf's songs about euphoric (when not broken-hearted) lovers in the working-class faubourgs, pitiable streetwalkers, and accordionists; from songs about the humble quarter Ménilmontant sung by Maurice

Chevalier and Charles Trenet; from famous paintings by the likes of Renoir, Monet, Toulouse-Lautrec, and Steinlen; from photographs by Atget, Brassaï, Willy Ronis, and Robert Doisneau; from movies by René Clair and Marcel Carné showing the people of the faubourgs and outer quarters; and more recently from scenes in the hit movie *Amélie* (2001), featuring a small Montmartre café and its colorful habitués.[86]

.　.　.

Paname and the other dominant identities of modern Paris—progress, pleasure, and the old picturesque—were all ways of covering over or denying the capital's revolutionary history and its reputation for revolt. They not only appealed to the dreams of people around the world, but also suited many in France—from government and business leaders to writers and ordinary Parisians—any and all who wanted to downplay (or forget) the recurrent revolutions and bloody street battles. Leaders of the Republic enhanced their regime's standing and French prestige in world opinion by promoting the capital as a showcase of a happy modernity. Writers on the city's pleasures, arts, and Old Paris pleased readers by presenting their subjects as the enduring, charming bases of Parisian life and history, relegating the revolutions to a neatly finished past and ignoring contentious politics. Every Parisian profiting in some way from the city's visitors stood to gain from encouraging the Paris-paradise dreams.

To be sure, the memory of revolutionary Paris still had many faithful guardians, militants on the Left (Radical, Socialist, syndicalist). They worked through the Municipal Council to mark public space with statues embodying their cause—the Republic (nicknamed "Marianne," a classical woman wearing a Liberty Cap), Voltaire, Rousseau, Danton. As part of their struggle against the political power of the Roman Catholic Church, they tried repeatedly to stop the construction of the counterrevolutionaries' basilica of Sacré-Coeur. And they fought hard for the Revolution's principles of human rights and equality during the Dreyfus affair. But they did not have enough power to direct the course of Paris in the late nineteenth century (or most of the twentieth). The state-appointed prefect who administered Paris was there to constrain the Municipal Council, and by law the capital had no elected mayor. Paris's Left and the Republic itself were on the defensive against crowd-inciting enemies—monarchist, clerical, anti-Semitic, Bonapartist—who threatened and even attempted coups periodically. To garner the widest support possible for the beleaguered Republic, the moderate republicans carefully avoided reminders of the capital's rebellious, regime-toppling past and instead emphasized themes of patriotism and progress, folding Paris's revolutions into the Ville Lumière narrative. Nonetheless, the Left lost Paris by 1900: the capital went over to conservatives and nationalists in the elections (municipal and legislative) of 1900 and remained a stronghold of the Right for decades.[87]

Besides diverting from political contention, the attractive identities so ardently trumpeted at the century's close also served to counter denunciations of Paris as an avatar of decadence—a sinkhole for morals, traditional artistic quality, and community life. Behind the pinnacle-of-glory boasts were not only fears of decadence, but also fears of destruction, nightmares of Paris in ruins.[88] Educated Parisians knew well about sinful cities meeting with doom and punishment in centuries past. But anxious ones had more than Sodom and Babylon on their minds in the late nineteenth century. They shared a painful memory of the devastating civil war and fires ending the Commune in May 1871. All those burnt-out buildings and piles of rubble made a future destruction of Paris easy to imagine.

In the decades after that "terrible year," Parisians not only rebuilt the destroyed buildings of the city, but also added new constructions that embodied a range of bright dreams—from the City of Light and the Capital of Pleasures to "Old Paris" and Paname. All of those imaginaries had their advocates and promoters, each presenting a version of the capital as the important authentic one. Officials of the Third Republic demonstrated commitment to the Ville Lumière project by building new public schools, hospitals, new town halls (*mairies*) in the arrondissements, and the engineering marvel that is the Eiffel Tower, while also erecting a legion of statues of "great men" and the symbolic figure Marianne, the now peaceful feminine heir of the Revolution.[89] Enterprising businessmen, for their part, built diverting simulations drawn from a more playful imaginary—heaven-and-hell theme-cabarets, for example, and dives trumped up for slumming tourists. The commercial creations that succeeded became iconic landmarks that attracted not only tourists, but also Parisians eager to venture beyond

FIGURE 1.8. Pride in the modernized city co-existed with fears of its destruction. The memory of the fiery repression of the Commune in 1871 haunted Parisians through the rest of the century. The "bloody week" of civil war in late May left many ruins around the city, such as this burned-out shell of the Hôtel de Ville (town hall). The Hôtel de Ville was rebuilt in the same Renaissance style as the original in the years 1873–1882. Photo by Alphonse Liébert in *Les Ruines de Paris* by Alfred d'Aunay (Paris, 1872).

their everyday worlds. A notable handful of them became legends integral to the reputation of Paris: a fake red windmill that housed a glamorous night spot, an imitation English elite pub-and-restaurant named Maxim's, and play-acting cabarets featuring down-and-out locals, sophisticated Bohemians, and hot-blooded delinquents. In patronizing such places, individuals defined themselves and Paris at the same time.

Around the turn of the century, then, Paris was both modern and "old." It was fashionable and elegant, but also "naughty," vulgar, fun, and thrillingly disgusting. It was a world capital (or "capital of the world," some asserted), but it was also a cluster of ingrown villages. It was a modern metropolis, but it still harbored back-alley wildernesses, inhabited by "savages." Its many sites "worth seeing" ranged from the refined to the revolting—with such distinctions often deliberately blurred by entertainment producers and customers alike. In the face of the capital's prodigious variety, observers looked for some unifying character and tried to sum it up in some single catchword, such as City of Light or Paname. For historical understanding, a better approach is to see all the identities as parts of a large, unwieldy whole, each revealing some truths and dreams about the city—while concealing others.

CHAPTER 2

The Memory of a Certain
Belle Époque (1914–circa 1960)

Or How the Turn-of-the-Century
Lived On Beyond Its Time

The Paris of 1900 lived on in the cityscape for more than half a century, surviving wars, economic crises, changes of regimes, and shifting aesthetic tastes. Neither of the World Wars brought large-scale destruction to the capital. None of the governments of the late Third Republic or the Vichy regime made major changes in the city's physical fabric. The Paris of 1900 also lived on in memories and dreams, sustained by a stream of nostalgia-spurring books, plays, paintings, photographs, and movies. When all was said and remembered, the city that was famously modern in the late nineteenth century became a dear "Old Paris" for the twentieth century. Historians usually dwell on change and the reasons for it, but in this case it is important to understand why there was so little change—why the turn-of-the-century remained so fixed in both the physical structures and the mental images of the city.

Contrary to what historians have commonly written, a rosy collective "memory" of the era around 1900 did not emerge right after the Great War with all its sorrows and stresses. It took years of mourning, remembering, and forgetting for a constellation of cheery images to crystallize in the selective recollection known as "the Belle Époque," the turn-of-the-century viewed as a singularly happy time, a vanished golden age. In that now-familiar memory, the City of Light was recalled at its brightest and the Capital of Pleasures at its most enjoyable, leaving out warts, slums, rats, hatreds, political strife, and the grim suburbs (*banlieue*) of workers, factories, and squalor. In this chapter we will see how that memory developed and became an emotional touchstone in thinking about Paris's present and future—with important long-term consequences for the city.

FIGURE 2.1. The memory of the Belle Époque lives on—visibly in postcards
and posters, in restaurants and cafés boasting "1900" décor, Guimard's art
nouveau métro entries, and of course at the legendary nightspots Maxim's and
the Moulin Rouge. More mundane set pieces of nineteenth-century modernity
are also still prominent: Morris columns (for *spectacle* advertising), cast-iron
newspaper kiosks, and Wallace fountains. All those pieces of "street furniture"
date from the period 1868–1900, as did the 1,200-some urinals once installed
around the city but almost all removed in the twentieth century—many in the
1960s. (Photos by the author.)

MOURNING AND NOSTALGIA

The four years of the First World War dimmed the luster of the prog-
ress-generator Ville Lumière, but the Capital of Pleasures continued to
flourish. Music halls, cinemas, cafés, and bars did a booming business,
thanks in large part to added demand from French and allied soldiers on
leave. For most Parisians, however, the enjoyment found in those places
paled beside their private worries and fears for the men on the battlefield. From time to time, fears for the home front also gripped the people
of Paris, as bombs and cannon shells (all told, over a thousand) fell on
scattered parts of the city and the suburbs, killing a total of 522 people
and wounding 1,223.[1]

FIGURE 2.2. The capital in the large escaped destruction in the First World War, but some buildings here and there suffered damage from time to time. Bombs dropped from a Zeppelin destroyed this apartment building in Belleville, for example (88 Rue Sorbier), in the night of January 29, 1916. The seventeen bombs that struck Belleville that night left 75 killed and 33 wounded. (Lansiaux collection, Bibliothèque historique de la Ville de Paris.)

After the guns of 1914–1918 fell silent, the French public looked backward not to the antebellum "good old days" but rather to the searing experience of the war years. While families nursed memories of lost loved ones, France's national and local leaders did their utmost, through patriotic speeches and ceremonies, to consolidate a collective memory of the heroes who "died for France"—the 1.4 million men killed on the battlefields north and east of the capital.[2]

At the same time, without any official patronage, a few places emerged as memory sites of prewar Paris. First to gain attention were the earthwork fortifications surrounding the city since the 1840s. Soon after the armistice, authorities deemed those *fortifs* useless for modern military purposes and announced plans to dismantle them in 1919, opening them up to new development. The prospect of losing those open spaces touched off waves of sadness and nostalgia among ordinary Parisians. For the humble folk living on the edge of Paris, the fortifs were a precious playground, a free space where young lovers made love, children played, *apaches* like "Jo the Terror" and "Jean the Tattooed One" fought, and some of the poorest of the poor lived in shanties or camped out. Parisians who had suffered so many painful losses through the four years of bloodletting now faced the loss of a cherished part of their city. Its death warrant symbolized the passing of a pastoral side of the city's outskirts—quiet natural terrain for leisure and play, open to even the poorest. The disappearing fortifs became a focal point of sentimental memory, expressed in popular songs for years.[3] Authorities promised to develop the now liberated terrain as green space for the congested city, but instead they allowed housing to be built on much of the land through the interwar years.

History-minded Parisians felt similar regret over the decline of the once-chic Grands Boulevards and the continuing demolition of rundown

FIGURE 2.3. Ecstatic throngs filled the Grands Boulevards to celebrate the end of the "Great War" on November 11, 1918. On that unforgettable day Parisians united in joy not known again until August 1944 when the capital celebrated its liberation from German occupation. (Bibliothèque nationale de France.)

old houses. Even the razing of an outmoded dusty arcade, the Passage de l'Opéra, in 1924–1925 touched off sadness and nostalgia. The most resounding response to its demise was Louis Aragon's *Le Paysan de Paris* (1926), which offered a guidebook-like appreciation of the old arcade's shops, cafés, theater, bathhouse, bookstore, and brothel—together with surrealist reveries about everything strange, marvelous, and sexual therein.[4] More common in its approach was Élie Richard's *Paris qui meurt* (Dying Paris) (1923), a tome of historical scholarship interspersed with personal remembrance and nostalgia. Richard affectionately chronicled the many streets and buildings destroyed by "the pitiless demolishers" since his school-boy days. Though sad and embittered, Richard was in no mood to fight, and he knew that most Parisians felt likewise. "So go the times," he mused. "Everything degenerates, is transformed, and is commercialized *sans relief*. . . . But people get used to everything, even to novelty, to slum-clearings, vacant blocks and gaping holes: to the point where the baron-prefect [Haussmann] appears sometimes quite modest and old-fashioned."[5] Here Richard exaggerated: compared with Haussmann's operations, the post–Second Empire demolitions were scattered and small-scale, and the pacing slower. Nonetheless, to wistful older Parisians, signs of Paris's dying seemed abundant. Yet anger and sadness readily settled into resignation.

Preservation efforts were small and ineffectual. The Paris historical commission that might have spearheaded such efforts was sapped by the same resignation that Richard expressed. The Commission du Vieux Paris, a semi-public advisory body, had no legal clout. Its stated purpose was to inform Parisians about the city's history—the "vestiges of Old Paris" and particularly their "picturesque aspect"—hence its devotion to compiling an inventory of Old Paris, "street by street, house by house," and to acquiring photographs of everything that might disappear.[6] When confronted with a proposed demolition, the commission could merely put in its opinion as a consultative voice, which city and national authorities generally ignored. The public also ignored it. The minutes and reports of the commission's meetings were published only infrequently, sometimes ten years late. In some years, only one meeting in ten made it into the records. No reports at all appeared between 1932 and 1955.[7] Parisians who might have looked into the commission's proceedings found dry, detailed notes on old buildings that were slated for demolition or already being razed. Only the buildings that were centuries old—eighteenth century at least—seriously interested the commission. When some members wanted to obtain state protection for the art-nouveau métro entries of Hector Guimard in 1918, they got nowhere. (Guimard's creations were not designated historical monuments until 1965.) Whenever state authorities wanted a privately owned building preserved for historical reasons, they had to obtain the consent of the owner, and the latter usually opted for demolition to make way for something new and more profitable. Monetary compensation also had to be provided to the owner, and the state funds for such purposes were perennially scant, especially for Paris properties, whose prices ran high. Frustrated and despairing, the lovers of Old Paris perpetually raged against the "legion" of "vandals," who continued their "attacks" and "crimes" "with a tireless tenacity."[8]

Unlike the passionate history-lovers, the great majority of Parisians did not focus on old buildings per se, nor did they rage. Their response was rather a generalized sense of loss and a quiet nostalgia for lost good times. It was a longing for an era that seemed to be free of the heartaches and daily-life struggles left in the war's wake. The very memory of places associated with those better times seemed to offer some consolation. Perhaps the most warmly regarded vestiges of Old Paris were the once-outlying villages of Paris, sites of memory that were even more widely cherished than the *fortifications*. Eleven suburban communes and parts of thirteen others had been officially absorbed into the city back in 1860 under the Second Empire, but their identity as "villages" remained strong in the minds and hearts of their inhabitants—and many other Parisians as well.

Like the fortifs, the villages were associated with poor and modest working people who lived apart from the grand historical Ville Lumière. Montmartre, a legendary site of Bohemian life and religious pilgrimage, was the most celebrated of the former villages and the prime focus of nostalgia. Untouched by Haussmann's renovations, the hill offered extraordinary panoramic views of the city and a quiet refuge from the busy boulevards below. But in the early twentieth century big new commercial buildings and six- and seven-story apartment buildings had cropped up along the main arteries on the lower slopes. After the war, tall apartment buildings went up all over the hill, filling lots once covered with brush and large trees, small old houses and sheds, gardens and farm-style courtyards. The construction of new streets (the Avenue Junot, for example) and the widening of older ones (the Rue du Mont-Cenis) brought the city onto the north and western sides. Altogether, most of the Butte was besieged by developers in the years between the world wars. By the end of the 1920s only the Place du Tertre and a few nearby streets retained a provincial village look.

In 1920 a group of colorful Montmartre characters took a symbolic stand against the encroachments of modern Paris: assembled in the cabaret Au Lapin Agile, they proclaimed their quarter free and independent—"la Commune libre de Montmartre." They were not only harking back to Montmartre's pre-1860 local autonomy, but they were also playfully reclaiming the independent political life it briefly experienced under the Paris Commune of 1871. And they were renewing the half-in-jest electoral campaigns of Rodolphe Salis and Aristide Bruant in the fin de siècle. Some of them presented themselves for mock elections as the "anti-skyscraper list," calling for an end to buildings over one story. Some denounced water and the municipal Campagnie des Eaux, endorsing absinthe instead. Another list of their candidates (*la liste sauvagiste*) promised to turn the basilica Sacré-Coeur into a municipal swimming pool and pledged to make a daily *apéritif* "free and obligatory" for all voters.[9]

But when writer Francis Carco declared in 1919 that "Montmartre no longer exists," he was not referring to a political or administrative entity. He meant the quaint old village of artists and writers that he had known as a youth living in the rustic dwellings high on the Butte, away from the fast-paced boulevards below. He meant the now-legendary Bohemian Montmartre of the prewar years, a community of young artists and writers sharing their poverty and camaraderie. That *vie de bohème*, he sadly noted, lived on only in the "credulous imagination of adolescents in the provinces." The Butte that his circle of young Bohemians knew "ten or fifteen years ago" was as much a bygone as their youth.[10] While admitting that "We need legends," he insisted that the "le bon temps" had ended. A period of glorious vitality had succumbed to dreariness. Carco viewed it as historical inevitability. Just as Bohemian Montmartre had disappeared, so eventually the new artistic quarter of Montparnasse would go, turning into just another of the "vague and drab intersections" in the modern city.[11]

A small group of Montmartre writers and artists, led by such well-known figures as Willette and Francisque Poulbot, organized to fight back against the developers, project by project. The defenders of Old Montmartre won a few battles, but they lost many others. Most notably, they did not prevent the destruction of the house of Berlioz (1925) or the one called the house of the fabled Parisienne Mimi Pinson (1926) on the Rue du Mont-Cenis. Their biggest victory was to ward off the construction of an apartment building on the sloping open lot known as La Belle-Gabrielle. With the support of the city, they transformed that parcel into a vineyard. Their first grape harvest was celebrated in October 1934 with the president of the Republic in attendance, and every year thereafter a well-publicized village festival took place (and still takes place today). The old rural tradition of the grape harvest, thus revived in the heart of the *grand-ville*, became an annual good-news story featured in movie newsreels shown throughout France. It was newsworthy, however, because it was exceptional, and a striking counterpoint to the widespread sense that old Montmartre, like Vieux Paris as a whole, was dying.

Yet, amid the repeated death notices, Montmartre kept alive its own micro-culture, capitalizing on nostalgia. The paintings of Maurice Utrillo, depicting postcard-quaint old streets, found eager buyers on both sides of the Atlantic. Poulbot's drawings of poor Old-Montmartre gamins, wide-eyed and soulful, became famous archetypes, enjoying strong demand from tourists and Parisians alike. Memoirs of prewar Montmartre culture were also popular. Writers Francis Carco, Pierre Mac Orlan, Roland Dorgelès, and André Warnod worked the nostalgia vein with an outpouring of books and articles recounting the youthful life of Bohemians and their high jinks in cabarets of the Butte. "We don't conceive of Montmartre without Carco, nor Carco without Montmartre," noted a book reviewer in 1929.[12] Memoirs like Carco's nurtured the Bohemia legend of the Butte, stirring the hopes and dreams of youths far from Paris. "As adolescents back in our little provincial towns, . . . [when] someone said the word Montmartre, our imaginations immediately took off," recalled a journalist two decades later. "Montmartre was the setting of creation, the smile and the tears of youth." "We couldn't imagine that anyone could write elsewhere than in Montmartre, under the arbor of the Lapin à Gill, in the presence of Frédé."[13]

A populist variant of the legend, enshrined in a hit song of 1925, filled the imaginations of Parisians who were neither Bohemians nor artists. In the slangy lyrics of "Où est-il donc?" ("Where is it now?"), a poor Parisian immigrant in New York City sadly recalls the good old days in Montmartre—his corner bistro, his favorite dance halls, and his pals (copains) around the Place Blanche and up the hill around the Place du Tertre. Then he describes the ongoing destruction: "They're demolishing our old houses. / On the empty lots of the Butte / Big banks will appear soon." The song ends on a funereal note: "Lamenting the bygone times [and] thinking of Salis, / We'll sing, Montmartre, your 'De Profundis.'"[14]

Other old villages of Paris lost even more of their character than Montmartre did, but none of them attracted as much attention from outsiders. By the 1920s the Butte-aux-Cailles, deep in the poor thirteenth arrondissement, was one of the very few to retain an old provincial atmosphere: it was "admirable in resisting the modern" and keeping its semi-rural character, noted the author of Paris qui meurt.[15] "Village," however, meant more than old-fashioned buildings and roads; it also meant an old-fashioned community life idealized and popularly known as Paname—a close-knit neighborhood of Parisians whose lives were interwoven by working, shopping, and socializing together. With so many people going daily far beyond their home turf by métro and bus, and moving in and out, the old kind of inward-looking community was in decline all over the city. A certain Paris was dying—the familiar old Paris of small local worlds cherished by old-timers.

ENDURING SITES OF PLEASURE AND MEMORY

Melancholy and nostalgia crystallized, too, around some celebrated turn-of-the-century places that, far from dying, flourished after the war. Those survivals of 1900 became symbols of an authentic old Paris of pleasures that somehow escaped the ravages of the twentieth century. In the late 1920s a Guide des plaisirs à Paris confidently reissued the old boast: "There is no city in the world where pleasures are more numerous and more varied than in Paris."[16] Many of the "Parisian paradises" listed in the guide were entertainment places of the sort that had become famous in the late nineteenth century. For example, the theme cabarets Ciel (heaven), L'Enfer (hell), and Le Néant (nothingness or death) were still amusing customers with playful evenings out-of-this-world. The original Chat Noir cabaret had gone out of business long ago, but numerous imitators and reproductions were available. Among them were Montmartre nightspots called the Chat Noir and Les Quat'z'arts. The Chat Noir got special notice for its distinguished ancestor: "The Chat Noir . . . the 'father' of the cabarets of Montmartre is still very amusing." Unmentioned was the fact that it had no connection with the original. The guide went on to assure readers that "the old cancan" was "not forgotten at the Tabarin dance hall (Rue Victor-Massé)." Happily, it seemed, the past lived on.

A cabaret named Bruant (84 Boulevard Rochechouart) featured a performer impersonating "the popular *chansonnier*" of the fin de siècle. A string of Aristide Bruant successors had taken up his act, wearing his signature costume—red belt, large felt hat, tall boots—and performing with all his "mordant verve," reported the *Guide des plaisirs*. Each evening one of them led audiences through the classic routine: greeting newcomers with the old insults—"ah, what a mug!" ("ah, c'te gueule, c'te binette!")—and yelling "pigs" at those who left.[17]

Every day a cluster of these Montmartre "cabarets" opened just for a crowd of tourists arriving in "Paris-by-night" motor-coaches. As expected, the shows featured *chansonniers* and a cast of extras in period-piece costume—men wearing "long flaxen wigs, baggy trousers, flowing neckties" and "girls" wearing red aprons and "golden casque"-like wigs.[18]

The famed "tour of the Grand Dukes" was still available, too, for visitors wanting to see the underside of the capital—"a strange, often horrible, sometimes dangerous, but so interesting Paris," noted the *Guide des plaisirs*. Particularly fascinating were somber places that resembled "the old Paris of the fifteenth century and dives that seem to belong only to the novels of Eugène Sue, Gaboriau and Montépin." To enter into these "true Parisian hells," the *Guide* advised, the visitor should take along two or three companions or—better still—go to the Préfecture de Police and hire a plain-clothes "agent de la Sûreté."[19] The warnings (probably unwarranted) reinforced the promise of pleasurable frissons in a noirish Old Paris.

Many of the classic boulevard restaurants and cafés of the nineteenth century were gone by the '20s (the Café Anglais, for example, disappeared in 1913, and the Café Riche in 1916) or were in their death throes. Many cafés-concerts and music halls had also disappeared or were converted to cinemas by the late 1920s, and the great majority met those fates in the 1930s.[20] But some of the most chic nightspots from the prewar era were still flourishing. Among the most famous survivors were Maxim's, the Moulin Rouge, and the Folies-Bergère. Why did they last while so many others did not? Much of the answer lies in the special historic associations that each enjoyed. It also lies in the adroitness with which their managements worked and reworked the Belle-Époque memory.

. . .

Maxim's art-nouveau décor was a museum-worthy survival of another era's taste for exuberant luxury, and it was an ideal stage-set for partying like the fabled elite of the past. But Maxim's was also a fine place to dine—one of the best Parisian restaurants and "one of the most fun and cheery," testified the *Guide des plaisirs à Paris* in the late twenties. Prewar traditions still governed the fun: "many *jolies femmes* after 9 p.m.," dancing from 10:00 on, and around midnight *soupeurs* and *soupeuses* filling the great hall at the back of the restaurant. "Champagne flows like water there, and well into the night a crowd of *viveurs*, theater people, mondaines and demi-mondaines have a noisy wild time."[21]

While Maxim's evoked memories, it also induced a happy amnesia. "At Maxim's you can easily forget that there was the war," attested the author of *Dancings* (1927). For the old elites who were still its faithful customers, it was a pilgrimage shrine and a refuge. It was "the last capital of the Grand Dukes," whose high life as well as lowlife tours remained legendary. The postwar "dukes" were not only Russians, but well-heeled people generally—many from Central Europe. Their world had collapsed in the maelstrom of the war, and now they found in Maxim's a rare sanctuary for old-fashioned privileged pleasure. Nowhere else, it seemed, were they so sheltered from revolutions and the encroachments of modernity. "Everything dies, everything disappears, everything declines and disintegrates: the old gentlemen in white gaiters, [horse-drawn] coaches, the gray top hat for the racetrack, gallantry toward women, the *grandes courtisanes*, . . . all. But Maxim's remains."[22]

A principal reason for its long life was that Maxim's adapted to changing times while also maintaining its original high-society cachet and historic charm. In its earliest years it had drawn aristocratic Parisians on their way home from evenings at the theater and clubs along the Grands Boulevards. Then it attracted an international clientele of wealthy and socially prominent visitors. An in-crowd of artists and writers also became habitués, including such notables as Sem, Caran d'Ache, Jean-Louis Forain, Jean Lorrain, Georges Feydeau, and Marcel Proust. In the early twentieth century a circle of business elites, too, had frequented the restaurant—including Louis Renault and other pioneering entrepreneurs of the automobile and aviation industries. Stars of the theater and music hall partied there as well. One glittery group after another added its patronage and luster to the place. Its central location—just off the Place de la Concorde on the Rue Royale—had always made it a convenient stop for late-night revelers, particularly those who lived in the fashionable western quarters of the city. After the war, it was still well positioned as chic nightlife shifted to the nearby Champs-Élysées from the old Grands Boulevards.

The Moulin Rouge, in contrast, was far from the center. Yet its Montmartre location and offbeat glamour still worked to draw crowds there when it reopened in 1924, coming back at long last after a devastating fire a decade before. The shimmy and the Charleston were the exciting fashions for Parisian moderns, but the cancan was still the climactic spectacle at the Moulin Rouge, as it was at the Tabarin nearby. To French commentators it was "le french cancan," the English word (rather than simply "le cancan") marking the dance as a tourist favorite, which it had been since the late nineteenth century. As performed in the 1920s, it evoked a set of vivid memories from its early glory days. The sight of eight dancers performing "in the tradition of Grille d'Égout et Madame la Goulue" was "like the resurrection of an old world," journalist Léon Werth observed in 1925. It was "moving," like "a scent of old Paris." For those who remembered the old days, the resurrection was neither wholly convincing nor joyous.

The dance that once symbolized gaiety was now "a melancholy spectacle," Werth noted, for it was artificially preserved, like "a dried flower stuck between the pages of a book." Cut off from Parisian life, it was "not a living tradition," but a "dead tradition."[23] Yet for audiences night after night it was good fun—a must-see spectacle of world-famous "gay Paris."

The Moulin Rouge and Maxim's enjoyed a further advantage: a legacy of prestige bestowed on them by famous artistic and literary works of the turn of the century. Artists Jean-Louis Forain, Sem, and Caran d'Ache not only frequented Maxim's, but they also depicted it in their art. Maxim's was also the setting of plays by Georges Feydeau and Yves Mirande (*La Dame de Chez Maxim's, Le Chasseur de Chez Maxim's*), the operetta *The Merry Widow*, and several movies.[24] Before the war Maxim's had already become an iconic fixture familiar even to foreigners who had never visited Paris. Lehar's operetta put Maxim's chic clientele on display throughout Europe—first in Vienna in 1905, then in Paris four years later (April 1909), and then in other capitals. The Moulin Rouge, too, had become famous in the world of the arts far and wide. It figured as an archetypically Parisian dance hall in the paintings and posters of Chéret, Toulouse-Lautrec, and Steinlen; young Picasso painted it too. Beaux-Arts students had held scandalously wild arty parties there, replete with parades of lightly clad models and masquerade balls—all reported in sensational manner by the Parisian press. In sum, both establishments were lively places of pleasure that drew together the high and the low of society, mixing moneyed, high-status customers with courtesans and prostitutes. Both succeeded with an alluring blend of artistic celebrity, glamour, and (to borrow guidebook writer Basil Woon's term) the "naughty-naughty."

At the end of the 1920s the Moulin Rouge ran into financial troubles due to costly management miscalculations and disputes with such key players as the star Mistinguett and the master of revues, Jacques Charles.[25] Production costs in that era of lavish revues were high, and competition among the leading halls and with cinema (now enhanced by sound) was fierce. Abandoning tradition, the Moulin Rouge was turned into a movie theater in 1929. It did not return to its variety show format with the can-can until the 1950s, whereupon it once again flourished as a music hall (and is still going strong today). The Folies-Bergère, in contrast, stuck to its proven formula of the sumptuous revue—with a profusion of semi-nude show-girls—even through the difficult 1930s and 1940s. Under the strong, steady direction of the same director for almost a half century, Paul Derval (from 1918 to his death in 1966), the Folies-Bergère brought out a new revue every year except for a couple during the Second World War—with new themes, costumes, dances, and songs. Yet the overall forms of the show remained predictably familiar, fulfilling expectations built on decades of word-of-mouth tourist reports and guidebook notice. Over the decades Derval even kept to a tradition of having every revue title contain thirteen letters and the word "Folie" or "Folies" (out of superstition). While playing on the "Fol'Berg's" Belle-Époque past and reputation, its directors were quick to hire the latest stars of the times, such as Joséphine Baker in the season (1926) right after her sensational Paris début. Conservative yet changing, the Folies-Bergère thrived as an iconic monument of the Paris of Pleasures through most of the twentieth century.

EVOCATIONS OF (GOOD) TIMES PAST

The 1920s were famously preoccupied with things modern—jazz, airplanes, international travel, art deco sleekness, "flapper" fashions, and bobbed hair—yet memories of the preceding century often claimed public attention. Whenever an old celebrity died, obituaries and articles retold the story of the star's rise and triumphs in now-legendary venues back around the turn of the century. Time after time a stage curtain seemed to be falling on the prewar past. Following the deaths of superstar actress Sarah Bernhardt and engineer Gustave Eiffel in 1923, and writer Anatole France in 1924, the sudden passing of singer Aristide Bruant in 1925 struck chords of memory with exceptional force.

Through his songs Bruant had identified himself with the poor districts (like Montmartre) and the lowlife of Paris more than anyone else. A string of singers from Montmartre's glory years had died since the war (Jules Jouy, Marcel Legay, Léon de Bercy, Montoya), and death-notice articles about them had occasioned elegies to the golden age of Montmartre. But none of those others had been so celebrated and so colorful as Bruant. His image and songs had become emblematic of the fin de siècle. Toulouse-Lautrec's posters immortalized his cabaret image, and his songs lived on in his recordings and in performances by others. Bruant had retired to his country estate in 1900, but in early 1925 he had come out of retirement to sing at the Empire music hall. Audiences and critics cheered his comeback, combining warm nostalgia with tributes to a now-old great performer. His reappearance in 1925 "made an entire epoch come back to life, the one that Steinlen and Toulouse-Lautrec fixed" in their works, noted a reporter for Le Journal.[26] Just weeks later, he died, setting off another round of articles recalling that vanished epoch, recollections imbued with affection and regret more pungent than before. Bruant's passing, the writer added, made that time "appear to be a little farther removed from us." Such losses made remembering more important than ever.

The immediate postwar period with all its economic difficulties and anxieties had *not* touched off any conspicuous public expressions of nostalgia for lost times. People old enough to remember knew that life had been better before the war, and they had no need to read or write historical accounts of it. But in the later 1920s, many did feel such a need. As the prewar era receded into the irrevocably dead past, a remarkable stream of memoirs and histories emerged, portraying a time now viewed as the calm before the storm, an era blessedly free of the pain and turmoil known afterward. Laced with regret, those accounts rendered detailed pictures of the city that older Parisians had known in their youth. The year 1930, as the beginning of a new decade, spurred even more reminiscing, now framed by comparisons with that other round-numbered year, 1900—the past serving as counterpoint to the troubled present. As the Depression years unfolded, memories turned brighter and more expansive, while '20s-style enthusiasm for faster, freer "modern" times faded. Jazz, exotic travel, aviation, and avant-garde snobbism were no longer fresh and exciting, observed a journalist in 1931, and a "new master" appeared—"love of the past," meaning particularly a certain not-too-distant past.[27] It became "chic to sigh after the French cancan" and hoop skirts and to hum (the old waltz) "Sourire d'Avril," he added.

"One of our most cherished, intimate, profound joys is to have known the prewar period," declared writer André Warnod in his 1930 book on Paris.[28] Memoirs of the "good old days" like Warnod's recalled an singularly fortunate time in the years around 1900. In fact, the most common term for that era remained simply "1900" through the 1930s. "Perhaps because we were young we have found those times so beautiful," Warnod conceded, but he went on to describe more than youthful illusions. He and other memoirists now saw 1900 through the lens of 1930s discontents and difficulties.

Most striking in 1930 was how low the cost of living had been at the turn of the century. Warnod spoke of it as "this beauty—negative it is true, but enchanting—of being able to live in Paris almost without any money, without doing anything, living badly certainly, but living." That was especially true of young people, who once managed to fill days and nights with socializing and artistic pursuits, scraping by without an onerous job, as Warnod knew from his own Bohemian experience.

Another "negative beauty" of the old days, according to the later memory of many, was that foreigners were almost inconspicuous in Paris life. Paris before the war, as Warnod described it, showed its true self—with its classic charms intact—in contrast to the city "invaded" by "Negroes . . . with their jazz and their dances, . . . Jews of *Mitel Europa* [sic] with their spirit of destruction, . . . [and] Americans with their banks."[29] Outside the districts overrun with foreigners, he conceded, "true Paris" lived on—in "the street and the faubourg," a Paris unchanged by the war and postwar crazes. But it was in constant danger.[30]

When Warnod wrote those lines, the number of foreigners was at an all-time high (over 9 percent of the total Parisian population), and xenophobia was rampant. Sentimental fantasies of a lost Paris that was more purely *French* waxed in tandem with alarms about new immigrants and their cultures.[31] Sometimes the anxieties about foreigners and their menace were not made explicit but took cover in warm and loving talk about the good "little Parisians," especially the old-fashioned common folk—or "Paname" before the war. In the first published album of Eugène Atget's photographs (1930), for example, Pierre Mac Orlan's introduction praised the late photographer for having captured the poetry of the Paris of François Villon and of humble working people in shadow-filled streets—as opposed to the capital of international fashions and bright modernity. In stark black-and-white clarity Atget's photos brought back to 1930 eyes the peaceful sights of automobile-free streets and such period-piece characters as the organ grinder and itinerant vendor of umbrellas.[32] Alternatively, fear of the foreign came couched in classical rhetoric about Paris the hub of the Enlightened world, the Ville Lumière. Paris, the delicate organ of rational and refined thinking, was under life-threatening attack, maintained poet Paul Valéry in a 1927 essay. Endangering the city and "the spirit of Paris" were "the growth of credulity . . . due to weariness with clear ideas [and] the accession of exotic populations to civilized life." The historic "capital of quality and the capital of criticism" was in grave danger.[33]

Above all André Warnod, like other nostalgic Paris lovers around 1930, looked back fondly to times he saw as an era of equilibrium, or at least slow, manageable change. Although it had not been "the golden age," it was "a singular and prodigious epoch, still attached to traditions by a thousand ties and one which harbored potentially formidable new forces." "Politics weren't overheated [then]," he maintained, forgetting about the Dreyfus affair (or not considering it politics?).[34] Paris was then "a city where the past remained living, but which greeted the new times harmoniously and evolved gently." Automobiles, the first auto-taxis, the first auto-buses, and airplanes were appearing, but horse-drawn fiacres were still there too. The styles back then were still formal, and "people still had a sense of decorum and correctness"—with men in starched collars and top hats and women in long dresses, tight corsets, and swishing petticoats (dessous froufroutants). Electricity was replacing gas, but gradually. "The Boulevard had already lost much of its prestige, but it still existed." The café-concert was dying, but slowly, losing out partly to spectacular music halls and even more to proliferating cinemas.[35]

One feature of the turn-of-the-century, however, stirred universal scorn in 1930: "le modern style," also known as "art nouveau." From the beginning the Guimard métro entries had been controversial, condemned by mainstream architects and officials as eccentric and not dignified or classical enough for a prominent place in the beautiful City of Light.[36] The style had even lost favor with its avant-garde supporters shortly after 1900, and in the postwar years it became the odd old antithesis of art-deco modern. Warnod derided it as "bad taste 'fin de siècle'"—an aesthetic that was "complicated and wimpy [mou], too artificial, too literary to be viable, . . . employed more for decoration than architecture."[37] Warnod and his contemporaries saw only fussy excesses—"everywhere only moldings, sculptures, patisseries, intrusive ornamental details." It was also a style that could be traced to suspect foreign influences—Austro-Hungarian, for example. And its spectacular feminine forms seemed excessive to anxious (male) critics.[38] From the perspective of 1930 it was simply a ridiculous out-dated style, and more than a minor aesthetic aberration, but for most it was not a damning fault. So much about the old days remained appealing—in contrast with the present.

.   .   .

The most important catalyst of the Belle-Époque memory appeared the next year (mid-1931): a book titled *1900*, by writer Paul Morand. Reprinted dozens of times the first year, it had more impact than did any other retrospective.[39] By sparking an emotional debate, it provoked a round of fonder-than-ever remembrances, which provided touchstones of public memory for decades to come. At the time it was written (1930), Morand was best known for his novels and travel literature, devoted especially to the most modern of cities. In writing *1900*, he took a journey back in time, with a keen eye for the distinctive features of prewar Paris.

Morand's *1900* was a series of historical tableaus, fuller than what others had produced, though it was not a full-scale history. Rather it was a belles-lettres memoir, filled with the author's personal recollections and judgments, free of nostalgic romanticism but also disengaged from modernist enthusiasms. It was the first to undertake a measured, comprehensive assessment of 1900, blending picturesque details with a historian's broad characterizations and critiques.

Morand recalled some famous scenes of Paris 1900 with amusement and affection, though he never used the glowing term "Belle Époque." His longest and most positive chapter described the Universal Exposition of 1900. What he relished was the exciting variety that the fair brought so close to his Paris home: the exotica of mosques and minarets and belly dancers; sideshows featuring Parisian beauties such as dancers La Belle Otéro and Cléo de Mérode; a simulated naval battle; and especially the "Wagon of the Trans-Siberian," which took fairgoers on a simulated railroad trip through a faraway empire. Other chapters evoked the city itself circa 1900—as a world epicenter abounding in "pleasures." He recalled the summertime cafés-concerts near the Champs-Élysées, the brilliant Sarah Bernhardt, the many colorful writers and plays produced, electric cars, the first airplanes, and the popularity of sports—from boxing (French-style—using feet) to *footing* in the Bois de Boulogne. Much of the book, in short, was a gallery of nostalgic vignettes that became the prime clichés of the Belle-Époque memory: portly bearded men in top hats, fiacres sharing the streets with early automobiles, the elegant dress of the "high-life" crowd at the Longchamp horse races, and of course the motley mix of peoples and cultures at the Universal Exposition that so optimistically opened the century.

But Morand gave a disparaging treatment to other features of the period. Recalling his boyhood in his home near the Champs-Élysées, he remembered chafing at the restrictions of bourgeois life—the long, multi-course family dinners, the onerous and joyless social obligations. The era's emblematic style came in for even stronger reproach. Morand not only ridiculed art nouveau as the "noodle style," but he went on to disparage the era's aesthetics more generally—in architecture, furniture, novels, and the theater. Then he lambasted "1900" for its moral failings. The era's noodle aesthetic was matched with a "noodle-morality," as he called it. The elite's "high life" and fondness for low life made 1900 the "low epoch" (*la basse époque*). Aristide Bruant's popularity with the well-off seemed to him symptomatic of that decadence. Further, he recalled, the nation was torn by hatreds and political extremes—anti-Semites, nationalists, anticlericals, anarchists—and seething passions over government scandals and the Dreyfus affair. Capping off the sundry negatives, Morand ended with sweeping reproaches. In contrast to the introduction's tribute to "these giants, our fathers," he concluded by condemning the naïve optimism and the self-satisfaction of his father's generation. Why, he asked those of 1900, did you lead "a life of a jumping jack and make us carry your cross? Why show off your Charvet cravates and have dirty feet? Why, every other minute, show your teeth and leave us with the war? Why have you been so ugly, so rich, so happy?"[40]

A few reviewers agreed that much about "1900" was "stupid" and deplorable, and not just its "noodle style." "The Paris of the old days was not all beautiful," concurred one journalist. Morand's book "offers those who haven't known [1900] . . . a very strong image" of "a base époque" in politics and art.[41] Most reviews, however, took exception to Morand's harsh judgments. The reviewer for *La Nouvelle Revue française*, for example, pointed up the "profound values of 1900," citing the victory of the defenders of Dreyfus and justice, the entry into public life of long-excluded social groups, and the artistic accomplishments of Claudel and Colette, Gourmont and Gide, Monet, Renoir, Cézanne, Seurat, Vuillard.[42] The ambivalence that ran through the book went almost unnoticed.

Art editor Louis Chéronnet weighed into the debate (1932) with an album of pleasant old photographs of turn-of-the-century Paris and an introduction analyzing his contemporaries' fascination with 1900. Their interest in history, he observed, did not stem from a simple nostalgia, but from a profound dissatisfaction with the past and the present. The era around 1900, that is, charmed people who could no longer believe in "progress."[43] Anxious and disillusioned with postwar life, they were eager to grasp whatever they could of that era from which they had been so brutally expelled.

Chéronnet and his generation, born around 1900, did not have personal memories of the turn of the century, but many of them enjoyed learning about it and discovering its vestiges. After the war, they had delighted in the short, simple movies from cinema's infancy. Later, after a period of enthusiasm for jazz, they rediscovered the waltz and the café-concert. Around 1930, Chéronnet explained, they were ready to do battle—against the superficiality of the moderns who scorned the past as well as against an escapist, ahistorical romanticism. Unmoored and unhappy in their own time, they refused to let go of a past that remained so unfulfilled. Feelings ran high not just for a lost era of peace and ease, but for a vibrant time that had been cut short prematurely by the war.

Chéronnet himself clearly delighted in evocations of a now-vanished Paris: "strolling the boulevards without fear of gasoline-powered machines," horse-drawn omnibuses and fiacres, organ grinders and street sellers of lampshades, sentimental old songs and singers, soldiers in red trousers, bakery demoiselles carrying bundles of baguettes (*porteuses de pain*), and posters of the hefty comic singer Jeanne Bloch.[44] The sixty old photographs that followed showed just such sights, capturing in death-like stillness the look of another era's women, fashions, social elites, stars, and streets. The charm of the women, even thirty years later, was difficult to resist, wrote Chéronnet. So was virtually everything that the book presented to his "anxious" (his word) contemporaries—images and recollections of an era that now seemed so innocent of war and misery, so regrettably lost and gone.

In the years around 1930, then, living memory passed into written history. Giving last rites to the prewar years, memoir writers took several steps fundamental to historical thinking: they defined a period (centering on 1900), marked its contours, and spelled out the differentness of the past.[45] The publication of the old photos confirmed the historical discontinuity. Some of them revealed details that had eluded later memory. The images, seemingly objective and obvious to all, conveyed appearances laden with mysteries and secrets that viewers were free to interpret. Imaginations in 1930, Mac Orlan and Chéronnet reported, revisited the scenes of 1900 with sympathy and melancholy.[46]

Several years later, writer Léon-Paul Fargue penned the most forceful rejoinder to those who had "denigrated the epoch called 1900" and "dragged it through the mud," singling out Morand as the prime culprit. In essays that together became the widely read book *Piéton de Paris*, Fargue (born in 1876) dismissed Morand (born 1888) as too young to have known 1900. Then he launched into a fresh evocation of 1900—indeed a paean to it, along with a critique of the moderns. In the "epoch called 1900," he began, Paris was more Parisian. Although he had grown up in a gritty working-class quarter of the city (La Chapelle), Fargue evoked memories of urbane and chic Parisians. The 1900 that he chose to recall was a time of "quality," of "festivity," of "good grace, wit, politeness," "all of it seasoned by delightfully nasty remarks and mischief." That "vanished time," he maintained, "was marked by many good things that we will never know again: charm, the *froufrou* of women, the Parisian spirit itself!"[47]

The clincher for him was how the Parisian women of yesteryear contrasted with those of the present. In that golden past, the city's dames and demoiselles, actresses and princesses, foreigners and dancers (like Otéro and Liane de Pougy) were Parisiennes first of all because they "made Paris talk." They even made foreign cities talk. "They were Parisiennes because they considered that life should be exclusively devoted to pleasure, to frivolity, to snobbism, to drunkenness and showing off [*tapage*]. In the execution of these games, they showed a facility, an ease, a charm and a verve that were the very cornerstones of the [prewar] attitude." The era around 1900 was a time when "pleasure was an art," and "love was elegant, not rushed and serious."[48] In counterpoint to that idealized 1900, Fargue laid out his jaundiced views of later times: Parisian women of the 1930s had lost their charm and playfulness. They had become preoccupied with partisan politics and economic matters. Modernity's close-fitting fashions, equal participation in sports, massages, and nudes on music-hall stages meant that women's bodies were no longer a fascinating mystery. Altogether, the era of "exquisite feminine tyrannies" had ended. The true Parisienne was on the verge of disappearing, and Paris life was the poorer for it.

Modernity, in short, meant decline to many who remembered the old days. Fargue summed it up as well as anyone: modern times were rushed, humorless, and industrial. "Great restaurants become banks, theaters are transformed into cinemas, *maisons de couture* no longer clearly set the tone for the civilized world." Moneymaking and politics blighted the contemporary world—particularly the turbulent politics of the 1930s that Fargue chose not to discuss: frequent cabinet crises, riots and street battles (most notably, February 6, 1934), demonstrations and counterdemonstrations, the radical Right and the Popular Front. "Modernity" and "progress," he concluded, meant war, noise, "grill-rooms," "daily catastrophes," huge dynamos and factories running full-steam . . . merely to sharpen a pencil.[49] The worse the present appeared, the better the turn of the century looked.

By the end of the thirties the bright flattering versions of 1900 had carried the battle over memory, leaving disturbing parts of the past largely in the shadows. Forgotten or obscured were the anarchists' bombings, the violent repression of strikes, the wretchedness of disease-ridden Paris slums, the bitter fight over the Dreyfus verdict, and the rampages of anti-Semites. One reason Morand's critical memoir drew fire for years was that it gave considerable space to the virulent politics of the past. Most people in the crisis-ridden 1930s preferred to remember pleasant images that became shorthand for the entire epoch—top-hatted gentlemen, stylish women in whale-bone corsets and rustling petticoats, the cancan, and streets full of fiacres and horses. What lodged most firmly in the minds and hearts of Morand's contemporaries was the memory of a quaintly amusing, untroubled lost Paris—a cheery collage of Paname and Paris-*Plaisirs*.

(RE-)PRODUCTIONS OF THE PAST

The many who were nostalgic found multiple ways to hang on to prewar Paris. One way was through entertainment—in music-halls, cabarets, and movies evoking the past. The deaths of old-timers like Aristide Bruant did not mean that their personas and performances died. For many decades after Bruant's demise, music-hall agencies maintained "le Bruant" as a standard act, meeting the unremitting public demand with a steady supply of impersonators.[50] A cabaret called the Mirliton was still doing business in 1951, the centennial of his birth, in the original locale on the Boulevard Rochechouart (#84), and the decor was still what it had been in the late nineteenth century. There a "false Bruant," the fifth in a line of successors, greeted customers with the master's joking insults and sang the old standards.[51]

The turn-of-the-century lowlife featured in Bruant's songs also lived on—in music-hall productions and movies. The 1920 hit song and play *Mon Homme* gave new life to clichés that went on to entertain for decades more—scenes of molls with a passion for their "man" and delinquent males violently quarreling over a desired young woman. Cabaret acts and movies such as Jacques Becker's *Casque d'or* (1952) served up the apache tale again and again. Even in the leading venue of jazz and youthful entertainment of the 1930s, the A.B.C. music hall, the aging "realist" singer Fréhel starred in 1938 with a "tour de chant 1900," dressed as a streetwalker (*pierreuse*) out of a Toulouse-Lautrec painting. Those reenactments, catering to an old fascination with the dark underside of the City of Light, kept alive clichés that after the war became, like the cancan, familiar markers of Parisian identity and its most fondly recalled period. As representations of an authentic old-time Paris after the war, they were a comfortable counterpoint to such emblems of modernity as "cosmopolitan" artists, jazzy *boîtes* (nightclubs), and the auto showrooms of the Champs-Élysées.[52]

The memory of old-fashioned friendly Paname also endured as a staple of popular songs and movies. One of most successful films of 1930, René Clair's *Sous les toits de Paris*, re-created a village-like modest quarter resembling Montmartre, complete with traditional artisans, street singers, small-time crooks and a pimp, small dance halls (*bals musettes*) and bistros. In contrast to Paul Morand's ambivalent and critical representation, Clair's movies in the 1930s depicted the Paris of yesteryear with undiluted sentimentality and affection—particularly the modest faubourgs of the "little people." "Let's say it's Carco in images," one reviewer observed.[53] For French audiences it was entertaining relief from Hollywood's offerings of gangsters, cigar-champing detectives, and cowboys. When *Sous les toits* played in capitals across Europe, foreign audiences also showed a fondness for the old-time Paris. Back home, French critics, reporting the film's success abroad, pointed up anew the special charm of quarters that had eluded the whirlwinds of jazz-age modernity. A couple of years later, Clair's *14 juillet* again enchanted movie-goers with an old-fashioned Paris—a slower-paced city devoid of traffic jams, buses, and tramways and also free of foreigners. The sets by Lazare Meerson provided "all the outdated charm of a Paris that no longer exists except in the films of René Clair and the paintings of Utrillo," noted a reviewer.[54] The public greeted these nostalgic works with enthusiasm, leaving behind the postwar vogues of "Russians, Negroes, Argentines," and exotic travel.[55]

Clair's earlier silent film *Un Chapeau de paille d'Italie* (1927) had already set out the most characteristic details of the turn-of-the-century. Talking pictures, through the 1930s, brought back more old comedies set in what a reviewer in 1933 called "the good time" ("le bon temps")—period pieces ranging from the tale of red trousered soldiers' fun in the barracks (*Les Gaîtés de l'escadron*, based on Courteline's 1913 novel), to *La Dame de Chez Maxim's* (1932), based on Feydeau's old play. "The good time," noted the reviewer, was when *cafés-crèmes* cost only 10 centimes and croissants only a *sou* (20 centimes), and Maxim's was the chic playground of the Prince de Sagan and Emilienne d'Alençon.[56] All through the decade of Depression, fascists, and bitter political strife, popular movies and popular memory looked back to that Paris of 1900, a Paris that sparkled with song and dance, lighthearted love and pleasure.[57]

THE PERSISTENCE OF
NINETEENTH-CENTURY PARIS

That popular way of remembering—predicated on the willful forgetting of an era's hatreds, poverty, and crises—accompanied a widespread reluctance to see anything seriously wrong with contemporary Paris. City and national officials looked backward fondly and helped perpetuate an old-time Paris.[58] Haussmann's cityscape, once scorned as boring and soul-less, now stood revered as beautiful and classical. When authorities undertook urban improvements in the first decade of the twentieth century and again in the 1920s, they followed the lines laid down by Haussmann. They finished constructing the Boulevard Haussmann in 1927, and they completed the central Halles of the Second Empire in 1936 by adding two last iron pavilions—in the style of Baltard, the original architect, of course.

They also continued the long-standing neglect of many parts. Almost all the slums untouched by Haussmann persisted. All but a couple of the *îlots* that had been declared public-health menaces since the fin de siècle remained in place through the Second World War. One exception was a slum in Clignancourt, which was cleared away in response to an outbreak of disease following the Great War. The only other notable slum clearance took place in the heart of Paris: on the "plateau Beaubourg," designated *Îlot insalubre* no. 1. Several blocks of decaying buildings there were leveled in the early 1930s, and the new open space became a parking lot for workers and customers of the nearby Halles. Otherwise the Paris of Haussmann and of 1900 lived on, providing support for memories at every turn.

The working-class banlieues to the north and south, devoid of such memories, continued on a course of uncontrolled, unsightly development— as an anti-Paris of factories, gasworks, dumps, depots, warehouses, sand and rock quarries, scatterings of poorly built bungalows (*pavillons*), and shacks. Building regulations and restrictions were virtually nonexistent in the banlieues through most of the 1920s, a decade when the population there grew from 1.5 million to over 2 million. Subdivisions sprang up without municipal water and sewer systems, paved streets, or other infrastructure. Yet they were a place of dreams—initially, at least, for people who moved there. The suburbs were the only remaining places where Parisian workers and modest employees could hope to buy a plot of land

and build their own homes, live without having noisy neighbors on top of them or down the hall, sleep in quiet and breathe good country air (at least sometimes), have space for a garden and children's play, and be forever "freed from the concierge." But the net effect was something else. The growing population and unchecked sprawl made the poorer outskirts an overpopulated "no man's land," Jean Giraudoux observed in 1930—a "dreadful zone of misery," "ugliness and sorrows."[59]

Residents of that "dreadful zone" elected Socialist and Communist mayors and city councils, producing a "red belt" of leftist municipalities around the capital (from Saint-Denis and Clichy in the north, Bobigny and Noisy-le-Sec in the northeast, Suresnes and Boulogne-Billancourt toward the west, to Ivry and Alfortville in the south). Red-belt officials were able to make improvements in housing and services in some communes (Bobigny, Suresnes, Saint-Denis, most notably), but overall the working-class banlieue continued as a dismal antithesis to beautiful historic Paris. Bourgeois Paris and its conservative city council regarded the *ceinture rouge* as menacing and beyond the pale. "Few cities have suburbs more depressing than the Parisian suburbs," observed an American travel writer in the mid-1920s. "They do not, however, mar Paris. They have no influence upon her at all."[60] Indeed, from the viewpoint of tourists and Parisians, Paris in all its glory remained "within her wall," and the ugly banlieue languished in "the outer darkness."

.   .   .

The unending praise lavished on the core city could only reinforce satisfaction with the status quo. Visitors, expatriates, and guidebooks in the 1920s and '30s reiterated the classic tributes to the beauty and charm of the city. Their appreciation was bolstered by a sense that life in other European capitals (Berlin and Vienna in particular) was not anything like what it had been before the war. M.-V. Vernier's popular guidebook of 1927–1928 declared Paris as ever "the true capital of the civilized world," a city whose beauty lay not so much in fine buildings and monuments as in "her intimate intellectual, artistic and social life."[61] Prominent Parisian writers also continued to sing the city's praises, ignoring the nostalgic critics and the invidious comparisons with 1900. "It's the city of the world where life is the freest," blessedly free of "cant and aristocracy and arrogance," historian Gabriel Hanotaux assured readers of the *Paris-Guide* in 1926.[62]

In an often-quoted essay of 1927, Paul Valéry described Paris as a capital at the pinnacle of its historic destiny, fulfilled and vital, providing an array of essential functions for the nation while realizing the highest potential of all that was France.[63] It was, in short, "the most complete city in the world." Only Paris was so singularly "the political, literary, scientific, financial, commercial, pleasure and sumptuary capital of a great country, representing all the history of that country and absorbing and concentrating all its thinking substance." "This Paris," Valéry concluded, "has made itself the metropolis of diverse liberties and the capital of human sociability." The German writer Friedrich Sieburg struck a similar note in his widely read book on France in 1930, affirming that "in Paris everything is finished: city and people; development has not ceased, but immortality has begun." The great harmonious city adapts its "forms of life not to the uncertain future, but to the past with its sure values." In the splendid unity of the past and present, "one sees nothing new, nothing fresh": "the charm of the finished" reigns. Even the "architectural errors, so numerous in modern Paris, are integrated into the infinite chain of marvels."[64]

The praise of Paris—ever "the most beautiful city in the world"—was so ingrained that few Parisians could begin to comprehend appeals for modernization. The choice they saw before them was either to save or to destroy the historical city—either to preserve the beauty bequeathed by centuries past or to sacrifice it for "what a great modern capital requires today," as Warnod put it. Defects, when acknowledged, were not taken seriously. The "city of light" actually lacked light in many places, Warnod conceded, but he quickly added: not quantity but *quality* gave Paris its distinction.[65] Vernier's guidebook described the "once fashionable" Marais as "now one of the meaner sections of the city," full of squalid buildings and industrial workshops, but also "exceedingly rich in picturesque vestiges of the past." Exceptions to the rule drew notice: "The Place des Vosges, delightful in its coloring and its spaciousness, is a quiet relief from the present squalor of the rest of the quarter."[66] In sum, lovers of Paris zeroed in on the historic places they prized and rendered the whole a hallowed, glorious place overflowing with the rich heritage of twenty centuries, a "harmonious combination of the past and of modern life."[67] Such visions of an ever beautiful, felicitous Paris were particularly alluring and consoling in a time dogged by cosmopolitan incursions, the Depression, violent clashes of fascists and antifascists, short-lived governments that disappointed or disgusted the Left or Right, and the terrible menace of another war.

After the war erupted in September 1939, and after Nazi German forces rolled across France in June 1940 and quickly occupied the capital, Parisians had even more reason to remember better days and to ignore the city's defects. With German troops everywhere in sight, Parisians no longer sang the classic praises of Paris in the present tense, nor did they trumpet hopes for its future. Their beloved city was no longer the capital of France, and it was no longer the "Ville Lumière"—and not just because of imposed blackouts and curfews. It was a "skeleton city," "nothing more than an artificial display," recalled Jean-Paul Sartre at the end of the war. "Everything was hollow and empty: the Louvre without paintings, the Chamber without deputies, the Senate without senators, the Lycée Montaigne without students." He should have added: Jewish neighborhoods without Jews and synagogues. In the "skeleton city" many houses, stores, and bars were closed up, their owners "deported, dead, or disappeared." Most of the ordinary Parisians concentrated on survival day-to-day, coping with hunger and long lines for rationed food, shortages of clothing and shoes, the biting winter cold, electricity outages, sickness, worry and sadness about missing loved ones, occasional Allied bombardments, and the Gestapo. Before the Allied invasion of Normandy in June 1944, a small minority of Parisians risked joining the Resistance, engaging in courageous and symbolically important acts, which ranged from printing underground papers to taking up arms. As for Parisians in general, "we could not take a step, could not eat, nor even breathe, without demonstrating complicity with the occupier," Sartre acknowledged. "We felt ourselves to be outside the game." "Paris suffered in shame and despair."[68]

French wartime authorities lacked not only money and materiel for urbanist projects, but also the desire to make changes. Now officialdom had firm ideological grounds for inaction: the capital was overdeveloped, too big and all-powerful for the health of the nation. So the new regime headquartered at Vichy adopted "reforms" shifting power from the over-

FIGURE 2.4. The unscathed conquerors claimed the best of Paris's famed pleasures in late June 1940: the most chic cafés on the Champs-Élysées, for example, shortly after the armistice signed on June 22. (Bibliothèque nationale de France.)

grown city to regional administrations. Paris was left to fend for itself, to make do with the old. Urbanists made plans, but authorities did not act on them. No major urban operations took place for the duration of the war, except for the clearance of a city-center slum long identified as a Jewish ghetto (Saint-Gervais in the Marais) and the razing of shacks in the desolate "zone" surrounding the city.[69]

The Germans built blockhouses, but they made no great efforts to change the cityscape. They were eager most of all to enjoy an unchanged, world-famous Paris, which was now theirs. For officers and high officials that meant the renowned sights and pleasures of Maxim's, the Tour d'Argent, the Folies-Bergère, the Tabarin (with its nude revues and can-can), the Lido, and elegant cafés on the Champs-Élysées. German officers and dignitaries gathered nightly at Maxim's (Goering's favorite haunt) to drink champagne and dine, sharing it with favored collaborators. They also took over the grand hotels, the biggest movie theaters, and the best brothels for themselves. Ordinary German soldiers on leave, like tourists before the war, went on group tours of Versailles and the Louvre, but on their own they flocked nightly to the fleshpot cabarets and nightclubs of Montmartre. Adolf Hitler, who flew in to see Paris for the first time in his life three days after the armistice (June 23, 1940), gave it a hurried tourist's visit, breezing through the Opéra, the Champs-Élysées, Sacré-Coeur, Sainte-Chapelle, and the Place des Vosges (showing little interest in the latter three), lingering a bit at the tomb of Napoleon in Les Invalides, and posing for a photograph in front of the Eiffel Tower.[70]

The new authorities renamed some streets to make them more ideologically correct: the Boulevard Pereire (a Jewish financier), for example, became the Boulevard Édouard Drumont (the leading anti-Semitic journalist of the fin de siècle). They blew up synagogues and ordered Jews to wear a yellow star (May 29, 1942), before carrying out mass arrests of Jewish Parisians a few months later. The German conquerors also attacked France's

FIGURE 2.5. Between the summer of 1941 and the summer of 1944, Jewish prisoners were interned in the 1930s housing project of Drancy, about seven miles northeast from the center of Paris—a transit camp before the long train trip to the Nazi concentration camps. Photograph dated December 2–3, 1942. (Bibliothèque nationale de France.)

nationalist symbols in Paris: they demolished the Vincennes monument to the French war dead of 1914–1918 and melted down bronze statues of French heroes and allegorical figures (monuments to Victor Hugo, Voltaire, Hector Berlioz, Emile Zola and symbolic works such as *La Victoire*). Many of these changes were readily undone by postwar governments after the summer of 1944. The same cannot be said of the scars left by the physical and mental sufferings of Parisians, those who survived and mourned the killings and premature deaths of friends and loved ones.[71]

In outward ways, everyday life during the Occupation slipped back in time to the turn of the century. Traffic jams and pollution disappeared, as automobile driving by ordinary people was prohibited, and most city buses ceased running. A strange, old-fashioned quiet reigned. Pedestrians and bicycles dominated the streets. Carts and wagons pulled by horses reappeared. Even horse-drawn fiacres from the Belle Époque reappeared— with drivers wearing top hats—though charging fares too high for most people to afford. The métro, the mainstay of public transportation, was packed with record-setting numbers of riders (121 million riders in November 1942 compared with 50 million in July 1939). Electricity was in ever shorter supply from 1943 on. The sale of radios was prohibited at the end of March 1943. The next year, Parisians had to cope with even more limited availability of gas, electricity, and food, especially after the Allied invasion in Normandy in June.[72]

To a population suffering from scarcities of food and other necessities, German reprisals for Resistance attacks (from summer 1941 on), roundups and deportations of Jews and resisters, and Allied air raids, the "good old days" before both World Wars looked more attractive than ever. Entertainers used "1900" as the setting for scenes of a happy past free of war, suffering, and quotidian problems. Old singers came back to sing old songs. In the revue, *À ta santé ... Paris*, in 1941 (at the Théâtre des Optimistes), a sketch entitled "Madeleine-Bastille" conjured up the Grands Boulevards and celebrities of the "1900 era."[73] When a program titled "Le bon temps" opened at the Moulin de la Galette in April 1943, a journalist hailed it as "the resurrection of the old café-concert," "the Caf' Conc' 1900 with all its legendary characters—the flirtatious beauty [*la gommeuse*], the comic soldier [*le comique troupier*], the proud acrobat with the triumphant mustache." Their reappearance in the harsh times of 1943 was enough to "resuscitate" "the charm" of better days, he declared—meaning "that so envied and decried epoch" before the wars.[74] For the war-and-occupation weary public, only recollections of a charming past had appeal.

FLOODTIDE OF MEMORIES

Rose-tinted memories of 1900 did more than bring comfort in a time of crises and hatreds. They also reinforced a prevailing inertia, a reluctance to do much about Paris's problems, such as the shortage of decent housing. Since the First World War, new construction in the private sphere was stifled by rent controls and high land prices. The state, for its part, built subsidized low-rent apartment buildings on the periphery but made no effort to improve housing in the core city before the 1950s. With the passing of decades, the housing stock as well as the street network grew increasingly dated and dysfunctional, contrary to the endlessly repeated classic descriptions of the city, the paeans ever fixed in the superlative. Preservationist efforts like those of the Commission du Vieux Paris were less effective preservers of the old than were attitudes nurtured by memoirs, movies, and songs, continually reinforcing an uncritical pride in Paris's past. Minds basking in remembered glory were not disposed to welcome new initiatives. Even shabby and dilapidated remnants of Paris-before-the-deluge could pass as memory sites of a familiar yesteryear.

After the Second World War, recollections of the "good ol' days" became even more beguiling. Now they sometimes included the interwar period, in retrospect taking on some of the estimable traits earlier attributed to 1900. "Before the war, Paris had arrived at a kind of maturity, of plenitude," wrote Léon-Paul Fargue in a piece published in 1955.[75] "Elegance, . . . knowledge, the sense of the comic or of moderation, the taste for discovery or embellishment [ornement], the spirit of examination, femininity, flânerie, games of intelligence and desire equally widespread" were all there in full flower. By Paris, he meant of course a select constellation: the Place Vendôme, the Latin Quarter, the Marais, the Place des Vosges, Madeleine, the Grands Boulevards, and the Bois de Boulogne.

For most people, a more distant time was the most attractive: the already-celebrated period around 1900. While the nation's new postwar leaders geared up to modernize on a grand scale, France's popular culture still kept an affectionate gaze on the lost time before the Great War. That period, long designated by the neutral term "1900," became known after 1945 by the bright label "Belle Époque," conjuring a time of ease, enjoyment, and innocence. After two horrific wars and the defeat of France in 1940, the turn-of-the-century looked more "beautiful" and fortunate than ever before. In the limelight was a Paris that was at once a quaint and convivial Paname, the Capital of Pleasures, and the brilliant City of Light. Movie audiences in 1947 saw scenes of it all beautifully recreated in a short documentary titled *Paris 1900*, by Nicole Védrès. Her montage of old film clips began in a lighthearted tone with scenes of the Moulin Rouge, the 1900 Universal Exposition, the fiacre-filled boulevards, and the overflowing market of Les Halles, followed by some comedy sequences and celebrity spottings—before shifting to ominous sights of preparations for war. Following Védrès, seasoned directors René Clair, Jacques Becker, and Jean Renoir returned to the same era for wistful stories that they made into some of the most popular movies of the postwar years—notably, *Le Silence est d'or* (1947), *Casque d'or* (1952), and *French Cancan* (1955). At the same time, a cascade of histories and memoirs regaled readers with tales of the good life in the good old days.[76]

After the Liberation in late August 1944, the era around 1900 appeared blessedly free not only of wartime agonies, but also of postwar hardships. A month of fighting, during which 2,873 Parisians were killed, ended decisively with the expulsion of the Germans, but the euphoria of Liberation did not last long. The sunny days of August 25–26 were two of the most joyous in the city's long history, following the saddest four years, but those glorious days did not end the shortages of food, electricity, gas, shoes, and jobs. Liberated Parisians had to suffer through another frigid winter with chilblains on their hands, "dining in their overcoats on a meager soup of carrots and turnips," "colder than they have been any other winter of the war," and "hungrier than they have been any other winter of the war," reported Janet Flanner.[77] They still stood for hours in line for necessities, and they still worried about thousands of loved ones who remained in Germany working in factories or, in the case of Jews and deported Resistance members, in prison camps somewhere to the east, perhaps alive, perhaps . . .

Upon hearing of the defeat of Germany on May 8, 1945, Parisians packed the streets, marching body pressed against moving body, shouting with joy, singing refrains of "La Marseillaise," momentarily forgetting their hunger. But worry and fear did not leave those still waiting for the return of relatives and friends from concentration camps. Batches of French prisoners returning since April had shocked Paris with their hunched, skeletal forms and their reports of atrocities suffered and of the deaths of many. Three hundred women liberated from Ravensbrück were met by "a nearly speechless crowd" at the Gare de Lyon, Janet Flanner observed. "There was a general, anguished babble of search, of finding or not finding. There was almost no joy; the emotion penetrated beyond that, to something nearer pain. Too much suffering lay behind this homecoming, and it was the suffering that showed in the women's faces and bodies."[78]

Trials of the "collabos" (the official part of the nation's purge of those accused of collaborating with the Germans) dragged on until July 1949. Bread and dairy products, remaining in short supply, were meagerly rationed until early 1949. Prices were high and rising in those same years, while the franc was falling. Rents went up sharply in 1948 after being freed from the legislated controls dating back to the First World War. Waves of strikes crippled Parisian life for days and weeks at a time. The weak and crisis-ridden governments of the Fourth Republic only worsened the postwar malaise.[79]

Besides distracting from trying postwar conditions, the consoling memory of the Belle Époque also helped distract from troubling memories of the Occupation. Most people had grave and compelling reasons to forget much about that nightmarish period. Memories of the humiliating defeat and occupation, the hundreds of thousands deported to Germany, Jews handed over to the Nazis, and the wartime collaboration of many ordinary citizens were pushed away, relegated to shadowy recesses. National leaders did their part by avoiding those sources of bad conscience and division: keeping silent about the war and occupation, they directed public attention to the Resistance, memorializing the fallen heroes with plaques on walls around the city.[80]

The alternative memory of a "beautiful era" did not need state support: songs, movies, and popular history amply supplied visions of a happy

Paname and youthful romance in the years before the wars.[81] Nonetheless, the state did lend support by coming to the rescue of a quarter that was an iconic scene of Belle-Époque evocations: Montmartre. Montmartre was not only a favorite setting for nostalgic retrospectives, it was also the quarter that had the most active and most prominent defenders and promoters. The Old-Montmartre Society (Société d'histoire et d'archéologie du Vieux-Montmartre) kept up a long campaign of preservation efforts. Well-known writers, artists, and architects lent their ideas and influence to the cause. In the middle of the Second World War architect Claude Charpentier (nephew of the composer of the Montmartre opera *Louise*) presented the first plan for preserving the historic character of the Butte. Yet, after the war, developers continued to push for new projects that threatened the old-time atmosphere. In 1948, for example, some entrepreneurs set out to build a modern amusement park from the Rue Norvins to the Rue de l'Abreuvoir. Writer Marcel Aymé and other notables protested and aroused enough opposition to kill the project. The next year, the state handed the preservationists a more sweeping victory: the Ministère des Beaux-Arts put "the site Montmartre" on its list of "natural and legendary monuments." So Montmartre became the first protected historic district of Paris. Some important restoration work followed. The lovers of Montmartre prevented the demolition of a seventeenth-century house that had belonged to an actor of Molière's troupe, and the City of Paris began restoring it in 1956. The house, at 12 Rue Cortot, became the Musée de Montmartre, an indispensable repository of history and memory ever since.

Claude Charpentier worked not only to defend what was left of a postcard Belle-Époque Montmartre, but also to push back the clock and remove everything added since 1900 (his hope). In 1955 he and his associates mounted an exhibition in the Hôtel de Ville showing just how to create "a new Montmartre that will be an old Montmartre" (as the sympathetic prefect of the Seine put it). The goal was to "resuscitate the Montmartre of the canvases of Utrillo," declared Charpentier—that is, to re-create the painterly look of a circa-1900 village.[82] With the artist's paintings as the blueprint, the plan called for removing the upper stories from tall buildings and requiring property-owners to remove fake half-timbering and brick façades. The costly height-reduction did not take place, and most views over the city were never opened up again, but 1900-style façades were put back in place around the Place du Tertre. Old Montmartre received exceptional public and state support for several reasons. First of all, it was the district most identified with the Belle Époque and the galaxy of artists, songwriters, singers, and writers of that period. Second, decades later, noted artists and writers—Poulbot and Marcel Aymé, among others—took up the cause with fervor. While making the case for Montmartre's importance to the cultural heritage of Paris, they also invoked the down-to-earth argument that preserving the famed quarter was a key to attracting tourists from all over the world.

More generally through the city, many survivals of the Belle Époque were disappearing. From the mid-century on, elderly witnesses and celebrities of the era "1900" were steadily dying off, and many of its landmarks were succumbing to the assaults of wrecking crews. Colette died in 1954, Mistinguett and Gustave Charpentier in 1956, Charles Pathé in 1957, Francis Carco in 1958. Valedictory tributes and warm retrospectives greeted each demise. The closing and demolition of one 1900 landmark after another similarly stirred memories and nostalgia. Piece by piece, the world of 1900 was disappearing. The Tabarin music hall, long a rival to the Moulin Rouge, closed in 1952 and was demolished in 1966. Nearby, the out-of-this-world cabarets Enfer and Ciel (Hell and Heaven) were razed in 1953 to make way for a supermarket. The Vél d'Hiv (Vélodrome d'Hiver) was torn down in 1959, its Belle-Époque origins tarnished by its role in 1942 as the detention spot for thousands of Jews before their deportation to Nazi concentration camps. The Grand Guignol theater ended its long spree of horror and humor in 1962. The beloved old Médrano circus gave its last performance in 1963. The Alhambra theater (in the Rue de Malte) was razed in 1967. Twenty of the surviving art-nouveau métro entries were replaced by plain new ones in the decade of the 1960s (only seven had been dismantled in the 1950s).[83] And these were only some of the most famous of the vanishing emblems of 1900. No public outcry or notable resistance accompanied their disappearance. The Belle Époque was loved, but it did not become a basis for decision-making about Paris's future—with the notable exception of Montmartre.

So the memory of the "beautiful epoch" flourished through the 1950s as a pleasant daydream and entertainment, offering the nation distractions from painful memories of war, strife, insecurity, and misery. For the capital more specifically, the golden-past version of 1900 added a rich layer of dreams and memories to the long tradition of Paris idealizations. A host of cultural productions since the late 1920s has stocked and restocked that imaginary—plays, movies, chansons, posters, photographs, and paintings (from the Impressionists to early Picasso). Emblematic vestiges of the period are prominent throughout the city today—the Eiffel Tower, the Guimard métro entries, art nouveau sign lettering, the Musée d'Orsay, and the vintage decor of cafés and restaurants in many quarters. Altogether, through the twentieth century, the memory of Belle-Époque Paris remained more popular than any other—more popular than the Second Empire, July Monarchy, Revolutionary era, or any old-regime monarch's reign.

The reason for its special appeal is not just a French need for recalling a paradise lost of peace, economic stability, cultural brilliance, face-to-face community, and plentiful entertainments. The reason is also that the Belle Époque was a relatively compact period near enough back to be readily recalled and placed in history, in contrast to the long spans of centuries marked by the city's churches and monarchical monuments. Its handlebar-mustachioed men and its women in bustled long dresses seemed more like vaguely familiar ancestors in a family photo album than distant predecessors in a history book. Doubtless the memory has remained so strong, too, because it encompasses such a wealth of attractive period pieces—bright paintings and posters, novels and plays, glamorous pleasure spots mixing social elites and the demimonde, everyday sociability in public spaces, and an old-time populace of classic artisans, soldiers in red-white-and-blue, street-corner singers, and pretty Parisiennes (*midinettes*) gracing the sidewalks.

But there is still another reason above all why the Belle-Époque memory has played such an important role in *Paris* history: it highlighted the multiple faces of the city more than any other period memory has, drawing strength from them all. It included the winding lanes of Old Paris and Belleville, Haussmannian streetscapes that were wide and modern but still filled with horses and fiacres, mold-breaking creativity, pleasure and beauty in many forms, and a colorful cast of Parisians in their favorite haunts—from the most fashionable elites to amiable ordinary folk and fearsome lowlife. Its cache of vivid images and works represents a good-old-days Paris that was both cosmopolitan and local, traditional and new, high-life and lowlife. Bolstered by this wide-ranging appeal, it has contributed more than any other "memory" or period to the modern city's mystique.

. . .

Not until the '60s and '70s did the Belle Époque's hold on the popular imagination weaken dramatically. In the 1960s, famously, restive and critical youths and intellectuals called into question the comforting old stories. A counterculture of irreverent singers and movies nurtured discontents and disillusionment with customary ways and backward-looking mentalities. By the early 1970s, Paris was more than ever open to things new from outside France. Love of the past, that is, reached a low ebb at the very time that the modernists were mounting their greatest assault on the historic city, inserting new and alien landmarks into it, breaking up the traditional scale and skyline. What those future-obsessed state officials and urbanists thought and did is the subject of the next chapter.

Postwar Modernizing and the Resistance of Memory (1945–circa 1980)

> After all her wartime trials, Paris has come to life again. . . . Those
> who love Paris will return to find her beauty unchanged, her
> charm intact, her deep belief in human values unshaken.
>
> —JOHN L. BROWN,
> Introduction to Clara E. Laughlin, *So You're Going to Paris!* (1948)

> Paris is an unaccommodating, noisy and dirty city, and the "city of light" is, in
> most of its quarters, one of the most badly lighted capitals in the world. [Paris
> est une cité incommode, bruyante et malpropre et la "ville lumière" est, dans
> la plupart de ses quartiers, une des capitales du monde la plus mal éclairée.]
>
> —PHILIPPE LAMOUR (1963)

POSTWAR HOPES AND HESITATIONS

After four years of German occupation and general impoverishment,
punctuated by Allied bombing raids (and, at the end, German bombardments and rocket attacks), the fundamental question for Paris was how
and when it would recover. After all the ordeals of the first half of the
twentieth century, could it regain its City-of-Light brilliance? Although
the historic core came out of the war largely unscathed, it was scarred and
shabbier than before. Yet lovers of Paris managed, as always, to look beyond the scars and shabbiness. The charms of the city were still "intact,"
Clara Laughlin's 1948 guidebook declared, and its intellectual and artistic
life made it "still the most exciting and dynamic of European capitals."[1]

Was such praise just trite flattery? It was hard for most people to tell.
Readers of the press on both sides of the Atlantic knew that exciting cultural life was flourishing in postwar Saint-Germain-des-Prés. Writers and
artists who frequented cafés there included such celebrities as Jean-Paul

Sartre and Simone de Beauvoir, Albert Camus, Raymond Queneau, André Breton, Picasso, André Gide, Marguerite Duras, and Boris Vian; an illustrious group of expatriate writers (including the African Americans Richard Wright, James Baldwin, Chester Himes) came together there as well. Saint-Germain-des-Prés and spots nearby were also the epicenter of exciting jazz, cabaret, and *chanson* performances (new songs by such rising stars as Juliette Gréco and Léo Ferré). Altogether, these Existentialist literati, avant-garde artists, and the new popular-culture talents combined to give the postwar Left Bank the kind of heady attraction that Montmartre had enjoyed at the turn of the century.[2]

In 1948, for the first time since the war, Notre-Dame and the Eiffel Tower were bathed in floodlights through the tourist season. Shops throughout the city were able to stock and sell almost everything, even though average Parisians were still unable to buy much of it. Most of the art (though not all) looted by the Germans was back in French hands. The city's theaters, music halls, and nightclubs were in full swing. The Folies-Bergère's show was more spectacular than any since the early 1930s: the revue *C'est de la Folie*, in two acts and thirty tableaux, served up a dreamscape of "splendid girls" and an "orgy of colors and lights."[3] Tourists came back that summer (1948) in numbers not seen since 1929—Americans above all. Recycling century-old boasts, a brochure from the city's tourist office in 1948 hailed Paris as once again the "capital of the world" and the "city of art par excellence." After suffering terrible ordeals the "grand coquette" had regained her smile.[4]

Yet even the tourism boosters had to admit that the flattering title "city of light" was not fitting just then. There was work to do before the sparkle returned. French urbanists were the most emphatic about how much needed to be done, and they had in mind more than cosmetic touchups or even a facelift. Unlike tourists rejoicing to find famous monuments still there, urbanists saw near-disastrous disorder and a moribund city. Appalled but undaunted, they dreamed of constructing a brand new "modern Paris," a twentieth-century version of the Ville Lumière, radically breaking with Haussmann's model. Once in power, they undertook renewal projects on a scale greater than any since the Second Empire, realizing their dreams in concrete forms that are prominent throughout much of the city today.

In the view of their foes and critics, they did more violence to the beloved cityscape than did the German army or the battles of wartime. This chapter examines their vision of modern Paris and tells the story of their key accomplishments—those against-the-grain works they provocatively imposed on a city long priding itself on architectural harmony and historical beauty. It also attempts to explain why the modernizers fixed so single-mindedly on just one of the faces of Paris (Ville Lumière) to the detriment of others—the historic, the picturesque, and the village-like sense of community known as Paname.

The long overdue work of updating Paris did not get underway until a decade after the war for several reasons. The nation's first postwar priority was the reconstruction of bridges, roads, ports, and factories in areas devastated by the war. At the same time huge sums from the public treasury were going into France's colonial war in Indo-China until 1954, and then another war in Algeria, until 1962. Barely coping with crisis after crisis, the weak and short-lived governments of the Fourth Republic gave little attention to Paris's chronic problems. Meanwhile the capital's slums expanded, and the wretched shantytowns (*bidonvilles*) on the edge of the city grew larger. Tens of thousands of laborers and their families, drawn by hopes of jobs in construction and industry in the suburbs (Nanterre, Saint-Denis, La Courneuve, among others), essentially camped out in cobbled-together huts and trailers, packed in mud-trash-and-rat-filled ghettoes. Most of them were immigrants from southern Europe (Spain, Portugal, Italy) and from northern Africa (Algeria, Morocco), but a fifth or more were from the French countryside. Regardless of origin, they were on the bottom of the social ladder—or not on the ladder at all—and beyond the ken of establishment Paris. Their housing plight did not begin to show up in public discourse until the mid-1950s.[5]

Even if state finances had not been so limited, the nation's leaders in the immediate postwar years were not disposed to support any project for the greater glory of Paris. Rather, they aimed at reducing the capital's importance and its huge population, to the benefit of the provinces. The old argument that France was overly centralized had gained the upper hand during the war and its aftermath. So, like the Vichy leaders before them, postwar officials adopted policies designed to end the overwhelming dominance of the capital, the tentacular "monster," shifting the balance in favor of the rest of the country. That policy position gained a huge boost from the forceful case made by the geographer Jean-François Gravier in his book *Paris et le désert français* (1947), which argued that the state should end the capital's suffocating hegemony and should revitalize the provinces—the "French desert." Adopting that line of thought, state officials and economic-growth commissions worked through the 1950s to redistribute industries and population over the whole territory. While the lovers of Paris yearned for the restoration of old splendor, official circles worked to dethrone the queen of cities. The long neglect of Paris did not end until a new (Fifth) republic, with a strong president (Charles de Gaulle), replaced the floundering postwar republic in 1958.

THE MODERNIST IMAGINARY AND MOOD

The planners and administrators of the Fifth Republic, like their immediate predecessors, did not bring to their work any of the awe and affection for Paris that so many had expressed over the centuries—far from it. Their sense of the city did not include strong feelings for its historic character, atmosphere, charms, or pleasures. Rather, they dreamed of remaking the city, designing it like a sleek machine whose parts would function more smoothly and efficiently than ever before.[6] To them, the critical imperative was to overhaul Paris so that it could serve the needs of a twentieth-century society and a full-speed-ahead modern economy.

To the modernizers, the capital was shockingly archaic and dysfunctional. Its infrastructure was hopelessly inadequate for a dynamic industrial society. "Paris is no longer a modern city," declared the president of the National Commission for the Management of the Territory, Philippe Lamour, in 1963. Nothing had been done to adapt Paris to "modern needs" since Haussmann and the creation of the first métro line, he declared. In fact, some subway cars still in use dated from the time of the very first métro in 1900. Soot and grime covered the city's once-splendid buildings. Paris "is full of inconveniences, noisy, and dirty," he continued, and overall "the 'city of light' . . . is one of the most poorly lighted capitals in the world." "Paris lives on a literary legend that is no longer justified by anything."[7] Not a single big hotel had been built since the Second World War. The city lacked convention halls and international stadiums. Housing was scandalously antiquated and in short supply: half the dwellings in the Parisian region did not meet modern standards and were "not technically transformable." Some 400,000 of them were public-health menaces (*insalubres*). Almost 100,000 families of three or more persons (sometimes as many as nine) lived in just one-room apartments. A full 20 percent of the dwellings did not have running water, and 80 percent had neither bath nor shower.[8]

Some modernizing efforts were only making things worse. With trees being felled and sidewalks whittled away to make room for thousands more automobiles each year, "Paris has become a vast parking lot," declared the Inspecteur des Finances in 1965. Lamour concurred: the spreading chaos of cars was obstructing the famous views; monuments could no longer be seen in their proper perspectives, and people were no longer able to stroll or stop easily. Simply put, the city had "lost its charm."[9]

As well-placed observers pointed out, the crisis went beyond infrastructure problems. Paris was suffering a decline of creativity, a malaise of the artistic spirit, declared magazine editor Françoise Giroud. The city could no longer claim to be home to the most innovative and best painting, filmmaking, dance, and theater. It was losing its status as "capital of the arts." In short, Paris was on its way to becoming merely a "museum-city," the modernizers warned.[10] So the old fear of the death of Paris came back in force. In the 1960s, however, the mortal danger no longer seemed to be revolution and civil war, but a paralyzing congestion, disorder, and decay.

Obviously the political forces long hostile to Paris—regionalists, decentralizers, and the ruralist reactionaries of Vichy—bore heavy responsibility for the capital's failures to adapt to the twentieth century. But the lovers of Paris were also responsible, some clear-eyed critics pointed out. While admirers repeated the mantra "the greatest and the most beautiful city in the world," all manner of problems went ignored. Some of the nation's most revered authors came in for special rebuke. "The worst thing that has happened to Paris is the creation of a myth of Paris for which Balzac and Hugo are largely responsible," contended the chief architect of state buildings, Pierre Dufau, in 1967. He blamed Montaigne, too, as the source of the familiar attitude of love for Paris, warts and all. Fondness for the picturesque and the past had become obstacles to renewal and the future. The lovers of Paris had created complexes and taboos that became straitjackets on posterity.[11]

Long thwarted and exasperated, urban planners were impatient to build a new Paris with a full panoply of modern structures: skyscrapers, freeways, underground parking lots, a state-of-the-art business district with high-rise office buildings and apartment complexes, along with a series of eight new towns and nine redeveloped old towns (Saint-Denis, for example) around the capital. Half measures would no longer do, they insisted. The city had already experienced too many decades of that, and now it was time for thorough-going transformation, remaking the capital for the new times, for the growing population, and for economic expansion. Planners anxiously fixated on a symbol of the future—the milestone year 2000. To make Paris a capital of the twenty-first century, there was little time left—only forty years to overcome "a hundred years of inertia" and "decadence," as the Inspector General of Buildings and Palaces Henry Bernard wrote in 1967.[12] More than the physical condition of Paris was at stake. A revitalized Paris would lead France to unprecedented economic strength, the planners maintained. In the process, the French capital would become the capital of Europe.[13]

The models for the new city came from abroad. One inspiration was a plan for London (1943–1944) that was designed to reduce the population, create a green belt on the periphery, and direct future development to ten new cities to be built more than twenty miles from the center. France's minister of Reconstruction (1948–1953), Claudius-Petit, framed similar objectives for Paris. Although he was unable to carry out such an ambitious plan in the postwar recovery years,[14] his successors in the 1960s followed up on the ideas and began building a ring of satellite new towns (*nouvelles villes*), providing modern apartments for poorly housed Parisians and newcomers to the region.

More spectacular sources of inspiration were the skyscrapers of Manhattan and Chicago. As icons of modernity, tall towers had inhabited French imaginations since the '20s. Towers were dominant in 1930s plans for redevelopment of the area west of l'Étoile, along the "triumphal way" from the city limit at the Porte Maillot to the Rond Point de La Défense, five kilometers beyond the Arc de Triomphe. The designs of Le Corbusier exerted a particularly strong influence. His famous Voisin plan of 1925 had called for clearing away most structures from the history-saturated Right Bank to make room for a grid of new towers, forming a spacious ensemble of perfect regularity in spacing and height. Expressing an aversion to the "dantesque" skyscrapers of New York City, he preferred "cartesian" versions, more orderly, better proportioned, harmonious in height and spacing. Though never realized, his vision of sweeping rational renovation and vertical construction shaped the minds of planners decades later.[15]

An official plan for La Défense in 1964 called for a new city of towers about twenty-five stories high—a formal regularity more like Le Corbusier's model than the ragged skyline of Manhattan. The towers would surround the quarter's first big building, completed in 1958: a horizontally huge hall (100,000 square meters), whose vaulted concrete roof covered a world-record-setting 230 square meters. It was to be used as exhibit space for the newest industrial and technological products, a showcase of modernity named the Centre national des industries et techniques. Altogether the new quarter was to be Paris's Manhattan, offering new office space in abundance for the many corporate headquarters that the old central city could not accommodate.

The influence of the American skyscraper was strong and obvious in the district's first "tower," the Tour Nobel, which went up in 1966. Although the two architects were both Frenchmen, one of them, Jean de Mailly, had made frequent trips to the United States for study, and he adopted American designs not only in the overall form, but also in the windows, which featured curved glass that had to be specially made by an American manufacturer.[16]

The Nobel Tower with its twenty-eight floors of office space was quickly surpassed by taller towers after authorities raised the permissible height from twenty-five stories to forty-five or more.[17] In 1972 the forty-two-floor Gan Tower (170 meters high when completed) cropped up on the horizon behind the Arc de Triomphe. Its intrusion into the historic vista from the Louvre westward touched off a storm of criticism—including strong disapproval voiced by Minister of Finance Valéry Giscard d'Estaing. President Pompidou and La Défense officials dismissed the outcry, and the construction of seven other towers proceeded to completion over the next several years. One of them made explicit the New York inspiration: the

Tour Manhattan, an office building completed in 1975. Nearby, the Tour Fiat (completed in 1975), though designed by two French architects, derived from another distinctly American source—Hollywood: the 570-foot-high tower with smooth dark granite walls and smoked glass windows was inspired by the mysterious black monolith in Stanley Kubrick's film *2001: A Space Odyssey*.[18]

By the mid-1970s some of the new towers rising at La Défense were three to four times bigger than the early ones. The district was becoming a specialized business quarter for the largest French and international corporations, rather than the mix of offices, stores, and apartments envisioned in the 1950s. Responding defiantly to critics of the new Manhattan visible from central Paris, President Pompidou in 1972 called for "a forest of towers"—not just a timid five or six—as a backdrop to the Arc de Triomphe.[19]

FIGURE 3.1. Paris's international business district, La Défense, emerged in the 1960s as the epitome of futurist modernity under the Fifth Republic. Located just outside the city limits but fitting squarely in the Ville Lumière tradition, it was a state-backed development zone of skyscrapers on a deck (dalle) for pedestrians with roads below for vehicles (following Le Corbusier's principles). (Photo by the author.)

The energy crisis and economic downturn of 1973 slowed down new development and brought out more energy-efficient designs, but skyscraper construction continued on at La Défense through the 1970s. And a "new generation" of a half dozen more followed in the 1980s.[20]

While the tower-filled district was rising outside the historic city, promoters of modernity prepared to build skyscrapers in central Paris as well. The state prepared the way (in 1956) by eliminating the old code that restricted building heights to 31 meters—the seven-story structures of Haussmann's Paris. Over the next decade and a half, dozens of tall towers sprouted up, far above the historic horizon, in central Paris. The first high-rise public housing (22 floors) went up in the Rue Croulebarbe behind the Place d'Italie in 1958–1960, conspicuous not only for its height but also its stainless-steel exterior (see Figure 3.2). Even more conspicuously, a 27-story tall university science building cropped up near the Seine at Jussieu in 1965, its profile showing up behind Notre-Dame.

On the western side of the city a large complex of office and apartment towers called the Front de Seine was being built (1961–1975). And a huge new business center with a tower taller than any at La Défense was being planned for a spot beside the old Montparnasse railroad station. In addition, if President Pompidou had his way, a big world trade center was to rise on the grounds long occupied by the central market Les Halles. Skyscrapers were emblematic of the new scale of the city that "the needs of tomorrow" required—for both new office space and new housing, argued the modernizers. Some advocates added that the towers would also be useful for Parisians' survival in the new age of atomic warfare: the underground levels could hold reserves of food and water and offer protection against radioactive fallout for hundreds of thousands.[21]

Replacing low buildings with tall ones was the way chosen to provide much more housing and to end the long-standing shortage in the congested central city. The 1959 "Plan directeur de Paris" called for urban renewal of about one-tenth of the surface of Paris, areas where the homes of 367,000 Parisians were located. The 1961 plan went further, calling for housing renovation affecting about a million Parisians in an area almost six times greater than the remaining îlots insalubres.[22] To make room for large new apartment-and-office buildings, old industrial workplaces—big factories, ateliers, warehouses, and garages—were to be forced out of the city. Tax incentives and zoning changes would de-industrialize Paris.

The biggest of the modernizing projects was the construction of a new Montparnasse railroad station and an adjoining Maine-Montparnasse business complex capped by a skyscraper that would be the tallest tower in Europe. The extraordinary height, its proponents contended, was necessary to balance the expansive mass of lower buildings in the complex.

FIGURE 3.2. The Tour Albert. Paris's first "skyscraper" apartment building, designed by architect Édouard Albert, was built in 1958–1960, far from the center—in the thirteenth arrondissement (the Rue Croulebarbe). Its neighborhood, chosen as the first to modernize by the Ministry of Reconstruction and Housing, was full of decaying dwellings around former tanneries (bordering the polluted, though covered, Bièvre River); it was also near the historic state-owned Manufacture des Gobelins and the Mobilier national (national furniture depository and workshop.) (Photo by the author.)

The new structures, planned since the early 1960s, would provide needed office space, new apartments, a shopping center, and numerous public facilities that the quarter lacked.

Critics attacked the proposed tower as a blight on the historic skyline, an ugly "colossal wall" ruining the view of the nearby classical domes of the École militaire and Invalides. To its opponents, the Maine-Montparnasse tower was also a glaring symbol of the Americanization of Paris and the modernizers' arrogant disregard for the capital's heritage. Although the four architects were French, the developer was a New York firm, and the consulting architects and engineers were from Chicago and New York.[23] A city councilman who railed against the proposed skyscraper in 1965 called it "the tower of General Motors" and the "tower of money and profit" that threatened the very "Soul of Paris." But he was unable to muster any sizeable following in his efforts to stop the planned "monstrous block" and to "save our city." The prefect of Paris, not the elected city council, held the authority to grant the building permit. He and other modernizers working for the state were unyielding. And they put their opponents on the defensive by recalling a famous protest against a tall tower in the last century: critics of the Montparnasse project had to argue that they were not undiscerning reactionaries like the ones who had angrily petitioned against the Eiffel Tower.[24]

Modernity meant not only skyscrapers, but also automobiles, more and more of them. Therefore the new Paris was to abound in free-flowing thoroughfares and parking for the increasing numbers of cars that ever-greater prosperity brought. The traditional street with its mix of walkers, shoppers, and vehicles was to be relegated to the past, along with such quaint pastimes as aimless strolling and leisurely conversations along the way. Many of the new high-rises were built on platforms and decks to distance residents from the street level below and its fast-moving traffic. New *autoroutes* were to go over-and-under the congested historic streets, and over waterways and train tracks as well, instead of cutting through densely built areas as Haussmann's boulevards (*percées*) did. A four-lane, double-decker thoroughfare was to go over the Canal Saint-Martin, and another one was to cover the Seine. "Paris must adapt to the automobile" and give up "a certain estheticism," insisted President Pompidou.[25]

The automobile had pride of place in the modern city as a swift and stylish transporter of residents thriving in the postwar economy. Further, it made possible a new aesthetic experience of Paris, its champions maintained (most notably, President Pompidou). Speeding through the city by car opened up new views of the cityscape, an official planning document of 1965 explained. In contrast to the pedestrian taking in such fixed sights as the sculpted front (*portail*) of Notre-Dame, the automobile passenger could enjoy the beauty of "grand perspectives viewed from different angles" and large volumes of colors, lights, and masses.[26]

Certain of the course of history, uncompromisingly sure, Pompidou had no patience for objections to anything new. As a former professor of French literature and author of an anthology of avant-garde poetry, he knew well that foes of the modern had inveighed against the paintings of the Impressionists, the Eiffel Tower, and the poems of the symbolists. He could only scorn their latter-day counterparts, those clinging to retrograde tastes and thinking about the city. The automobile was a fact of modern life, and Paris simply had to adapt to it. In his brief for the automobile, Pompidou acknowledged only one problem—the poor driving habits of Parisians: for the sake of order in the city, those at the wheel must "discipline themselves."

The first new autoroute project was an expressway hugging the Seine on the Right Bank (the Voie express rive droite), begun in 1964 and finished in 1967. A similar expressway on the Left Bank was to follow, passing close by the Gothic majesty of Notre-Dame. Pompidou backed both of them enthusiastically. "Twenty-three million automobilists have already taken the Right-Bank Expressway, which proves that it is good for something!" he declared in 1971. Also planned was a network of radial autoroutes leading in and out of the city, following designs formulated back in the 1930s. Under construction all through the 1960s was a ring expressway just outside the city limits, occupying terrain where the fortifications had stood: the *Boulevard périphérique*, completed in 1973, became both a new traffic-filled artery and a new barrier around the capital.

As the numbers of automobiles in the city increased from one million in 1960 to over 2 million in 1965 and then 2.5 million by 1970, urban planners had to find ways to provide parking spaces for them. In 1968 only about half of the cars registered in the capital had a place to park: for 900,000 automobiles, only 470,000 places were available, reported the prefect of police. Curbsides and courtyards were hopelessly insufficient. So in many quarters, parked cars were crammed onto every sidewalk and square not fenced off, making endless obstacle courses for pedestrians. The planners' solution was to build underground parking garages, beginning with one in the Rue Saint-Honoré (1,100 spaces) in 1960. Underground construction peaked in the Pompidou period with 35 "parkings" completed between 1969 and 1973. The new facilities put more and more automobiles out of the way and out of sight, but only after years of heavy construction and dusty disorder around such revered monuments as Notre-Dame and Saint-Sulpice.[27]

RENOVATION–EVISCERATION

Parisians saw modernizing at its most radically transforming in two mostly poor arrondissements—the thirteenth and the twentieth, where one large slum after another was gutted and replaced with high-rise apartment buildings. One of the first to be remade was a populous neighborhood around the Rue Nationale (Îlot no. 4) in the thirteenth. When demolition began in 1956, dilapidated low dwellings were overflowing with some 6,400 people, most of them hand-to-mouth poor. Many a large family lived in just one room. The streets in the quarter were lined with some 180 retail shops, selling basic food, drink, and other necessities. Cafés were also numerous—48 of them in all, nearly one café per 130 inhabitants. And scattered through the quarter were artisans' workshops, factories, and warehouses.

Most of the inhabitants worked, shopped, and socialized near where they lived, as sociologist Henri Coing reported tellingly in his study of the *îlot* (published in 1966). Many had no need to leave the neighborhood. When they did go outside the thirteenth arrondissement, they spoke of "going to Paris" (or "expatriating themselves"). Despite the overcrowded, squalid housing, and lack of green space, the residents were strongly attached to their neighborhood. They spoke of feeling like members of "a big family." Merchants allowed poor families to buy on credit. Customers could pick out cuts of meat or a baguette to suit particular tastes. Shopkeepers, knowing most their clients' preferences, addressed each regular with "Well then . . . the usual?" With apartments so crowded and lacking amenities, many of the residents spent much time in cafés and in the street. People greeted each other with a friendly "bonjour" and exchanged news as they crossed paths each day. They talked with immediate neighbors going to and from the shared W.C. and the water faucets outside the apartments. The concierge, watching it all, knew the habits, and even the secrets, of most. The quarter was "un petit village," the locals often remarked. The razing of the old buildings and the new construction of the quarter ended that sense of intimate community, dispersed the inhabitants, and destroyed the Rue Nationale as a vibrant market street.[28]

FIGURE 3.3. The thirteenth arrondissement, far from the splendors of classic Paris, before modernization: the Rue Baudricourt (circa 1900), near the Rue Nationale, was full of hardscrabble drinking places and furnished-room tenements, housing workers near their workshops and factories. (Photo UPF/ Archives de Paris—11Fi 2854.)

FIGURE 3.4. The Rue Clisson (in 2005). Gentrification in the de-industrialized, massively redeveloped thirteenth arrondissement. Large apartment buildings constructed in the late twentieth century—with all the modern comforts but soul-less?—have replaced the low structures filled with shops, cafés, and workers' tenements before 1960 (compare with figure 3.5). (Photo by the author.)

Other areas of the thirteenth underwent similar metamorphosis. Houses and apartment buildings of one to four levels were demolished, and new ones—mostly of eight to twelve stories—went up in their place. The biggest "operation" was the "secteur Italie" (south of the Place d'Italie), where re-development included the construction of the thirteenth's tallest high-rises, the Olympiades, on land vacated by the Panhard automobile factory (in a triangle between the Avenue de Choisy and the Avenue d'Ivry). Named after such Olympic sites as Helsinki and Squaw Valley, the 36-floor apart-ment towers and horizontal slabs (barres) were ready for occupancy in the early 1970s. Altogether the new buildings of the thirteenth provided many more apartments than the old structures had (10,000 old dwellings replaced by 16,000 new ones). Yet many of the inhabitants did not stay in the quarter but instead left for the fourteenth arrondissement or the nearby suburbs Ivry and Vitry—for financial reasons or to be near work and friends. A third of the new apartments were subsidized public housing (H.L.M.—*habitation à loyer modéré*), but that did not come close to meeting the demand.[29]

Across the river in Belleville, urban renewal was just as spectacularly destructive of old neighborhoods and community life. Clearing out the old began in 1955 on Îlot no. 11 (Quartier des Amandiers, Ménilmontant), where 19,000 people lived—a population density even greater than in the Rue Nationale (750 persons per hectare compared with 520). Up on the hilltop around the Place des Fêtes, demolition began in 1966 in a neighborhood of some 9,600. There (the Hauts-de-Belleville), for the first time, the operation was turned over entirely to private developers.[30] The

FIGURE 3.5. Profiles of 1970s modernity: the Olympiades, a complex of apartment towers (33 floors) and low-rise barres (14–18 levels), is now the heart of the largest Chinatown in the capital, occupying land formerly filled with industrial buildings (the thirteenth arrondissement). (Photo by the author.)

tall concrete towers that replaced the old houses provided good modern living space for many more people, but the stark new Place des Fêtes, like the new Rue Nationale, was bereft of all but a few of the traditional nodes of community life. Lower on the hill, bulldozers also wiped out Îlot no. 7 in the picturesque, winding Rues des Couronnes, Julien-Lacroix, and de la Mare—a steep hillside neighborhood of miserably housed Parisiens who, again, had long enjoyed a close-knit sociability.

The urban planners looked at shabby areas and saw only poverty, wretched housing, public health dangers, criminality, and wasted space. They hailed the demolitions and new constructions as indubitably good, the upward course of progress whose proof lay in striking statistics—so many dwellings added, greater floor space per apartment, and new public facilities opened: new schools, nurseries and daycare centers, playgrounds, cultural centers, and green spaces. But to uprooted inhabitants and the many who venerated Paname, the massive projects were catastrophes, destroying neighborhood social life, the traditional scale of the cityscape, and a time-burnished beauty.

Although the urbanists seemed like soul-less technocrats to their critics, they were not exactly cool-headed rationalists. Long frustrated, impatient for change, and exasperated by everything hindering it, they wanted action, and they were ready to fight for it. "Only those who are in the battles win them," the prefect of Paris declared in 1968, quoting Racine and Saint-Just. To sum up their cause, they used the language of battle: *reconquête urbaine.*[31] Their weapon of choice was the bulldozer. In one targeted sector of the city after another, they deployed bulldozers with the same grim resolve to destroy and clear away that they showed in razing the scrap-built shantytowns on the periphery and in the nearby suburbs.[32] They fought not only against "insalubrity," but also decay and decadence. In their view they had to act quickly to "reconquer" Paris—to rescue it from the grip of creeping rot, the encroaching riffraff, and ugly, outmoded industry. Alarmed by how much needed to be done by 2000, they threw themselves into an urgent offensive, struggling against the rooted resistance to modernity, forcing Paris to make a leap from yesterday to tomorrow. Their actions were necessary to save Paris, they proclaimed, just as their opponents, the partisans of "old Paris," did. The modernizers were saving it from "asphyxia" and "gangrene," while their foes were rescuing it from "vandals" and "assassins."

Both of the warring sides appealed to a common stock of Parisian values. Both declared their love of Paris with all its beauty and monuments (the urbanists clearly speaking defensively). Sometimes the modernizers even spoke of the "soul" of Paris as important, though their use of the term was even more vague than was their opponents'. Despite their talk of sentiment and soul, the planners and political leaders of the 1960s showed none of the usual traits of Paris lovers. President Charles de Gaulle took little interest in the capital and left its renovation to others, such as his minister of Culture, André Malraux, who cared most about the city's museums, art, and famous old monuments. Malraux's main accomplishment was to clean the dark, sooty façades of Notre-Dame, the Louvre, and other iconic structures. Georges Pompidou, as prime minister and then as president, felt most strongly about the city—in his own blinkered way. What he cared about was not the historical Paris or the life of neighborhoods, but rather an emergent modern metropolis that was to be an international business hub. None of these leaders wrote much about Paris or strolled in it the way the loving flâneurs did. Rather they rode through it as quickly as possible in their black limousines with darkened windows rolled up.[33]

The Gaullist officials and urbanists of the 1960s, refusing to brook more delays, wielded extraordinary power to carry out the most far-reaching urban operations undertaken in twentieth-century Paris. With the opposition weak and ineffective, their promises for Paris carried preponderant weight in public opinion—until late in the decade.

NEW CULTURE, NEW *VILLES*

While international modernism was cropping up on the Parisian skyline in the late fifties, new forms of international popular culture began to captivate Parisian youth. The movies of James Dean and Marlon Brando provided alluring models of adolescents in revolt. American rock 'n' roll singers and dancers showed how to have rebellious fun—to a raucous beat. Imported music and festive rock concerts became the core of a new culture of French youth in the early 1960s, a culture of young Parisians rejecting their parents' preoccupations with work and economic gain along with

their elders' memories of deprivation, political strife, and German occupation. They forged a social identity of their own and a new sense of community, reaching out to unknown other youth as "buddies"—*copains*—with
much in common. They read the magazine *Salut les copains* and listened
to a radio program of the same name on Europe 1. When the radio station organized a concert and celebration (a *fête de la musique*) for the copains at the Place de la Nation in June 1963, some 150,000 young people
showed up. The capital had never before seen such a gathering of youth.
Social commentator Edgar Morin, writing in *Le Monde* (July 6, 1963),
declared the concert a watershed event, crystallizing the emergence of a
"new adolescent class" as a social force.[34] It was the first of many such
festivities enjoyed by Parisian youth in the years that followed.

More and more of those young people lived not in central Paris, but
out in the large, built-up area around the capital—the *agglomération* (also
known as "le Grand Paris"), extending some twenty kilometers from the
center of the city. The population of those outlying parts increased by more
than a million three hundred thousand (from 6,436,000 to 7,830,000)
between 1954 and 1975, while the population of Paris proper declined
by a half a million (from 2,850,000 to 2,300,000).[35] Together the postwar "baby boom" and the growth of Greater Paris placed enormous new
demands on the state and the administration of the metropolitan area.
The new realities also undermined traditional conceptions of Paris—as
a historical wonderland bounded by Montmartre, the Latin Quarter, the
Champs-Élysées, and Bastille—and challenged preconceptions of the suburbs (*banlieue*) as an "anti-Paris," an ugly hodgepodge rightfully kept out
of the picture (if not out of mind). The state's failings in dealing with the
new Greater Paris led to long-simmering social disorders and periodic
upheavals that continued though the rest of the twentieth century—and
into the twenty-first as well.

By the early 1960s it was clear that growth-limiting policies for the
capital were producing major spillover problems for the outskirts, requiring
a more coordinated system of administering the whole region. For decades
government projects for the banlieue had routinely run aground due to
opposition from one or more of the competing powers in charge—three
departments, 1,305 communes, and several state ministries. Addressing

the problem, the young Fifth Republic created the *District* of the Region of Paris in 1961, a new administrative unit for an area extending about 60 kilometers from the center (much of the Île-de-France). The new regional authorities were able to collect taxes for the district, design infrastructure improvements, undertake long-range planning, and carry out projects for the region. Further adapting to the new demographics, a reform law of 1964 replaced the old Department of the Seine (encompassing the city of Paris) and two others nearby with eight new departments for the region.[36]

Anticipating decades of steady growth, the regional planners proposed building ten metropolitan expressways (*autoroutes de dégagement*), two new beltways (*rocades*), and a regional express rail system (the RER).[37] Like the city planners, they were looking ahead anxiously to the milestone year 2000, when the population of the region, they projected, would reach 12 or even 14 million—or 18.2 percent of the French population, in contrast to the 8,470,000 inhabitants there in 1961. The pressure was on. Five million more people (at the least) would demand services within thirty years. The rising population would increase demand not only for housing (100,000 new units each year to be built), but also for mass transport—a third more, at the least—and for recreational facilities as well.[38]

To help end the long-standing housing shortage in Paris proper, the state sponsored the construction of huge concrete apartment complexes called *grands ensembles* from the mid-1950s into the early 1970s, implanting them out in semi-rural communes such as Sarcelles, in nearby working-class suburbs such as La Courneuve, and in more distant, planned new towns (*nouvelles villes*), such as Cergy-Pontoise and Marne-la-Vallée. Designed for 30,000 to 40,000 inhabitants, those suburban housing projects were built not for the immigrant workers who ended up in them years later, but rather for provincials moving into the Île-de-France, Parisians living in miserably substandard housing, and their counterparts in the banlieue, including the inhabitants of the shantytowns. Though close to the city, most residents of the suburbs and new towns lived apart from it. The métro lines ended at the gates of the city. Even trips to and from the near banlieue involved time-consuming changes to buses and trains. A Greater Paris for commuters began to materialize only when the first line of a regional express train (the RER) went into operation in 1969. A few years later (1974), a new word was coined for the residents of that urbanizing region: *Franciliens* they became.[39] But neither the neologism nor the regional train system came close to being enough to give outlying residents a sense of being Parisian or living like one.[40]

The expanding population of Franciliens and Paris youth were a new kind of Parisian: they led lives removed from reminders of centuries past, and they felt no nostalgia for the Belle Époque or long-favorite memory sites such as Montmartre and Les Halles. On the one hand, their memory void made the slate-cleaning work of the modernizers easier. But on the other, they did not lend support either. The new youth culture, stirring hopes for a less repressive society, was at odds with the technocratic urbanism of the de Gaulle era. In its more anti-bourgeois manifestations, it also contested the material "progress" of the "Thirty Glorious" postwar years—especially the older generations' satisfaction as new consumers of automobiles, washing machines, and television sets.

The youthful rebellion of 1968 that became the near-revolution known as "the events of May" erupted first in the forlorn suburb of Nanterre (five miles out beyond the Arc de Triomphe), a town full of stark postwar housing projects and the largest Algerian *bidonville* population in the region. It started at a raw, new university (opened in 1964), occupying a poorly built campus, devoid of the amenities of the traditional university and the Latin Quarter. The full-scale revolt of May, which caught the powerful by surprise, grew out of some important discontents that went beyond the university and Paris—discontents with the Gaullist government, shortcomings of the postwar economy, and entrenched social constraints that were national in scope.[41] But dissatisfaction with the modernizers' Paris did play a part, as we shall see. And out of the contestation that flowered in 1968 came long-term changes in Paris life and governance.

THE BATTLE OVER THE
HEART AND BELLY OF PARIS

The battles of spring '68 were fought in many places—from the grim new university at Nanterre and the Renault factories on the edge of the city to the old streets of the Latin Quarter, but one place emerged in the late 1960s as the prime symbolic site of struggle for the future of Paris: the central market Les Halles. The importance of that battle was not evident to most people (historians included) even years afterward. Yet, as the following pages will show, those who joined in battle understood well and articulated well the alternative futures that were at stake.

State officials had decided as early as 1943 to remove the congested, inadequate market from the city center, and their successors reaffirmed the decision in 1948, but it was not carried out—because other problems and projects took precedence in the difficult times of war and postwar. By the 1950s proponents of the move, more convinced than ever, marshaled a host of reasons for getting rid of the central market. The nightly invasion of trucks caused large traffic jams in the very center of the city. The market generated disgusting-if-not-dangerous mounds of smelly, rotting fruit, vegetables, animal scraps, and hordes of rats. Above all, the nineteenth-century facility was too small and primitive to serve the needs of the vast city of the twentieth century. Finally, in February 1959, the Council of Ministers made the decision to transfer the market to Rungis, seven kilometers outside the city. Yet the actual move was delayed for years, largely because of resistance from established merchants of Les Halles.

Planners saw in the relocation a grand opportunity for modernizing the very heart of Paris. Clearing away the pavilions would free up a huge space (some 69 acres) for new office space and public facilities needed in the city center. With discussions confined to the inner circles of state officialdom, office buildings for government ministries took priority in the early stages of planning. The minister of Finance wanted to bring together all his employees in one new building. The minister of Equipment wanted a big new building for his staff. Some in the highest echelons of the state envisioned a new international commerce center, to be surrounded by banks and first-class hotels. The prefect of Paris had in mind a business complex on the scale of 200,000 square meters of office space. The minister of Cultural Affairs wanted to construct a major facility in the quarter together with a big library that would relieve the overcrowded Bibliothèque nationale.[42]

As objectionable as the market was to some, it was beloved to others— as a reserve of old-time popular life and memory. Local associations and advocates for Old Paris fondly depicted Les Halles as the living heart of the historic city. The central market had flourished as a vital hub of plebeian

life since its creation in the twelfth century. The "belly of Paris," as Zola
had described it, in all its hurly-burly and crazy-quilt colors and smells,
was also the heart of a humming neighborhood filled with *charcuteries* and
crémeries, butcher shops, workers' cafés and bistros, hefty porters, and
salt-of-the-earth prostitutes. Drifters and homeless men gravitated there
to find some hours of work, quick pay, and food. The poor went there
to glean discarded produce from the pavement—or to filch an apple or a
pear. Some with a few coins purchased a portion of warm mystery stew
(*l'arlequin*) made of leftovers from restaurants good and bad. Social elites
often went there at the crack of dawn to cap a night of partying with the
simple enjoyment of hearty onion soup in workers' cafés. "All true Parisians adore this quarter," noted André Fermigier, columnist for *Le Nouvel
Observateur*, in May 1967: "those who live in it, those who come to it
to dine, to buy their flowers or their crate of tomatoes, to hear an accor-
dionist, to breathe the scents [*parfums*] of former times, to seek—in their
poverty alas! and their solitude—a little warmth and comfort, or simply
some work."[43]

Les Halles may have been dear to many Parisians, but most did not
come to its defense when the transfer of the market grew imminent. They
either accepted the case for modernization or simply acquiesced in it. It
was hard for many to believe that the old Halles was in real danger. Talk
about the move had gone on so many years with nothing happening. The
move seemed so drastic that it was reasonable to expect de Gaulle and
Pompidou to not allow it.[44]

Finally, in the night of March 4–5, 1969, the drawn-out drama came to
a decisive end. The nightly bustle of wholesale buying and selling stopped
abruptly. Six hundred trucks from forty-eight moving companies showed
up to pick up tons of food and to transport it to the new facilities on the
outskirts, at Rungis, near the Orly airport. The urbanists had won a decisive round, but they wanted nothing less than total victory. That meant
razing the market and then building something new befitting the capital
of modern France.

Since 1967, the defenders of the old Halles had mounted campaigns
on several fronts to save the Baltard pavilions. The case for historic preservation was made in a barrage of pleas and protests by local associations

and their supporters—through petitions, letters, editorials, and books. Prominent architects and historians of art in France and around the world argued for the historical importance of the well designed iron-and-glass structures, built some twenty-five years before the Eiffel Tower.[45] Some argued for preservation of the surrounding neighborhood as well—on aesthetic grounds. Many of the buildings, they showed, were once beautiful exemplars of Parisian architecture from the seventeenth and eighteenth centuries—some even from the sixteenth century. "Picturesque dwellings [logis]," "magnificent" stairways, "noble façades," splendid works of wrought iron—the quarter was brimming with "riches of art," the authors of an impressive architectural survey of the *quartier* in early 1968 demonstrated "house by house."[46] Bordering Les Halles was the splendid Gothic church Saint-Eustache, "one of the largest and most beautiful of Paris, which saw the first communion of Louis XIV, the burials of Colbert, Molière, La Fontaine, Mirabeau. . . ." Destruction of the quarter would be not only an "inconceivable" loss of the capital's "artistic heritage," but also the loss of a historic "liaison between the Marais and the Palais-Royal." The quarter was, in short, the "heart of the capital," and the safeguarding of its historic character and "vocation" was nothing less than essential.

A battle over the fate of the pavilions began on the site itself within months after the transfer. On one side were organizers of cultural activities, who filled the now-free spaces with art and entertainment for residents of the quarter and all Paris. The pavilions took on new life as venues of exhibits, plays, concerts, circus acts, and movies. An ice-skating rink was installed in one of them; in another, a Picasso exhibit, which drew seventy thousand visitors. Back in June 1967 sixty-seven leading artists, intellectuals, and entertainers had signed a petition demanding that cultural facilities be given priority in any future development. They insisted that the quarter of Les Halles be made "a home [foyer] for culture in the heart of Paris . . . a place of all expressions of art and culture, a place where the spirit of Paris will breathe."[47] That would not only enhance the quarter, they argued, but also "maintain Paris in its role as cultural capital of the world." For a few years after the transfer, with the former market full of attractions drawing crowds there, local associations took hope. To partisans of the 1968 revolt, Les Halles was "the natural place for creativity in a popular setting and the starting point for a cultural revolution."[48] But for the Pompidou regime the specter of "cultural revolution"—or even festive gatherings with a potential for contestation—was all the more reason for moving ahead with the planned transformation of the quarter.[49] That required first ripping out the old iron structures.

An American banker offered to buy the pavilions for 30 million francs with the intent of reconstructing them somewhere in France or in the United States. Telegrams urging preservation flooded in from notables all over the world—from the curators of major American museums and celebrities such as John Lennon, Max Ernst, Andy Warhol, Alexander Calder, Robert Rauschenberg, and Jean Tinguely. Nine members of the architectural jury for the Beaubourg cultural center wrote to President Pompidou pleading that he save "at least some of the pavilions of Baltard." The structures were important, they argued, not only as masterpieces of French architectural history, but also as a flourishing theater of cultural activity complementing the future Centre Beaubourg—and necessary for the success of "the work which will remain attached to your name." In July 1971, two to three thousand people came out to demonstrate around the former market, demanding that Les Halles be a cultural center for ordinary Parisians.[50]

The state's officials remained unyielding. Opposition to the slated demolition, in their view, represented a test of their authority by the troublesome forces that had brought about the 1968 uprising. If authorities delayed or agreed to preserve some pavilions on the site, they believed, the agitators would not be satisfied and would take the concession as a sign of weakness and as cause for further agitation. At the end of June the prefect and other officials decided that "the essential [part] of the demolition" had to be "done before the end of August"—specifically the six pavilions on the eastern side—"in order to create an irreversible situation."[51] In early August 1971, when most Parisians were away on vacation, bulldozers moved in and began demolishing the famed pavilions. By the end of the month they had reduced most of them to debris. Over the next several years they finished off the rest, except for one, a single pavilion that was moved to the suburb of Nogent and reconstructed there in 1976 (and dedicated in 1978). All the others, smashed into large heaps, were sold as scrap iron. The destruction could not have been more brutally efficient.

Somehow the "army of rats" that had lived in the buildings and cellars made a quiet exodus to new homes without spreading disastrous ills. In the historic "heart" of Paris there was now simply a large "hole," soon to be made bigger by deep excavation. The sight of the ruins was a shock for Parisians returning from vacation at the end of the summer 1971. How could it have actually happened so quickly? "Heart-rending sight, disgrace of a regime, . . . wound that will not be closed in this heart of Paris," wrote André Fermigier in the *Nouvel Observateur*. "They killed the pavilions," onlookers cried, voicing the same poetic sense of the organic city. "They have killed the architecture of Baltard right in its youth, when it was taking on a second life"—as a foyer of artistic creation and popular participation outside official sponsorship and control, wrote urbanist Marcel Cornu.[52] Demolishing the pavilions was the sure way of eradicating the new life that had sprung up in the dead market. The twofold destruction produced a sense of loss that the hole seemed to symbolize for years.[53]

The "operation of the Halles" included more than removing the market and bulldozing the pavilions. It also entailed demolishing many old buildings in the quarter—entire streets-full of apartment houses built centuries before the structures of Baltard. They included the historic treasures inventoried and publicized by scholarly lovers of Vieux Paris—the many "noble façades," handsome ironwork, and sculpted cornices. Though preservationist writings and exhibits in the late sixties had won considerable public support for the cause, it was not enough to stop authorities from carrying out most of the demolition work. Altogether fifty-six buildings were destroyed, some of them among the oldest in Paris and some still in good condition.[54]

But the most glaring and mourned loss was the destruction of the market. Sorrow mixed with outrage at the assaults on "the heart"—and belly—of the capital. Some *amoureux de Paris* like historian Louis Chevalier considered the wounds to be life-threatening for the living body of the city. Talk of the "massacre" and the "murder" of Paris, which had earlier emerged around the proposed demolition of the old Gare d'Orsay, now focused on the destruction of Les Halles and the surrounding quarter—a double murder.[55] Les Halles was nothing less than quintessential Paris for many lovers of the traditional city. The market district was "the center of centers," containing "the essential of Paris," maintained the shocked and angry Louis Chevalier.[56] Its destruction meant the doom of all the adjoining quarters and thus the entire city center, he was convinced. Several years after the August massacre, Chevalier critically analyzed the technocratic mentalities and political powers responsible for "the assassination" in his resounding book L'Assassinat de Paris (1977). Delivered with magisterial force, it was a withering attack on the modernizing project. But it was more than that, hence doubly memorable: it was also a loving elegy for a vanished, richly human Paris that was already being forgotten.

CHANGING COURSE

The debate about what to put in the now-hollow heart of Paris was long and passionate. Multiple possibilities were proposed by competing imaginaries, all of them grounded in centuries of Paris tradition. Proponents of each possibility knew that they had at hand a unique opportunity to create a defining new center of the capital. At the same time, Les Halles became the stakes in some larger struggles, too. Much of France was going through a tumultuous post-1968 reworking of attitudes toward political leadership, society, culture, and urbanism. In that exceptional time of flux, decisions about the market district became choices about fundamental alternatives for Paris and even the nation.

The razing of the pavilions came at a time when critics of the new Paris were already furious about the concrete towers rising on the Front de Seine, the Place d'Italie, and Maine-Montparnasse. The new structures were aesthetically offensive, lacked essential human qualities, and did not fit into the traditional fabric of the city—so went the principal criticisms.[57] There were others. According to some, the architectural concept of the tower itself was outdated and foreign, having been conceived in Germany in the 1920s, redesigned in France, exported to the United States, and reimported. The skyscraper struck some, moreover, as the monstrous offspring of a phallic and infantile obsession. It was also "the perfect expression of isolation, in time and in space not only of the volumes which compose it but also of the individuals who inhabit it . . . ," charged architect Ionel Schein in 1972. Its very structure and its one-dimensional functionality worked against human communication and festivity in the city.[58]

In the early 1970s as the Tour Montparnasse rose up and up above the cityscape, it drew ever-stronger outcries. It became a defining totem of Parisian modernism, standing out provocatively in more ways than its unprecedented height. Almost all the earlier high-rise buildings were planted several miles outside the center at La Défense, where they did not intrude on the classic monuments and skyline of the capital. Neither the construction of the large circular Maison de Radio France (1956–1963) nor the complex of towers called the Front de Seine provoked widespread outcry, because those were built on old industrial sites on the edge of the historic center.[59] But inserting a skyscraper in the central city, rupturing the most venerable historic fabric, was quite another matter. The 690-foot-tall shaft towering over every other building was conspicuous from almost everywhere in Paris. Reactions of angry disapproval simmered away in the press and the populace, but the public authorities and the developers pressed forward with construction in the early 1970s (unlike the Les Halles project, the Tour Montparnasse was a private venture, though backed by the state). The tower was officially opened in September 1973—without much fanfare, while President Pompidou was on a state visit to China.

Coming to fruition together in the same period, the renewal projects at Montparnasse and Les Halles demonstrated more glaringly than any other the modernizers' brazen disregard for historic Paris and the little-people's Paname. Those operations also, more than any other, catalyzed the emotional charge that the old cityscape held for many Parisians. And next in the works was the Left-Bank expressway, one of President Pompidou's pet projects, to be built right in the shadow of Notre-Dame. Public outrage over the brutalist protrusion at Montparnasse, combined with dismay at the demolished pavilions and the planned expressway, galvanized a groundswell of opposition to Gaullist urbanism. By 1974 it had become strong enough to force urban redevelopment away from the skyscraper-and-freeway forms of the 1960s.

The battle over Les Halles also led to fundamental change in the way urbanist projects were chosen and shaped. By the end of the 1960s redevelopment had become associated with realty speculation, corruption, and heavy-handed dictation by the state.[60] Secrecy and authoritarian decision-making, critics charged, were at the root of the problems. The planning for Les Halles was the epitome of that closed-door approach: state authorities and their "technocrat" planners made decisions without open discussions or architectural competitions. Opponents of the closed process demanded local citizen involvement through neighborhood associations, hoping for a more democratically planned city, one better attuned to the lives and aspirations of the people.

For the Halles district, vigorous local associations emerged in the late '60s, even before May 1968, and quickly demonstrated their effectiveness, exerting pressure and articulating responses to the state's projects. One pioneering association, the Union des Champeaux, organized an exhibit of photographs of the neighborhood's old buildings in February and March 1968. That exhibit attracted 30,000 people and did more to awaken public opinion than anything else had. In May the demand for *participation*, meaning democratic discussion and decision-making, gained tumultuous force with the outbreak of student and worker revolt. From 1968 on, a variety of local organizations energized by the battle over Les Halles carried on long-term campaigns to win public support and to make government officials heed grass-root concerns. In the aftermath of May 1968 the prefect of Paris took the unprecedented step of establishing a liaison with the association leaders.

Public disenchantment with the urbanists and the pressure of activist associations became great enough to move President Pompidou to break with the old secret manner of deciding for Paris. Open architectural competitions (beginning with one for the new museum complex at Beaubourg) and regular public exhibits of projects became the norms in the 1970s. But that was not enough to satisfy the mounting demands for a more democratic Paris. In the wake of the Halles battle, opposition leaders—Left, Center, and even some Gaullist city councilors—called for a fundamental change in the governance of the capital, demanding that Paris be allowed to elect its own leader, a mayor, to stand up to the president and his prefects. Eight bills to that effect were submitted to the National Assembly in 1973 and 1974. Finally a law authorizing an elected mayoralty for the capital was passed under the next president, Giscard d'Estaing (December 31, 1975).[61]

The Blitzkrieg on the pavilions, in addition, contributed to a new appreciation of nineteenth-century architecture. The first round of that aesthetic revaluation occurred in the late sixties when connoisseurs of old Paris began denouncing the slated demolition of the ornate fin-de-siècle Gare d'Orsay, a Belle-Époque basilica of a train station. In response, state authorities decided against its demolition in April 1971, only months before the destruction of Les Halles. The Gare d'Orsay officially became part of the nation's "patrimony" in 1973, when the façade and decorations of the station were entered into the inventory of *Monuments historiques*; five years later, the whole structure won the same protection. The razing of the Baltard pavilions, showing how quickly and easily events could take a different turn, helped awaken a larger public to the preservationist cause. In the aftermath, the remaining structures of the nineteenth century took on new value as precious pieces of the city's architectural heritage.[62] The city of Haussmann and the Belle Époque became the new "Old Paris."

REVIVING THE HEART

For more than five years, the huge hole at the former market was the city's biggest *chantier*, a site of excavation and subterranean construction. Heavy-duty earthmovers dug deeper and deeper and then laid the foundations for a new network of subway and RER lines. All the while, fierce debates over the site's future development raged on. People from the neighborhood came daily to watch the construction work with consternation, anger, curiosity, or admiration. For years the vast *trou* was an ever-changing stage full of moving cranes and machines, workmen and supervisors. No one knew what was coming next. Certainly no one expected the gun-fighting cowboys on horseback who showed up there for weeks in 1973, when the desolate "hole" served as a movie set for the making of a Western (*Touche pas à la femme blanche*, directed by Marco Ferreri).[63]

State authorities had been screening several scenarios of their own since the late 1960s. They decided in 1967 and 1968 that a mass-transport hub and a retail center called a "forum" would go into the market space. In search of a model for the "forum," redevelopment officials visited and documented Montreal's underground shopping mall, the Place Ville-Marie.[64] Next, President Pompidou and the Parisian Chambre de Commerce added the idea of building a new international trade center nearby, along with an infrastructure of hotels and cultural attractions for the business travelers and tourists who would be drawn there. If any sizable open space were left, the president feared, it would be occupied by hordes of "hippies." Pompidou's vision of the "heart of Paris" was squarely in the Second Empire tradition of the City of Light—Paris as an economic dynamo and an international capital. It was also squarely in the Haussmannian tradition of urban renewal without regard for the "little people" or their sentiment toward a vital quarter of Paname. The overriding objective was to fast-forward the central city to the future by replacing the archaic market with the latest forms of work and leisure.

When Pompidou died in early April of 1974, most of his projects died with him—or they were killed by his successor, Giscard d'Estaing, elected president in May 1974. Within his very first weeks as president, Giscard canceled the proposed expressway on the Left Bank and other *autoroutes* through the suburbs. Following his lead, authorities halted the proliferation of high-rises in the city center and even lowered the permissible height of the office towers at La Défense.[65] For the western end of the Halles site, Giscard decided against an international trade center and instead opted for a French-style public garden. "For the first time in a century," a new green space—"a zone of shade and charm"—was to be created inside Paris, observed André Fermigier in *Le Monde*.[66]

Rejecting the international modernism of his predecessor, the new president announced his preference for aesthetics "à la française." By that he meant "an architecture of reason" and "harmony" befitting the classic Ville Lumière—a style that was "natural" and "strongly tied to the environment and local geographical diversities" instead of "cold, impersonal, and willfully imposing" models from the New World.[67] In closing the era of modernist rupture, Giscard opened an era of growing concern for French heritage (the nation's "patrimony")—and direct presidential involvement in Paris projects, presented with fanfare as the *grands projets* of the president.

Overall, Giscard shifted the planning focus from modernizing to improving the "quality of life." For the capital a "better quality of life" meant more green spaces, less congestion, more public transportation, less pollution. The state now returned to a planning policy of limits for Paris. A special new tax was levied on industries seeking expansion in the central city, while subsidies were reserved for the creation of firms and jobs outside the capital.

Optimistic projections about the future had shriveled in the aftermath of the oil crisis of late 1973. After a thirty-year phase of extraordinary growth (*les Trente Glorieuses*), economic hopes were brought down by soaring oil prices, general inflation, and fast-rising unemployment. But even before the downturn, the postwar express-train called "progress" had left many Parisians disappointed. By the end of Pompidou's presidency, the gap between the capital's glorious reputation and its condition was too glaring to ignore. Three authoritative reports in 1973–1974 attested to the decline of Paris. Two of the reports criticized the recent assaults on the city's historic character, and all three agreed on the need for limiting the growth of Paris.[68] Without reading any reports at all, Parisians could see that ever more automobiles were clogging the streets and polluting the air, even though the central city's population was declining. They could also see the gaping "hole" at Les Halles, which epitomized a Paris immobilized at a crossroads . . . and a center stripped of its famed liveliness.

Among proposals for the heart of Paris, one notable modernist project survived the new regime's vetoes: a museum of contemporary art that President Pompidou had decided to locate somewhere in the area of Les Halles (a decision announced on December 11, 1969). The site chosen was a large open block called the Plateau Beaubourg, empty since the razing of slums known as *Îlot insalubre no. 1* in the 1930s. An international architectural competition took place in 1970–1971—the first ever for Paris—with the judging done by a jury that included only one French architect. The winning design, out of 681 entries, was a strikingly modernist building proposed by two foreigners, the Italian Renzo Piano and the Briton Richard Rogers. It made not even the slightest gesture of accommodation to the historical neighborhood. Amid streets lined with old-regime stone buildings, the Beaubourg Center was a brash intruder with its industrial metal frame, expanses of glass, and its brightly colored ducts and elevators stuck on the exterior—its "tripes out in the air." Critics likened it to an oil refinery, a vessel from outer space, and a horizontal Eiffel Tower. Its architects preferred to call it a "great machine," an overtly functionalist, polyvalent structure unlike the city's old "palace"-style museums of culture.[69]

The architects left almost half of the building lot open for a plaza. The very antithesis of a modernist provocation, that part was inspired by the past, by historical models and the personal memories of an architect. The sources were not of Paris, but of Italy—the grand Piazza of Sienna and the ever-changing seaport of Genoa. In Renzo Piano's vision, the bustling Beaubourg with its adjacent open space was like the Genoese port juxtaposed to the "reassuring, protective, and immutable" old city.[70]

As construction advanced in 1972 and 1973, critics relentlessly attacked the ultramodern design. President Giscard d'Estaing considered blocking its completion in 1974, but then backed away. Its opponents were unable to do anything more than to get the height reduced slightly—to 42 meters—or 136 feet.

From its opening in early 1977, the new Beaubourg with its Pompidou Center (Centre national d'art et de culture Georges Pompidou) attracted Parisians and tourists alike in record-setting numbers—more than twenty thousand visitors a day in its first seven months, twice the anticipated number, and far more than for the Eiffel Tower and the Louvre. The avant-garde architecture grabbed attention, but the excellent cultural facilities made it a steady popular draw: the open-stack large public library (the only big one in Paris), the temporary exhibits of contemporary art and design, the museum of twentieth-century art, and an array of free performances outside on the sloping plaza.

While the new Beaubourg moved quickly to completion, debate over the redevelopment of Les Halles dragged on. President Giscard d'Estaing wanted a monumental park to dominate the surface of the Halles site, and he found what he liked in a plan by the Catalan architect Ricardo Bofill in the fall of 1974. Bofill designed a large formal garden that was to cover ten acres, leaving another five acres to be occupied by the sunken shopping center called the "forum." In choosing that proposal, Giscard embraced the royal tradition of embellishing the city with grand formal spaces, designed to impress visitors with the power of the state and the importance of its capital. Bofill's project paid homage to such classical *grandes places* as the Place des Vosges, the Palais-Royal, the Place Vendôme, and the Piazza of

Sienna. For an influential bloc of Parisian architects and city councilors, the plan with its formal monumentality was too laden with the past: they mounted effective opposition to it in 1975.[71]

The politics of the fray shifted radically in 1977 when, for the first time in almost two centuries, Parisians were allowed to elect a mayor of Paris. Advocates of the governance reform, including Giscard d'Estaing as a presidential candidate in 1974, had all believed that it would work to their political advantage. But the first mayoral election upset the expectations of almost all of them, especially of the Giscardiens, when the Gaullist politician Jacques Chirac, a leading rival of Giscard, won the office in March 1977. Now a strong new Parisian leader joined in the jostling over Paris's future.

The new mayor immediately announced his opposition to the state-dictated urbanism of the 1960s and early 1970s. Chirac was not known for his love of the capital, although he was a longtime Parisian and deputy from a Left-Bank district. Nor did he have any expertise in architecture and urban design. Yet shortly after assuming the new office he announced that he would be the chief architect in the contentious matter of Les Halles: he would end the impasse. The national authorities had long ignored the feelings and wishes of the common Parisians, and now the "people" had their spokesman, who understood his role well and played it with relish. So Mayor Chirac adopted the populist tradition, speaking for Paris-Paname and playing off the aristocratic airs and princely power of Giscard. For his part, the president of the Republic decided to back out of the fray and to concentrate instead on creating a new science museum at La Villette.

Les Halles should "smell of French fries," declared the mayor. That was to say: no more cosmopolitan or neo-classical architecture (à la Bofill) and no more precious world-capital designs. To preserve some of the popular character of the neighborhood, some architects and Communist leaders proposed building thousands of new low-income housing units there. Advocates for the district also pleaded for cultural and sports facilities—a public library, a theater, a swimming pool, a skating rink—and not just shops and offices for people who lived elsewhere. And local associations called for "green space," as they had for every redevelopment project since the mid-sixties.

No one wanted a tall building at Les Halles—especially after seeing the Tour Montparnasse. All sides now rejected the bulldozer-and-skyscraper urbanism of the Pompidou era. The pioneering models of that modernity, the towers at La Défense, had become conspicuous disappointments by the mid-seventies. Employees disliked the working conditions in the office buildings—the poor lighting, inadequate sound-proofing, and unreliable air-conditioning—while employers found expenses there excessive after the drastic hike in oil prices in late 1973. Office space at La Défense—about 100,000 square meters of it—went unsold for five years after the '73 economic shock. The showcase of planned modernity was failing.[72] The city of Paris itself returned to old-style regulatory traditions and greater respect for the historical cityscape in 1977 with a revision of the municipal code for construction.[73]

Two years after Beaubourg opened, the sunken shopping center called the Forum des Halles opened for business on the eastern side of the former market, finally filling the "hole" and occupying five of the fifteen acres total. In response to Parisians' desire for cultural and recreational resources in the quarter, authorities had tried to recruit businesses that would help meet that demand. The biggest store in the Forum fit the cultural category in some ways: FNAC, a cooperative that sold books, records, and concert tickets; it also provided spaces for debates and photo exhibits. In addition, the three-level Forum included six movie theaters and a branch of the famous old Grévin wax museum, featuring Belle-Époque tableaux of such celebrities as Louis Pasteur, Jules Verne, and the can-can dancers of the Moulin Rouge. For all that, the Forum was mostly a shopping center, whose customers were not the long-standing inhabitants of the quarter. Prominent among the Forum's 250 stores were many boutiques bearing names like Yves Saint Laurent, Pierre Cardin, and Ungaro.

While nostalgic lovers of the capital endlessly lamented the death of the heart of popular Paris, spokesmen for the Forum and the mayor gamely—and lamely—emphasized that the new Les Halles remained in the tradition of the old . . . as a marketplace. Retail businesses there benefited from the accessibility that the mass transport crossroads provided (four métro lines, two RER lines, and thirteen bus routes, not to mention 4,000 parking places). But amid the crowds in the Forum were youth from the poorer banlieues, whose presence aroused old fears of the "uncivilized," the "dangerous classes" amassed in the very heart of the city. Drunks, homeless men, and pickpockets caused little concern in comparison with the green-and-red-haired Punks and Rockers, gangs of "Iroquois" and gangs of black leather jackets, given to fighting the others. Despite sensationalist newspaper reports of robberies, violence, gangs, and drugs, the crowds kept on coming—and shopping.

Debate continued on the question of how to develop the rest of the site. In 1979 an association created by Parisian architects opened an "international consultation" to get new ideas. This time the proposals were made public—some six hundred of them, and this time a report on them emphasized the history of the quarter and ways of tying the new to the old. The chosen project, announced by the mayor in January 1980, provided for shops, apartments, and an office complex on the edges of the site—with roadways and parking underground. The new buildings followed tradition in scale and in such details as mansard roofs and dormer windows. Additional modernist architecture was limited to the underground annex to the Forum, completed in 1985. Unlike the original Forum, the new part was filled with long-promised public facilities: a swimming pool, a gymnasium, a billiards hall, a vidéothèque, an auditorium, meeting space for associations, a children's library, and a lending music library of CDs and cassettes.[74] The next year another round of stores opened in the "New Forum."

FADING MEMORIES, BURIED MEMORIES

Laments for the old Halles died down with the passing of years, and attention shifted to criticism of the new. The new Halles was "chic and *choc*," a journalist concluded in 1985. It was a "subtle mixture of old and modern," a place for flânerie but also a rapid-transit center; a neighborhood of fast-food outlets and famous old restaurants, the latest fashions—black sunglasses, black boots (*godillots*), black pants—all existing together with the shabbiest of clochards.[75] Business in the underground mall boomed. By 1989 the Forum grossed more than any other shopping center in France. The centuries-old, storied Parisian market had become the nation's most thoroughly international emporium. The neighborhood, too, had drastically changed its character, anguished critics stressed. The makeover was lamentably deficient in new housing. Many old residents of the quarter had lost their homes in the redevelopment and moved out of the center. More than six thousand residents of the neighborhood (34.6 percent of the quarter's population) left in the period of expropriations and "the hole" between 1968 and 1975. The number of housing units diminished by 1,716 between 1968 and 1982 (by 2,412 from 1968 to 1975, the years of the most demolitions).[76] Les Halles ended up not at all a showplace of clean-slate modernizing, but rather a motley mix of the new laced with traces of the old—something for almost everyone, though not nearly enough of the traditional to satisfy former residents or lovers of Old Paris and Paname.

Outside the center, the modernists' Paris continued to take on concrete form. A new generation of skyscrapers cropped up at La Défense in the late 1970s and 1980s. The Front de Seine complex filled out in the seventies with the construction of some twenty towers, most of them around thirty stories high, built on platforms for pedestrians only. And ever more parking lots were constructed throughout the central city, despite the new environmental awareness and efforts to increase "green spaces."

When the battle over modernist renovation finally died down, each side had left its mark on the city, but neither had won completely. After the battle of Les Halles in particular, it became clear that the urbanists of international modernism no longer enjoyed the momentum that was theirs in the 1950s and '60s. New skyscrapers, new freeways, and *grands ensembles* no longer dominated the planners' agenda. But other consequences were not so clear-cut. In the main the outcome was a series of compromises—with the automobile (and the rats) as with modern architecture. The result, examined in the next chapter, is the contemporary Paris we find today—a postmodern pastiche of old, new, and newer.

CHAPTER 4

New Varieties of a
"Nouveau Paris" (1974– . . .)

BACK TO FRENCH IDIOMS

In the early 1970s, when modernist Paris was still new and jarring to many, President Pompidou testily responded to critics that each era has the right to create its own architecture. Upon his death in April 1974, a new era was left to define its own Paris. But support for ambitious urban projects was at low ebb. The upheavals of 1968 and the drawn-out battle over Les Halles had left many Parisians weary of fierce clashes and skeptical of urbanists. International modernism was out of favor. The drive to create a Manhattan-sur-Seine was sputtering to a stop. Discontent with the modernized metropolis was rife: the back-to-the-land communes of chastened veterans of '68 were a colorful symptom. Yet the city that anti-modernists considered "assassinated" found new life in the last decades of the century—in a stunning variety of forms that neither Pompidou nor his opponents had imagined. Renewal in many forms, this chapter will show, came through reworking the city's stock of identities and memories—from modernity-forging Ville Lumière, pleasure capital, and multicultural world capital to populist Parisian. Paris after Pompidou returned to familiar old French notions . . . with some new twists.

In the late twentieth century just as many times earlier, glowing tributes drawn from tradition deflected attention from the recent conflicts and ruptures. A city Tourist Office booklet (1977) recited the classic motifs: Paris is a universal city with a grand past (Goethe), "Paris is a fête" (Hemingway), a place of wondrous "light and atmosphere," a city of revered monuments and great modern architecture, a showcase of prestigious fashion, a "gastronomic capital," a cultural and educational hub, where a marvelous diversity of entertainment flourishes as well.[1] In the view of the latest boosters, the capital's contrasts of old and modern, sophisticated and

119

simple, formed a harmonious whole, every part precious and impressive. "To see Paris" now meant visiting not only Notre-Dame and the Eiffel Tower, but also the Pompidou Center, the Maison de la Radio, La Défense, and the Montparnasse Tower, the new skyscraper in the heart of the city.

Missing from the recycled accolades was the perspective of ordinary Parisians, whose neighborhoods and jobs had fared poorly in the throes of modernizing. The push for more office buildings, towers, and express-ways left most Parisians feeling left out, their desires ignored and their "village Paris" mangled. To them, the harmony of the new whole was simply out-of-date rhetoric. All too plainly, the quality of life and the his-toric charm of the city had grievously deteriorated under the leadership of Pompidou and company.[2]

Pompidou's successor, Valéry Giscard d'Estaing, ended the era of leap-to-the-future urbanism in 1974. As the last chapter noted, he took a stand against the construction of new towers in central Paris, killed the project of a Left-Bank freeway, and chose green space instead of a huge Center of International Commerce for the western part of the Halles site. Giscard was neither a preservationist devotee of Old Paris nor a populist champion of Paname (though he played the accordion), but he was deter-mined to change the direction of Paris redevelopment. His tastes ran to the classical, in contrast to the avant-garde modernism of his predecessor. But his thinking about Paris was far from backward-looking. Rather it reflected several critical changes in attitudes and economic conditions oc-curring in the year or so just before his election to the presidency: the oil price shock of late 1973, and the downturn in the economy, bringing the postwar thirty years of rapid economic growth to a close.[3] At the same time, ecological concerns were gaining support. Instead of a future of more towers and automobiles, Giscard envisioned more green space and better public transportation.[4]

If Paris was not to be the "New York of the old continent," as President Pompidou had wanted, what was it to be? More like Paris of the past, it turned out—apart from the Beaubourg Center and the Forum des Halles. The new land-use plans (*Plans d'occupation des sols*) that the city coun-cil adopted in late 1974 and in 1977 favored continuity with the historic urban fabric—traditional building heights and forms, mixed-use streets, and monuments.[5] And a new generation of architects (among them, Christian de Portzamparc) took a similar turn, designing innovative but modest structures that fit into the historic profile.[6] To be sure, a complete "return to tradition" was not possible. The Tour Montparnasse was there to stay, and so were the towers of the Front de Seine and the high-rises near the Place d'Italie. But those landmarks of Gaullist-era urbanism were to remain period pieces, not models for future development.

The old motifs City of Light and Capital of Pleasures posed more difficult challenges than did modernist architecture. Signs of Paris's decline—as an international cultural leader and urban masterwork—worried serious observers and planners through the seventies. How could Paris again be the world's cultural and arts hub? London and New York were flourishing as global cultural centers, Paris leaders knew well.[7] The primacy and creativity of Paris could no longer pass as self-evident, even to the usual boosters of the city. "After being a cultural capital, Paris is becoming a parking lot," wrote the respected columnist André Fermigier in 1972. The decline of "urban creativity," he maintained, was tied to the difficulties of moving about and exchanging ideas in the car-clogged city. Creativity also suffered as core districts went heavily over to office space, with consequences even more deadening once the period of economic expansion ended. The city's population increasingly comprised executives, professionals, and old people, which accounted for much of the "reduced social and cultural vitality."[8] Could the famed vitality be restored? And the fun too?

Paris "no longer knows how to receive and entertain its visitors" and "has been living on its reputation for some time": "Gay Paris is boring," concluded tourism advocates in 1971. The famed "gaiety of its streets" was gone. Traffic and parking made the daytime city unpleasant, and after work so many people left for the suburbs or stayed home watching television that the center seemed empty. On weekends and holidays, better-off Parisians fled to the countryside in their automobiles. "Festivity has deserted the city," lamented Parisian writer Michel Ragon (1971), echoing 1960s critiques of postwar modernization.[9] This withering of festivity was particularly disconcerting because it followed a 1960s groundswell of dreams of community celebration—and some all-too-brief festive days for participants in the May 1968 revolt.

The committee in charge of organizing the annual Fêtes de Paris in 1971 had to work with a paltry budget of 250,000 francs.[10] City authorities tried to do more, for their part, by lighting the major monuments later into the night, and they sponsored classical music festivals. But they could not overcome the dampening effects of the weakening economy as the decade unfolded.

The world-famous nightspots, even more than Paris as a whole, were living on their reputation. They no longer presented star singers and comics who could attract crowds of Parisians. Instead, they reproduced set pieces of a legendary past and played to tourists. The Moulin Rouge and the Lido still featured the cancan, though updated with some choreography borrowed from Las Vegas. But by the 1980s the iconic dance was dying, according to music-hall insiders. One reason, leaving aside the possibility of declining audience interest, was that dancers could no longer get into the spirit of it and did not want to do rigorous training for it. "It's a world which is coming to an end," remarked a Lido dancer who had grown up in Montmartre.[11] Another reason was that the classics of the music halls were losing out in competition with the fresher shows produced by newcomers like Le Paradis Latin (1977). Parisians, famously novelty-loving, went for the newer entertainment. The famous old music halls, increasingly dependent on audiences of foreigners and seasonal tourists, faced high production costs and charged high admission prices. By the late 1980s the most traditional of the showplaces, the Folies-Bergère, was unable to fill its worn seats with customers and had to lay off a dozen singers and dancers. Tucked away as it was in a small street near the long-declining Grands Boulevards, the Folies-Bergère lacked the association with Montmartre—artistic, Bohemian, and Belle-Époque glamorous—that still bolstered the prestige of the Moulin Rouge. Finally, in 1993 it abandoned its traditional variety-act formula and began presenting musicals, such as *Les Années Twist*, *Fame*, and *Cabaret*.

Neighborhood movie theaters and dance halls fared even worse than the big music halls: they just declined and died with little or no public notice. The oldest *bal musette* of Paris, Le Petit Balcon (hidden in a back alley near Bastille), was demolished quietly and quickly off-season (February) in 1989. It had survived since the 1930s by staging performances of clichéd, old-fashioned lowlife for "Paris-by-night" tours—with the *apache* dance as the pièce de résistance. But it could not make it through the wrenching redevelopment of the neighborhood.

None of the national or Paris authorities in those closing decades of the century made any effort to bring back the vanishing Paname of the "little people" or the old-time places of pleasure. Yet they no longer pressed on single-mindedly toward a modernist future. Incongruously, a socialist president named Mitterrand added a kingly series of monumental edifices to the capital's cityscape (detailed below), but his projects were not driven by the vision of economic expansion that excited his Gaullist predecessors. After years of willfully breaking with the past, Paris's leaders and the public turned *back* to it, revisiting memories and traditions, retrieving "mythic remains" such as Bastille Day street dancing, and reusing pieces of the "good old days." The drive toward an individualist and productivist modernity, epitomized by office towers and expressways, gave way to a fresh appreciation of local community, culture, festivity, and play—a configuration known as the postmodern.[12]

To give just one illustration of that cultural turn before going into it further, I would point to a change in Parisians' use of the Georges Pompidou expressway, which was built in the 1960s for the automobiles of commuters rushing to work: since the mid-90s, every Sunday as well as several weeks in the summer, that riverside "voie rapide" has been closed off to traffic and given over to leisured pedestrians, rollerbladers, and bicycle riders. In such ways, breaking with the technocratic modernism of the '60s, post-Pompidou Paris evolved into the lively postmodern city of our time.

CELEBRATIONS AND CULTURE

Years after the May '68 rebellion, the counterculture dreams of festivity and leisure continued to challenge the postwar priorities of work, productivity, and consumption. Parisian youth found festive experiences on their own all through the 1970s—at rock concerts. Young audiences "grooving" on maxi-decibels worked themselves up to beat-driven highs, sometimes laced with a lingering '60s-style spirit of *contestation*. In the 1980s many also participated in new festivities in the streets, explicitly

FIGURE 4.1. Taking Paris back from the automobiles and their urbanist advocates of the 1960s: cyclists, strollers, and rollers enjoy the Rive droite expressway Sundays and holidays (and sometimes entire weekends, since 1996). The riverside thoroughfare, strongly opposed when constructed in the 1960s, is officially named the Voie Georges Pompidou in honor of the prime minister who dedicated it in 1967 and later defended it as president. (Photo by the author.)

expressing social and political concerns. A carnival-like Gay Pride parade became an annual revel early in the 1980s. Even bigger draws were star-studded public concerts that doubled as demonstrations against racism. In 1985, for a protest rally against anti-immigrant prejudice and the rise of the Front National, the association S.O.S.-Racisme (created in 1984) organized one of the most resounding concerts of the decade, attended by some 300,000 people. Staged in the Place de la Concorde the night of June 15, 1985, the Nuit de la Fraternité featured twenty-five top performers and music from many cultures in celebration of a "France of all colors," standing up against the growth of the xenophobic Right.[13]

The biggest annual political festival in the 1970s and 1980s was the party each fall sponsored by the French Communist Party, the Fête de l'Humanité, held three days and nights in September in a large park in the northern working-class suburb of La Corneuve. The "Fête de l'Huma" regularly drew 400,000–500,000 people, most of them not party members. Many attended simply to have a good time, eating, drinking, and enjoying concerts featuring such headliners as Johnny Clegg and Patricia Kaas on a big stage. It was, at once, an international fair of political activists, an end-of-summer-vacation party, and the "Woodstock" of the French Communist people.[14]

National and municipal authorities, for their part, stepped up publicly funded programs to make Paris festive, responding to both 1960s social critics and to hard-headed tourism advocates. They also looked for ways to enhance cultural life for the general public in the '80s and '90s. Shifting their focus away from concert-and-arts festivals for the well-off, national and local officials made unprecedented efforts to enrich the everyday lives of ordinary Parisians through arts and leisure activities.[15]

Before 1968 municipal administrators had concentrated on subsidizing classical concerts for the summer tourist season, beginning with the Festival du Marais, then adding the Festival Estival de Paris and Paris Quartier d'Été, in venues around the city. New kinds of concerts began to proliferate in 1977—municipal programs featuring amateur musicians in June, for example ("Journées de musique amateur"), and others organized year-round by arrondissement-based associations.[16]

After 1977, when Paris elected its first mayor since 1870, the municipal government and the national government became rivals in the cultural arena—to the great benefit of the city. Mayor Jacques Chirac and President Mitterrand's Minister of Culture Jack Lang each developed his own ambitious program for the capital in the 1980s, but overall the part played by the mayor was much more substantial. The new mayor and the political Right generally were determined to discredit the presumption that only the Left could be a generous public patron of culture. The municipal budget for culture under Mayor Chirac quintupled by 1985 and increased eight-fold by 1988.[17] City hall created an extensive network of local arts workshops (more than 400 "ateliers d'expression culturelle"), devoted not only to the classical arts of the theater, painting, and sculpture, but also to such popular arts as cartooning, jazz, metal work, computer-based textile design, holography, and laser art—altogether some 175 artistic, artisanal, and technological specialties.[18] The city government also created a new Vidéothèque de Paris, which opened in the Forum des Halles in February 1988, offering a rich collection of films on Paris as well as classics from afar. And in the fall of that year it opened a new public center for Paris architecture and urbanism (the Centre d'information, de documentation et d'exposition sur l'urbanisme et l'architecture de la Ville de Paris), housed in the Pavillon de l'Arsenal.

Mayor Chirac supported classical music and dance performances, but also jazz and other forms of popular culture. The municipality helped create the Festival de Jazz (1980) with concerts in the Théâtre de la Ville. And it established a new Municipal Office of Fêtes, which provided subsidies for such events as the Race of the Garçons de Café, folkloric dance-and-song performances, the Marathon of Paris, and the Montmartre wine harvest celebration. It also worked to assure the celebration of the July 14 national holiday in every quarter of the city.

Following Socialist François Mitterrand's victory in the presidential election of 1981, his administration made new efforts to create still more Paris fêtes with a decidedly populist appeal. The chief impresario was Jack Lang, primed for the task by an education and experience in theater. Lang showed his talent for orchestrating celebrations on the very night of the inauguration of President Mitterrand, when a joyous throng gathered at the Place de la Bastille for a victory party with performances by some of the nation's most popular singers. The following year, Lang as minister of Culture organized a city-wide music festival in which amateur musicians of all kinds participated simply by performing in local venues, including street corners, all over the city. That event, named "la Fête de la Musique," became an annual, hugely popular "invented tradition," a revamped summer solstice celebration. And to enliven public spaces with quality entertainment over the long term, Lang's ministry created a national center for researching and teaching "the arts of the street."[19]

By 1999, the municipal cultural budget had multiplied by more than twelve since the election of a first mayor in 1977, increasing from 109 million francs to almost 1.4 billion francs. The city supported sixty-four libraries, seventeen conservatories, and fifteen museums, and it was bringing festive events and artistic activities to all twenty arrondissements. By the end of the 1990s, the municipality was doing more culturally than any other city or even any nation-state, Mayor Tiberi proudly noted. Looking ahead, he resolved to confirm Paris's "role of international capital of art and culture" in the twenty-first century.[20]

Arguably the most notable successes of the mayor's office have been the new festivities that it has created. Tiberi's successor, Bertrand Delanoë, came up with several particularly imaginative programs. In the summer of 2002 he turned the right bank of the Seine (along the expressway) into a giant beach where Parisians and tourists could sun themselves, lounge on sand (180 cubic meters of it hauled in for the occasion) and gravel (25 tons), relax in the shade of palm trees (80 specially implanted) and

FIGURE 4.2. Since 2002, a central stretch of the Right-Bank expressway has been turned into a beach for Parisians to enjoy in the summer vacation periods. Paris-Plage is one of Mayor Bertrand Delanoë's successful initiatives, seeking to make the city more "convivial" and enjoyable in automobile-free spaces. (Photo by the author, August 2003.)

beach umbrellas (150), play volleyball, and build sand castles. Next, the following fall, he invited Parisians to stay up all night one Saturday to enjoy extraordinary events at thirty-five locations throughout the capital, beginning at dusk the fifth of October. That first Nuit Blanche gave the public the opportunity to hear classical music in a Montmartre church, visit artists' galleries in Montparnasse and Oberkampf, ice skate at Bercy, swim in the Pontoise pool, or watch a huge interactive light show on a façade of the new National Library, the windows turning bright or dark in response to commands sent by the public to a central computer via the internet and mobile telephones.[21] In such novel ways the capital's leaders combined the old dream of a pleasure capital with the post-1968 effort to make the good times accessible to all. The catchword "Paris is a fête" has taken on new meanings and new forms in our time.

CITY OF A HUNDRED VILLAGES

Amid the return to old motifs, one old trope was not dusted off, at least explicitly, for official or mainstream use: the slang term of endearment, "Paname." Its folksy, backward-looking imagery was doubtless too alien to the social realities of the post-1960s metropolis. Too many neighborhoods had lost their long-familiar character, along with the small old-fashioned anchors of their daily life: many bakeries, *charcuteries*, cheese shops, fish shops, and small *épiceries* had disappeared, falling victim to consumers' preference for one-stop shopping and lower prices at supermarkets. A long-preponderant population of artisans, factory workers, and shopkeepers moved out or died off. The familiar old faces of concierges in their entryway apartments disappeared too, replaced by entry doors with keyless digital locks. With rents rising and apartment buildings undergoing gentrification, the poor were finding it more and more difficult to live in the center, just as they had following Haussmann's renovations a century earlier.

In the 1960s many poorly housed Parisians moved to the *banlieues*, along with provincial newcomers. The total population of the intra-muros city declined from the early 1960s through 1999 by over 600,000 (from 2,753,014 to 2,125,246). At the same time, the number of foreigners living in Paris increased sharply until 1982 (from 4.7 percent of the city's population to 16.6 percent).[22] In the 1970s immigrants from North Africa and Southeast Asia flooded into big new apartment buildings and still-run-down (hence affordable) dwellings in the east end of town.

The old notion of the Parisian *quartier* as a village, however, did not fade away. In fact, it enjoyed a revival. Jacques Chirac as mayor worked hard at promoting it, making the arrondissements the locus of an officially sponsored sense of Paname. Chirac ally Jacques Toubon made a point of contrasting the mayor with Haussmann, the misguided champion of bigness and uniformity. Chirac himself spoke often of his city's "villages of a provincial character" and the "small Parises" within the "immense urban agglomeration." Downplaying the memory-killing transformations of many *quartiers*, he urged Parisians to cherish and cultivate the local.[23]

The mayor directed his appeals not to the intellectual and artistic elite ("open to foreign influences") but to the "people of Paris" as "sung by the poet," meaning the good common people who were "attached to their city as to their province." He talked of "giving Paris back to the life of its quarters, restoring what was the soul of its former villages."[24] At a time when rising crime rates, new immigrants, and the decline of the small merchants were causing general alarm, the mayor offered cheery iterations of the Paname myth, fuzzy evocations of close-knit Parisian communities in vaguely distant "good old days."

The new monthly city magazine worked the village theme regularly. The cover of the very first issue of *Ville de Paris* (October 1978) featured a photo of a Parisian market with the caption saluting "Paris the capital, but also Paris of a hundred villages."[25] Each issue contained a section entitled "Life of the arrondissements," reporting on local happenings, as though modernity's depredations were being reversed. Then, beginning in April 1981, a series of supplements entitled *Villages de Paris* presented anecdotal histories of the quarters, depicting "what makes the personality of the villages of Paris." From December 1979 on, a regular column presented a retrospective on provincials in the capital: the Bretons, then the Alsacians, the Savoyards, and others, each group making its own community or "colony" within the big city. Evoking a Belle-Époque portrait of French immigrants from the countryside, the city's image-makers ignored the many Parisians who had come more recently from lands beyond Europe.

After the National Assembly created the office of elective mayor for each of the capital's twenty arrondissements (1982), those new local leaders too became ardent promoters of the village image.[26] Chirac reacted by insisting on the unity of the whole municipality over which he presided: "Paris, in the diversity of its quarters, is a great united [solidaire] and living body. Paris beats with a single heart."[27] And he spoke as though the city had lived its history with a single identity—"Paris la 'grand'ville,' the Paris of Villon and that of Hugo, the conquering Paris of 14 July and the martyred Paris of the occupation, Paris compagnon of the Liberation. . . ." Yet he did not lessen city hall's efforts to invigorate local life.

While marshalling the rhetoric of villages, municipal personnel supported a number of programs to revitalize community life in each district. Creating and backing local festivities was one of the most important—with

FIGURE 4.3. The annual Fête des Vendanges de Montmartre is the high point of the year for fun-and-wine loving aficionados of old Montmartre (including visitors from distant lands) who celebrate its memory as a "free commune" separate from Paris, enjoying a distinctive village and Bohemian community life. (Photo by the author, October 2002.)

highest priority given to the most popular national holiday, Bastille Day. "The national fête is the occasion to create the ambiance of village festivities of bygone times in the capital," declared the municipal magazine in June 1979.[28] The mayor's deputy in charge of tourism now took on the additional role of organizing holiday activities in every arrondissement—above all, neighborhood dances officially known the *bals 'Paris-villages' du 14 juillet*, held in the streets or at firehouses. Other local events followed, such as neighborhood flea markets (*brocantes*), public concerts, and fairs featuring provincial products.

Throughout the year, the city's street markets have also produced a semblance of village life—at least one or two days a week, especially weekends, in almost every quarter. In the early 1990s there were eighty-one of them. A few of them occupied old glass-and-metal structures that offered shelter from rain and wind; most of them were simply open-air stands lining the sides of a street. Though supermarkets were gaining an ever larger share of the food business in the last decades of the century, many Parisians frequented (and still do) the street markets to buy farm-fresh tomatoes, lettuces, mushrooms, fruits, eggs, and cheeses (or even live chickens), sometimes directly from the producer. In that traditional ambiance, too, they engaged in old-fashioned social exchanges with neighbors and sellers, revitalizing old Paname imagery.

DESTRUCTION AND RENEWAL

Paris after Pompidou has also been marked by ongoing urban renewal—still called the "reconquest" of Paris, meaning above all the elimination of its slums. Since the '70s, however, renewal has taken some new turns, which can be labeled postmodern. The most striking difference has been the targeting of substandard buildings dating from the 1950s and 1960s, rather than just pre-1940 eras. Municipal authorities, that is, began to redo modernist renewal projects. They revisited, for example, the complex of tall cement towers around the Place des Fêtes and added new aesthetic touches and human-scale structures to the stark open space at the base of the high-rises. More spectacularly, they began demolishing postwar buildings that they judged not worth renovating. The first such operation, televised as a major symbolic event, was the dynamiting of the run-down apartment block named Debussy (February 18, 1986) in the Cité des 4000, a '60s *grand ensemble* in the immigrant and working-class suburb La Courneuve just outside intra-muros Paris. Other demolitions in "the 4000" followed in 2000 (Renoir) and 2004 (Presov and Ravel)—with still more planned for the near future.[29]

In Paris proper, the renewal projects created a host of new housing and commercial properties that were more expensive than the old. Many long-term residents, unable to afford the raised rents, moved on and out, making way for new businesses and tenants. Working people in poorer east and northeast arrondissements—the thirteenth on the Left Bank and the nineteenth and twentieth on the Right—were particularly hard hit. Both areas had long been full of workers and the poor, living near workplaces that were losing their viability. Both areas had been home to the last of the nineteenth century's great political revolutions—the Paris Commune of 1871; both had been battlefields where the diehards of that rebellion had fought to the end. Belleville (the nineteenth and part of the twentieth) has also been a long-standing refuge for immigrants from distant parts— Poles, Maghrébins, Africans, Chinese, Pakistanis, and Jews from North Africa and Eastern Europe. In the 1980s as the condemned buildings met their fate and the modern housing went up, waves of young professionals, artists, and working families moved into the new apartment buildings. Some, too, settled in the run-down-but-salvageable dwellings that remained. New life sprang up, often in unexpected forms, after even the most massive demolitions and dislocations.

In the thirteenth arrondissement the highest of the high-rise apartment buildings began to open in 1972, south of the Place d'Italie. The complex, called Les Olympiades, comprising nearly 4,000 dwellings, consisted of towers thirty-three stories high (80 meters), tied to horizontal blocks of 14–18 stories, all built on a platform eight meters above the street level, filled with stores and offices, with parking underneath. By 1974 the sale of the apartments was slowing due to the national economy's downturn, and the outsized towers were the targets of growing criticism. In 1975 President Giscard d'Estaing took a stand specifically against building more towers in the thirteenth arrondissement. Over the next few years, many of the first occupants of the Olympiades chose to move to the banlieue or elsewhere in eastern Paris, leaving space for newcomers. In the same years, coincidentally, waves of refugees from Southeast Asia (Vietnam, Laos, Cambodia) and from Hong Kong, Taiwan, and mainland China began to arrive in France. Numerous Asian families gladly moved into the Olympiades and then helped relatives and friends find lodging nearby—or in the same apartment. Studios and two-room apartments often housed 8–10 persons. The foreign population in the quarter rose from 2 percent in 1954 to 18.4 percent in 1984. By the early 1980s some 10,000 Chinese were living there, making it Paris's newest and biggest Chinatown.[30]

The historically protected quarter of the Marais also underwent fundamental changes in the 1970s. As shabby buildings were renovated, artisans and the poor were priced out, and the solidly bourgeois moved in. Workshops and cafés long frequented by workers died and disappeared. New boutiques, coiffeurs, bars, and restaurants made the Marais a new destination of the in-crowd from around the city as well as tourists. And a new subculture took root there in the 1980s: after a gay bar opened and flourished early in the decade, others sprang up nearby, forming a lively enclave of hangouts and shops catering to free-spending, fashionable, sociable gay men.[31]

In the Latin Quarter's medieval streets near Saint-Michel, Greek restaurants and kebab stands proliferated, especially after the Saint-Séverin area became a pedestrian zone in 1972. Throughout the Latin Quarter, pizza parlors and McDonald's restaurants sprouted and thrived. On the Champs-Élysées, meanwhile, fast-food outlets and shopping malls were taking over prestigious locations associated with an image of luxury and distinction that was the cachet of "the most beautiful avenue in the world." In the quarter of the renovated Montparnasse, as rents rose sharply in the 1980s, artists, modest families, and old-fashioned bistros gave way to young professionals, chain restaurants, pizzerias, and new eateries with Greek, Chinese, Indian, and Mexican specialties. Around Bercy (in the twelfth arrondissement), the old neighborhood of wine warehouses, cafés, and shabby small structures was turned into a modern quarter of large office buildings, business centers, hotels, apartment buildings, and a big new park, which opened in 1994–1995.

Yet while these and other neighborhoods were losing their old character, many Parisians were strengthening local life by joining voluntary associations in record-setting numbers. The number of associations in Paris increased from 60,000 in 1977 to 120,000 in 1993. Each year some 4,500 were created, twice the average of the preceding years. In 1992, 8,000 of them received subsidies from the municipality. Many neighborhood associations offered activities and courses ranging from aikido to jazz—for children, adolescents, adults, and the elderly. Particularly active and numerous were sports organizations, 1,500 of them, devoted to swimming, gymnastics, and soccer, to name only a few.[32]

Many of the political associations sprang up in the defense of neighborhoods against urbanist projects and unilateral decision-making by the state. Historical memories of resistance helped. The most active defense associations emerged in the areas that had been the most fiercely fighting strongholds of the Commune in 1871: the Butte aux Cailles, Belleville, and Montmartre. Mobilizing quarter by quarter, the anti-urbanists won some notable battles in the late 1980s. Residents around the Canal Saint-Martin blocked bulldozers to stop development on a small but much-frequented green space, the Villemin Square. Neighbors around Bercy were able to prevent the felling of two hundred century-old trees. Others succeeded in saving some twentieth-century structures whose fame had been assured by popular movies—the façade of the storied Hôtel du Nord and the house of the apache moll known as Casque d'or. Altogether more than sixty associations were actively combating municipal projects by 1993. They combined their grassroots militancy with cultural and social events, such as an annual festival of the Canal Saint-Martin, art exhibits, and neighborhood flea markets.[33] The urbanist projects that destroyed the long-familiar cityscape and life of many neighborhoods also sparked resistance and new local life—in some.

A MAYOR MAKES A DIFFERENCE

From its very inception in 1977 the office of the mayor was a bastion for resistance to the fast-track urbanism of the Pompidou era. Mayor Chirac and his successor, Jean Tiberi, couched their opposition in voguish watchwords such as protection of heritage and ecology, and they spoke warmly

FIGURE 4.4. A semblance of convivial community lives on within the post-industrial metropolis—at least in places on fine spring Sundays. This former convent garden, the Jardin Villemin along the Canal Saint-Martin, was opened to the public in 1977. When a part of it was later ceded to a developer by the municipal government, residents organized and stopped the bulldozers. An administrative tribunal annulled the building permit in 1991. (Photo by the author, April 2005.)

of historic, picturesque, and affective Paris, aligning themselves with the lovers of Old Paris. Yet they did not take an unequivocal stand against change. While defending historic Paris in speeches at opportune moments, they also endorsed renovations along with the ideal of a "mixed" city. In 1996 Mayor Tiberi approved of more supple building regulations that encouraged construction adapted to the historic character of the varied neighborhoods, so that, despite being modernized, they would keep "their own charm, the particular structure of their architecture, of their streets." It was urbanism with a "more human face," "on the scale of the *quartiers*," the municipal magazine declared. Using language borrowed from the defenders of Vieux Paris, city officials promoted their new policies as measures for the "protection of the most picturesque sites of Paris" and "the historic and affective patrimony." Special protection came into play for "certain sectors . . . bearing a strongly affirmed character" in their "typical, symbolic, or picturesque aspect."[34]

Two symbolic thoroughfares received special treatment in the 1990s, though neither was picturesque or classically "old Paris." Rather they were legendary sites of Parisian glamour and pleasure that had lost their luster in the course of the twentieth century. First, in 1989, Mayor Chirac created a much-publicized commission to restore the once-chic "most beautiful avenue in the world," whose sidewalks had become obstacle courses of parked automobiles, café tables, and signs. The "Mission des Champs-Élysées" returned the broad promenades (contre-allées) to strolling crowds and café sitters by installing new granite underfoot together with barriers against autos, planting new rows of trees, and imposing new stricter regulations on storefronts and signs.[35] A similar effort to rehabilitate the Grands Boulevards began under Mayor Tiberi in 1997. New street lights and benches were installed for pedestrians, and ninety buildings along the way were marked for historical preservation. But to lend a new sparkle to the relatively narrow, traffic-clogged old boulevards was harder than to restore the expansive Champs. It was also difficult, if not impossible, to reverse a century-long decline of commercial activity and "conviviality": prestigious and wealthy customers and residents had long ago shifted to the west, leaving most of the Grands Boulevards stranded in less supportive plebeian neighborhoods.

Most conspicuously of all, Mayor Chirac undertook a major campaign early in his administration to make the capital cleaner, using showy technology. New motorized scrubbers and motorbike vacuum-cleaners (motocrottes) swept regularly across the sidewalks, and new self-scouring public-toilet cubicles were installed along the bigger streets. The street-cleaning machines made for impressive displays of speed and efficiency befitting the Ville Lumière, but they were not wholly effective. Years later, even several decades later, the battle was far from won—particularly the battle against dog droppings, deposited daily on public pavement by many of the city's 200,000 dogs. Sixteen tons of it a day fell on Parisian sidewalks, reported Le Monde in late 1999. Municipal workers removed twelve tons a day, leaving much of the remaining four tons to end up on pedestrians' shoes, despite the threat of fines for the pet owners and media campaigns urging the masters to take responsibility.[36] Trying a new tack, the newly elected administration of Mayor Bertrand Delanoë in June 2001 announced that the *motocrottes* were to be abandoned and other approaches taken—imposing more fines on offending dog owners while mounting another campaign for compliance with the law.

The mayors also made well publicized efforts to build more underground parking and provide more green space in the city, never calling attention to the long-run contradiction. And they grappled with the old problems of slums and insufficient public housing. Mayor Tiberi, for example, made a new commitment to attacking the blight of slums in 1995, when the number of dilapidated and insalubrious buildings, officially identified as such, stood at 136. At the end of 1999, 51 of the 136 "had already been demolished or renovated."[37] Successive mayors, having identified hundreds of buildings unfit for habitation, continue the struggle to upgrade or demolish them. Still today, however, a stubborn core of substandard buildings and poorly housed Parisians remains, along with unknown numbers of the homeless and squatters.

Recent mayors have also worked to combat the most flagrant public nuisances, such as excessive traffic noise. About 38,000 dwellings most exposed to the noise were made eligible for new acoustical windows subsidized by the municipality in 1999.[38] In the old battle against the city's two million rats, mayors have less progress to report. Each spring the municipality launches a campaign of *dératisation*, but "de-ratting" the city has never meant elimination of the big gray pest. That is simply too much to hope for. Authorities, communicating through the municipal magazine, have in effect tried to lower expectations by explaining that the rats have "remarkable intelligence": when given poisoned grains to eat, the rodents quickly figure out which products cause death and then avoid them. Usually the city officials fill the magazine with news of accomplishments, but in this case they share their pessimistic conclusion with the public: there is to be no definitive resolution of the problem. Resigning themselves to an unending war, they struggle just to maintain the status quo, doing what they can to check a population increase. Besides, they tell the public, rats are not all that bad: they play a helpful role as sewer cleaners (*éboueurs des égouts*).[39]

So, despite continuing efforts by one administration after another, slums and assorted public nuisances—noise, dirt, pollution, traffic—remain a part of the everyday city, irreconcilable counterpoints to the dream images of a heaven-on-earth Paris. Successive mayors have made some improvements, notably in street cleaning; as for the rest, they have reported every measure taken, including every palliative, as noteworthy progress. To lovers of Paris the city's defects have always been merely "warts and blemishes," insignificant compared to the beauty of the beloved. Or they have even been part of the beauty, as Montaigne held. To less smitten inhabitants, the quality of life in Paris has left much to be desired—and still does.

CAPITAL—OF WHAT?

In the late twentieth century, the title *capital* more than any other served to assert the importance of Paris. Paris's identity as the seat of the French state for more than a thousand years has inspired admirers to extend that notion of capital in many ways, all designed to underscore the city's unchallenged preeminence over the rest of France. In 1988 Europe's ministers of culture bestowed on Paris a new international version of the title: "the cultural capital of Europe in 1989." In the middle of that banner year, the bicentennial of the French Revolution, the proud mayor emphasized that Paris was not only a "museum city," but also "a great cultural capital, without doubt the leading one in the world"—a "permanent home of intellectual creation, in the domain of the plastic arts, music, theater, dance, as well as fashion and decorative arts." And it was a "center of university and scientific research of the first order." It was also number one in the world as a convention site, a ranking that it had held for more than ten years. Everything was in place, Mayor Chirac added, for Paris to be not only the cultural capital, but also the *première* of the capitals of the new Europe, only a few years away from becoming a fully integrated common market.[40] Commercial publicists made the case similarly. In 1990, for example, a special promotional section in the weekly magazine *L'Express* was emblazoned with the grandiose title "Paris, Capitale du Monde"; inside, a half dozen specific claims spelled out the case: "Paris is the world capital of business tourism [*tourisme d'affaires*] for ten consecutive years," the "Capital of convention halls," the "Capital of gastronomy," the "Capital of luxury products," and even the "Capital of interpreters" (an assertion resting on the slender base of an École supérieure d'interprètes et de traducteurs, which trained thirteen to fifteen professionals a year).[41] The boosters further asserted that their city was (still) "Capital of culture and the joie de vivre," a claim supported by references to its extraordinary galaxy of museums, places of entertainment, and "grandiose projects" such as the new Grande Bibliothèque.

In the early 1980s President Mitterrand planned to reclaim the historic "world capital" role by having Paris host a Universal Exposition in 1989 (as in 1889), celebrating the French Revolution and its heir, the Fifth Republic under socialist leadership, champion of human rights. He also urged that Paris host the Olympic Games in 1992, the centennial year of their modern revival, and fully backed the city's bid. But neither the world's fair nor the Olympic Games came to fruition in Paris. The reason was largely that both undertakings entailed too many disruptions and complications for the normal life of the already crowded city, and the costs were too great. Both events also fell victim to political rivalries between the president and the mayor.[42]

In the late '80s Paris was a credible candidate for the title of capital of Europe, as the mayor maintained, but that claim weakened after the revolutions of autumn 1989 in Eastern Europe. The fall of the Communist regimes and the unification of Germany in 1990 led to the emergence of Berlin as a new central European capital. The reunified metropolis, endowed with potential greatness by almost any standard, could lay new claim to European leadership in the not distant future. In the post–Cold War, Paris was better described as one among several European metropolises with a global role.[43] But it has been hard for political leaders and writers to give up the old rhetoric. The references to Paris as capital roll on and on: "international capital of art and culture" (Mayor Tiberi in 1999), an "Arab capital," diplomatic capital, "capital of exile," a capital of cinema (mainly for the international diversity of films showing in the city's 386 theaters), and "capital of the rollerskate" (an exhibit in the Hôtel de Ville).[44] Ritualistically invoked, the title remained an irresistible staple of Paris clichés—and a strong alternative to the more ambiguous and shopworn image "Ville Lumière."

MITTERRAND'S MONUMENTS

For centuries, ambitious kings and Napoleonic emperors made a practice of dressing up their capital and giving it monumental éclat. The early presidents of the Fifth Republic continued the tradition, imposing their ideas of modernity and monumentality on Paris, until Giscard d'Estaing in the mid-70s backed off from that kind of dictation by the state. A revival of monarchical practices was certainly not expected of Giscard's successor, France's first Socialist president. Yet in François Mitterrand's first press conference as president on September 24, 1981, he announced an epoch-defining agenda of big projects for Paris: they included redevelopment of La Villette for cultural purposes and a new grand monument at La Défense, along with mounting a "universal exposition" in the capital in 1989 marking the bicentennial of the French Revolution. His predecessors had taken on one, two, or three major projects; Mitterrand spoke of seven, eight, even nine. His choices could scarcely have been more varied: a new museum of science, a music center, a huge new national library, a "popular" Opéra at La Bastille, an institute for Arab studies (moving ahead on planning begun under Giscard d'Estaing), and a towering "grand arch" at La Défense, intended to house a human rights exhibit.[45] All were in the Ville Lumière tradition of showcasing modernity and cultural leadership, updated with some populist touches—but with no wistful concern for Paname, Old Paris, or the Capital of Pleasures.

In public statements into early 1982 the president and his aides emphasized the importance of "grand architecture." From the outset Mitterrand was determined to leave an enduring Socialist mark on the city. His minister of Culture Jack Lang, and top city planners rode around Paris one Sunday morning in September 1981 looking over potential sites for construction. They had their eye especially on the eastern side of the city—the poorer end, long neglected by the nation's governments. Some outmoded, under-utilized industrial areas along the Seine were easy to spot, and were readily taken by the state. But the ambitious plans quickly added up to staggering expenses for taxpayers, and by 1983 it was clear that something had to be cut. So Mitterrand chose to give up the 1989 world's fair in order to save his architectural "grand projects" for Paris. Instead of building housing for the poor or public recreational facilities, he and his aides held out for new monuments in the grand royal and imperial tradition.

As president, Mitterrand took a strong interest in architecture, more than his predecessors had. He made it clear that he would decide on such matters, and in the case of renovations to the Louvre (1984–1989), he managed to choose architect I. M. Pei without even a preliminary competition, though the law then required competitions. Neither Mitterrand nor French architects associated with the Left had a definite architectural style in mind at the outset, but they began by rejecting Giscard's cautious neo-classical tastes. With an eye to his legacy, Mitterrand dreaded most of all the prospect of modernist structures in the style of a "freeway tollbooth." In the end it became clear that his tastes ran to classical forms and materials—cubes and rectangles, granite and marble. Yet the grand structures built under Mitterrand ended up as varied in their styles as in their functions. In different ways they all made a break with France's traditional high culture and the tastes of the traditional elite.[46]

They also broke with the centuries-old orientation of official and elite Paris toward the west—toward the aristocratic Champs-Élysées and the royal Versailles. In an effort to correct the historic imbalance, Mitterrand's administration concentrated the new projects in the less prosperous side of the capital. The westward movement of elites dated from the late seventeenth century when aristocrats began leaving the Marais and the center to take up residence in the Faubourg Saint-Honoré, the Faubourg Saint-Germain, and outlying areas closer to Versailles. The eastern side of Paris became largely the domain of the working classes and the poor—and only a few places that drew tourists, such as the cemetery Père Lachaise and the Carnavalet Museum.

One of the biggest projects on the east side was the development of a new park and museum complex around the old stockyards at La Villette. The large site (140 acres) provided an extraordinary opportunity for a major operation, one that was most similar to Les Halles in scope. The history of its redevelopment shows how much the battle over the central market changed thinking about the city and its public spaces. Like Les Halles, La Villette had been a center for the city's food supply: it was both a slaughterhouse and a wholesale meat market—with Baltard-like iron structures dating from the Second Empire. After years of talk and debate, construction of an enormous new abattoir dragged on through the sixties with completion nowhere in sight. Astronomical overruns and stories of corruption made La Villette synonymous with scandal. Finally, in 1970 the municipal council turned the huge space over to the state for a "prestigious operation" of urban renewal "unequaled in the entire world."[47] Debate over proposed uses and plans then began in earnest, while the stockyards and slaughterhouses shut down in stages, with the last closings in March 1974.

The most favored proposals resembled those that had come up in the long controversy over the redevelopment of Les Halles—ideas for cultural facilities, a public park, and new housing. But at La Villette, well after the destruction of Baltard's Halles, sentiment for preserving the great iron hall ran strong, particularly as many people thought it to be Baltard's work (it was actually by Louis-Adolphe Janvier). The vast interior seemed wonderfully suited for exhibits and shows. For the rest, constructing new apartment buildings on the edges of the park, providing perhaps three thousand dwelling units, seemed the right choice to political leaders most tuned to local needs. The municipal council wanted housing too. But President Valéry Giscard d'Estaing wanted a large green space and a new science museum. Having turned over Les Halles to city authorities to decide, Giscard reserved La Villette for his own designs and tastes. The architect he chose was a safe establishment figure, Adrien Fainsilber, who favored a classical French layout of geometrical pools, walkways, and a well-proportioned museum, rendered contemporary by such environmentalist touches as solar panels and abundant greenery covering the building's facade. Critics with Parisian interests at heart immediately attacked the president, or "the prince," as they called him, for making such big decisions on a Paris question. The tug of war continued through Giscard's term in office. All the while, almost all eyes remained on Les Halles, where emotions ran higher and the stakes for the city's future seemed bigger.

After the May 1981 presidential elections, La Villette became one of President Mitterrand's *grands projets*. To the plans already made, Mitterrand's minister of Culture added a rock concert hall and a music center, the last comprising a conservatory, concert halls, a museum of instruments, and collections for education and research. The first piece of the project to be completed was the portable hall for rock concerts, Le Zénith, a canvas-and-metal structure erected like a circus tent, installed in a corner of the park in 1983.[48] One of a new generation of huge halls, Le Zénith could seat about 6,000 people—in contrast to the nineteenth-century Olympia with its 2,000 seats and the Bobino with 1,100.

Finally, in 1986 the new science museum complex—the Cité des Sciences et de l'Industrie—opened in the vast, renovated slaughterhouse. Placed in front of it was a huge shiny stainless-steel sphere called La Géode, housing a hemispherical movie screen of 1,000 square meters, one of the biggest in the world. The grounds around the museums and canals became one of the city's biggest parks (75 acres), landscaped with gardens, sidewalks, and whimsical small structures in the tradition of old-regime *folies*. Parisians flocked to the new green space and the *folies*, and many, including tourists, took in the science displays. By the nineties the science complex was attracting more visitors than any other museum except the Louvre. As a whole, La Villette was clearly one of the most successful of President Mitterrand's additions to the capital.[49]

Other big projects for the east end included a sports arena called the Palais Omnisports de Paris Bercy (1984), a new park (about 33 acres) near it, and a huge new national library, the Bibliothèque nationale de France, built on the Left Bank in the once-industrial thirteenth arrondissement. Construction of the library began in 1991, and the building, renamed the Bibliothèque François Mitterrand by President Jacques Chirac, opened to readers (many of whom found it to be poorly designed) in 1996. Nearby, on vacated industrial sites, a new university for eastern Paris was built (Université Paris 7).

Across the Seine, an abandoned elevated train track between Bastille and the Gare de Lyon was turned into a walkway and green space, filled with rose bushes, shrubs, and flowers ("la coulée verte") nine meters above the street. In 1994 the renovated arches underneath it began filling with arts-and-crafts galleries, and the old structure was renamed the Viaduc des Arts. All these projects spurred the upgrading of apartment buildings, restaurants, and office space in the surrounding neighborhoods.

To critics such as journalist Claude Dubois, the policy of bringing the east of Paris up to the level of the west (the "rééquilibrage de l'Est parisien") was only a "technocratic alibi" for a "sociological revolution" against the poor and their culture. The new Opéra constructed on the Place de la Bastille in 1989 symbolized it powerfully, he wrote. In the French Revolution's bicentenary, the "new bourgeoisie" took the Bastille from the common people: the new Opéra Bastille was "the death of 'la Bastoche,'" Dubois declared, meaning the death of a quarter of workers and poor people and the demise of their culture of old-time cafés and accordion dance halls. Once again, the poor were being driven from the city.[50] By the end of the twentieth century the east side in general was still not equal to the western *beaux quartiers* in its residences and businesses, but it had become more prosperous—and more bourgeois. It lost its old mix of provincial and Paname cultural life and became up-to-the-minute trendy—in part due to the new state-sponsored cultural installations and in larger part due to an influx of artists and young people with some disposable income and more leisure time.

PARIS IN THE PLURAL

Julian Green's notion of Paris as plural became even more apt in the years after he articulated it in 1972.[51] The metropolis that had long been a magnet for people from the provinces and the rest of Europe attracted waves of new immigrants from all parts of the globe in the late twentieth century. As the newcomers poured into low-rent neighborhoods, they created densely settled colonies whose shops, languages, and dress were foreign to the French. The villages of Paris, traditionally reminiscent of the provinces, became cosmopolitan enclaves. In the late twentieth century, more than two hundred nationalities were living in the capital. The number of foreigners in the Parisian population was twice as big as it had been a century before.[52]

Parisians who had long relished the exotic (in small doses) now found it in restaurants, food markets, bookstores, craft shops, and concerts throughout the city. At the end of the twentieth century, the quarter of Oberkampf, for example, became one of the most lively and "hip" villages with the global flavor. Oberkampf with its Chinese *cantines*, Balkan grocery stores, kosher butcher shops, Indian bazaars, and French bakeries "reflects well the world spirit of Paris," declared a *Télérama* special issue on the capital in 1997.[53]

Late-twentieth-century Paris and many of its suburbs became a mosaic of world cultures as never before. It became, in particular, "le melting pot mondial de la musique," "where jazz performers mixed with raï singers, accordionists, African musicians and, of course, techno DJs."[54] Paris was where the stars of African music were made. Zairean singers who were successful in their own country dreamed of going to the place they called "Paname." Rastas migrated with the same dream to the city they called Babylon. In Paris they found not only a large African audience, drawn from many nationalities, but also recording companies such as Sonodisc and Safari Ambiance, which distributed their music throughout Europe and Africa.[55]

In the spring of 1978, Parisian aficionados of African music gathered for Africa-Fête, a large festival with a series of concerts in such venues as the nightclub New Morning. Activist Mamadou Konté, who had emigrated from Senegal in 1965, took a leading role in organizing the festival after a French government crackdown on African organizations in Paris. French jazz star Claude Nougaro joined the African singers the first year, helped pay them, and even helped put up posters.[56] Africa-Fête became an annual event for more than a decade. In the 1980s it doubled as a response to political attacks on immigrants by the right-wing politician Jean-Marie Le Pen. Audiences numbered five thousand at first, but grew to twelve thousand within a few years. Africans made up 70 percent of the first audience, but five years later 70 percent of the spectators had white faces.

The most omnipresent sounds of plural Paris came via local radio. After lawmakers liberalized the audio-visual system in July 1982, Paris quickly went from having a few state-run stations to eighteen authorized private stations, with many more added in the months and years that followed. Unauthorized ("pirate") broadcasters also started up regularly, crowding into the frequencies of others. "The F.M. band is totally saturated," noted a media official in 1987.[57] New stations filled almost every niche of interest and identity. Radio Montmartre, Radio Nostalgie, Radio Classique, Radio-Shalom, Radio Notre-Dame, Radio-Beur, Radio-Latino, Fréquence gai, Radio-Libertaire (offering programming 90 percent French), and numerous others found a following. The station with the most listeners, however, did not cater to particularist political, or religious groups.[58] The most listened-to station by the mid-1980s was N.R.J., a powerful "national radio" that featured the latest rock and pop music (much of it *not* French) and hip, energetic young DJs.

In the banlieues, some local radio stations serving ethnic and foreign groups did much more than simply entertain. In the working-class suburb Saint-Denis, for example, a station called Fréquence Paris Plurielle served as "a place of dialogue" for "foreigners residing in France" (a.k.a. *immigrés*). Working in a few dingy rooms in a blind alley, about 150 people a week kept the broadcasts going. Associations of Malians, Kurds, Latin Americans, and Maghrébins shared the airwaves, offering programs that were cultural, social, political, and musical in roughly equal doses. The station was "the echo of the world," a Babel of cultures, although a minimum of 50 percent of the programs were in French, according to a policy set by the directors. To aid newcomers to Paris (many of them also new to France), the associations taught listeners how to get their legal rights while also staying in touch with their cultures of origin around the world.[59]

Even though Greater Paris has become more than ever before a cosmopolitan "world city" in recent decades, it has notoriously failed as a "melting pot" for many immigrant groups. In the neighborhood that the French call "Chinatown" in the thirteenth arrondissement, for instance, the Asian residents have largely remained socially separate in their enclave, despite efforts of local associations to bring the immigrants and their neighbors together. In Belleville—long the most "pluri-ethnic" part of the capital—Black Africans, Arabs, and Jews have their own cafés, where members of other "communities" do not go. Some French customers drop in at times, but Asians of the quarter do not. "The mixed population does not mean interactions," observed a young Frenchman. "Everyone has his or her little clan," added an older man. In the famously multiethnic quarter of the Goutte d'Or, the Senegalese immigrants have their cafés and bistros, while those from Zaire, Kabylia, and Oran have their own. The quarter is home to two mosques, a synagogue, a Protestant church, an evangelical church, and a Japanese Buddhist temple.

Far from being a village, it is a patchwork of different villages. And it is certainly not a part of a culture-sharing Paris-Paname. The inhabitants' participation in the life of the rest of the city is negligible. So are their interactions with the 40 percent of the quarter's population that comes from old French stock.[60]

The immigrants and their children out in the poorer banlieues, too, have remained grievously separate from Parisian life, despite some improvements in public transportation. Their growing numbers in the last decades of the twentieth century met with waves of anti-immigrant fears and antipathies. The large majority of the immigrant population, which is of North African and Black African origins, has been subject to racial and ethnic discrimination. The percentage of the unemployed in some of the large housing projects (*cités*) runs four times higher than the national rate.

Frictions between young men of the suburbs and the police have built up over years. The long-simmering alienation, frustration, and anger that exploded into widespread rioting in late October and early November of 2005 had been long-standing subjects of public discussion and alarming sociological reports since the 1980s. The media, politicians, and administrative reports regularly deplored the grim, dilapidated, graffiti-covered housing projects and called them "ghettos." In 1995 the state inaugurated a "Pact de Relance pour la Ville" aimed at bringing a fuller range of society (*mixité sociale*) into quarters that had become segregated by class and ethnicity.[61] But the government programs—subsidized housing and education—and French society have obviously fallen short of what is required for social integration.

In Clichy-sous-Bois, where the violence first broke out in late autumn of 2005, the rate of unemployment was 25 percent, striking particularly hard the third of the families who were of foreign origin, most of them poor and crowded into substandard housing. Fifty percent of the residents were under twenty-five years of age. Young males, finding community in local gangs, took the lead in setting fire to cars and some public buildings, actions quickly spread by youth in other banlieues. Altogether they burned hundreds of vehicles nightly for several weeks (over 10,000 total for all France).[62] Old notions of the banlieue as the disinherited, dangerous, anti-Paris appeared to be newly confirmed.

The prejudices encountered by the second- and third-generation children of immigrants have not been just those ingrained in the old-stock French. "Racism . . . exists even between foreigners," as an unemployed twenty-year-old woman from Algeria living in La Courneuve observed: "I mean like me. . . . I am Arab. . . . Between Arabs and Blacks . . . Racism . . . exists already among us the Maghrébins [peoples of northwestern Africa], between Moroccans, Tunisians, Algerians. Racism, you sense it between Africans, Black Africans and West Indians [*Antillais*]." Long-term residents of Maghrébin origin living in the suburb have deprecated newcomers even of the same origin as they (the "anciens" against the "nouveaux").[63]

In the suburb Aubervilliers, for example, successive waves of immigrants since the nineteenth century have struggled to establish themselves and to maintain their social cohesion and traditions as others moved in. After working their way into the ranks of the propertied, the Auvergnats as landlords then rented to North Africans, who in turn rent to sub-Saharan Africans now.[64] Everyone has a plethora of "others" to disparage and exclude, if so inclined. Fifty-two different nationalities were present in the *grand ensemble* of La Grande Borne (at Grigny) at the dawn of this century. The banlieue communes of Montreuil, Saint-Denis, and Sarcelles were home to more than eighty different nationalities. A nationality such as Algerian or Senegalese covers three different ethnic groups each—and different religions as well.[65]

In addition, old prejudices against Jews—that is, against long-established French citizens of Jewish heritage—found fresh fuel in the early twenty-first century, some of it spilling over from distant Arab-Israeli conflicts. The old hatreds and racism erupt periodically in the form of anti-Semitic insults and graffiti, attacks on individuals, and violence against Jewish restaurants and synagogues in central Paris as well as in the heavily immigrant suburbs to the north.[66]

Each ethnic "colony" finds "a form of security" (or relative safety from rejection) within its own housing project and suburb. Paris, only a métro stop or two away, is "a distant, mythical land" to the young residents of northern suburbs like Pantin. "When you live in the suburbs, you wouldn't even think it's France; you wouldn't even think that we live in Paris. It's another world," remarked a young African immigrant in Nicholas Stern's documentary on a housing project in Pantin. The adjoining suburbs are generally just as alien and segregated. "In a single kilometre, you move from one world to another," the banlieue residents told François Maspero as he made his journey of eye-opening reportage "through the Paris suburbs" in the late 1980s. For a lifelong inhabitant of Aubervilliers like Akim, "even neighboring La Courneuve was a different planet"—or more prosaically, an unknown ghetto.[67]

In the famously cosmopolitan central city itself, the old vibrant social diversity of centuries past has been steadily disappearing. For decades the poor and the working class have been moving out to the banlieue, most of them not forced by expropriation, but leaving voluntarily in search of affordable housing. The supply of subsidized housing units (*logements sociaux*) has long lagged far behind demand.[68] Low-income people have opted for the suburbs also in order to have new and more spacious apartments, less pollution and noise, and some land for a garden. And some moved because their jobs in factories, warehouses, and railroad yards shifted to the outskirts. In sum, Paris has lost its traditional workers—and their Parisian-defining slang, songs, cafés, and dance halls. The population of the central quarters especially has become less varied, and more exclusively middle- and upper-class ("bourgeois" say the Parisians).[69] Accordingly, many of the city's neighborhoods have become less interesting and lively. That conclusion has come not just from nostalgic populists such as Louis Chevalier and Claude Dubois, but also from city officials and urban planners in the late twentieth century. The drumbeat of appeals for socially "mixed" quarters—conventional political wisdom since the 1990s—is eloquent testimony to the widely shared sense of regret over the loss of modest residents since the 1960s.

A DEAD CENTER?

Alarm about Paris's dying re-emerged in new form at the very height of Mitterrand's efforts to bring new life to the city in the late twentieth century. All through the century the partisans of modernization had feared that urban decay combined with inertia was bound to turn Paris into a museum-city, a "ville-musée" like Venice. They worried that awe of Paris's past together with historic preservation was stifling current life and creativity, leaving an embalmed corpus. That fear grew much stronger as new museums mushroomed in the last decades of the century—the Pompidou Center (1977), the Musée d'Orsay (1986), the Cité des Sciences at La Villette (1986), and the enlarged Louvre (1993), to name only the biggest—along with a growing industry of "cultural tourism" centered on museums and historical monuments.

No one argued the old fear in contemporary terms more forcefully than a prominent Paris museum curator, Françoise Cachin, in 1994. The city center, she maintained, had been given over to the past.[70] New museums and the enlargement of old ones had added over 70,000 new square meters of display space in fifteen years. The heart of the city was filling up with museums and offices for museum personnel. Cultural and tourism forces were taking the place of long-standing political, financial, and commercial powers, whose activities moved out to the periphery. More and more of the central city was living off a host of international tourists who came to visit such shrines as the Louvre and Notre-Dame. At the Louvre 70 percent of the visitors were foreign tourists; 15 percent of the French visitors were from the provinces. At the Musée d'Orsay 55 percent of the visitors were foreigners. At least half of the Parisians who went to the museums were students going there on a school trip. Instead of being a crucible of new creation and a showcase of the latest in modernity, Paris was becoming a place devoted to things old and dead. The city itself was dying in its core, according to Cachin's diagnosis.

At the same time, a new challenge to the city's tourist attractions materialized in a nearby "new town": a Disneyland for Europe opened in 1992. Just twenty miles outside Paris, it offered visitors its own hotels, restaurants, and rail link to the airport. Euro-Disney brought to Greater Paris the sanitized New-World imaginary of Walt Disney, giving Europeans a chance to walk on "Main Street USA" rather than a historic Parisian boulevard a half an hour away. Visitors could spend their day in Frontierland and Adventureland rather than in the famed old quarters and museums of the capital. After several years of unexpectedly small crowds and big losses, the park began to make money. A commercial simulacrum of the American past successfully colonized the outskirts of Paris. But it did so only after adapting to European expectations (food, drink, and prices)—

and after adding the magic word "Paris" to Europe's magic kingdom in 1994, making the theme park "Disneyland Paris."[71]

Yet the old capital, so famously museum-like and rich in museums, still captivates legions of visitors and immigrants with its flourishing cultures and creations of today. The number of museums has only increased since Cachin's alarm cry. Among the most notable are the Musée des arts premiers (the Musée du Quai Branly), which opened in June 2006, and a museum of immigration history (the Cité nationale de l'histoire de l'immigration), which opened in 2007 in a former "palace" built for the 1931 Colonial Exposition. Those two reflect a new effort to reach out beyond the familiar tradition of European art and history, but the city also added a museum, the Pinacothèque de Paris (open in 2007 in a central location, Place de la Madeleine) that offers more exhibits in the grand Western tradition (Picasso, Soutine, Utrillo, et al.).

Amid the many museums, all manner of artistic and intellectual creativity continues, though much of it well outside the central city, in peripheral lower-rent districts like Belleville and increasingly, the nearby suburbs. Two major new centers nurturing contemporary art have opened in recent years, both updating the Ville Lumière tradition with democratic emphases on dialogue and exchange, and both bringing together cutting-edge artists and the general public. One is the renovated Palais de Tokyo, formerly a museum building dating from the 1937 International Exposition. Reopened in 2002 as a center of "contemporary creation," it showcases temporary exhibits by experimental artists, French and foreign, and serves as a lively, open-till-midnight haven for artists and visitors. The other is the Centquatre (named for its address, 104 Rue d'Aubervilliers), a former municipal mortuary in a poor neighborhood alongside the railroad tracks behind the Gare de l'Est. In the beautifully renovated space (40,000 square meters) once full of coffins and hearses, dozens of artists in residence work in their own studios and regularly greet the public that comes there to learn about the ongoing creative activities—in everything from the visual arts, music, dance, and design to cinema and video.

Shops and cafés in the museum-rich center continue to flourish—most of them not life-dependent on the tourist trade. Although the number of French food retailers (butchers, fishmongers, *crémeries*, *pâtissiers*, etc.)

and traditional cafés has been declining throughout the city for decades (while Chinese, Japanese, Middle Eastern, and American-style fast food outlets have been proliferating), Paris still boasts an extraordinary number of cafés-restaurants—over 12,000—and a thousand art galleries.[72] And many streets in the center still offer lively urban theater and entertainment daily. Underground, in the métro stations some 250 authorized entertainers, half of them coming from outside France, perform music of many lands.[73]

On boulevards around the city, several demonstrations a day provide spectacles of placard-bearing marchers chanting, singing, and playing to crowds on the sidewalks. Wherever the marchers and spectators appear, so do hawkers of beer, soda, and grilled *merguez*, lending a holiday air to the streets. May Day regularly draws a big spirited demonstration of left-

FIGURE 4.5. Street demonstrations are a regular part of the capital's political life and were, in critical times in the nineteenth century, serious, sometimes violent, threats to governments—and the prelude to revolutions (1848, 1870). In contemporary Paris, often (but not always) the marchers participate with a festive spirit and create a diverting spectacle for crowds of bystanders. Here, students along with some teachers and parents, march on the Grands Boulevards against a national educational reform and budget cuts in the spring of 2005. (Photo by the author.)

ist partisans and unionists from France and abroad, reactivating memories of the Popular Front's euphoric demonstrations (1935–1936).[74] Most
of the other demonstrations through the year are protests or clamorous
responses to government proposals and current political events. In the
wake of anti-immigrant and anti-Semitic acts and political demagoguery
of that ilk, for example, thousands of demonstrators took to the streets
in May 1990 to denounce attacks on Jewish cemeteries, and in spring
2002 tens of thousands turned out to denounce the first-round success
of the right-wing presidential candidate Jean-Marie Le Pen, leader of the
Front National.

New festivities, added to traditional ones, also enliven public spaces.
They range from neighborhood street fairs and fêtes to spectacles and
concerts in the major *places* and parks (La Place de l'Hôtel de Ville and
La Villette especially). For youthful Parisians, a particularly popular one
is the annual Techno Parade, the first of which rolled and rocked its way
through the streets of Paris in September 1998—forty floats, each booming
some 1,200 watts of (ear-splitting) sound, each a moving stage filled with
dancers and DJs, all winding up at the park of Reuilly for "a giant rave."
In sum, although the central city's streets are no longer filled daily with
anything like the host of colorful circus-style performers (*saltimbanques*)
and peddlers of old, they are far from the monotonous, dead spaces that
critics of urban renewal and historical preservation long feared.

POSTMODERN WORLD CITY

As the twentieth century drew to a close, Parisians did not fixate anxiously
on the future as the 1960s urbanists had. While still vibrant and open to
new things, the city settled back and memorialized pieces of its recent
past. In the last decades of the century, authorities added hundreds of
commemorative plaques to the hundreds already in place recalling events
of the Second World War. Most of those are in memory of Resistance and
Liberation heroes and martyrs. In 1994 the city added two new museums
also devoted to that memory: the Musée Jean Moulin and the Mémorial
du maréchal Leclerc de Hauteclocque et de la Libération de Paris. Then
beginning in 2000, the commemorative effort extended to youthful victims, whose deaths were recalled with sadness and shame: the city began

fixing plaques (332 to date) on the walls of public schools in remembrance of the 6,403 Jewish children deported to Nazi camps.[75] Other official-memory efforts have gone into honoring and protecting historic sites and notable buildings from the latter half of the nineteenth century and the twentieth century. Designated as historical monuments were such diverse places as (1983) the Wall of the Fédérés (the place in the Père Lachaise cemetery where the last Communards were executed—a powerful memory site for the Left) and (1989) the Belle-Époque workingman's restaurant Chartier (still open at 7 Rue du Faubourg Montmartre). The caretakers of public memory also granted historical recognition to such modernist architectural works as the building for the French Communist Party headquarters (designed by Oscar Niemeyer, built circa 1970, and added to the historical registry in 2007). They even extended official protection to the city's first residential skyscraper, the Tour Albert (described in Chapter 3), protruding above the neighborhood's bleak nineteenth-century buildings since 1960: it was designated a historical monument in 1994.[76] Official Paris memory became more eclectic than ever before.

How much of all that history has taken root in popular memory? In a city saturated with historical monuments, statues, and commemorative plaques (over 1,300), most Parisians and visitors apparently give little or no attention to most historical markers, including the many plaques recalling the high dramas and tragedies of the Occupation and Liberation. It may be that the war memories, like memories of more-distant traumas in Paris's long history, are seemingly too remote from most people's busy lives in the present, however painful and disturbing they remain for some. The plaques, like the import of the métro-station-and-street names honoring Resistance heroes (Colonel Fabien, Jacques Bonsergent, et al.), fade into the quotidian background. Yet movies, exhibits, and books about the Occupation, the Resistance, and the Liberation of Paris have met with strong public interest in recent decades. Those extraordinary times are doubtless lodged firmly in the collective memory of Parisians, yet they have not been integrated into the familiar imagery of the city. The old, long-established identities of the city still hold sway in the minds of most Parisians, as opinion surveys have shown again and again[77] (more on that in Chapters Five and Six).

FIGURE 4.6. Traces of embattled memory: the basilica Sacré-Coeur vs. the Paris Commune. Political and religious conservatives organized the construction of the basilica (built between 1875 and 1914) as penance for the Commune and other revolutionary sins—or acts against God and the Church. Anti-clerical city council members struck back by setting out reminders of their side of history— naming the park at the base of the Butte after Communard's fiery heroine, Louise Michel, and erecting a statue to a victim of the Church's intolerance (Le Chevalier de la Barre) near the front of the basilica. Now with the historical references no longer common knowledge, these once-warring mementoes go unnoticed by most visitors to Sacré-Coeur. (Photo by the author, 2009.)

Critics of the postmodern city have argued that officialdom's efforts to bolster collective memory and a sense of community have been superficial, incoherent, and unsatisfying. The occasional festive event, for instance, has not mattered much in the face of the disintegrating economic and social bases of the quarters (cafés, shops, parish life). Restoration projects like the makeover of the Rue Montorgueil (near Les Halles) leave behind artificial fragments, pieces of nostalgic window dressing. Missing is a sense of the living and historic city as a whole. Some also charge that the promotion of fantasy, festivity, and a semi-fictional local community simply covers over or denies the realities of "lop-sided power relations"—political-economic processes that constrain workaday opportunity and community participation for many, as cultural theorist David Harvey notes.[78]

In response, it should be noted that these critics of the postmodern city are caviling at traits that have long characterized Paris—for being "a patchwork of incongruous leftover pieces alongside a set of artfully designed compositions."[79] Moreover, the dressed up, traffic-free Montorgueil with its numerous cafés and shops *does* sustain a level of liveliness and diversity greater than most other streets in the center. Although the social life in such places falls well short of the level associated with the old Halles (as described by Louis Chevalier and others), and though much of it *is* fragmentary and relatively ephemeral, it is more than enough to belie the old cry about Paris's assassination decades ago.

After all the debates about the city's "destiny" and after much redevelopment, it was still not clear at the century's end whether the city's star was rising relative to others or not. It was also not clear where Paris's optimal future lay: where should Paris be concentrating its efforts to strengthen relationships?—toward France's provincial cities (now only a few hours away by the new fast trains, the T.G.V.), toward neighboring regions in France and others nearby like the Lombard region, toward other capitals of Europe, or other great cities around the world?[80]

Paris entering the twenty-first century was certainly more international in culture than ever—with its many sushi bars, couscous cafés, Chinese take-outs, Egyptian *salons de thé*, kebab shops, and American barbecue chains (not to mention McDonald's and Starbucks) and its large population of foreigners, but it was hardly the leading-light "world city" or Ville Lumière that Victor Hugo and Napoleon III had envisioned. Modernist dreams of unilinear progress and primacy were no longer compelling. Paris could no longer claim to be a "world city" in the Second-Empire sense of a capital with dominant power and influence. Managing an unstable mix of modernity and nostalgia, the city (and the state) grappled with ambivalence even about its primacy in France.

At the same time, contemporary scholars have made a strong case for Paris as a "global city"—in the sense of being one of several international "command-and-control" centers, powerful metropolises linked in a worldwide network of economic and cultural relations.[81] As such, it competes not only with London, Frankfurt, Berlin, and Milan, but also with Toronto and Tokyo. In size it is dwarfed by such non-European cities as Tokyo, Mumbai, São Paulo, and Lagos (Nigeria), but it still surpasses all of them but Tokyo as a thriving "global city." When Western writers referred to Paris as capital of the world in the nineteenth century, Europe meant "the world" to them; now Paris can no longer pass for being even the capital of Europe. Yet its importance and roles go far beyond its own continent. Although Paris no longer leads in global politics and culture, it still makes its cultural mark on many societies and civilizations far from Europe. It is, above all, the place where an extraordinary enchanting imaginary is firmly anchored, a city viewed through a hyper-realist lens of collective memories and dreams that have resonance around the globe. With its remarkable pastiche of historic riches, cosmopolitan communities, and international mystique, Paris has a unique claim to the title of world city.

CHAPTER 5

Paris in Comparison

INCOMPARABLE?

After viewing Paris's personas in historical perspective (Chapters 1–4), it seems to me worthwhile now to double back in search of answers to a fundamental question: what makes Paris different from—and greater than—other great cities of Europe? This chapter focuses on the motifs that have most commonly recurred in the many answers given over the centuries. Looking through them, one can quickly see that contemporary notions about Paris's unique charms are not just city-hall boasting and tourism puffery. Rather they are old stock ideas that long ago formed a tradition, a collective memory nurtured by a host of contributors—travelers, guidebooks, writers, songsmiths, poets, and scholars. Like the tradition of Paris descriptions as a whole, those comparisons have set up expectations, guided perceptions, and framed views over generations.

From the beginnings of the tradition to the early twentieth century, by far most of the comparers have presented the city as superior in various ways. Paris's most enthusiastic admirers have simply declared it off-the-scale, making specific comparisons pointless. In the Middle Ages, they proclaimed Paris "without equal," without a rival, the queen of cities, the city of cities. Of course, calling it "paradise" also put it beyond reach of the competition. Alternatively, they declared Paris incomparably superior to the greatest cities of all time, citing glorious names from history. Without ever having set foot in Jerusalem, Alexandria, Athens, or Rome, they issued their unequivocal judgment. Later admirers continued the tradition of imaginative praise. Goethe, for example, hailed Paris as the "universal city," though he never visited it.

Another old way of exalting Paris was to create a glorious, fanciful prehistory for it. Medieval scholars spun stories telling of its origins back in an antiquity of fabled cities and bigger-than-life heroes. One account ascribed Paris's foundation to refugees from the burned city of Troy, who named their new home after their hero Pâris, the husband of Helen. Another version traced Paris back to the Arcadian city Parrhasia, whose men of war (the Parrhasians) were installed on an island in the Seine by none other than Hercules.[1]

In recent centuries, the fabulous ancients have moved to the wings, and Parisian writers have more often produced accounts of Paris that reflect their own experience and self-conscious literary ambitions. Avoiding the contention that most national issues entailed, they put their talent to work as connoisseurs of the extraordinary capital city that was their own hometown. Among other things, they vaunted its historic luminaries and the institutions that produced them—as well as many of the contemporary writers themselves. Thus identifying themselves with the city's glory, the cultural elite happily affirms that Paris is ever home to the finest. So a systematic "capital narcissism" (as Christophe Prochasson has put it) has flourished.[2]

Working-class and lower-middle-class Parisians, too, have been blatantly narcissist—in their own way. Like the Cockneys of London, they prided themselves on their identity as true Parisians—"Parisiens de Paris." While singing the praises of their hometown, they scorned the rest of the world without knowing any of it, and they presumed people from outside the capital—provincials and foreigners—to be doltish, backward, less-than-civilized. That "militant lack of understanding," observed Valéry Larbaud in the 1920s, made Parisians more provincial than ever before.[3] A stream of popular songs through the twentieth century has etched the points of pride into collective memory: the most romantic city, the most beautiful, "the "ville idéale," "a veritable corner of Paradise"—the rhyme of Paris and *paradis* making the flattery irresistible to lyricists.[4]

Today some of that boosterism and provinciality may still exist in the French capital (though not in anyone I know!), but a complete blindness to rival cities became nearly impossible with the growth of international travel and communications in the course of the nineteenth and twentieth centuries. Comparisons, favorable and unfavorable, have become common currency in public discourse. This chapter puts a spotlight on those comparisons, the reasons behind them, and the characterizations of Paris that they fostered. A look back at that comparative tradition can help us see the ways in which the Paris imaginary has been shaped by a self-conscious rivalry with other great cities, such as London. That comparative perspective may help explain why certain attractive traits have been highlighted as the most distinctive and important. The extollers of Paris, that is, have long told a great deal about what Paris was *not* (much more than they acknowledged). Noteworthy, too, are the comparisons that have *not* been favorable to the French capital—in particular, those that reform-minded Parisians made to point up their city's shortcomings.

GREATER THAN . . .

The most general measure used in ranking cities is a catch-all notion that needs to be clarified at the outset: specifically, what does it mean to call Paris a great city? First of all, there is its relatively great size. The capital city has stood out for centuries as France's "grande ville" (or simply "grand-ville"). Guidebooks for French and foreign visitors alike have opened with that fact: "Paris, the capital, is by far the largest and most important city of France. It occupies about 20,000 acres and has a population of nearly 3,000,000"—so began an American guide of 1920, for example.[5] Although the authors went on to call the emphasis on "bigness" characteristically American, it should be noted that it also has been a commonplace in French writing on the capital city. Until the end of the nineteenth century, Paris was in fact huge compared to other cities in France and in the entire world except one: London. It was still second in the world as late as 1875, but at the turn of the twentieth century it lost that rank when New York City overtook it.

The phrase "grande ville" referred not only to size, but also to "greatness" in qualitative respects. Its numerous claims to superiority were already set out in the early seventeenth century by the leading guidebook: "the most beautiful city presently known," also remarkable for its "surprising diversities worthy of admiration," for the "illustrious persons that it has produced," "the magnificence of its buildings," "the immense wealth of some of its citizens," the unparalleled flourishing of "the fine arts," and its high reputation in the world, as evidenced by the "great number of foreigners of quality and princes even" who came there to study the language and the "distinguished manners" of the Parisians.[6] Phrases of that tenor were still commonplaces in the centuries that followed. But were they well founded over the centuries? Were they tenable when tested against what could be found in other great cities of Europe?

The most formidable challenger to Paris's claims in the nineteenth century was the much bigger metropolis across the channel: London. The two capitals were frequent subjects of comparison in guidebooks and travel literature, as historian Claire Hancock has shown in a comprehensive study.[7] National rivalry, not just hometown pride, was involved, the capitals serving as symbols of the nation-states. On the French side, most observers made comparisons with London to point up the uniqueness and, of course, the superiority of Paris. The immensity of London did not impress them as a bragging point. But other claims were hard to belittle or rebut—notably, London's world financial and commercial power and such widespread home "comforts" as running water. French writers chose instead to dwell on their capital's beauty, charm, intellectual leadership, and the gaiety of the populace. The French and the English guides did agree on some points—on the abundance of amusements in Paris and the contrast between the great *ville de plaisirs* and the smoky, foggy metropolis of work, world commerce, and modern industry. English guides, however, regularly added disparaging remarks to that pleasure motif, noting Parisians' rampant frivolity, idleness, and gross appetite for public spectacles. English judgments of this kind, along with the overall challenge presented by London, surely helped kindle some of the French boasting about Paris.

After Germany defeated France in war in 1870–1871, Paris faced a growing challenge from a newcomer, Berlin, now the capital of the new German empire. Imperial Berlin made every effort to catch up with Paris, building grandiose state buildings, museums, grand hotels, department stores, theaters, music halls, and opera houses. Ambitious Berliners even tried to appropriate the proud title of "Light of the World" for their city—in the very same period that Paris was beginning to be known as the Ville Lumière.[8]

Yet for all its extensive new building and impressive dynamism, Berlin of the late nineteenth century did not overtake Paris in drawing power and prestige. Even Berliners declared their own hometown shapeless and ugly in comparison with Paris and Vienna. A leading art critic, Karl Scheffler, claimed for his city the distinction of being "the capital of all modern ugliness" (1910).[9] Nor could Berlin begin to compete with the established capital of "pleasures," especially the ones that attracted multitudes of visitors. The German emperor, recognizing his capital's lack of appeal, decided against attempting to mount any world's fair. "Paris is the whorehouse of the world; therein lies its attraction independent of any exhibition," he explained.[10] Berlin was also in no position to challenge Paris's leading role in the international art world. Even as a cultural center within Germany, Berlin did not attain the level of dominance that Paris had over France, as historian Christophe Charle has shown. Around 1900, Paris as cultural hub was already living on its past, Charle concludes, but it had accumulated such a rich heritage that it could afford missteps and wasted effort. Berlin was the parvenu, trying to catch up but unable to be more than "an epigone without genius."[11]

Vienna, capital of an old empire, was the close rival of Paris in cultural inventiveness, perhaps even the leader, but its reputation lagged far behind. More than any other city, Paris had won world attention regularly with huge world's fairs and wave after wave of brilliant avant-gardes—well before Vienna's fin-de-siècle flowering.[12] The Austrian capital, further, was a much smaller city, more distant for travelers from the west, and (like Berlin) not so closely connected to English and American centers of power.

In relation to all the provincial cities of France, the primacy of Paris was indisputable and overwhelming. It had been so since the seventeenth century at least. The population of metropolitan Paris maintained a lead of *seven* times that of the next biggest city in France between 1831 and 1990.[13] That demographic gap, along with Paris's concentration of power and cultural institutions, gave it a national importance on a scale quite different from that of its English, German, and Austrian counterparts. Within France the enormous differential produced the common Parisian attitude of disdain for provincials—and a corresponding resentment among provincials.[14]

Paris had everything, and it had more of everything than any other French city. Its nineteenth-century boosters went further and asserted that its total sum of resources and functions made it greater and more complete than any other city in Europe. As Eugène Pelletan put it in the *Paris guide par les principaux écrivains et artistes de la France* (1867), "London is only a market; Berlin . . . only a university; Vienna only a concert; Florence . . . only a museum; St. Petersburg, only a garrison." But Paris was "a city that was at once commercial, industrial, poetic, artistic, literary, learned. . . ." Extending the view of the historian Jules Michelet and others that Paris was a marvelous concentrate of all the rich variety that made France so extraordinary, Pelletan maintained that the French capital best represented all of Europe and its peoples—and therefore should be their choice for "capital of Europe."[15] Toward the turn of the century, when Parisian poet François Coppée repeated the old tribute that Paris is "the world," containing an "infinite variety" of things human, he added the down-to-earth conclusion that "the true Parisian could, if need be, dispense with any travel."[16]

No one in the nineteenth century pushed the microcosm-and-apogee argument further than the widely revered writer Victor Hugo. In his introduction to the 1867 guide and in a later essay, he declared his beloved city "the sum" and the successor of the greatest cities of the past—Jerusalem, Athens, and Rome. Paris—building on their legacy of the True, the Beautiful, and the Great—had moved the world upward toward the ideal. Paris represented the highest achievements of humankind and all history. "Paris is a totality." "Everything that is elsewhere is in Paris." "All civilizations are there in summary form, and all barbarisms as well." "Paris is synonymous with the Cosmos. Paris is Athens, Rome, Sybaris, Jerusalem, Pantin [an industrial suburb]." "The city of light," "this masterpiece," was the highest expression of all humanity.[17] And Hugo's acclaim was the highest expressed in modern times. Coming from such a prestigious writer, these high-flying phrases carried exceptional weight, though they merely reiterated ideas that had been developing for centuries.

The poet Paul Valéry updated these paeans in 1927 in an essay that is noteworthy for its eloquent and remarkably direct answer to the question of Paris's greatness. In pointing up the city's exceptional range of functions and creations, his argument went far beyond the intellectual and cultural roles highlighted by Hugo. "Every great city is cosmopolitan and diverse," he observed, and every great city "is an immense gambling casino," where people come to get ahead and to take their chances, knowing that such places offer "the greatest number of chances and the greatest number of preys available—women, posts, knowledge, contacts, facilities of all kinds." But Paris stands out with its "essential character":

It is . . . in my eyes the most complete city in the world, for I do not see any place where the diversity of occupations, industries, functions, products, and ideas is richer and more intermingled than here.

To be, solely, the political, literary, scientific, financial, commercial, pleasure [*voluptuaire*], and luxury capital of a great country; representing all history, absorbing and concentrating all the thinking material as well as all the banking and financial facilities—and all this [at once], good and bad for the nation that it crowns, is what distinguishes the city of Paris from all the other giant cities.[18]

Although "complete" sounded like praise, Valéry acknowledged that the centralization of so many activities in Paris could be both good and bad for France. For more than a century, worried analysts of French society (since Louis-Sébastien Mercier just before the French Revolution) had decried the concentration of so many functions and resources in the capital as excessive and harmful to the whole country. It was a diagnosis that was made with increasing frequency in the interwar period. "Isn't there the risk that this big head will someday be too heavy for the equilibrium of the country?" asked the geographer Albert Demangeon in 1933, suggesting that the "tentacular" "monster" be scaled back by the government.[19] Valéry's essay with its all-stops-pulled-out fervor was the last notable tribute of its kind. Through the rest of the twentieth century the critics of the outsized capital held the upper hand in the debate, enjoying the support of national authorities and public opinion, especially outside Paris. From the perspective of the provinces the damage done was already alarming in the 1920s and '30s: while the "bloated city" grew ever bigger, once-lively villages and hamlets were dying.

This view of Paris as too large and powerful was later adopted by the ruralist and regionalizing Vichy state and the postwar (fourth) republic.[20] A series of decentralizing measures were put in place—from the 1950s to the 1990s. Yet the capital with its region remains as preponderant in population as two centuries earlier (with 11 million inhabitants in 2006 compared with 1.7 million for the closest provincial metropolis, Lyon).

And its "tentacular" power is still dominant, though the old cultural and economic gulf between it and the provinces has narrowed. Paris has remained a more "complete" great city than any other in France and more fully the all-purpose center of the nation than (even) London or any other European capital.[21]

INVIDIOUS COMPARISONS

Through the twentieth century, more than ever before, critics of the French capital pushed aside the panegyric tradition of Paris and pointed to other European cities as models to follow. The comparisons they made as would-be reformers tellingly highlighted serious shortcomings and problems in the capital. After the First World War, for example, as the liberated periphery and nearby *banlieue* around Paris began to fill up willy-nilly with shacks and bungalows, the playwright and reform advocate Jean Giraudoux pointed admiringly to Berlin's vast tracts of green space and more ordered, attractive outskirts. Paris's banlieue, wrote Giraudoux, had become "an appalling zone of wretchedness," "ugliness and sorrows"—a "no man's land, but [an] overpopulated [one]."[22] After the Second World War, urban planners once again pointed to the example of Berlin, whose well-designed reconstruction included ample public parks and gardens with trees in abundance. Berlin, Rome, London, and Vienna each provided nine times or more green space per resident than Paris did, reported a contributor to *Urbanisme* in 1957.[23] French urbanists also looked to postwar London as a model of regional planning, aimed at decongesting the core. Most resoundingly, the geographer J. F. Gravier, the chief Jeremiah of the anti-Paris set, lauded English plans for a "massive reduction of the central metropolitan area," shifting industry out and creating new satellite towns.[24]

While the old mantras—the most beautiful city, the capital of the civilized world—echoed on, Paris had already passed its pinnacle in several respects. It had lost its status as the third biggest city in the world by 1925, when Tokyo surpassed it (after London and New York). And it continued to drop in rank through the rest of the century. By 1950 it was sixth in population (after Shanghai), and by 1975 it was down to eleventh. In 1990 Greater Paris was fourteenth in the world—after such non-European metropolises as Tokyo, Mexico City, and São Paulo. At the end of the twentieth century Paris was no longer in the top twenty largest metropolises of the world, having been overtaken by such faraway newcomers as Bogota, New Delhi, Karachi, and Bangkok.[25]

A more serious blow to Parisian pride was a growing sense of the city's declining cultural leadership, epitomized by the loss of primacy in the art world after the Second World War. New York began claiming that it had taken the lead in the late 1940s, a challenge that French observers did not acknowledge for another decade. But American military and political hegemony was indisputable, along with the weaknesses of postwar France and its loss of great-power status. The onslaught of American merchandising (symbolized by Coca-Cola), the English language, and Hollywood movies was also obvious and, in the view of defenders of French civilization, an alarming danger. In that context came the strident American claims that the United States, long disparaged for vulgarity and superficiality, had become the world powerhouse of modern art too. French cultural leaders (Minister of Culture André Malraux in particular) reasserted Paris's importance in world art history by taking such masterpieces as the Mona Lisa and the Venus de Milo on tour abroad in the 1960s, but they could not deny New York's emergence as the new "capital of art"—as the matrix of the latest and boldest creations of the avant-garde (abstract expressionism above all) and the city where the most affluent market for art was flourishing.[26] Postwar London, too, took on increased importance as an international art market, challenging the longtime leader across the channel.[27]

More generally, Paris was losing its star-quality attractiveness and prestige, lamented observers of all stripes. The aggressive modernizing operations in the 1960s and the early 1970s produced intense discussion of not only the declining quality of life, but also the now-uncertain "international vocation" of Paris. Both the critics and defenders of the urbanists worried about the capital's diminished luster, its image and influence abroad—or what the French call its *rayonnement*. Polls in 1973–1974 revealed that only one out of a hundred foreigners, when asked if they would like to live in Paris, answered in the affirmative.[28]

That kind of report only confirmed what Parisians knew from everyday experience about their city's pollution, traffic jams, and high prices for housing and food. In 1973, Parisians learned that even the capital's famed restaurants were in decline. The bad news originated with the *Times* of London, which trumpeted it to the world: the food served in the "temples of 'la grande cuisine,'" such as Maxim's, Lasserre, and Allard, was no longer anything extraordinary. On the music scene, too, the news was bad: the city simply did not have the concentrations of "clubs, cabarets, pubs, and coffee houses" featuring rock that made its rivals "London, New York, Amsterdam or Berlin the cities that swing [*villes qui swinguent*]."[29] And in the creation of high fashion Italy had become a strong challenger to Paris, while "the prêt-à-porter" (ready-to-wear) industry of Broadway was taking the lead for the mass market.

Within Europe, London emerged as a particularly strong rival in the 1960s and 1970s. While Paris was slipping as a cultural center, London was getting notice worldwide for its bursts of creativity—in pop music (the Beatles, the Rolling Stones), fashion, design (Terence Conran), theater (Tom Stoppard, Harold Pinter), and art (Henry Moore, Barbara Hepworth). London's importance as a financial center strengthened in Europe with the United Kingdom's joining the Common Market in 1973. But in the 1980s the balance shifted back. Paris's ambition to be Europe's capital surged once more as London's economic and social problems escalated, and its infrastructure went into rapid decline under the budget-slashing government of Margaret Thatcher. Yet London still held the lead as a world city thanks to its long-standing role in international banking and investment and its close ties to the huge American market. It also had the advantage of having a language that was spoken by far more people around the world than French, facilitating the global marketing of its cultural products and financial services.[30]

In the 1990s, after the reunification of Germany, Berlin began to stand out as a potential capital of a Europe whose center of gravity was shifting toward the east. The restored capital plunged into a whirlwind of rebuilding the eastern half and the central zone where the infamous wall had run. Reuniting the sectors long divided by the Cold War sharply increased Berlin's museum-and-monument attractions. "The city possesses everything in double," noted *Le Monde* in 2001. Its more than 2,300 permanent institutes, 170 museums, nine symphonic orchestras, more than a hundred choirs, and three opera halls added up to a wealth of cultural offerings hard to match anywhere.[31] The energy and excitement of renewal—in the economy, the infrastructure, and the arts—threatened to make Paris the stodgy, feeble elder of European capitals.

After the Iron Curtain fell, Prague too became a new standard of comparison. With its new accessibility, it quickly emerged as a fresh and exciting destination for international tourism. Although much smaller than Paris and economically weak, it was stunningly rich in beautiful old buildings, and its historic urban fabric was unspoiled by freeways, parking lots, and office towers. As early as 1991 the anti-urbanist organization S.O.S. Paris editorialized with an unprecedented nod to the east: "Without the ravages committed over the last century Paris would be as beautiful as Prague, where Parisians rush headlong today."[32]

By the late twentieth century, the increase in travel and exchange of information throughout the European Community yielded a greater consciousness of all Europe's major cities, making it harder to toss off the old self-regarding Paris tributes. For example, Paris could no longer claim its historic status as the mecca of carnal pleasures, reported a French guidebook to "Sexy Paris" in 2000. While providing an ample listing of addresses for "sex-shops, pick-up places, swingers' clubs [clubs échangistes], gay bars, [and] erotic bookstores," the book added the deflating comment that the Parisian scene was no longer what it had been in the heyday of Le Guide Rose in the 1920s: much of the clientele had "disappeared with the closing of the legalized brothels" in 1946. The guide, traditionally the kind of publication to boast, frankly acknowledged that the French Babylon had been outstripped by Madrid, Amsterdam, and Hamburg in the second half of the century. "Sexy Paris" was no longer "the capital of love at a price [l'amour tarifé]."[33]

In many more important ways, Paris around 2000 still boasted plenty of attractions, special appeal, and mystique. And even with its diminished international standing by a number of measures, it remained the world's most popular tourist destination and convention site. Its tourist attractions are well known and easy to enumerate. More difficult to pin down are the unique attributes and winning distinctions of the city as a whole. The next two sections offer a historical perspective on these matters by highlighting the traits and comparisons that well-informed, authoritative French observers have emphasized in portraying Paris.

SINGULARITIES

In trying to capture what makes Paris unique, observers have pointed to everything from particular visible features to general, highly subjective characteristics—its beauty, its genius, its atmosphere, and its "soul" (to be examined in the next chapter). Paris, historian Alfred Fierro tells us, is the only city in the world that has bookstalls along its riverbank (about 250 of them today)—an odd detail, but in historical context a detail that underscores the city's long-standing distinction as an intellectual center. Similar in effect are boasts about the city having the most beautiful "square" in the world— the Place de la Concorde—and the most beautiful avenue in the world—the Champs-Élysées: these fit together into the generalizing acclaim for "the most beautiful city in the world." Such accolades have been passed on as articles of faith among admiring writers and Parisians for more than a century.[34]

For grand assertions about Paris, no one since Hugo has outdone the patriotic and deeply religious writer Charles Péguy, passionate in both his love and hate for the capital. His essay of 1913 on "temporal glory" set

FIGURE 5.1. Admirers of Paris's beautiful boulevards have habitually turned a blind eye to the traffic that choked streets—even before the automobile era. The Place de l'Opéra, looking toward the Boulevard des Capucines (circa 1900). (Postcard, private collection.)

out a long litany of superlatives and paradoxical contrasts that set Paris apart. He begins with variations on the "capital" theme: "always capital in the history of the world, temporal capital of the world, intellectual capital of the world, . . . and spiritual capital." Then he hails it (with italicized emphasis) as "the city that has suffered most for the temporal salvation of humanity." Thus begins a cascade of tributes that continues for over ten pages—a prose poem cadenced like classical oratory, sentences flowing on and on without a break, clause building on clause, stretching into entire paragraphs and even whole pages. "Unique city in the world, the most intellectual . . . for the intellectuals, and . . . the most pleasurable for the pleasure seekers, the most carnal for the carnal; . . . the most modern, the newest . . . of all the modern cities, the oldest, the most historic, the most authentic, the most traditional of the ancient cities." "City . . . of the most solitude . . . city of the most gathering together." "The most serious city, the most frivolous city. . . . City of the most culture. City of the most empty chatter. . . . City where the most vice is sold, where the most prayer is given. City of perdition. City of salvation. . . . City radiating . . . the most intelligence in the world. . . . Brain where the most thought is elaborated. . . . Heart whence comes the . . . truest prayer."[35] Thus, rising rhetorically into the high thin air of the unverifiable, Péguy penned the ultimate exposition of the capital's distinctive and antithetical traits.

Celebrations of Paris's uniqueness pass lightly over the fact that the city has copied some of its most prominent features from other metropolises. Ancient Rome inspired the triumphal arches (the Portes Saint-Denis and Saint-Martin) and the classical domes (the Invalides and the Collège de France) constructed in the seventeenth century. More Roman-style monuments appeared during Napoleon's reign. His Arc du Carrousel was modeled on that of Septimius Severus in the Roman Forum; the column in the Place Vendôme was modeled after the Trajan column; and the church of the Madeleine was inspired by a Roman Temple of Victory. Napoleon's nephew, the Emperor Louis Napoleon, drew inspiration rather from a great modern city, London, and its spacious parks and squares: his idea for developing the Bois de Boulogne, for example, derived from Hyde Park. A century later, Manhattan and Chicago provided Parisian urbanists with models of skyscraper modernity.

But Paris is much more than its borrowings, and it is unlike any of its models. Its structures represent the incremental work and accumulated styles of a long history, a history going back many centuries further than Berlin's. Its centuries of construction have been unbroken by caesuras like London's great fire of 1666. Paris's continuity through two millennia has given it a "permanence through the centuries that Rome and Athens do not have to the same degree," historian Jean Bastié observed in concluding his recent history of the city in the twentieth century.[36] Thus the leading French historian of contemporary Paris reissued, with only a slight qualification (about degree), the grand historical note of distinction asserted long before by Hugo and Valéry—that the city embodies and represents all preceding Western civilization.

Some other important ways in which Paris is distinctive can be demonstrated precisely by quantitative comparisons. One of those is population density. The central city is home to more people per square kilometer than that of any other European big city—and Tokyo as well. The eighty quarters of Paris (an area of 10,539 hectares or 26,042 acres) are home to 20,421 inhabitants per square kilometer, compared to London's 4,482 inhabitants per kilometer (with a total surface area of 1,578 square kilometers). *Greater* Paris (the "agglomeration") is also more densely populated—at a rate of 5,000 inhabitants per square kilometer compared to Greater London's 3,800 per square kilometer and New York's 2,900.[37] The old intra-muros core, in other words, retains more of a residential function than do the centers of other metropolises. Yet that central city, which made the claim to greatness in the nineteenth century, declined in population from the early 1920s: by the end of the century it had only 2,116,000 residents (1999), and that placed it at the *hundredth* rank of cities in the world. The 2007 census showed a small increase (68,000), marking a reversal of the twentieth-century's long-term decline—largely the result of more tall high-density housing.

One regular source of such precise data is the municipal magazine (titled *À Paris*), distributed by the mayor's office to all residents. Though it is given to Paris boosting at every opportunity, it also sets out exact figures on all manner of comparative urban matters from time to time, allowing readers to check for inflated impressions. Take, for example, the matter of the city's well-known wealth of museums. "Paris is the greatest museum city [*ville-musée*] in the world," referring to the capital's wealth of museums, monuments, and art, Jacques Bonnet declares in a 1994 book on world "métropoles." To support his claim, he gives the tally of museums in the Île-de-France as 200, half of them in Paris.[38] The number is impressive, but it is dropped on the reader with no comparable count given for London, Berlin, New York, or other contenders for that title. More helpfully, the mayor's publication *Paris en chiffres* gives a total of 134 for Paris, 167 for Berlin, and 150 for New York.[39]

Sorbonne historian Jean Bastié's recent tome in the series *Nouvelle Histoire de Paris* illustrates even better than the mayor's publications a Parisian reflex tendency to consider the city the world leader and to stretch as far as possible in marshaling evidence of it. Both the first and last chapters are filled with statements declaring the singularity and superiority of Paris. Twice Bastié points out that "geographically, Paris is at the center of the world." His explanation calls upon us to see for ourselves: if you take a globe in your hands and turn it to put France in the position of the north pole, you will see Paris in the center of the northern hemispheres and the most heavily populated land masses. London enjoys "the same advantage," he concedes, "but . . . New York, Tokyo, Los Angeles, and many other metropolises" do not.[40]

A table in the first chapter shows "the world rank of Paris" on a number of scores, listed alphabetically, beginning with the stock market.[41] In that domain, Paris ranked eighth, measured by the totals of funds and of trades made—behind London, New York, Boston, Tokyo, San Francisco, Zurich, and Los Angeles in 1998. Altogether Paris places first in five categories: as a tourist destination, a place for international meetings and conventions (*congrès internationaux*), a center of luxury and fashion, a "gastronomic center," and a rail "platform."

Some of these assessments of Paris's importance are readily quantifiable, while others are not. In the matter of tourism, Bastié's statistics show Paris enjoying an impressive lead in the number of tourists (foreign and provincial, stays of any length, all kinds of lodging), but the figures for the total of nights involved or the total amount of money spent are not known. To give a (very) rough estimate of the number of visitors in a recent year

(1999)—70 million—he adds an estimated 50 million foreign tourists, who at least passed through the capital, together with an estimate for provincials and French overseas residents, many of whom stayed not in hotels but with friends and family. (Official figures put the total of foreign tourists at 25 million in 2004, 26 million in 2005, and 27 million in 2006.)[42] For the distinction as the world's favorite convention city the statistics are more precise: Paris was host to 280 of them in the year 1999, counting gatherings of more than 300 participants, at least 40 percent of whom were foreigners, and at least five nationalities, spending a minimum of three days.

In most of the categories, Bastié's table does not provide figures for other cities, leaving unclear the degrees of difference in the comparisons. On tourism, for example, contemporary London has been not far behind in attracting tourists (19 million compared with Paris's 21 million in 1998), according to other sources.[43] For the distinction of being the world's leading center of luxury, fashion, and gastronomy, no supporting evidence is offered. As a "center of telecommunications," publishing, and scientific research, no rank is indicated or comparative data provided. The ranking of Paris as the world's leading rail center is supported by a combined statistical total—with no breakdown given—of travelers, arrivals, and departures for all stations, adding up to 99.5 million.

A number of other statements about the city's extraordinary standing, scattered through the book, are plausible and noteworthy though difficult to support with statistics. Paris, one of the world's most cosmopolitan cities (he lists nine), "is perhaps the one that most attracts the persecuted and the proscribed of the entire world."[44] "Paris is the best known city in the world through literature, poetry . . . , theater, music, painting, the arts, cinema and especially popular song," the master historian writes. And: "For the rest of the world, it's a magical city." "What appears to us the essential characteristic of Paris," Bastié declares, "is its extraordinary aptitude for creativity." At another point he notes that "Paris is one of the best equipped cities of its size in the world, and one of the least polluted, where one can move about the most easily by public transport. All that in a physical and architectural environment [that is] the most pleasing of any. The possibility of finding entertainment and taking in cultural or leisure activities is at least as great as in all the other great cities of the world, and safety is not less there."[45]

Putting it into international perspective, Bastié concludes: "In reality, the sole rivals of Paris are London, New York, Los Angeles, and Tokyo"—all of them world or "global cities" of the first rank, above a second order of about twenty cities, such as Berlin, Moscow, Amsterdam, Chicago, Buenos Aires, Shanghai, Beijing, Singapore, and Hong Kong.[46] While acknowledging contemporary rivals all over the globe, this assessment reflects the city's long-standing reputation but does not provide historical perspective. Other recent historians *have* offered it: as extraordinarily attractive, dynamic, and creative as present-day Paris is, the Ville Lumière is no longer the premier beacon of progress that it was known to be in 1900.[47]

TERMS OF ENDEARMENT

In the end, several affective notions of Paris's distinctiveness stand out as the most commonly held and most important over the years since the nineteenth century. Grounded in emotional response more than comparative data, they take us back to the question of what makes Paris so beloved: this section provides an examination of the classic answers, passed on in a variety of formats. Foremost are the city's aesthetic and optimally human qualities, as described by proud Parisians and visitors. Perceptions of those qualities, like most judgments of Paris, are inescapably subjective and manifold, but they are not boundlessly diverse. Most follow the channels of long-standing conventions, prearranged ways of thinking that have shaped dreams and characterizations of Paris over many generations. Clichéd and impressionistic though they are, they can help us see the city as many have seen it over generations, and that can give us a better understanding of the thinking and feeling behind oft-repeated accolades.

A longtime favorite theme in the praise of Paris is the cityscape's peerless beauty, in which harmony is a major element. What the critics of Haussmann's work decried as stultifying uniformity, its admirers (including Haussmann himself) lauded as a splendid balance of regularity and variety, its many parts artfully united. In his memoirs Haussmann quoted with pride the municipal architect who stated the ideal as accomplished reality: "The transformation of Paris is a multiple work, embracing several great divisions, which join together to form an ensemble, a complete and harmonious whole ['un tout complet et harmonieux']." "Everything fits together in a beautiful city," proclaimed a defender of Paris's historic styles of architecture around 1900. In Paris, Péguy boasted, "so many beauties of so many ages are directly wedded to each other, all work together in accord . . . with the beauty of the city, with the total beauty."[48] Phrases like "harmonious whole" became commonplace in books and articles praising the Haussmannian core—while ignoring the lack of harmony outside it.

Other talk of the splendidly harmonious has referred to a seamless interweaving of past and present in the city. "Whereas in cities such as Athens or Rome, the past dominates or effaces every presence, and in the cities of America the present hides the absence of any past, in Paris there is harmony, [an] equilibrium of the two," declared Parisian writer Léon Bopp in 1957, adding: "for Paris knows how to remember and to exist at the same time." "Survivals and relics of more than two thousand years— Roman, Gallic, Christian, barbarian, medieval or Gothic, renaissance or classical, modern, revolutionary or ultra-modern"—all have their place

FIGURE 5.2. Away from the celebrated "beau Paris" and boulevards of Haussmannian order and harmony, disparate beautiless buildings abound, like the ones shown here near the périphérique (the ring expressway) in the eighteenth arrondissement bordering the suburb Saint-Ouen. (Photo by the author, 2006.)

and there is no "dissonance," he insisted. "All the epochs fit together like the pieces of a puzzle, or they blend like perfumes or tastes or sounds or colors that are complementary, harmonic, in this immense Paris that is conservative and conservatory, collector and conciliator of so many memories of the past."[49]

As opponents of urbanist operations in both the nineteenth and twentieth centuries saw it, the harmony of the cityscape was the result of a long process of *natural* growth and evolution that had been had brutally disrupted by Haussmann in the 1850s and '60s and then again by the modernizers of the 1960s. Yet in important ways that "natural" growth has not been well proportioned and harmonious. It has resulted in an imbalance between the poor eastern side and the fortunate west, which has long concerned twentieth-century planners and commentators. And it has produced a stark imbalance between the expanding agglomeration and the intra-muros city, increasingly so since the 1950s.[50]

But admirers of the city's unique beauty have had in mind much more than architectural harmony and Haussmannian order. "Paris is indisputably the greatest and the most beautiful city known up to now," maintained an early, best-selling guidebook in 1706, echoing lines commonplace since the Middle Ages. [51] That aesthetic judgment has been perhaps the most subjective and variously understood of all the claims made about Paris. What exactly makes it beautiful in the eyes of its admirers? Each Parisian has his or her own vision of the city—a vision shaped by childhood and youth, values, and dreams, as Parisian-born Julian Green noted, and each has "a secret preference for the Paris he has tucked away in his memory as being more beautiful than that of his neighbor's."[52] Those personal preferences, of course, have been much more disparate than the notions of beauty perpetuated by literature of tourism. Some, such as Jacques Prévert and Brassaï, have appreciated above all "the beauty of sinister things"—"those deserted quays, desolate streets, that district of outcasts, crawling with tarts . . ." so commonplace in the thirteenth and fourteenth arrondissements. Some have found beauty even in the most derelict old slums (*îlots insalubres*) of the twentieth century. Many have loved the Old-Paris look of ramshackle dwellings and rustic streets in hilly Belleville-Ménilmontant, as photographed by Willy Ronis in the 1950s. And some have even delighted in the homely villages and wastelands of the poor people's banlieue, prior to the modernizing projects of the 1950s.[53]

Much more often, the natural setting of the city has been extolled for its beauty. Péguy, for example, described Paris as "the city of three hills, equidistant, equilateral, equitable, this circle of hills, . . . wisely, intelligently spaced, discreetly, elegantly disposed."[54] Since the Romantics, the aesthetic favorites of most people have been the Seine with its *quais* and its twenty-eight bridges, the parks (especially Luxembourg, Monceau, the Bois de Boulogne), and cemeteries (especially Père Lachaise)—peaceful

FIGURE 5.3. The Square du Vert Galant, a serene oasis on the tip of the Cité island, is surrounded by archetypical elements of Parisian beauty—the Seine at its most charming, the picturesque Pont Neuf ("new" when completed in 1607), and monumental masterworks on each side—the Louvre in all its grandeur on the right bank and the domed Institut de France on the left. (Photo by the author, 2004.)

places where nature inspires reverie. La Seine—not too wide and not too narrow—is a key "amenity" in the center, as Georges Sand observed. The gentle river and "the soft clarity of its reflections" worked together with the temperate climate, moist air, and silky-rose or pearl-toned skies to produce a "cheerful" setting. Fondness for the Seine, like the love of Paris generally, was selective, to be sure. It did not extend to the industrial eastern part—around the Tolbiac Bridge, for example, where the banks were strewn with rusting iron and broken glass through most of the twentieth century. "There are really two Seines: the rich and the poor," observed journalist Henri Calet, a lover of Paris who hurried to the more attractive part of the river with an almost erotic passion, viewing "her" as "young, fresh, [and] lovable," especially in the springtime.[55]

Other perennial favorites include the ordered perspectives of Paris, especially the long vista stretching from the Louvre through the Tuileries garden, the Place de la Concorde, and the Champs-Élysées to the Arc de Triomphe and beyond to La Défense—a thoroughfare known as "the triumphal way" since the French "victory" in the First World War. That famed vista reflects classical reason and taste, as the guidebooks emphasize, but it also owes much to the fury and destructiveness of the Communards, who opened up the view by burning down the Tuileries Palace in 1871. When the newly created Commission des Perspectives Monumentales parisiennes made its choices of beautiful sites it believed to be in imminent danger in 1930, it obtained protection for the Esplanade des Invalides and the Champs-Élysées from Concorde to the Rond-Point, along with some outlying places of natural beauty, such as the Île de la Folie in the Bois de Boulogne.[56] The perspective preferred by lovers of Old Paris—the view of the Seine and the riverbanks from the Pont Neuf, the border of antique buildings, the other old bridges, the islands and their quays—received state protection in 1973, followed by UNESCO designation as a World Heritage Site in 1991, after years of development nearby threatening the historic setting and the skyline.

Still another oft-mentioned part of Paris's beauty is its great assortment of "monuments," a term that has included churches and the Louvre as well as the Arc de Triomphe and statues. "Paris is the first for the number and beauty of its monuments," declared the guidebook *Paris Complete*:

FIGURE 5.4. The most prestigious classic vista of the City of Light: the Champs-Élysées as it looked circa 1900 from the top of the Arc de Triomphe—without automobiles. (Courtesy of the Library of Congress, LC-DIG-ppmsc-05202.)

A New Alphabetical Guide for the Traveller in Paris (1855), following the standard practice of not offering any specific comparison with, say, Rome or Venice.[57] But the beauty of many monuments has been debatable and sometimes quite controversial. The basilica Sacré-Coeur and the Eiffel Tower were as heatedly denounced in the nineteenth century as the Pompidou Center, the Montparnasse Tower, and the Bastille Opéra were in the twentieth.[58] Strong objections, however, have generally died out with the passage of time. By the 1920s the Eiffel Tower, for example, had become widely accepted as a beautiful structure, and not merely as a gigantic novelty and engineering tour de force. What helped sway opinion, no doubt, was that leading artists and poets (Robert and Sonia Delaunay, Raoul Dufy, Apollinaire, Jean Cocteau, Charles Trenet) imaginatively invoked images of the tower in their works.

In contrast, the hundreds of statues of "great men," which the early Third Republic erected in parks and squares throughout the city, did not even begin to win public acceptance after decades in place. Opinion polls in the 1920s showed that the Third Republic's statues (550 statues added between 1870 and 1914!) were considered the ugliest features of the capital—especially the big overwrought ones. During the Occupation the Germans destroyed many of those monuments for their own ideological reasons—and to reclaim the metal. After the war, Parisian authorities, accepting the public's verdict of decades before, made no effort to replace the missing figures.[59]

For many, the beauty of Paris lies first and foremost in the *ensemble* of monuments, streets, squares, buildings, rooftops, and perspectives. Tourists and hometown connoisseurs alike have long taken great pleasure in seeing the whole from such vantages as the Butte Montmartre, church towers, and—from 1889 on—the Eiffel Tower. A guidebook of 1828 recommended the tower of Notre-Dame, the Vendôme Column, "and especially the Buttes Chaumont" for views of the "magnificent panorama" of the "immense capital."[60] The Romantic poets of the 1830s were most struck by "the sea of roofs" and the view, in all directions, of countless chimneys, mansards, rain gutters, weather vanes, and sparrows.[61] Historian Jules Michelet, who climbed to the top of Notre-Dame and the Arc de Triomphe regularly for years to admire the view, found the sight beautiful in its "immensity" and "uniformity," but paradoxically he also found it "beautiful in its variety, the gathering together of all styles, representing the résumé of the world." Often repeating the cliché "the most beautiful city in the world," he was that rare observer who had actually seen Rome, London, and other capitals of Europe and had come away certain that "the form of Paris is more beautiful."[62]

This was not just hometown favoritism. In the nineteenth and twentieth centuries, leading citizens of rivals Berlin and London readily agreed with Michelet's judgment. Worldly-wise Londoners in the late nineteenth century considered their city downright ugly: lacking axial vistas, it had more extensive slum housing and traffic congestion than Paris and fewer splendid public buildings. After having visited Paris, Lord John Manners wrote to the prime minister in the late 1860s: "As F[irst] C[ommissioner] [of the Metropolitan Board of Works] I do not think that I can ever hold up my head again having witnessed the contrast between the two Capitals."[63] Berliners who decried their city's lack of beauty early in the twentieth century

FIGURE 5.5. The Parc de Belleville, built in 1988, provides a spectacular panoramic view of the city—but no trace of the old hillside neighborhood that was destroyed. The eleven acres of sloping green space (below the Rue Piat) were formerly filled with winding narrow streets (the Rue Vilin, the Passage Julien Lacroix), stairways, and small houses. (Photo by the author, June 2002.)

("the capital of all modern ugliness"—"shapeless, prosaically commercial-industrial, and short on historical edifices") had no reason to change their minds decades later. Hitler's opinions on the matter were shared by most Germans; he found Berlin ugly and considered Paris the most beautiful.[64]

From our present perspective how can it be so clear that Paris was and is more beautiful than, say, Venice and Rome? Given the multiple standards for judgment and the incommensurable entities being judged, one might conclude that it is futile to try to compare the beauty of Europe's great cities. Clearly, Paris lovers have not broached that thought. Centuries of their enthusiastic advocacy, combined with Paris's undeniable charms, have made the notion of its superior beauty virtually axiomatic in minds around the world.

Finally, the rhapsodies about Paris have long emphasized the city's exceptionally *human* qualities. On this theme, Parisians have given us many commentaries—vivid disquisitions steeped in their sensibilities and cultural memory. Even the topographical form of Paris is human, laid out like a prone body, according to imaginative minds in the nineteenth and twentieth centuries, building on a poetic tradition that has developed since the fourteenth century. "The [main] artery is the river; the heart, the Île de la Cité that surrounds Notre-Dame; the lungs, the Bois de Boulogne and the Bois de Vincennes; the artistically curved nervous system, the outer boulevards; the epidermis, the rail line circling Paris [*la petite ceinture*]," explained the German writer Friedrich Sieburg in 1930, reiterating and updating the Parisian poetic tradition.[65] More commonly, poets and songsmiths have focused on the many human activities and the various emotions of the city-person: Paris laughs, sings, dances, works and plays, drinks and eats, sleeps and awakes, rejoices, mourns, weeps, grumbles, and rages.[66]

After the nineteenth-century revolutions, as we have seen, Paris personified has usually been cast as a woman—commonly an alluring, charming, seductive, capricious young woman. Yet French writers over the last century have not been consistent in the choice of Paris's gender—any more than those in the nineteenth century were. They have invoked a masculine figure when discussing the city in its political and nation-governing roles. Otherwise, popular imagery has typically pictured it in a feminine form and with a lively, flirtatious personality, in contrast to the staid classical feminine forms representing French provincial cities, most visibly in public statues. As for rival cities elsewhere in Europe, some of them too—notably Berlin and London—have been represented in feminine forms in some periods of their history (Berlin in the 1920s, for example). But in neither case was that imagery enduring and dominant. More generally, Berlin and London have appeared with a masculine face and character.[67] Far more than for these rivals, Paris's feminine representation has been etched in imaginations far and near, associating the city with such stereotypically feminine interests as love and fashion.

Along with its beauty, Paris has long been identified with extraordinary human intelligence—or a brain, as Péguy put it. From the earliest flowering of the Sorbonne in the late Middle Ages, the city was a renowned intellectual center. Victor Hugo, perhaps most famously, portrayed Paris as a great thinking being, generating world-transforming ideas for humanity's liberation and greater happiness. As the progenitor of humanizing progress and democracy, Paris was the *civitas humana*, succeeding the *civitas Dei* that was Rome.[68] Historian Charles Simond, reflecting on outbursts of anger and joy in the city, stressed in 1900 both intellectual and emotional bases of Paris's special humanness. The novelist and poet Jules Romains took this line of thought even further by portraying individual squares and streets as living beings with different personalities and minds.[69]

Historian Louis Chevalier is the only notable scholar to have anchored notions of the city's human character in a verifiable demographic singularity: intra-muros Paris's great population density (over 20,000 inhabitants per square kilometer). That density results in an exceptionally intense collective experience—shared daily rhythms of work, eating, sleeping, and even a shared affective life, he argues.[70] Although his conclusions about a collective Parisian personality (to be examined in the next chapter) are far from convincing, his observation about the almost constant human presence does ring true for most quarters of the city (the *beaux quartiers* to the west being an exception): human faces, eyes, voices, and gestures are almost omnipresent (and unavoidable) in streets, shops, cafés, métro, parks, and squares. In Paris, "it is hard to be lonely; there is always another pair of eyes, not unfriendly, appraising you," American writer Adam Gopnik noted at the end of the twentieth century. "We go to cities to be invisible, or to be invisible and visible by turns, and it is hard to be invisible in Paris."[71]

But in historical perspective, as older Parisians can readily testify, that plethora of human presence had diminished markedly over the second half of the twentieth century: disappearing were street singers, pushcart vendors, newspaper hawkers, concierges at every entrance, ticket punchers (*poinçonneurs*) in the métro stations and on the buses, along with many small shopkeepers and artisans. Still, to an extraordinary (if not unique) degree, Parisians go about daily life crowded with others in small spaces and in virtually unavoidable social contact. On this aspect of the famously "human city" in our time, the essayist Adam Gopnik again offers clear-cut, unabashedly personal observations, based on a comparison with New York—and apparently not shaped by the long tradition of commentary emphasizing Parisian sociability. One of things he missed most, he tells us, is the "consensual anonymity" and "the comforting loneliness of life in New York": in Paris, "no relationship, even one with a postman or a dry cleaner, is abstract or anonymous; human relationships are carved out in a perpetual present tense."[72]

The city's exceptionally human character became a key point of pride for twentieth-century defenders of its historic scale and architecture. Even before the First World War, urbanist Eugène Hénard called for preserving Paris as a beautifully crafted masterwork, "a penetrating poetry made of grace and art," which stood in stark contrast to London with its expansive, "tumultuous Thames" and the "crushing aspect" of Manhattan with its "gigantic suspended bridge, its colossal statue, [and] its twenty-story houses."[73] As outsized buildings and new freeways made inroads on the historic cityscape in the 1960s, the human measure found in the old norms became a commonplace in critiques of the new—with fresh appreciation of the building heights that did not overwhelm people in the streets or extend upward beyond their view.

But to the anti-urbanists and lovers of Paris generally, the humanity of the city went far beyond the dimensions of buildings. As the militant organization S.O.S. Paris put it: "We want Paris to remain a human city where it's good to live, where different social layers and trades remain intermingled, even if each quarter has its own distinct character." The old vision of an intimate, convivial community—the populist Paris called Paname—re-surfaced in nostalgic older Parisians as well as anti-urbanist circles.[74] While mourning the passing of that more "human city," some have also taken up the cause of nurturing a memory of it, championing nostalgia as a much-needed enhancement of the present.[75] But for many today (as the next chapter shows), the city is still delightfully human—when viewed through the lens of a beloved, familiar neighborhood, its street market and remaining small shops, and walking-distance compactness.

All in all, through the vicissitudes of recent centuries, the chorus of voices exalting Paris over other cities has been stronger and more continuous than any that its principal rivals have enjoyed. Comparisons with London, in particular, have been most important for defining Paris's distinctiveness. London has consistently been ahead in population, territory, and power as a financial center, but its superiority by those measures has not dimmed Paris's star status. London's great size has been disparaged by, among others, Disraeli and Henry James, as a crushing immensity, dull and plain . . . or worse. "London has always been an ugly city," declares the distinguished English historian of the city, Peter Ackroyd, adding: ugliness "is part of its identity."[76] In the same manner of generalizing about hard-to-compare variables, Paris has been deemed beautiful and harmonious—and lauded for its human-scale, village-like sociability, and pleasure offerings, all unmatched by London.

"No city [is] more beautiful, more complete, more human," the historian Michelet concluded succinctly, writing well before Haussmann's operations.[77] That triad of comparative praise is clearly still in circulation and can still pass as plausible, remarkably, given the many drastic changes seemingly diminishing those qualities. Remarkably enduring, too, is the general tradition of idealizing description that (as we have seen) has fastened onto a historical core of Parisian worlds. Today, recognizable forms of those worlds, enhanced by memories and dreams, clearly win over many besides history buffs. The "city's appeal and the quality of life that it can offer should not be underestimated," concludes a recent study of *Capitals of Capital*.[78] Thanks to its appeal and possibilities it offers for living well, the economic historian observes, Paris not only surpasses other great cities as a tourist destination, but also rivals Frankfurt as a financial center and, more than any other continental city, can "hold its own with London" as an attractive place for doing big business. In this realm of appeal, mystique, and perceptions, more than in matter-of-fact data, there are strong grounds for maintaining, as of old, that Paris is nonpareil.

CHAPTER 6

Contemporary Paris—
Images, Spirit, Soul, and Sites

Characterizing the personality or the "soul" of Paris has never been more difficult than it is now. The inherited tropes do not provide much help. The image of a beautiful seductive woman seems incompatible with to-day's traffic-clogged boulevards and expressways and the crazy quilt of *banlieues*. The vision of Paris as a paradise surrounded by "a circular pur-gatory" is similarly far-fetched.[1] So is the "Paname" image of a village-like French community for the de-industrialized, gentrifying world city (its old working-class café-and-street life almost gone). To portray the city as a pleasure dome is even more obviously inadequate, describing only a small number of places and times. And there has never been a popular image for Greater Paris in all its sprawling diversity.

An alternative approach, taken by generations of writers, has been to offer sketches of the people of Paris, especially colorful types, as a por-trayal of the metropolis. A handful of distinctive types long served: the elegant Parisienne and the *midinette* (the vivacious working girl), the stal-wart *mécano*, the street-smart brassy gamin (the *titi*), and the *maquereau* ("mackerel" or pimp). But in the second half of the twentieth century with all its modernizing transformations, they all but disappeared. The *titi* and the *maquereau*, for example, were gone by the 1980s, as historian Louis Chevalier sadly noted, and no replacements have emerged. Recent efforts to characterize Parisians, such as Louis Chevalier's *Les Parisiens* and Alain Schifres's *Parisiens*, have produced a large gallery of portraits that point up diversity above all—the differences between the born Parisian and the resident still attached to provincial roots, the bourgeois and the worker, women and men. The dissimilarities come through more convincingly than generalizations about the whole population. Parisians themselves see their differences as readily as their commonalties.[2] Even in the realm of the imaginary, as we have seen, Paris has been plural and heterogeneous in its historic guises and character—as a grand world capital, as a garden of pleasures, and as an assemblage of villages.

To understand Paris we must some somehow encompass its vast complexity without reductionism. What we need is a way of comprehending that does justice to the city's multiple facets and moods, the many functions and roles it performs, and the unending series of deaths and rebirths that its parts undergo. This is an old problem that is arguably even more difficult now than in the nineteenth century when such imaginative writers as Balzac and Hugo, Baudelaire and Zola devoted their genius to capturing the emergent "grande ville," turning out volume after volume of tableaux and story-telling.[3] Now more than ever, it takes imagination, combined with first-hand knowledge, to understand Paris. Contemporary Parisians who bring both to the task—writers, artists, everyday people—may be able to help us. What follows is an exploration of the images, places, and memories that matter most to them.

IMAGININGS, SYMBOLS, AND MAPS

Most Parisians and visitors know only parts of the city from direct experience, but have picked up images of the whole from literary depictions, paintings (the Impressionists above all), movies (Hollywood's as much as French), histories, and guidebooks. How to relate the parts to the whole is an old question that requires us to choose from several possibilities. At one end of the spectrum is the answer given by poetic *flâneurs*, unhurried strollers who closely observed everything from the street and relished both the surprising sights and the familiar dear "old stones." They loved the Paris they discovered daily—in random fragments—and they felt no desire to change it. Other street-level versions of the city come from ordinary working Parisians going about their daily routines: their "blind" individual trajectories form unrecognized networks that collectively constitute a mundane whole.[4] At the other end of the spectrum is the rationalist planner who conceives the city as a legible system of functions and structures. The urbanist focuses particularly on the malfunctioning parts and envisions wholesale correctives. Passing over the picturesque and the incidental, this approach looks to an imagined, abstract order in the future.

Both the sentimental and the rationalist ways of viewing are inadequate and misleading in important ways. Neither offers understanding of the ever-changing nature of the city. Both have tended to treat Paris as a living being in decline, and both have led to alarm about its approaching death—with the dreaded end always just ahead. Even the great historian Louis Chevalier fell into that mode of thinking instead of taking the longer view of the city as continuously dying and reborn. Why did he not see that as distinctive old structures have disappeared, others were emerging—in different forms or in different quarters? Deeply attached to the old popular Paris that he had known his entire life, he could not conceive that the new Beaubourg, for example, could be grafted into the living city—and could be *liked* by many Parisians, especially younger ones (Chevalier, born in 1911, was in his late fifties and early sixties during the Pompidou presidency). Many Parisians in the late twentieth century in fact embraced the new.[5] The city that Chevalier declared "assassinated" in the 1960s and 1970s lives on four decades later—and even thrives.

While thinking of Paris as a changing but enduring being, we need not think of it as possessing a single personality or soul—or one gender. There is too much to fit into any one image, especially a human one. Long ago, it took a big leap of imagination to picture the city as a beautiful and charming woman. Now the challenge is to think of the city as having multiple faces, multiple "hearts" or centers, and multiple personalities, the plural helping capture more facets of the city. Yet a plural image is more difficult to conjure and to hold in mind. We are left wondering if some unifying form can be found for the diversity of representations.

On a fundamental level Paris is a richly built-up site on a stretch of the Seine valley packed with famed old churches, palaces, monuments, vistas and squares, dwellings of diverse sizes, stores, theaters, music halls, restaurants, and cafés. How to visualize it all? Usually it is done by a resort to that classic of reductionist selectivity—synecdoche. Prominent monuments such as the Eiffel Tower and Sacré-Coeur have commonly served as emblems for the whole. Tourism promoters and artists have made those monuments familiar representations of Paris recognized everywhere. Alternatively, there is the city's official symbol—an armorial seal displaying a ship surmounted by a crenellated-castle crown and a band of fleurs-de-lis.[6]

Better yet: a map. The mapped lineaments of the city—with the sinuous course of the Seine through the middle—have become an emblem familiar to many, especially in France. Perhaps most widely recognized is the métro map. The station names along the most frequented lines have long been evocative sites of memory for Parisians, and the ability to recite them like a litany confirms one Parisian to another.[7] The outlines of the arrondissements form another orienting pattern that is uniquely Paris's: spiraling out from the center, they look like an escargot's shell, as the popular writer Alexandre Arnoux has pointed out.[8] But for most writers the mapped outline of the city has been the prime image to conjure with: its oval form obviously resembles . . . an egg . . . or a pumpkin (to Mercier) or a baroque Chinese fish (to Arnoux) or a brain (to Julian Green) . . . or an *entrecôte* (to butchers). To even more imaginative observers, Paris resembles a heart. For some of them, the topographical form corresponds miraculously to the city's political function as the vital center of France. Or the telltale form marks the city as a place for romance and sexual flings. "In Paris love is the music to which all pleasure goes. . . . If you look at a map . . . , you will see that this city has the shape of a human heart. A strange coincidence, is it not?"—an English guide to "nocturnal pleasures" (1889) pointed out.[9] In sum, the schematic forms are many, but none have caught on as emblems of the city in the way that the Eiffel Tower and Notre-Dame—beautiful historic monuments—have.

Besides, to focus on mapped outlines is to lend a fixity and concreteness to Paris that has not been there historically. The métro system, the arrondissements, and the boundaries have changed from time to time, and the edge of the city has never been so well defined as the lines on a map suggest. A large metropolitan area or "agglomeration" outside the central city has filled in, mixing together old and new in an uneasy process fraught with conflicts and dysfunctions. The outskirts (the banlieues), where about 50 percent of the Greater Parisian population lived back in 1944, were home to 80 percent of the population a half-century later. Yet the public imagination has not caught up with the changes. It has always been hard to grasp the totality, which no one could actually see or experience, but today the problem is one of visualizing an even more vast metropolis than ever before, one that does not have clear boundaries.

SOUL AND SPIRIT

Writerly talk of an underlying spirit or "soul" of Paris has been one way out of these quandaries. Should we even try to identify and describe something so nebulous? Historians usually do not. But such notions, difficult to pin down as they are, have so permeated thinking and writing about Paris that surely they merit examination in an account of the city. We do not have to take them (or dismiss them) as renderings of some ineffable je-ne-sais-quoi. Rather we can regard them as expressions of how Parisians feel about the city and the qualities they judge to be key. Writers have done most to shape a tradition about such themes. On the subject of soul they have usually expressed themselves with unabashed affection, conjuring a passel of hopelessly subjective, beloved qualities they consider to be quintessential. But we do not have to limit our inquiry to the literary set. The idiom of soul has reached beyond them to a range of ordinary Parisians, whose views are reflected in such sources as the popular press, opinion surveys, and sociological studies.

Commentaries on the "atmosphere" and "soul" of Paris tell us about several key characteristics. One is the Parisian sense of the city's long, rich history—its cumulative past that endures as an affective "atmosphere" for succeeding generations. The "soul" of Paris is the living, felt presence of memory and history, enshrined in centuries-old streets and buildings, embodying layer upon layer of time and the contributions of generation after generation, as Louis Blanc put it in 1867. That soulful presence is not limited to famed memory sites, such as Notre-Dame and the Louvre, or a few "representative" parts. It also pervades the banal, homely corners that bear the accumulated imprints of countless events, both good and terrible, over centuries.[10] When contemporary Parisians have spoken of "soul" in their city, they have meant above all the parts of the city that escaped Haussmann's pickaxes in the nineteenth century and the bulldozers of the postwar boom years—the small streets and squares and small shops and cafés: places where people walk, work, and socialize without being overwhelmed by traffic or mega-blocks of concrete.

Along with a general sense of the city's time-honored glories, specific eras and historical experiences stand out in living memories. In the last decades of the twentieth century, with the bloom off the modernist vision, many in France took a conspicuously greater interest in memories of the yesteryears they had lived through. "Never so much 'rétro' among so much 'néo,'" observed the author of a 1993 book *Nostalgies françaises*.[11] "Never have people so much tried to retell the past, to dream of it, to understand it, to conserve it, to restore it, to display it in museums and palaces, but also to recompose and rewrite it."

A poll in late 1985 asked older French people (over 70) in which years or period in the twentieth century they felt happiest. The Belle Époque was now too far back for most of them to have known. Instead, a majority of them chose the interwar period (1919–1939) and the fifteen years between 1958 and 1973 (perhaps because, among other things, it was a period of economic growth and prosperity). When asked which no-longer-existing things they missed the most, the most common answer was the small trades that once filled the public spaces—the street singer and grinder (*rémouleur*) (33 percent of the responses), for example. Next came the old dances and accordion dance halls (*bals musettes*) (26 percent). Next were street fairs and traveling circuses (25 percent), processions and pilgrimages (20 percent), July 14 holiday parades (15 percent), and priests wearing cassocks (*en soutane*) (15 percent). These were all sights in the streets and modest neighborhoods that everyone shared—pleasant everyday features of the lost good ol' days. But older people also recalled vividly the dangerous times, difficult periods, and turning points in war: the defeat of the French army in 1940 and the German occupation (65 percent and 64 percent), the rise of unemployment in the 1980s (49 percent), the Allied landing in Normandy (37 percent), the return of General de Gaulle in 1958 (34 percent), the death of de Gaulle (30 percent), and the rise of Hitler to power (29 percent).[12]

Nostalgia has had to work around many bad memories, which insistently re-surfaced, one after another, in the late twentieth century. Memories of French collaboration with the Nazis grabbed attention from the 1970s on—with books, movies, and trials of collaborators keeping the spotlight on the "dark years" of German occupation.[13] Memory of the French role in deporting Jews to Nazi death camps came up with particular force in 1994 and 1995 on the anniversary of the 1942 roundup and detention in the sports arena called the Vél d'Hiv. The old vélodrome had been torn down in 1959, but in 1994 its nightmarish past became a news item and a painfully revived memory by virtue of a presidential ceremony on the site and the dedication of a commemorative monument representing seven Jewish deportees. In 1995 President Chirac embedded the disturbing memory squarely in the nation's history by acknowledging the responsibility of the French state in the crimes committed against the Jews. Several years later, a 1930s housing project in the dreary suburban town of Drancy, where around 80,000 Jews had been detained before being shipped

FIGURE 6.1. Commemorative plaques on Paris's elementary schools recall the memory of the more than 11,000 Parisian children who were deported to death camps by the Nazis and their French collaborators between 1942 and 1944. After decades of collective forgetting, more than 330 plaques have been affixed on schools since 2001, rendering a dark counterpoint to the official slogan "liberty, equality, and fraternity." The small lettering and the plaque's positioning, however, downplay the text in relation to the eye-catching emblem of the city of Paris (a ship surmounted by a crown) and upbeat slogan—"it is tossed by waves, but does not sink." (Photo by the author, 2009.)

to Auschwitz, also received belated recognition as a noteworthy site for the national memory. The deportees' transit camp there was designated a historic monument by the minister of Culture on May 30, 2001. In that same year Mayor Bertrand Delanoë dedicated a plaque on the Saint-Michel Bridge in memory of the scores of Algerians (perhaps hundreds of them) beaten and killed by the police on October 17, 1961. The victims had been targeted while marching to protest a curfew imposed on the Muslim community during the Algerian struggle for independence.[14]

More remote traumas also returned to disturb the present. During the 1989 bicentennial celebration, right-wing detractors of the French Revolution called attention to the bloody repression of the Vendée rebels by the Paris militants.[15] Bitter memories of the unjustly condemned Captain Alfred Dreyfus cropped up in the 1980s when a statue of the officer was ready to be placed in an appropriate spot. The minister of Culture and Communication Jack Lang, who commissioned the statue in 1985, wanted to place it in the École militaire courtyard where Dreyfus had undergone the humiliating ceremony of being stripped of his officer's rank after being sentenced to prison. The army refused to allow the statue there. Next, municipal authorities refused to have it placed on city property. Finally, after several years of argument, the statue was placed in the Tuileries garden in 1988 and then moved in 1994 to a small square off the Boulevard Raspail.

Evocations of the city's soul routinely pass over these disturbing memories. Conventionally (as noted above) soul refers rather to a generalized sense of a historical continuum, a mystical bedrock of reverence toward ages past. It can also refer to specific images in warm sepia tones, traces of history that are quaint and charming, like the antique storefront of the chocolate shop À la Mère de Famille (founded in 1761) and the perfumery Guerlain (opened in 1839) on the Champs-Élysées.[16] Either way, talk of Paris's soul-as-history invokes a consensus of sentiment, transcending all manner of Parisian divisions and conflicts.

The same can be said of another common definition of the city's soul and spirit: Paris's openness to difference. The capital, in this view, is the antithesis to the provinces, notorious for rigid, narrow attitudes. Paris, long celebrated and decried as "cosmopolitan," famously delights in the savors of diverse cultures, now more than ever before. Contemporary

FIGURE 6.2. A place that has what Parisians call "soul": the oldest chocolate candy shop (confiserie chocolatier) in Paris—À la Mère de Famille, founded in 1761, still open at 35 Rue du Faubourg Montmartre. (Photo by the author.)

Paris is the "eclectic city," full of contrasts and receptive to everything, declared the métro's weekly paper at the end of the twentieth century. As is standard practice in this kind of celebratory Parisian writing, tensions and conflicts among groups went unacknowledged. "What appears at first glance to be an incongruity is in fact the soul of Paris: its openness to all cultures."[17] The popular magazine *Télérama* introduced its special issue on "a cosmopolitan summer in Paris" ("the exotic guide to the capital") with the assertion: the city "welcomes like no other capital the cultures and the specialties of the five continents, without feeling its own integrity threatened." Balzac's declaration "Paris is the city of the cosmopolitan" is even truer today, the editorial continued, citing the abundance of "exotic" restaurants and galleries, bookstores, craft boutiques, dance and concert performances, and cultural centers.[18]

Though most immigrants and visitors to the city have found it difficult to integrate fully into Parisian society, many have echoed the centuries-old tributes to the French capital as an extraordinary place of freedom. Paris's historic role as a champion of revolutions and political liberties is a part of what is meant. Certainly the city has been a haven for refugees and the persecuted to an extent that only London has rivaled. In addition, it has offered considerable freedom in personal life as well. The *grand-ville* offers a multitude of choices along with an anonymity that is liberating. Other great cities have provided similar freedom, but arguably not so much as Paris or as consistently. In both its famous Bohemian communities and among ordinary people, a "mind your own business" attitude has reigned in such matters as drinking, intimate relationships, and sexuality. Parisians who once lived in villages and small towns have particularly welcomed the absence of scrutiny by neighbors and priests. English and American visitors have also been keenly appreciative. As the American Basil Woon wrote in 1931, "From the day you step from your train at the Saint-Lazare station you may—and do—cast prejudice, decorum and what'll the-folks-say-t'home to the winds. . . . This feeling of freedom is undoubtedly the dominating ingredient in the tantalizing, definition-defying thing that is the charm of Paris." To drive his point home, he noted that "there are no speed limits whatever in Paris."[19] The city's laissez-faire ways have never had more enthusiastic admirers than the fugitives from Prohibition-era America like Basil Woon.

But cosmopolitanism and tolerance have been only part of the story. Paris has indeed long welcomed "exotic" additions to its cuisine and arts scene, but that very receptiveness has made many Parisians feel that their city's integrity *was* in danger. Xenophobia has been commonplace since the Second Empire with its critics of "world city" newcomers. Fin-de-siècle Montmartre chansonniers targeted Jews and immigrants (*métèques*). In the interwar years Blacks and foreign workers came under attack.[20] Then the Vichy regime and Occupation authorities adopted and implemented policies of persecution and exclusion that sent tens of thousands to their death in Nazi concentration camps. In recent decades, too, anti-immigrant reactionaries make it manifest that the antipathies toward "others" persist. In short, talk about Paris's soul has been a prime vehicle for ahistorical generalization and airy flattery, which also serve to gloss over some ugly history.

To help us grasp the notion of the city's "spirit" there are more texts available and fuller explications than for "soul." Poets and essayists have spun conceits about that spirit for centuries, but scholars have held back— that is, until Louis Chevalier, master historian of Paris, wrote his analysis of Parisians in a book published in 1967 (and reissued in 1985). Chevalier's *Les Parisiens* made the most forceful scholarly case ever for the existence of a distinct "spirit" shared by Parisians. The remarkable "unity" and likeness of the Parisian people, he explained, have resulted from centuries of a continuous "collective existence" in an extraordinarily small urban space. Parisians, he emphasized, share an "intense" and "total" life together, marked by common rhythms of work, eating, and moving about the city. After living that way for centuries, the population has come to share a "Parisian personality," a set of common psychological characteristics, values, tastes, and concerns.[21]

Chevalier drew on his vast knowledge of literature and history, contemporary scholarship, and his own observations from living among Parisians for more than three decades. In explaining what he considered distinctively Parisian, he begins with attitudes toward the body. Competing in the big city for work and advancement as well as for partners and marriage, Parisians, especially women, have come to care about their bodies and their looks more than provincials have. Chevalier based that observation on evidence found in literature and historical records together with studies of expenditures on health and beauty products. Yet after emphasizing the physical aspect of the female body, he added that it did not matter most. Women who were truly *Parisiennes* had to exemplify the standards of mind and spirit required by Parisian "civilization." Chevalier cited as examples the archetypical *Parisiennes* of popular culture, Mimi Pinson and the *midinette*—artfully self-fashioned young women whose mind and personality above all made them physically charming and adorable.[22]

Spirit is a slippery word in any language, but in French (despite its reputation for precision) *esprit* can mean wit and intelligence as well. As clever humor, Parisian *esprit* shone famously in the *bons mots* of the boulevardiers and the satires of the *chansonniers* of Montmartre cabarets. But Chevalier's portrayal of the Parisian *esprit* went well beyond those various elites—and beyond the literary and scientific leaders that Victor Hugo acclaimed so resoundingly. Louis Chevalier reaffirmed the long-standing claim of extraordinary mental acuity for Parisians in general and, most notably, ordinary people. Centuries of living in the stimulating, densely populated city, he maintained, have fostered a Parisian mind characterized by a quick, perceptive intelligence. As the progeny of generations fleeing the countryside, Parisians have had in common a strong "will for liberation" and pleasure, gladly leaving behind the constraints and pettiness of provincial life, Chevalier explained. Confident of their judgment and understanding, the common people developed a famously critical, mocking, skeptical character. The irreverent but tender, wisecracking popular type known as the *titi* (a descendant of Hugo's character Gavroche) was the emblematic figure.[23]

In contemporary times the motif *esprit* comes up in discussions of the city's cultural vibrancy, but wit no longer appears as a defining trait. Writer and journalist Claude Dubois, current champion of old-fashioned popular life, maintains that the *esprit titi* died in the tumult of the "ravaging urbanism" of the 1960s and 1970s, which uprooted and dispersed "Paris canaille." "The soul of the people of Paris died" too, he maintains. It died in the physical destruction of Paname—the old, poor neighborhoods of working people and their cafés and accordion-orchestra dance halls. Now all that is left is a faint, distant reminder in the person of the young hood (*loubard*) of the banlieue public projects who speaks *verlan* (slang with reversed syllables) and jeeringly rejects pretension and authority—sometimes even engaging in violence.[24] In Claude Dubois the old popular-culture dream of a little people's Paname is steeped in bitterness and is more nostalgic than ever.

Through the twentieth century, romantic love figured in popular songs, novels, and movies as a prominent, essential part of the Parisian spirit. Glossy advertising for perfumes, liqueurs, and tourism, along with photographs by Robert Doisneau, helped make the theme familiar worldwide. Is there anything more to it than the stuff of romantic fiction and popular clichés? "It [love] is part of daily experience and the most banal experience that Parisians have of others and of themselves," insisted Louis Chevalier, scholar of Paris history and indefatigable flâneur. "Nothing seems so obvious." Chevalier even went so far as to assert that a "loving behavior," springing from a need for "moral and physical" love, is the distinguishing spirit of "Parisian civilization." What he called "les choses de l'amour" ran the gamut from sentimental love and passionate love to eroticism and sexuality: he thought it pointless to try to separate out the components. For him the "Parisian spirit" was about "pleasure" and "the drama of love" above all, as captured by novelists from the Abbé Prévost to Carco. Reflecting the influence of old-regime court models, love Paris-style was typically more sensible and playful than passionate and consuming. And Parisians' "loving behavior," characteristically, has taken forms that have varied from quarter to quarter. The Palais-Royal most famously served the demand for pleasure in the eighteenth century, and the Grands Boulevards in the nineteenth. For a later period, Chevalier maintained, Montmartre was *the* place—in the imaginary and in the lives of many.[25]

So Chevalier, like poets and writers before him, wrested crisp conclusions from the ether of Parisian subjectivities. Brushing aside empiricist qualms, he lent his authority to old conventional views. He gave explanations better than anyone had—broad-brush historical explanations, difficult to prove but not altogether implausible. Although his book with all its generalizing cannot be taken as an accurate description of "les Parisiens" in contemporary times, it is an indispensable compendium of classic views that have come down through recent centuries. Remarkably, after decades of studying Paris history, writing it, and observing it first-hand, Louis Chevalier affirmed long-standing notions about the centrality of love, pleasure, and sex in Paris.

SECRET PARIS

Long-term, older Parisians with the most memories are doubtless best at grasping such elusive subjects as the soul and the spirit of Paris. Even though many of them have never ventured into large areas of the city nor studied its history, they do have the advantage of having participated in Parisian life for an extended period. They may view the city's past through the emotionally tinted lens of their own past, merging personal memories with the capital's history, but their years of experience there arguably puts them in a good position to understand Paris's subtleties. Visitors, typically pressed for time, usually follow guidebooks that tell how to see a scattering of classic sites in a week or two. They miss what Julian Green has called "secret Paris," that which he believed to be known only to Parisians and not accessible to people in a hurry.[26]

Visitors miss not only most of the city, but also small and intangible aspects of the parts they do visit. Lovers of Paris have long insisted only people who wander with time to lose—time not measured in days or even weeks—can get to know the city. Only through such aimless strolls (flânerie) can one know its everyday "physiognomy"—"the thousand and one activities that give it its own cachet," a popular book for tourists explained in 1960. By walking and seeing close-up the "workaday insouciance and elegance" of the people's routine activities, one enters into "intimate communion" with "the Parisian spirit."[27] But, it must be added, to wander that way in today's metropolis is also to enter into "intimate communion" with rushing autos and buses and noisy, exhaust-filled intersections.[28]

It has also been said again and again that to know Paris requires an open, exploratory spirit. Many long-term residents are no more knowledgeable than visitors who have simply read guidebooks and histories.[29] And some of the locals' "secret Paris" is really not secret at all. When asked to name little-known places of beauty or interest, many Parisians answered with the same spots—the Canal Saint-Martin, for example.[30] Similarly, a recent guide titled Paris secret et insolite includes entries on such well-known places as the (now-reconstructed) Hôtel du Nord on the Quai de Jemappes, the Mosque of Paris, and Guimard's art-nouveau Castel Béranger along with "forgotten culs-de-sac" and "hidden gardens."[31] Another not-really-secret "secret Paris" is the one that Parisians don't talk about because it is so familiar and taken for granted: it is where their everyday routines take them. "It's the central chambers of the labyrinth that exert their magnetism on the city-dweller, those that he or she revisits indefinitely," observed writer Julien Gracq.[32] But such familiar circuits through the labyrinth do not move ordinary people to wax eloquent about the "soul" or "spirit" of the city. As for the unknown remainder of the city, which struck the imaginative Gracq as exotic and "half-dreamed," for many it simply remains unknown, undifferentiated space of no interest.

"Secret Paris" can also mean the kind of scenes that photographer Brassaï immortalized in the 1930s, though most of them were in public view almost any night. Brassaï was the first to capture that side artfully in photographs. Moved by a fearless love of images and armed with a small new Leica, he made unforgettable photos of lovers embracing on a park bench, lamplighters on their rounds, street-fair fortune tellers, "ladies of the evening," cesspool cleaners at work with their hoses and afterward eating together in cafés, bearded old *clochards* in the street, homeless men sleeping under the Pont Neuf, and rag pickers rummaging in trash bins. He took his camera behind doors usually closed—into an opium den, gay and lesbian bars, bordellos, a gay ball at the amusement park Magic City, and backstage at the Folies-Bergère, crowded with bare-breasted showgirls resting while stagehands changed scenery. Some of the nocturnal world of "pleasure, love, vice, crime, drugs" was "secret" because it was unlawful and dangerous, as Brassaï quickly learned. Many pimps and prostitutes, thieves, and hoods did not want to be photographed in their dives and dark streets, and they made that unmistakably clear: on various occasions someone stole Brassaï's bag of exposed plates, broke his cameras, threatened him at knifepoint, took his money, and chased him away. But he persisted out of fascination with the outcasts and strangeness of the Parisian nights. Brassaï believed that his photos of that underworld "represented Paris . . . at its most authentic" and in its enduring "folklore."[33]

Some of it was already old-fashioned when he published his album *Paris de nuit* in 1933—the sights of the horse-drawn milkman's wagon, the traveling fair, and the gas streetlights, for example. In 1976 when the album *Brassaï, The Secret Paris* came out, his 1930s photos evoked even more nostalgia. So much had vanished: the central market, the cesspool cleaners, the lamplighters, the always-lighted brothels like Suzy and Belles Japonaises, the street-corner urinals covered with Byrrh ads. Yet many of his images—of shadowy streets, the quays, and night people—are remarkably like what a stroller can encounter today.

The dark underside of the City of Light has also been captured in a marvelous written account by Jean-Paul Clébert—his book titled *Paris insolite* (1952). Although it was written before the big urbanist operations of the Fifth Republic, and many places it describes have changed drastically, its main points still hold for the contemporary city. Living hand-to-mouth and wandering day and night in the mazes of "the ever-mysterious capital" for years, Clébert came to know the underworld of sordid nooks and crannies that long before had entranced the legendary Grand Dukes—the outcast Paris of cheap bars and grubby bistros that harbored the homeless and jobless, beggars, *clochards*, ragpickers, aging hookers, and ex-cons. For men who slept on the sidewalks or on métro benches, in parks and under bridges, and those who scrounged for food and drink and cigarette butts every day, Les Halles was the providential cornucopia. There, Clébert recounts, the down-and-almost-out could scavenge discarded fruits and vegetables or find several hours of work carrying crates or weighing bananas.

Time and time again the roaming Clébert stumbled onto a hidden something that was extraordinary . . . and sometimes bizarre. Pushing open a door, stepping into a corridor and then a courtyard, he discovered "the unexpected landscape of an old well, its chain covered with ground ivy, [and] . . . the secret passage that cuts through a house and connects with another universe, that of farm yards filled with old paving stones, hay barns, stables for fiacres. . . ." Through a temporary job measuring walls for a contractor, he came upon an apartment full of mushrooms growing everywhere, another filled with birds flying around freely, and still another where floors were thick with slithering snakes. He discovered homeless men who spent their nights inside the chapel-like tombs of the cemetery Père Lachaise, and hustlers who went into the graveyard to remove human heads from recently buried corpses (after bribing the caretaker), carried them out in a sack, washed them off in a hotel room, and then sold them to interested shops (unidentified). He learned of a bistro where tattooed human skin, obtained from the morgue or from medical school labs, was bought and sold. "Out-of-the-ordinary" Paris is "inexhaustible," especially for venturesome explorers like Clébert.[34] If it is also "secret," one big reason is that most people do not want to know all of it firsthand.

Yet sightseers still line up to visit the Paris sewers, the skull-and-bones filled catacombs, and the police museum's displays of criminals and crimes. In counterpoint to the famed monuments and classical vistas—or as relief from them—they seek out places devoid of classic order and rationality, the kinds of bizarre or grotesque places that have fascinated and delighted many since the time of Eugène Sue's *Mystères* and the Grand Dukes' slumming tours. Though less common and less important now than in the Romantic era, anti-classical features remain a familiar part of Paris's identity and allure.

THE MOST LOVED — AND FAMILIAR

Going beyond the secret and the strange, we may now look more closely into aspects of the city's physiognomy that locals and visitors consider most lovable and quintessentially Parisian. For many people living far from the city, Paris remains a favorite setting for dreams and dream vacations—as a place of beauty, romance, and pleasure. Travelers by the millions have made it the world's leading tourist destination year after year. Yet the city so identified with beauty and elegance remains plagued by pollution, loud street noise, traffic jams, dog and pigeon droppings, slum housing, rats, street crime, and other "warts." How can it live up to its high reputation? How can the dreamlike imaginary hold up in the face of experience?

Foreign tourists and visiting provincials can overlook the warts and stay with the dreams more easily than can residents: visitors usually take in only postcard-famous parts in a matter of days—such as the Champs-Élysées, the Latin Quarter, the Cité, the quarter of the Opéra and *grands magasins*. At the top of the list of Paris's most visited monuments and museums is the cathedral Notre-Dame, followed by the basilica of Sacré-Coeur, the Eiffel Tower, the Louvre Museum, the Cité des Sciences at La Villette, the Musée d'Orsay, the Arc de Triomphe, and the Centre Georges Pompidou (Beaubourg).[35] The list reveals strongest interest in the most renowned historic places—plus a couple of more recent ones. Unfortunately, the records do not tell us what actually pleased or disappointed the visitors.

Paris residents cope daily with annoyances that never show up in the dream world. Few Parisians make public declarations of love for the city's warts and blemishes (as Montaigne put it). Those who complain about noise, traffic, and other nuisances are clearly the majority. According to survey results that appear regularly in the mayor's magazine, three complaints have ranked highest in recent years: street noise, crime, and dog dung on the sidewalks. These also figure in a book-length indictment of

Paris defects by journalist Anne Le Cam, who builds up to the dire conclusion that the condition of the city now precludes good living. With "the worst" so overwhelming, "the true Paris" is no more.[36]

That is one extreme. The account that follows examines a fuller range of testimony about how Parisians, in the majority, view their city and characterize it. Although their interests and criteria may be quite different from those of non-Parisians, they who have years of day-to-day knowledge of the city may be able to give some insights to the rest of us—especially about such subtle subjective matters as the lovable and soulful.

What, then, do Parisian "lovers of Paris" love about their city? At the most elemental, many of those who have not expressed themselves for the record probably share the diffuse and vague sentiments expressed by writer Francis Jourdain: "We loved Paris like we loved life, without saying it . . . perhaps because we didn't know it any more than the fish knows that it loves water." They might also agree with his explanation of "a quasi-organic attachment": "In Paris, and only in Paris, we were truly at home, or rather we were integrated, assimilated, we were Paris itself, a part of our Paris."[37]

For more specific answers, we can turn to public opinion surveys, popular magazines and papers, and the testimony of writers. Among the most beloved places in Paris are the tranquil, village-like squares and small streets scattered throughout the city. "The soul of a *quartier*," architectural historian François Loyer has written, resides in the secondary streets behind the broad boulevards. The famous boulevards lined with harmonious façades are the imposing exterior of a quarter, designed to impress the outsider. The dense interior is the setting of daily-life Parisian "bonhomie"—a disorderly space of diverse, "incoherent" building styles and small businesses fashioned by the locals for themselves.[38]

Back-street cafés, quiet squares, and restaurant terraces are particularly appreciated in the warm summer months, when many Parisians seek outdoor places (with "soul") for evening socializing. Each year popular magazines offer reports on the best of those spots. In June 2002, the weekly *Zurban Paris*, for example, featured a cover showing young people gathered around café tables in a pedestrian-only street (the Rue des Barres) behind a Gothic church (Saint-Gervais-Saint-Protais). The lead article,

"Paris côté village," describes places where one could "take the pulse of a provincial Paris" and "let the charm take effect"—calming remnants of the past, away from the din of the *périphérique* and the Grands Boulevards. In "the little, typically Parisian *place*" named Gustave-Toudouze in the ninth arrondissement, below the Butte Montmartre, "you'll hear only the sound of sparrows" and the tinkling of dishes. At night actors and artists of the quarter as well as stars of television and movies mix with the regulars. Likewise charming, the magazine noted, are the hip cafés beside the Canal Saint-Martin, those in the Rue Vercingétorix (fourteenth arrondissement) and the Rue des Panoyaux (twentieth arrondissement) with its quaint café Lou Pascalou ("the prettiest of the bars of Ménilmuche, the most charming of terraces—especially at night—in the glow of the street lamps"), and the Place Sainte-Marthe in the tenth ("a little corner of Provence, in the shade of trees in full flower").[39] An article on "secret terraces" in the same issue guided readers to other quiet spots, outdoor cafés to be enjoyed on summer evenings—from the Café Renard in the Tuileries garden to the panoramic "high place of *la dolce vita*," the café Au Rital overlooking the city from a corner above the Parc de Belleville. These refuges from modern Paris exist all over the city, even though critics of urban renewal since Haussmann's time have regularly mourned their demise. The disappearance of such intimate, human, and picturesque locales seemed inevitable in the era of pickax demolitions and new boulevards just as in the decades of bulldozers and tall towers, but they have not disappeared. They have ardent supporters, more than ever, and they are perhaps now more beloved than ever, having become rarer and so obviously endangered.

For residences that are village-like, the Parisian ultimate comes in the form of "villas," small houses with gardens lining quiet streets or pedestrian walkways—such as the Villa Montmorency in the posh sixteenth arrondissement or the Villa Émile-Loubet on the hill of Belleville (a lane of cottages practically in the shadow of their antithesis, the high-rises around the Place des Fêtes). Access to the villas is closed to vehicles, and some (like the Villa Montmorency) are even closed to pedestrians who don't live there. The widespread appeal of such village-like neighborhoods translates into high real-estate prices and quick sales for properties. But a small-scale layout in itself does not spawn close ties among neighbors. In

FIGURE 6.3. A now-rare "village" of small villas lives on in the shadow of high-rise apartment buildings on the Place des Fêtes, a prime example of slate-cleaning (memory-obliterating) renewal operations in the 1970s in Belleville. (Photo by the author.)

the upscale villas that are home to celebrities and business leaders, residents keep more to themselves than in the modest villas, like those of Belleville.[40]

Yet it does not always take an old-fashioned kind of physical setting for Parisians to develop strong feelings of attachment to their own street and their own quarter. After the radical urban operations of the 1980s and 1990s, Belleville became "a sinister clone of the banlieue"—or so it seemed to those who warmly remembered a time when "the street was convivial." "A river of cement has drowned this modest and simple paradise," lamented writer Thierry Jonquet, a Belleville resident. When the old Place des Fêtes with its nine cafés and decaying neighborhood of small dwellings was cleared away in the 1970s, only four cafés were left amid the new concrete high-rises. It all looked antithetical to conviviality, yet young women interviewed there in the early 1990s described it as a friendly "village." "Here everyone knows each other; the merchants call me by my first name." "When you go down [out from the apartment building], you are sure to meet someone [you know]; it's not like in Paris." These happened to be Jewish women who enjoyed a close community life of their own, but they were describing general relations among neighbors in the contemporary quarter. Black African workers living in the settlement house Bisson in Belleville expressed a similar fondness for their neighborhood and a strong desire not to leave it. In the revamped Les Halles quarter as early as the mid-1980s, too, a woman living there for the past five years told an inquiring journalist: "Our quarter is a village. In my building everyone knows each other. People go into each other's homes." Added the journalist: "it's a quarter of adventurers, actors, journalists, unconventional people, where a warm conviviality reigns among the residents."[41]

Such feelings of conviviality and rootedness are notoriously less common in the big housing projects in the suburbs. Yet many residents do participate in a variety of social networks there—through religious organizations, local associations, and neighborly exchanges. Young people commonly enjoy interethnic circles of friends in the same housing project (*cité*) and at school. Some young males, notoriously, belong to gangs that are in effect "a second family" and a small-scale society.[42]

Many residents in suburbs where immigrants have long been the most numerous (the Department Seine-Saint-Denis, notably) feel a sense of belonging to an ancestral land and culture as well as to their familiar suburb and housing complex. Teenage girls in an Aubervilliers *grand ensemble*, studied in the 1990s by ethnographer Tricia Danielle Keaton, thought of themselves as Arabs or French Muslims or at times simply French, and as residents of a project or a neighborhood in Aubervilliers, but not as Parisian suburbanites. "I was born in France," wrote one French Muslim girl in her journal. "I have French culture, but I live with Moroccans. Every year, for two months, I go to Morocco. I speak Moroccan, I eat Moroccan food. In fact, I have two cultures, French and the other. . . ." "My neighborhood, I love it and hate it," wrote another girl in her journal. "It makes me happy and sad, and I have so much against it, my poor neighborhood." Her sadness was in part a response to the projects' deterioration over the years and lack of aesthetically pleasing, intimate surroundings of the kind that have generated fond sentiments for historic Paris quarters. But it also reflected her discouragement and sorrow over the outer-city's ghetto-like conditions that, she observed, lead to older boys' losing hope, dropping out of school, and ending up jobless.[43]

Immigrants and their children, like the girl quoted above, cobble to-gether plural identities, including some newly assumed in France, such as "African" and "Creole." Myriad variations emerge, differences related to age, ethnicity, gender, socioeconomic status, educational level, and length of time lived in France. The tiny percentage of young Moslem women who wore the headscarf in school (until a law banned it in 2004) led lives that were, in many ways, adapted to French culture and in some ways to another culture. The children and grandchildren of different immigrant backgrounds have in common French schooling and a familiarity with an urban youth culture that is as international as it is French (with such elements as rap and hip hop), but most are by all accounts marginalized in French society and discriminated against in employment. Older immi-grants, generally less assimilated, do not share anything remotely like the nineteenth-century Parisian culture of workers (idealized as "Paname"). Nor do they merge socially into established neighborhoods in the suburbs (or Paris) the way Italian, Spaniard, and other foreign (but European) workers did before the Second World War. Socially their world centers on people in their housing project and immediate neighborhood within the suburb. Their sense of identity does not include an affectionate tie to Paris.[44]

The feelings that Parisians have for their own quarter in the central city are generally less ambivalent, yet often quite complex. A close sociological study of one street in the Latin Quarter sheds light on the varied ways that residents have felt about their immediate surroundings. "There are two Rues du Dragon," explained a young man: one is that of the merchants, the residents, the café, and two or three restaurants of regulars." That one was the endearing "little village" where people knew each other well. The other Rue du Dragon was the automobile-clogged street of fashionable shops and restaurants that people from outside knew. Another resident added, "Two Rues du Dragon? Very well, but that's simplifying to the extreme; I count more than sixty!" People who expressed love for the street did not give reasons, but the gist of their comments seems to be that their neighborhood was the Paris they had come to know and love most—and that to explain further was beside the point. Their love sprang from a sense of fulfillment of their needs and desires there where unfathomable fates had placed them. "I'm glad every day to have the chance to live in the Rue du Dragon." "I love my quarter because it is mine as I love my mother because she is mine."[45]

Besides sentimental attachments, Parisians have practical reasons for loving their *quartiers*, as a recent opinion survey makes clear. Unlike inhabitants of the suburbs and the countryside, Parisians have most of their daily needs met close by their homes. Within twenty minutes or less by foot, they can get to a post office, cafés, cinemas, schools, supermarkets, sports facilities, and libraries. More than 95 percent of Parisian households declared themselves "very well equipped" in their home quarters, whereas only 34 percent of provincials in towns smaller than 50,000 enjoyed such amenities. Consequently Parisians stay in their own neighborhoods for most of their activities outside work, except that they go to cafés more frequently near their place of work.[46]

Public opinion surveys have documented that, beyond their own home quarter, most Parisians have liked most and known best the old heart of the city—the quays of the Seine, the two islands, and the Latin Quarter. They also felt most positively toward the chic *quartiers* (eighth and sixteenth arrondissements) around the Champs-Élysées. They knew the least the outlying poorer quarters, like the nineteenth and twentieth arrondissements. According to an in-depth sociological study in the 1970s, most Parisians, familiar with a generalized map of the city, could locate somewhat accurately the major landmarks and monuments, but most also knew places of interest and beauty that are not famous—quiet, off-the-beaten-path places such as the Villa Montmorency and the Place des Peupliers. When asked where they would take a last walk through the city, most named the quays of the Seine and the Latin Quarter. The top choice as a place to live was the Île Saint-Louis—centrally located and quiet, an island neighborhood of prestigious old buildings, of course surrounded by the Seine at its most

FIGURE 6.4. Among the soulful places in the contemporary city are post-industrial sites such as the Canal Saint-Martin, once a working-class neighborhood where the humble Hôtel du Nord, a centerpiece of the Paname tradition, was located. (Photo by the author.)

beautiful. Next in preference came the sixth arrondissement (Left Bank) and the Marais. Overall, the famous historic center together with the river clearly ranked highest in Parisian affections.[47] The perennial popularity of songs about the Seine—affectionately evoked as beautiful and charming, an undulating feminine work of nature, and a favorite refuge of lovers and the homeless—is further evidence of those preferences.[48] So are the high real-estate prices for central locations.

Some notable places far from the historic center have become famous and beloved thanks to romantic fictions popularized by the press, novels, and movies. One example is the Hôtel du Nord, the subject of a semi-fictional book by Eugène Dabit, published in 1930 and made into a movie in 1938. The plain, fourth-rate Hôtel du Nord standing beside the Canal Saint-Martin had a tenuous claim to public support. What the film audiences saw and remembered was not actually the hotel by the canal, but a movie set erected on the outskirts of the city. Yet the facsimile served to win hearts and minds over to the unprepossessing original. New owners of the former hotel took the movie set as their model when they tried to restore the interior in the 1990s. Another prime example is the House of Casque d'or on the Rue des Cascades in Belleville, one of several places where a golden-haired gang moll lived early in the twentieth century. Its fame dated from 1952 when it served as a set for a hugely popular movie about the young woman (played by Simone Signoret) and her two warring lovers.

Unlike earlier buildings championed by the anti-urbanists, the run-down hotel and the rustic Belleville house were neither distinguished aesthetically nor associated with classical literature and the social elite. The two became causes for preservation only when developers in the late twentieth century threatened to replace the old small buildings with big new ones. Both were saved only after anti-urbanist militants made repeated appeals to public opinion and finally gained support from the City and the Ministry of Culture. Once again, as earlier with the Moulin Rouge and Maxim's, set pieces of the Paris imaginary triumphed and became emblematic heritage sites.

· · ·

Warm testimonials about life in contemporary Paris regularly appear in many publications, but among the most accessible to ordinary Parisians is the weekly newspaper of the métro *À Nous Paris!*, distributed free in numerous stations. In many issues an interviewed celebrity is asked is tell what he or she thinks of Paris and loves about it. Their responses are most often commonplaces and clichés. When asked what Paris represented for him, the star television newscaster Patrick Poivre d'Avor answered that it is "first of all the City of Light." It attracts and dazzles, he added. In his youth in Rheims the capital appeared beyond reach, but at sixteen and a half he went to Paris for his studies. What were his first impressions? "Paris is one of the most beautiful cities in the world." In her response to the standard questions, pop singer Patricia Kaas declared, "When I stroll in the evening, I find Paris very romantic." Like many provincials, she formed glorious images of the capital from her earliest years in the small town in Lorraine where she grew up (Forbach). "To know Paris is a child's dream." Now her favorite parts of the capital are the Marais—"a young quarter with many bars and small, very nice [*très sympa*] terraces"—and the Left Bank neighborhood where she lives (the sixth arrondissement), though she has the "impression that it's losing its old charm." Pop singer Jacques Higelin, famous for hymns to the old-fashioned people's Paris, told of his love for the small lively streets where he takes walks—the Rue de la Goutte d'Or, the Rue Vieille-du-Temple, and the Butte-aux-Cailles. He fondly recalled times during his youth when he missed the last train back to his banlieue home and "passed the night in the capital looking and listening," enjoying the "great night life among artists, workers, butchers" at Les Halles and the "warm, friendly ambiance" there.[49]

Perhaps the grandest bouquets tossed to the city came from a twenty-seven-year-old actor named Lorànt Deutsch, a self-described flâneur and amateur archeologist who told his interviewer in 2002 that he could not live without a view of Paris, that he was "a bashful lover" ("un amoureux transi") of Paris since childhood, that he owned hundreds of history books on the city, that he searched its walls and ruins in order "to capture the soul of the city" and "to go into it in depth." "Paris is my woman; I sleep with her!" he exclaimed. When asked if there was something he did not like, he mentioned only the closed carriage entrances ("portes cochères"), which prevented him from going into the courtyards of old buildings.[50] These unending tributes by celebrities reinforce in Parisians, as enthusiastic guidebooks have done for outsiders, the old belief in the city's singular beauty and greatness. Their declarations of love call up again the long-standard faces of Paris—Ville Lumière, picturesque Old Paris, and affable Paname—even the city as seductive woman.

For an understanding of these strong feelings, again historian Louis Chevalier has given us noteworthy insights, based on his incomparable knowledge and love of Paris. He loved not only the city's beauty "in a thousand forms," but also its omnipresent "little pleasures" and the jostling variety of people and their rush of activities. The city's exceptionally intense and stimulating collective life, he maintained, inspired thinking and sparked creativity in every domain from the arts and crafts to literature and philosophy. It lay at the source of the "particular beauty that made the glory of Paris." Chevalier found beauty "in myriad forms" throughout the city, and he loved it all—beauty "in the grubbiest streets, in the most neglected quarters, and in the most impoverished faubourgs." Like

Baudelaire (whom he quotes), he found "enchantments" even in the "horrible," so interrelated were the constitutive parts. But for Chevalier the best of the city as pleasure and inspiration was Les Halles. There more than anywhere else the daily experience of "intertwined destinies" worked to enhance individual lives. Through the "collective existence" there, "each person, whether working, having fun, taking a walk, eating, sleeping, whatever activity and at every moment, is transformed, exalted." For that, Chevalier loved Les Halles with an unwavering passion.[51]

The market quarter was all the more enchanting because its liveliest hours were at night, when the lighted pavilions overflowing with sellers and buyers stood out like a bright stage show against the surrounding darkness. The nightly attractions included the nearby cafés crowded with workers drinking and eating and bantering, the neighborhood's prostitutes in the streets and cheap hotels, and the drop-in appearances of society elites capping off their evening of pleasure. Today, decades after the "assassination" of all that in the 1970s, Les Halles is a shopping mall that is dark and locked up at night, leaving it to other parts of the city to carry on the nocturnal tradition.

"THE PLEASURE OF NIGHT"

Paris at night continues to cast its famed enchantment in numerous quarters, though certainly not everywhere. Brightly lighted cafés, cabaret signs, theaters, and streetlights lend an inviting sparkle to much of the city, especially along the principal boulevards and the Champs-Élysées, making the late nineteenth-century slogan "Ville Lumière" far more valid now than when it first took hold. Illuminated monuments—the Opéra, Notre-Dame, and other majestic buildings along the Seine—stand out as familiar stars of the first order. But the most spectacular of all is doubtless the Eiffel Tower, whose brilliant lighting top-to-bottom is visible for some fifty miles around.

For those who prefer the darker areas for pleasures and adventures, the choices are numerous and the promising areas widely scattered, extending to the heights of Belleville, the Bois de Vincennes, and the especially notorious Bois de Boulogne. Prostitution (male and female), the prospect of orgies (*partouzes*), and exhibitionism plus voyeurism have drawn many to the Boulogne park nightly since the 1920s, when automobilists became common on its roads after dark.[52]

Many a lover of Paris has maintained that the city is most alive and most itself at night. As Louis Chevalier explained it, in the dark hours people are more open to each other and to pleasure, which their incomparable city provides in particularly intense ways. "The pleasure of the night is the passionate love of Paris," he declared in his anecdotal book about Parisian nights (1982).[53] "Stories" (histoires), he held, are the best way of bringing out the nature of Paris at night—"pieces and bits," fragments and memories of many nights, characters and incidents that merge to form the basis of a history. So from his own memories and extensive reading, he put together a collage-like series of stories about brothels, night owls of all kinds, anecdotes and laughs enjoyed in favorite cafés and bistros, particularly among the working people of the old Les Halles.

As those nocturnal workers have become fewer, and as fewer workers spend their evenings in neighborhood cafés and bistros, the main actors in the nocturnal city have become young people, pleasure-seeking socialites, and tourists, ever more disproportionately. Those three groups have long been the mainstay clients for much of Paris's nightly commercial entertainment. Just before the First World War, the new magazine Paris-Minuit announced itself as the "organ of Tout-Paris that has fun and especially joyous Montmartre and the youthful Latin Quarter." Addressing itself to male readers, the opening editorial hinted at sensual pleasure with a soon-to-be-archaic discreetness: "we are devoted to the immortal religion of Woman, and we will celebrate her radiant beauty and her sovereign charm." In the late 1980s, by contrast, the magazine Paris Nuit boasted the abundance of sexual pleasures available (much of it in commercial form)—with a cover banner on the first issue proclaiming: "erotic telephone numbers for all incomes!"

Contemporary youth out on the town, known in French as "clubbers," flock nightly to dance-and-drink clubs featuring hot bands and singers. Most of those are concentrated not in the Latin Quarter and Montmartre, but in formerly working-class areas on the Right Bank. Old structures have come back to life in new incarnations: a former brothel—now La Jungle (in the Tiquetonne-Etienne Marcel quarter); a former public bath—now the discothèque Les Bains; an old tool factory—now the Mécano Bar in the Rue Oberkampf; a tannery (La Maroquinerie in Belleville)—now a cultural center; and an abandoned beltway train station—now La Flèche d'or café and disco (in the Rue de Bagnolet). On the quay François Mauriac in the formerly industrial thirteenth arrondissement, two old sea vessels—a Chinese junk named *La Guinguette Pirate* (then renamed *La Dame de Canton*) and an Irish-sea lighthouse boat called the *Batofar*—draw capacity crowds regularly. The habitués of such places speak passionately about the music and dancing, potential dates, and glamorous celebrities in one club or another, but they do not wax eloquent about the Parisian night per se. Nor do they care about the venerable Romantic practice of taking long solitary walks to discover the sounds and sights of the city after dark.[54]

For many others, quiet evenings out in the city are enjoyable, as the popular writer Alphonse Boudard's book *La Nuit de Paris* (1994) shows well—with photographs by Yves Manciet. Both men were 69 years old when the book was published, yet they did not look back and mourn the good ol' Paris that was gone. Despite his good memories of vanished places, Boudard stayed focused on the present: "No superfluous regrets. Must live with one's time." Night in Paris is better than day, he explained, because it is when people can slow down, escape the heavy traffic, and observe the landscape and others. At night they "can breathe. They can hear themselves think. They can watch each other live." The photos and commentary give us such tourist favorites as the illumined façade of Notre-Dame, the bridge Alexandre III, and of course the Eiffel Tower. But they also capture the shadowy quays with a scattering of quiet strollers, a dark scruffy courtyard in the Faubourg Saint-Antoine, late diners at the Brasserie Lipp, flâneurs idling in the Café des Deux Magots, a métro entry in a winter rainstorm, and a tiny plain café packed with smiling wine drinkers. "Old Paris" has died many times, but the night is still alive. Boudard gives the "anciennes Halles" only a brief mention and then waxes enthusiastic about an old bistro in the quarter that keeps the past alive. Although it is full of middle-class customers instead of the market workers of yesterday, the rest is unchanged: the crowded kitschy interior, the day's menu written on a chalkboard, the plates of traditional *charcuterie* and *tête de veau*, and the inexpensive good wine from the big oak barrel behind the counter.

Scarcely a glimpse of lowlife appears in this book, though Boudard knew that side well. Everywhere and in a thousand forms, changing with the seasons, "the charm of Paris nights" is manifest.[55]

Visitors wanting a more glamorous night out still fork over considerable sums for a sampling of the legendary capital of pleasure, taking "Paris by night" tours to "typical Parisian" cabaret shows. And they line up for nightly programs at the Moulin Rouge (its fame boosted in recent years by Baz Luhrmann's movie *Moulin Rouge*) as well as at such glitzy rivals as the Lido and the Crazy Horse. If they go to Maxim's, it is not for the food (no longer highly rated) or to mix with chic regulars, but for the experience of being in the legendary nightspot and seeing its spectacular art-nouveau décor, restored and classified as a "historical monument" since 1979. Dark lowlife places are much more out of favor than the old glitzy spots: the "pleasures" of slumming no longer exert the powerful attraction that they did back in the days of the Grand Dukes, perhaps because outsiders no longer have the same voyeuristic curiosity—and the same sense of security—as before.

For most Parisians of today, the city's fabled "pleasure of the night" has been for decades little more than a historical reputation. Since 2002 town hall has made an effort to bring back some of that pleasure once a year by organizing the special all-night program of Nuit Blanche, whose début under Mayor Delanoë was recounted in Chapter 4. For the "sleepless night" once every year since, the public has been invited to more than a hundred venues around the city to enjoy multimedia shows, dance, and concerts, some of which take place in historic buildings (the Hôtel de Ville, for example) normally closed at night. Most of the people who have stayed into the wee hours have been youth; older adults and families have mostly attended events earlier in the evening. By all reports, the participating throngs have greatly enjoyed the special performances and the break with routine. Although the early editions were marred by mishaps (the mayor was attacked by a deranged man the first year, and rain kept people at home the second year), Nuit Blanche is well on its way to becoming a tradition, an invented festivity making Paris livelier and more convivial—a fabled Paname quality prized by the current mayor. The public heartily approves, as a recent survey shows: Parisians want more opportunities for that kind of affordable, accessible special night out.[56]

With events like Nuit Blanche and the Fête de la Musique added to the myriad commercial offerings that have accumulated since the nineteenth century, the city's reputation for good times and sociability cannot be neatly subsumed under the rubrics of dream and myth. And by comparison, the poorer suburbs look impoverished, especially to visitors and Paris residents who do not take note of the many cultural events (theater, exhibits, and music festivals such as Banlieue Blues) that have emerged there in recent decades.

NEW SITES AND SYMBOLS

Besides being the site of centuries-old dreams and memories, the city is also the locus of multiple contemporary cultures, interacting with one another and with a common Parisian culture. Youth from the entire agglomeration periodically experience a sense of the whole in memory sites built in the late twentieth century, such as stadiums and arenas out on the edges of the metropolis—the Palais des Sports (1960), the Parc des Princes (1972), the rock concert hall Le Zénith (1984), and the Stade de France (1999). In such outsized untraditional venues, huge crowds of young people come together to enjoy concerts, sharing the rhythms of rock, the performance of superstars like Johnny Hallyday and Madonna, and the excitement of sporting events (most notably the final world championship soccer match in July 1998 when France's team won). In contrast to Mitterrand's monuments, those arenas and stadiums overflow with youthful energy and excitement periodically. And they matter more in the lives of ordinary Parisians than the presidential "grand projects."

Special occasions of celebration, bringing ordinarily scattered Parisians together in central memory-rich spaces, have arguably been the most important catalysts of Paris-wide community spirit. The prime rallying point has been the Champs-Élysées, where crowds of joyful celebrators (1.5 million) showed up after the World Cup victory in 1998, where throngs of spectators have gathered for Bastille Day parades and for the finish of the Tour de France each July, and where cork-popping revelers have amassed on New Year's eve in recent years. Holiday spectacles such as big fireworks shows in the Champ-de-Mars on the Fourteenth of July have also drawn people together across the different communities of the city.

In contrast, some recently created places serve as everyday centers and symbols of Parisian life in its latest incarnations, vying for visitors' attention with old standards such as the Eiffel Tower. A few of the most advertised recent attractions have nothing Parisian about them: the Hard Rock Café (14 Boulevard Montmartre), for example, with its restaurant, rock memorabilia, and boutique. Another is the Stade de France, located just outside the city in Saint-Denis, offering visitors an exhibit, guided tours, restaurants, and a gift shop (*boutique-souvenirs*). An even more widely advertised tourist destination is the most successful of all the recent creations—Disneyland Paris. With so many contemporary attractions beckoning, many visitors may fill their days in Paris without having time for the classic museums and monuments.

In recent decades clusters of trendy (*branché*) cafés and restaurants have sprung up in run-down neighborhoods whose low rents attract artists and young people. More new cafés, restaurants, and galleries have followed, and middle-class residents find the neighborhoods increasingly desirable; rents go up, and many of the youth and trend-setters move on, beginning the cycle anew elsewhere. In the last decades of the twentieth century, the most striking transformations took place in long-poor parts of eastern Paris, as decaying neighborhoods were reborn through renovation of the housing stock and the construction of new public facilities such as Beaubourg and the Bibliothèque nationale de France. The area around the Place Bastille became a hot new night-life district, especially for young Parisians, after the construction of the Opéra of the Bastille in the late 1980s. The old quarter of shabby tenements and artisans' workshops became a lively district of galleries, stylish cafés and bars (many featuring tapas and "happy hours"), and *dernier-cri* restaurants packed with young people.

But by 1997 Bastille was becoming too popular, market driven, and expensive for many, and a new stomping ground emerged farther to the north—in the neighborhood around the Rue Oberkampf in the eleventh arrondissement. There former industrial workshops, a local cinema (La Cithéa), a one-time café-concert (Le Charbon), and old dusty workers' cafés turned into designer boutiques and neon-lighted singles' bars, booming with amplified techno, house, garage, or salsa.[57] The galaxy of voguish cafés, restaurants, *boîtes*, and galleries is ever evolving. For youthful connoisseurs of the contemporary city, the monuments and museums of the glamorous Ville Lumière are barely noticed backdrops for the Paris that is alive today, made and remade by the flux of taste and fashion.

. . .

Most ordinary Parisians, however, do not find soul in the latest youth favorites or stadiums. They do not hold up any one soulful place as representative of the entire city. Well-known symbols of the city, such as the Eiffel Tower and Sacré-Coeur or Notre-Dame, convey only a small part of what the city is and has been, and they do not evoke the warm feelings that many ordinary or picturesque old places do. None of the classic symbols of Paris's preeminence comes close to representing all that Parisians find soulful, beautiful, charming, and lovable in their city.[58]

A figure of a bigger-than-life, undying being with multiple moods and experiences might help capture more than any of the old emblems do. Yet, despite the centuries-old literary tradition of personifying Paris, ordinary Parisians do not generally think of the city as a person endowed with a continuous core identity, let alone a soul and a spirit. Nor do they think of the city's history as a narrative or a series of biographies (genres most suited to eliciting personal identification). Few leaders of Paris and local heroes stand out over the centuries, and no invented character has emerged to represent the city in the way that the mythical figure Marianne has for the French Republic.

In recent times soulful Paris has stirred loving elegies from such engaging chroniclers as Louis Chevalier, Julian Green, Alphonse Boudard, and Claude Dubois. For them, soul talk has been a way of critiquing modernization and the losses it has entailed since the 1950s. Lovers of Paris, famous and ordinary, have identified soul with the historic, human-scale city surviving in the old central quarters—the pre-Haussmannian streets suited to strollers and small shops, the six-story maximum building height, the gently flowing Seine and its tree-lined quays, the many green squares and parks, and the intimacy and convenience of a familiar, compact neighborhood. The chorus of nostalgic laments, however, has not drowned out a steady, bright counterpoint of voices that affirm the vitality of the Parisian spirit and soul today. The mayor's magazine and local-events publications regularly report on that vitality, often using the old poetic language of the personifying tradition.

In this chapter's survey of contemporary attitudes and feelings, we can see how fully Parisians of our time have assimilated centuries-old ways of viewing and loving Paris. They have been exposed to an idealized imaginary of Paris all their lives; their minds are stocked with memories and dreams fixed long ago in phrases and images now inescapable. They do not have to read Victor Hugo, Baudelaire, or Péguy. Classic tributes to Paris echo endlessly in the popular press and municipal publications. Parisians do not have to go to museums or look in art books to see iconic images of the beautiful city and its pleasures and its Belle-Époque charms. Those images are endlessly recycled in magazines, advertising, postcards, and movies. Classic views of the common folk's Paname—as portrayed by Atget, Willy Ronis, and Robert Doisneau—also remain visible and on display in racks of photos, postcards, and posters. Evocations of it often show up in movies as well (e.g., the 2001 box-office hit *Amélie*). The old idealizing tradition lives on, still imprinting minds with inherited perceptions in spite of the dramatic changes in the cityscape and social life.

French imaginations have not yet invented new images to illumine current realities of Paris with its agglomeration. The best they have for the Paris region today is that of a mosaic, static and vague. But leading French planners are now engaged in imagining the future entire region as "le Grand Paris," one that will be better organized and equipped as a functioning whole. In 2007 the president of the Republic commissioned ten teams of leading architects and urban planners to propose ideas for a better "Grand Paris," projects for the region to be realized in the next fifty years. Some basic themes show up in all the proposals presented in 2009: more public transportation that will better serve the entire region, more and better-planned housing developments, more "coherent" organization of commerce and industry in the region, and a greener metropolis—more green spaces, systematically developed, as well as new measures for energy efficiency.[59]

Several important steps toward realizing the new regional Paris are already well underway. They include efforts to bring Parisian and suburban authorities together for administrative cooperation and inter-communal, as well as regional, coordination and planning. Other significant steps already begun are measures to break down the old barriers between the city and its suburbs. Those include covering the traffic-charged *périphérique* (the twentieth century's addition to a long history of successive walls), extending more métro lines into the suburbs, constructing new tramways, and introducing the city's self-serve bicycle rental system (*vélib'*) into thirty communes bordering the capital. Currently, too, more of the nation's cultural institutions are being installed in the banlieue—the Musée national du sport in Saint-Denis and the new Archives nationales at Peyrefitte near Saint-Denis, for example. At the same time, the long-snubbed industrial suburbs are beginning to gain new attention and respect as cultural tourism destinations—with old industrial infrastructures preserved as heritage sites and a growing number of banlieue festivals, expositions, plays and concerts.

Whatever proposals for "le Grand Paris" are adopted, the history of such efforts shows that many political and economic obstacles lie ahead, diverse local interests making it difficult to carry out a regional plan. It will also be difficult (if history is any guide) for the imaginary of Paris to expand outward beyond the historic center and catch up with the regional realities and the changes underway. Can a new "Grand Paris," even in fifty years, attain anything close to the emotional charge, prestige, and world-famous imagery associated with the classic central city for centuries? Not easy to imagine. In any event, for contemporary Paris it is worth underscoring that the important work of imagining the future metropolis is moving forward. A historically momentous step is now underway at the official level, and the public is being informed of the process.

As a historian, I will not attempt to invent a new figure to capture current realities (that is for Parisians to do), but I will make a few suggestions about what is needed in the Parisian imaginary. New representations will have to be more encompassing and complex than the historic ones traced in this study. They should help us envision the larger-than-ever whole without imposing a sham coherence on it. The prominence of so many diverse foreign presences (architecture, businesses, products, people) may seem to make the task more difficult today, but that may not necessarily be the case. For centuries, Paris's rich symbolism has included markers taken from outside French culture—from the Rome-inspired triumphal arches built by Louis XIV and the ancient Egyptian obelisk implanted by Napoleon to the Manhattan-like towers of Pompidou's time. Now, images of the post-colonial megapolis are needed to reflect the world city of the twenty-first century. They must be capacious enough to take account of the Montparnasse Tower and the high-rise Chinatown of the thirteenth arrondissement, Disneyland out on one side of town and La Défense on the other, as well as troubled suburbs like La Courneuve and Clichy-sous-Bois.

The difficulty is not only that the settlements of the Île-de-France region are so far-flung and disparate. It is also that so much of the long-neglected orphan called "Greater Paris" seems in most minds to lack what the French call soul, having grown up on the wrong side of formidable barriers (physical and mental) separating it from historic "beautiful Paris." The fertile imagination that for centuries has given us a poetic Paris, rich in symbols and soul, has new work to do.

To Know Paris

At the end of every accounting, the *grande ville* spills out over even the best-laid organizing schemas. Every attempt at showing the totality or a unified order ends up incomplete and inadequate. After the guidebook has finished describing "all that's worth seeing," and after the historian has re-counted the eras leading to the present (even in books far longer than this one), much is still left out. Paris is more than its parts, more than its physical fabric, more than its documented history. It cannot be squeezed neatly into a pigeonhole labeled "city of light" or "capital of the world." Nor can it be reduced to a singular "spirit" or "atmosphere." Moreover, it is always changing—from one end to another. Perceptions and memo-ries cannot keep up or take it all in.

The city that tourists visit and residents see daily is one that remains incompletely known, full of unexplored corners and unanticipated hap-penings. Paris eludes our grasp. Therein lies a fundamental condition of its mystique. Viewed as bottomless, always harboring secrets and surprises, the great city has long seemed to offer prodigious possibilities for fulfill-ing one's aspirations and living the good life, whether defined as artistic, intellectual, sensual, romantic, epicurean, or sociable. Abroad and out in the provinces, where many do not know Paris well, an attractive Paris imaginary is common knowledge, a montage of images drawn from paint-ings, novels, movies, songs, postcards, and guidebooks—the product of centuries of gilded memories and flattering descriptions. Imaginations fill in the blanks. Dreams of enjoyments and enchantments take flight. The celebrated places of beauty and pleasure become only a sampling of much more yet to be discovered.

As noted early in this book, wonder and longing have fastened onto the city since the Middle Ages, endowing it with an extraordinary imaginary: Paris as paradise, or the new Athens (or Babylon), the capital of pleasures, the warm community of easy-going "little people," and the hub of civilization and thought, whose magical atmosphere turns all residents into intellectuals and connoisseurs. Dreamland visions and wish-fulfillment tales long ago congealed into a tradition of exuberant paeans, which have echoed through the centuries down to our time. "Paris, while it is the capital of France, is still more the capital of dreamland," observed the English expatriate writer Richard Le Gallienne in 1936.[1]

Idealizing and dreaming have not only helped shape the city's identity and reputation; they have also gilded the images of particular landmarks such as the Moulin Rouge as well as Montmartre generally and such thoroughfares as the Grands Boulevards and the Champs-Élysées. Tales of those places in turn add to the luster of the whole. Like a movie star, Paris is "both ordinary and glamorous, . . . both real and mythical."[2] Its extraordinary mystique is the byproduct of representations and realities interacting over centuries, weaving together collective memory, fantasy, and selective personal experience. It has emanated from a process of image production and idealization to which many genres and countless imaginations have contributed. To be sure, the materials they had to work with have been exceptional: the city's natural endowments and wealth of beautiful monuments. But it is that old, long-term cultural process that has produced the lenses through which the materials are viewed in the best light. The process continues today with tourism promoters, Hollywood romantic comedies, branding advertisers, and travelers just-back-home contributing their variations on old themes.

Now, rather than trying to capture it all in any single image ("City of Light") or single theme, we can do better by conceiving Paris as a set of styles or frameworks that encompass many images and activities.[3] Better to think of the city as an unstable diversity—or an atonal medley—rather than a masterpiece of order and harmony (so dear to French observers and guidebooks). There is so much to work with, so much more than canonical sights and classic imagery. Back in the seventeenth century, guidebooks were already exclaiming over the infinite diversities of the *grande ville*. How can one comprehend it in all its vastness now? I close with a couple of suggestions.

Perhaps most difficult to capture and most likely to be slighted are scenes of everyday life, the kind that some of the famed flâneurs have savored: scruffy little cafés full of locals, homely streets and buildings, green oasis-like squares and parks, thronged street markets and deserted *impasses*. Those who can pull themselves away from the "prestige" of Paris's restaurants, theaters, and other shining attractions, wrote an ardent lover of Paris in 1900, can find more of the city's "infinitely varied riches" and can refresh themselves in "the picturesque qualities of old streets, the orderly activity of commercial centers, [and] the powerful impression of smoggy industrial *faubourgs*."[4] The key is to pay close attention to distinctive mundane particulars, as the German writer Paul Cohen-Portheim did in 1937:

When [the visitor] suddenly notices the infallible taste with which the flower-girl has arranged the masses of blooms on her barrow, the movement of the woman in the box as she lets the cloak slip from her shoulders, the walk of the mannequin coming out [dressmaker] Paquin's door, the crocheted woolen collars of the working women, the gesticulations of the men gossiping outside the *marchand de vin*, the chauffeur calmly lighting a cigarette in the midst of the most frightful traffic—when he suddenly begins to notice the thousand and one characteristic little things going on around him, . . . then these things will begin to form a perfectly definite and unique picture, and the name of that picture is Paris.[5]

Among my own favorites are the fresh baguette-filled bins in the *boulangerie* below my apartment, sidewalk café fronts brightly covered with gallery and theater posters, courtyard gardens and former ateliers in old working-class quarters, off-the-beaten-track bistros and cafés (in Belleville, for example), neighborhood flea markets (*brocantes* and *vide-greniers*), local fêtes in the Butte-aux-Cailles and Montmartre, the walkways along the Canal Saint-Martin teeming with strollers on sunny Sundays, street musicians singing old *chansons* with an accordion or hurdy-gurdy, the myriad delectables laid out in open-air markets, just about any view of the Seine and the quays on a spring or summer evening, and the now-few remnants of Old Paris (in the Marais and Latin Quarter mostly, but also in parts of Montmartre, Belleville, and the Faubourg Saint-Antoine). Delightful, too, are times when I encounter the kernel of reality that lies within the happy Paname myth: the amiable woman and her daughter working a rotisserie (on the Rue Lepic) with a cheerfulness that does not fade even on the hottest summer day, the banter of some hawkers of fruits and vegetables, the bonhomie of big-city neighbors sharing a glass in their local café (or an annual *repas de quartier*), and the nostalgic party scene (old songs and accordion music, dancing, wine drinking) fostered in riverside cafés (*guinguettes*) along the Marne.[6]

But "a perfectly definite and unique picture" would be incomplete and false without some of the less attractive "little things" as well. "It takes the special sensitivity of a Baudelaire or a Proust . . . to convey the charm of a certain kind of ugliness," Julian Green observed. He had in mind such mundane objects as "the plant adorned with a dreadful red ribbon, the worn leather bench spewing out tufts of black horsehair, the solid white marble tabletop, the oilcloth writing pad and the penholder that have served to write so many declarations of love and fine words of parting." About all those, he maintained, you can say "without hesitation: 'That is Paris'" (echoing the exclamation "that, that's Paris!" made famous by Mistinguett's hit song of 1926). The same was true of "one of those coarse brooms sweeping up the leaves at the pavement's edge in October with a sound like the sea, or an array of tired-looking volumes in a bookseller's box on the quays between the Pont Neuf and the Pont Royal." "Good or bad, what Paris produces is Paris, be it a letter, a bit of bread, a pair of socks, or a poem."[7]

That loving view of an all-observing writer, however, was not as all-embracing as it might appear from that line. "I have many times wished the Eiffel tower at the bottom of the ocean," Green admitted. He wished that the Grand and Petit Palais would disappear as well.[8] Later in the century, lovers of "old stones" would nominate the Montparnasse Tower for removal to the deep sea rather than Eiffel's. Yet both the towers remain, and so do such grand monuments as the Grand Palais, while much of what was popular Paris *has* disappeared in recent decades—most notably, Les Halles, that most Parisian of spots for the lovers of Paname. The economic and political powers devoted to Ville-Lumière aims have made their mark on ever more of the city. Even among most ordinary Parisians, it seems, the lure of more modernity has outweighed nostalgia for old-time life lived in modest-to-poor circumstances. And the famous old edifices are no longer considered the only essential symbols of the city. Some prominent modernist edifices of the late twentieth century have become icons too (the Beaubourg and the Louvre Pyramid, in particular). Despite the demolitions and international imports of the late twentieth century, the catalogue of world famous markers has only grown longer.

Today the famed attractions are so numerous and their symbolic importance so inescapable that the charms of the ordinary can be overlooked more easily than ever. They need to be highlighted more than ever before. The surrealists showed the way in the 1920s, finding the marvelous in everyday shop-windows filled with assorted body parts (of mannequins), and in parks and squares, where lions and sirens (lifelike statues) disturbed the otherwise civilized tranquility.

Whatever the specifics chosen, it would be a mistake to consider only things "purely" and uniquely Parisian. Borrowings from abroad have long been prominent components of the "that's-Paris" composite—from the Roman-style triumphal arches and the London-style parks to the central shopping mall known as the Forum des Halles. Foreigners' imaginings have shaped the creation of some of the city's defining emblems—from the dance that Parisians call "le French cancan" (because they recognized how much it fascinated English tourists thirsting for the "gay" and "naughty") to the host of tourist-dependent businesses catering to dreams of the "pleasure" capital. Foods, music, words, and fashions from all over the world—not to mention the swirling lines of hip-hop graffiti and "tagging"—are as much part of contemporary Paris as wine shops and *charcuteries*.

What is distinctive about Paris as a whole is not the enormous variety of its cityscape, attractions, and people (found in every great city), but the aggregate of particulars from its long continuous history, especially its locally stylized set pieces—mansard roofs, Haussmann-style buildings, Wallace fountains, Guimard métro entries, the bridges and quays of the Seine, statues of the once-upon-a-time-distinguished dead, imposing monuments to long-ago glories, all the cumulative residue of centuries, melded together in the cityscape we see today. What is distinctive is the unique ensemble of place-specific historical memories and imaginings that give meanings to the monuments, buildings, and streets. Reminders of revolutions and wars, deaths, occasions of mourning and celebration are strewn throughout the city—from the Bastille to the Arc de Triomphe and La Défense, from Père Lachaise cemetery to the catacombs. Where the physical remains have disappeared, collective memory and historical imagination come to the rescue, filling out the observable present with images and stories picked up from books, paintings, prints, movies, and photographs.

Of course, the stories and images can produce such high expectations that a first-time visitor may have difficulty avoiding disappointment. A mental image of the Moulin Rouge scripted by paintings and movies will bear little resemblance to the bauble of a building that one sees from the middle of the Place Blanche. Misleading more generally is the classic description of Paris as a splendid place of coherent beauty, as if finished to perfection. The catch phrase "the most beautiful city in the world" is as much a cramping shibboleth as it is an old compliment or boast. A better approach is to envision the city as discordant, ever-changing, and full of surprises. Some sense of this emerged centuries ago in images of the city as a living being and especially as a young Parisienne who is capricious and eager for the latest fashion. Paris remains as much as ever a place of endless inventiveness—not just on the part of the officials and event organizers, but also on the part of individuals improvising their own day-to-day lives and their own pastiches of the city, as Michel de Certeau has pointed out.[9]

The guidebooks were right to say that Paris does not readily yield up its secrets or its "soul" to the hurried visitor. But they were mistaken to suggest that they or any cognoscente could reveal the subtle essences and prescribe "must-see" spots, as though following the dictates of some universal standard. In the end, each visitor, immigrant, and Parisian creates a personal version of Paris, blending dreams and memories with on-the-spot discoveries. To know the city means endlessly rediscovering it and re-imagining it. Paris can still be expected to challenge our expectations (even in its elite City of Light manifestations—for examples, see Appendix 1). Fortunately it has not become the stiflingly ordered and homogeneous city that critics of modernity anticipated with dread. The gamut of beauty and ugliness, the elegant and the dreadful, is still there in full flower. Amid new touches added continuously, its historic identities remain palpable at many turns. Still richly human, and conveniently well this side of paradise, it is more than ever a "world" best understood in the plural.

Unusual and Unexpected Paris—A Sampler

Sights at variance with classical Paris can be found even in the very heart of the historical city—near the Louvre and the Palais-Royal:

- The Buren Columns (260 black-and-white striped pillars), in the court of honor at the Palais-Royal, the controversial installation of minimalist artist Daniel Buren in 1986.

- The Kiosque des Noctambules at the métro station Palais-Royal, Place Colette, is a brightly colored aluminum canopy strung with 800 large glass beads—the work of Jean-Michel Othoniel, dedicated on October 30, 2000.

- The "iron-lace"-covered Ministère de la Culture building, 182 Rue Saint-Honoré, by architect Francis Soler, completed in 2004.

Among the many other unexpected works of art scattered around the city:

- Street art and murals by Ben, Nemo, Jean le Gac, Jérôme Mesnager, Miss.Tic, and others. See "Profile: Paris pochoiristes" by Tara Mulholland, *International Herald Tribune*, November 10, 2006.

- The Big Thumb of César/*Le Pouce de César*—a 40-foot-high (12 meters), 18 ton cast iron sculpture, based on a mould of the artist César Baldaccini's own thumb. It was installed in the La Défense quarter in 1993.

- The Love Wall (*Le mur des je t'aime*)—a wall covered with tiles inscribed "I love you" in several hundred languages—is an artistic installation, dedicated in 2000, in a small square just off the Place des Abbesses (Montmartre).

Other sights beyond the guidebook canon:

- Street entertainers (musicians, mimes, magicians, marionettes, acrobats): performances can be found most often on weekends in pedestrian-only areas where many tourists and leisured Parisians pass by. Among such places are: the small bridge (behind Notre Dame) linking the Île de la Cité and the Île Saint-Louis, the plaza in front of the Centre Pompidou, the sidewalks near the church Saint-Germain-des-Prés, and near the Place du Tertre (Butte Montmartre) and in front of Sacré Coeur.

- Thousands of skaters rolling along together do a fun tour of the city almost every Friday night—since the late 1990s. For information about the itinerary set for a given week and the association in charge, see Pari-Roller.com.

- The greening of Paris: community gardens springing up on small lots throughout the city in recent years. For a list of these "jardins partagés" and the associations behind them, a map of their locations, and photographs of the beautiful flowers being grown, visit the city website "Paris.fr", then "Paris Loisir," and then "Paris au vert."

- A slice of authentic Old Paris . . . in the suburbs: the "Square du Vieux Paris" in Nogent-sur-Marne features a Wallace fountain, a Morris column, ornate cast-iron street lamps, signs, and park benches from nineteenth-century Paris—all set out in front of the only surviving Baltard pavilion (moved from Les Halles and reassembled on the banks of the Marne in 1976–77).

Landmark Paris Imagery

CITY OF LIGHT/VILLE LUMIÈRE (MODERNITY, PROGRESS, LIBERTY, BRILLIANCE IN ARTS AND THOUGHT)

Architecture: The Eiffel Tower (1889); the Palais de Chaillot and Palais de Tokyo (1937); the Maison de la Radio (1963); Montparnasse Tower (1973); the Centre Georges Pompidou (Beaubourg Center) (1977); the Arche de la Défense (1989), the Bibliothèque nationale de France (1996), and other *grands projets* of President François Mitterrand.

Images: The Champs-Élysées, Eiffel Tower, and boulevards featured on postcards, posters, in magazine advertisements, and movies—especially Hollywood films: *An American in Paris* (1951) and *Funny Face* (1957), for example.

Paintings: *Paris Street, Rainy Day* (1877) by Gustave Caillebotte; *Boulevard Montmartre at Night* (1897) by Camille Pissarro; *The City of Paris* (1913) by Robert Delaunay; *La Tour Eiffel, Le 14 juillet*, and *La Fée Electricité* (1937) by Raoul Dufy.

Songs: "Ça c'est Paris" (1926), music by José Padilla, lyrics by Lucien Boyer and Jacques Charles, sung by Mistinguett; "Paris je t'aime d'amour" (1930), lyrics by Battaille-Henri, music by Victor Shertzinger.

.   .   .

The modernized city (second half of the twentieth century):

Feature films: *Playtime* (1967), directed by Jacques Tati; *Chacun cherche son chat/When the Cat's Away* (1995), directed by Cédric Klapisch.

The contemporary *banlieue* and its housing projects (*cités*): *2 ou 3 choses que je sais d'elle/2 or 3 Things I Know about Her* (1967), directed by Jean-Luc Godard; *La Haine* (1995)/*Hatred*, directed by Mathieu Kassovitz; *L'Esquive/Games of Love and Chance* (2004), directed by Abdellatif Kechiche.

CAPITAL OF PLEASURES/"GAY PAREE"

Movies featuring the Moulin Rouge, Maxim's, the Folies-Bergère, such as *French Cancan* (1954), directed by Jean Renoir, and *Moulin Rouge* (2001), by Baz Luhrmann.

Songs about the Moulin Rouge, Montmartre, romance, sex: for example, "Pigalle" (1946), lyrics by Georges Ulmer and Géo Koger, music by Georges Ulmer.

Michelin-starred restaurants and gourmet shops (Fauchon and Hédiard on the Place de la Madeleine); cabarets and music halls: Moulin Rouge, Lido, Crazy Horse.

PANAME (THE LITTLE-PEOPLE'S PARIS):

Songs about young working-class men and women and marginal figures, their love life, and their strong attachment to neighborhood and Paris: "Tu le r'verras Paname" (1917), lyrics by Robert Dieudonné and Roger Myra, music by Albert Chantrier; "Mon Paris" (1925), lyrics by Lucien Boyer, music by Jean Boyer and Vincent Scotto.

Many songs by Maurice Chevalier and Édith Piaf, such as "La Marche de Ménilmontant"

(1942), lyrics by Maurice Chevalier and Maurice Vandair, music by Charles Borel-Clerc; Piaf's "Paris" (1949), lyrics and music by A. Bernheim; "Paris, tu es la gaieté" and "Bal dans ma rue" (1949), lyrics and music by M. Emer.

"À Paris" (1949), music and lyrics by Francis Lemarque; "Paname" (1960), lyrics and music by Léo Ferré, sung by Léo Ferré, Juliette Gréco, Catherine Sauvage.

Photographs: Works of Eugène Atget, the Séeberger brothers, Brassaï, Willy Ronis, René-Jacques, Robert Doisneau, Henri Cartier-Bresson, Édouard Boubat, André Martin, André Kertész, Izis, Peter Turnley.

Movies: *Sous les toits de Paris* (1930) and *Quatorze juillet* (1932) directed by René Clair; *Hôtel du Nord* (1938) and *Les Enfants du Paradis* (1944–1945), both directed by Marcel Carné; *Casque d'or (Golden Marie)* (1951), by Jacques Becker—Paname's colorful marginals and transgressors; *Amélie* (2001), directed by Jean-Pierre Jeunet.

MEMORIES, IMAGES, AND VESTIGES OF THE BELLE ÉPOQUE

Films such as *Paris 1900* (1947), directed by Nicole Védrès; *Le Silence est d'or* (1947), directed by René Clair; and *Gigi* (1958), directed by Vincente Minnelli.

Paintings by Jean Béraud, Jules Chéret (and posters), Auguste Renoir, Henri Toulouse-Lautrec, Giovanni Boldini.

Photographs by Eugène Atget, Jacques-Henri Lartigue, and the Séeberger brothers.

Memoirs by Francis Carco, Pierre Mac Orlan, and Paul Morand (especially Morand's book *1900*, published in 1931).

Sites and street fixtures: Guimard métro entrances—complete models at Abbesses and Porte Dauphine; the Eiffel Tower (1889), the Grand Palais and Petit Palais (1900), the Pont Alexandre III (1900); Castel Béranger by Guimard (circa 1895—14 Rue La Fontaine); Le Bistro du peintre (116 Avenue Ledru-Rollin), Maxim's (3 Rue Royale), Restaurant Chartier (7 Rue du Faubourg Montmartre).

Modern Paris Timeline

1841–1845: Construction of new fortifications (named after Premier Adolphe Thiers) around the city.

1852: Following a coup d'état by President of the Second Republic Louis Napoleon, he was crowned emperor—as Napoleon III.

1853–1870: Haussmann, as prefect of the Seine (the city of Paris then a department), directs urban renewal, which included construction of iron pavilions (designed by Baltard) for the central market, Les Halles (constructed 1854–1874).

1855: First "exposition universelle" in Paris.

1860: Annexation of communes (Montmartre, for one) and parts of communes within the fortifications.

1862–1875: Construction of the Opéra-Garnier.

1867: Second "exposition universelle" in Paris.

1870: From September on, Paris under siege by Prussian army.

1871: The Paris Commune, March 18 to May 28, ending with "the bloody week" of repression by the army and fiery destruction of important public buildings, including the Hôtel de Ville.

1875: Inauguration of the new opera, the Palais Garnier.

1878: First "exposition universelle" under the Third Republic.

1882: Inauguration of new Hôtel de Ville de Paris.

1883: Préfect of the Seine Eugène René Poubelle makes obligatory the use of metal trash cans, which take on his name.

1885: Funeral of Victor Hugo (May 22).

1889: Another Exposition universelle, for which the Eiffel Tower was built. Moulin Rouge opens.

1897: Commission municipale du Vieux Paris created.

1898: Dreyfus affair.

1900: Exposition universelle; Petit Palais and Grand Palais; Gare d'Orsay; first line of the métro.

1910: Flooding of the Seine.

1913: Last horse-drawn omnibus.

1914: Declaration of war (Aug. 3).

1918: Armistice (Nov. 11).

1919: Law authorizing destruction of the fortifications.

1925: Exposition des Arts décoratifs.

1931: Exposition coloniale—in the Bois de Vincennes.

1934: Deadly riot, Place de la Concorde (Feb. 6).

1936: Electoral victory of the Popular Front (May 3).

1937: Exposition universelle des arts et techniques: Palais de Chaillot and the Palais de Tokyo.

1939: Declaration of war against Nazi Germany (Sept. 3).

1940: German army enters Paris (June 14).

1941: Opening of internment camp for Jews at Drancy (August).

1942: Massive arrests of Jews (12,884), detained in the Vélodrome d'Hiver and then deported (July 18).

1944: Uprising of Parisians (Aug. 19); Liberation of Paris completed (Aug. 26).

1947: Jean-François Gravier's influential critique of the centralizing capital: *Paris et le désert français.*

1949: End of rationing tickets.

1950: Celebration of the bi-millennium of Paris (July).

1952: Movie *Casque d'or.*

1955: Decree instituting new policy of decentralization of industries.

1956: Beginning of construction of the *Boulevard périphérique* (beltway), completed in 1973.

1957: Construction of the housing project Courtillières in Pantin (finished in 1964).

1958: CNIT (a huge exhibit hall) at La Défense; Charles de Gaulle (June 3) is voted full power for six months, while a new constitution is written and approved by referendum.

1960: Regional planning: Plan d'aménagement et d'organisation générale de la région parisienne (PADOG).

1961: Law creating the District of the Région of Paris—with Paul Delouvrier as its chief administrator (*délégué général*); inauguration of Orly airport; deadly repression (hundreds killed) of Algerians demonstrating against curfew (Oct. 17).

1962: "Malraux law" establishing "safeguarded sectors."

1963: Inauguration of the Maison de la Radio.

1964: Completion of the Cité des 4000 at La Courneuve; seven new departments take the place of the old departments of the Seine and the Seine-et-Oise.

1968: Revolt of university students and union workers (May).

1969: Transfer of Les Halles to Rungis; first line of the RER (regional train system); resignation of President de Gaulle; election of George Pompidou as president (1969–1974).

1973: The Tour Montparnasse completed.

1974: Inauguration of new airport Roissy Charles-de-Gaulle.

1976: The Region Île-de-France replaces the District.

1977: Paris elects a mayor, Jacques Chirac (mayor 1977–1995), the first since 1870; opening of the Centre Pompidou (Beaubourg).

1979: The Forum des Halles inaugurated.

1981: Election of François Mitterrand as president.

1986: The Musée d'Orsay opens; La Cité des Sciences, des Techniques et de l'Industrie at La Villette opens.

1987: L'Institut du monde arabe inaugurated.

1989: The Pyramide du Louvre opens; L'Opéra Bastille inaugurated; La Grande Arche de la Défense inaugurated (July 14); Ministère des Finances building at Bercy completed.

1993: Le Grand Louvre—expansion completed: renovated Richelieu wing, other new exhibition spaces, and the Galerie du Carrousel.

1995: La Cité de la Musique inaugurated at La Villette.

1996: The general-public reading rooms (the upper-level) of the new Bibliothèque nationale de France (at Tolbiac or the "site François-Mitterrand") open.

1998: The library for researchers at the Bibliothèque nationale de France opens; the Stade de France opens in Saint-Denis.

2001: Election of Bertrand Delanoë (Socialist) as mayor of Paris; new efforts at cooperation between the city and the suburban communes.

2002: Creation of Paris-Plage.

2005: Youth riots in suburbs to the north of Paris after two adolescents were killed while fleeing from the police (Oct.–early Nov.).

2006: Inauguration of the first section of the tramway des Maréchaux. Opening of the Musée Quai Branly, "Le Musée des Arts premiers."

2007: Opening of the Cité nationale de l'histoire de l'immigration in the Palais de la Porte Dorée.

2008: Opening of the Centquatre arts center (104 Rue d'Aubervilliers).

2009: Beginning of construction of new Archives nationales in suburbs near Saint-Denis.

. . .

A more complete, much longer chronological table can be found in Annie Fourcaut et al., eds. *Paris/Banlieues: conflits et solidarités: historiographie, anthologie, chronologie, 1788–2006* (Grâne: Créaphis, 2007), pp. 417–76.

Notes

INTRODUCTION

1. Julian Green, *Paris* (New York: Marion Boyars, 1991). Bilingual edition with English trans. by J. A. Underwood. ("Julian" is the name his American parents gave him upon his birth in Paris in 1900; "Julien" is the form used by French publishers of the many works he wrote in French from the 1920s to 1992, literary works that earned him election to the Académie française in 1971.) See the chapter titled "A Secret City/Une Ville secrète" (esp. p. 48), first published in the *Oeuvres complètes* (Paris: Pléiade, 1972). I am also indebted to the thinking of Michel de Certeau, *L'Invention du quotidien*, vol. I: *Arts de faire* (Paris: Gallimard, new ed., 1990), esp. chap. 7, "Marches dans la ville." Other studies of Paris that have taken the pluralist approach in recent years—though with themes and analyses quite different from mine—include Eric Hazan's *L'Invention de Paris* (Paris: Seuil, 2004); Jean-Pierre A. Bernard, *Les Deux Paris: les représentations de Paris dans la seconde moitié du XIXe siècle* (Seyssel: Champ Vallon, 2001); and Karlheinz Stierle's *La Capitale des signes: Paris et son discours*, translated from German by Marianne Rocher-Jacquin (Paris: Maison des Sciences de l'Homme, 2001).

2. Altogether more than seven hundred of those images appeared in print by the era of Baudelaire, literary scholar Pierre Citron has shown. See his two-volume work, *La Poésie de Paris dans la littérature française, de Rousseau à Baudelaire* (Paris: Les Éditions de Minuit, 1961). For writers' treatments in the nineteenth century, see Christopher Prendergast, *Paris and the Nineteenth Century* (Cambridge, Mass.: Blackwell, 1992) and Priscilla Ferguson's *Paris as Revolution: Writing the Nineteenth-Century City* (Berkeley: University of California Press, 1994), in addition to Stierle's *La Capitale des signes*. On images of the city more generally, two classic treatises are Kevin Lynch, *The Image of the City* (Cambridge, Mass.: Technology Press, 1960), and Pierre Sansot, *Poétique de la ville* (Paris: Klincksieck, 1971).

3. On the importance and workings of memory, I draw on the ideas of Maurice Halbwachs (who published now-classic works on collective memory as early as 1925) and Pierre Nora, who conceived and edited the superb multivolume work titled *Les Lieux de mémoire*, 7 vols. (Paris: Gallimard, 1984–1992). My work, however, highlights sites of memory that for the most part are not the ones treated in Nora's collection (translated as *Realms of Memory* [New York: Columbia University Press, 3 vols., 1996–1998]). My account focuses on memories and dreams (especially wish images) that have been sources of the leading "imaginaries" surrounding modern Paris. I owe the term and concept "imaginaries" to contemporary French historians who have used it fruitfully: see, for example, the issue of *Sociétés & Représentations* (no. 17) titled *Imaginaires parisiens*, ed. Jean-Louis Robert and Myriam Tsikounas (March 2004). Other excellent contributions may be found in *Paris le peuple: XVIIIe–XXe siècle*, ed. Jean-Louis Robert and Danielle Tartakowsky (Paris: Publications de la Sorbonne, 1999). For an exposition of the theory of urban imaginaries or representations, see Marcel Roncayolo, *Lecture de villes: formes et temps* (Marseille: Parenthèses, 2002), esp. chap. 23, "Imaginaire." See also the excellent methodological study by Antoine Bailly, Catherine Baumont, Jean-Marie Huriot, and Alain Sallez, *Représenter la ville* (Paris: Economica, 1995).

4. In addition to the literary studies cited above in Note 2, see the useful anthology by Benjamin Arranger, ed., *Paris vu par les écrivains* (Paris: Arcadia, 2003). Studies of Paris paintings are too numerous to list here. A large scholarly survey of note is *The History of Paris in Painting*, ed. Georges Duby and Guy Lobrichon (English ed., New York: Abbeville Press, 2009). A shorter survey (perhaps useful as an overview) is Amélie Chazelles, *Paris vu par les peintres* (Lausanne: Vilo/Edita, 1987). For Paris in movies, see Gilles Nadeau and Jean Douchet, *Paris cinéma: une ville vue par le cinéma de 1895 à nos jours* (Paris: Éditions du May, 1987), and N. T. Binh, with Franck Garbarz, *Paris au cinéma, La vie rêvée de la capitale: de Méliès à Amélie Poulain* (Paris: Parigramme, 2005). See also Vanessa R. Schwartz, *It's So French! Hollywood, Paris, and the Making of Cosmopolitan Film Culture* (Chicago: University of Chicago Press, 2007), esp. chap. 1: "The Belle-Epoque That Never Ended: Frenchness and the Can-Can Film of the 1950s." For albums of memorable photographs of Paris, see Jean-Claude Gautrand, ed., *Paris mon amour* (Cologne: Taschen, 2004), and Virginie Chardin, *Paris et la photographie: cent histoires extraordinaires de 1839 à nos jours*, Préface, Patrick Modiano (Paris: Parigramme, 2003). Nineteenth-century photography is closely examined in Michael Marrinan's *Romantic Paris: Histories of a Cultural Landscape, 1800–1850* (Stanford, Calif.: Stanford University Press, 2009), and Shelley Rice's *Parisian Views* (Cambridge, Mass.: MIT Press, 1997). For popular songs that have made Parisian motifs widely familiar, convenient collections include: *Paris ses chansons: les 30 plus belles chansons sur Paris* (Paris: Paul Beuscher, 1995); Pierre Saka, *La Chanson française à travers ses succès* (Paris: Larousse, 1988); and (an anthology not limited to songs) Bernard Delvaille, *Paris, ses poètes, ses chansons*, preface by André Hardellet, photos by Serge de Sazo (Paris: Seghers, 1977).

CHAPTER ONE

1. See Pierre Citron, *La Poésie de Paris dans la littérature française de Rousseau à Baudelaire* (Paris: Éditions de Minuit, 1961), I: pp. 20–24. See also Stephen C. Ferruolo, "Parisius-Paradisius: The City, Its Schools, and the Origins of the University of Paris," in *The University and the City: From Medieval Origins to the Present*, ed. Thomas Bender (New York: Oxford University Press, 1988), pp. 22–43.

2. Citron, *La Poésie de Paris*, I: p. 21, and Boris Bove, "Aux origines du complexe de supériorité des Parisiens: les louanges de Paris au Moyen Age," in *Être Parisien*: actes du colloque organisé par l'École doctorale d'histoire de l'Université Paris I Panthéon-Sorbonne et la Fédération des Sociétés historiques et archéologiques de Paris-Île-de-France, ed. Claude Gauvard and Jean-Louis Robert (Paris: Publications de la Sorbonne, 2004), pp. 423–43.

3. *Paris pittoresque*, ed. G. Sarrut and B. Saint-Edme (Paris: D'Urtubie, Worms et Cie, 1837), I: p. ii.

4. *Conty's Pocket Guide to Paris*, English edition (Paris: Conty's Guides Office, 1898), pp. 30 ("gayest"), 51; *Cassell's Guide to Paris and the Universal Exposition of 1900* (London: Cassell, 1900), p. 1; Baedeker's *Paris and Its Environs* (Leipzig: Karl Baedeker, 1904; 15th revised edition), p. xxviii ("seductive capital"), and p. 9 ("indisputably the cradle of high culinary art").

5. On "horrible" Paris, see Georges Grisson, *Paris horrible et Paris original* (Paris: E. Dentu, 1882). Working the same vein were Hugues Le Roux, *L'Enfer parisien* (Paris: Victor Havard, 1888), and Charles Virmaître, *Paris impur* (Paris: Dalou, 1889). For a detailed description of the rats, see Henri d'Almeras, "Les Rats de Paris," *Le Magasin*

pittoresque, 15 Jan. 1900, p. 54, describing the "gigantic" russet-colored *surmulots*, which reigned "unrivaled" in the sewers of the city.

6. Jacques Lux, "Les Laideurs de Paris," *Revue bleue*, 17 Aug. 1907, pp. 223–24.

7. Jules Armengaud, *Nettoyons Paris* (Paris: Maurice Bauche, Éditeur, 1907), pp. xiii, 8, 17–18.

8. Henri d'Almera, "Histoire culinaire de Paris," *Le Magasin pittoresque*, 1 Mar. 1900, p. 147. In d'Almera's words, people no longer had enough "leisure" or "tranquility of soul" to "savor a good meal."

9. André Billy, *Paris vieux & neuf. La Rive droite* (Paris: Eugène Rey, 1909). His opening chapter is an essay on "L'Amour de Paris"; pp. 11 ("très inutiles"), 14, 18. Billy's declared purpose was to "reinforce" and "multiply" the "reasonable and unreasonable reasons" for loving "our beautiful Paris."

10. Roy Porter, *London: A Social History* (Cambridge, Mass.: Harvard University Press, 1994), p. 11.

11. Simon Schama, *The Embarrassment of Riches: An Interpretation of Dutch Culture in the Golden Age* (Berkeley: University of California Press, 1988), p. 298.

12. Michel de Montaigne, *Essays*, Book III, chap. ix.

13. Tournon, *Moyen de rendre parfaitement propres les rues de Paris* (Paris, 1789), p. 60, quoted in Alain Corbin, *Le Miasma et la jonquille: l'odorat et l'imaginaire social XVIIIe–XIXe siècles* (Paris: Flammarion, 1986), p. 67.

14. John Lough, *Paris Theatre Audiences in the Seventeenth and Eighteenth Centuries* (London: Oxford University Press, 1957, 1965), p. 209.

15. Nikolai M. Karamzin, *Letters of a Russian Traveler, 1789–1790* (New York, 1957), quoted in Johannes Willms, *Paris, Capital of Europe: From the Revolution to the Belle Epoque* (New York: Holmes & Meier, 1997), p. 13.

16. Marie-Jeanne Dumont, "Du vieux Paris au Paris nouveau: Abécédaire d'architecture urbaine," in *Le Débat*, an issue entitled "Le Nouveau Paris," no. 80 (May–Aug. 1994), p. 6. See also David P. Jordan, *Transforming Paris: The Life and Labors of Baron Haussmann* (New York: Free Press, 1995) and the still valuable work of David H. Pinkney, *Napoleon III and the Rebuilding of Paris* (Princeton, N.J.: Princeton University Press, 1958). For an excellent analysis of the economic and social processes at work, see David Harvey, *Paris, Capital of Modernity* (New York: Routledge, 2003). On the new sewers, as an engineering feat and as a tourist attraction (from 1867 on), see Donald Reid, *Paris Sewers and Sewermen: Realities and Representations* (Cambridge, Mass.: Harvard University Press, 1991).

17. Paul Léon, *Paris, histoire de la rue* (Paris: La Taille douce, 1942), p. 220 (". . . l'éclairage de Paris a centuplé de puissance, passant de trois cent cinquante millions à soixante-quinze milliards de bougies-heures.").

18. Richard Harding Davis, *About Paris* (New York: Harper & Brothers, 1895), pp. 78–79.

19. Léo Claretie, "L'Art de la réclame," *Le Magasin pittoresque* (1899), pp. 107–9.

20. Hugo, "La Vision de Paris dans l'exil," dated November 1875, originally in *Pendant exil*, reprinted in volume entitled *Paris*, p. 122, in *Oeuvres complètes* (Paris: J. Hetzel, n.d.).

21. Citron, *La Poésie de Paris*, vol. II—on images of Paris as the center, heart, brain, and "head" (*tête*) of the world and beacon (*phare*). Wladimir Berelowitch, "La France dans le 'Grand Tour' des nobles russes au cours de la seconde moitié du XVIIIe siècle," *Cahiers du monde russe et soviétique* XXXIV, 1–2 (Jan.–June 1993), pp. 193–210.

22. Rebecca Spang, *The Invention of the Restaurant* (Cambridge, Mass.: Harvard University Press, 2000), esp. chap. 7: "Putting Paris on the Menu." Spang notes that the guidebook image of Paris as a city of great restaurants preceded the reality (pp. 171–72). Mondion, *Paris Complete: A New Alphabetical Guide for the Traveller in Paris* (Paris: Alphonse Taride, 1855), p. 2.

23. Gautier wrote the preface of Édouard Fournier's book *Paris démoli* (1855). Françoise Choay, "Pensées sur la ville, arts de la ville," chap. 3 of *Histoire de la France urbaine*, ed. Georges Duby, vol. IV: *La Ville de l'âge industriel*, ed. Maurice Agulhon (Paris: Seuil, 1983), p. 182.

24. Reid, *Paris Sewers and Sewermen*, p. 39.

25. Edmond Texier and Albert Kaempfen, *Paris, capitale du monde* (Paris: J. Hetzel, 1867), p. 7: "Aussi Paris n'est-il plus seulement la capitale des quatre-vingt-neuf départements, il est proclamé *capitale du monde*." The comment on alignment appears on p. 3. Edmond Texier was editor of the popular magazine *L'Illustration*, and Albert Kaempfen, a pseudonym for Louis Courajod, was a curator at the Musée du Louvre.

26. Texier and Kaempfen, *Paris, capitale du monde*, p. 1—preface of editors: "Paris put on a new suit, society was about to make itself a new skin." See also pp. 7, 10.

27. Louis Veuillot, *Les Odeurs de Paris* (Paris: Palmé, 1867), pp. 352–53.

28. *Baedeker's Paris*, 1904, p. xxv. On the cosmopolitanism of Paris and the many foreigners drawn to it in the first half of the nineteenth century, see Philip Mansel, *Paris between Empires: Monarchy and Revolution, 1814–1852* (London: Phoenix Press, 2003).

29. *Paris-Guide par les principaux écrivains et artistes de la France* (Paris: Librairie Internationale, 1867). A reprinted edition (Paris: La Découverte/Maspero, 1983) provides only a couple hundred of the more-than-two-thousand pages in the original, but includes a valuable new introduction by Corinne Verdet. For Louis Blanc's essay "Le Vieux Paris," see pp. 17–18.

30. Alistair Horne, *The Fall of Paris: The Siege and the Commune, 1870–71* (Garden City, New York: Anchor, 1967), and Rupert Christiansen, *Paris Babylon: The Story of the Paris Commune* (New York: Penguin, 1996).

31. Arthur Rimbaud, "L'Orgie parisienne ou Paris se repeuple" (an often-quoted poem written May 1871).

32. Emmanuel Le Bail and Sylvain Ageorges, *Sur les traces des Expositions universelles: Paris 1855–1937* (Paris: Parigramme, 2006), pp. 79, 104. The 1900 Expo occupied ten times the terrain of the 1855 Expo. On "the capital of the nineteenth century," see Benjamin's two essays by that title ("exposés" of 1935 and 1939) in *The Arcades Project*, trans. Howard Eiland and Kevin McLaughlin (Cambridge, Mass.: Harvard University Press, 1999), prepared on the basis of the German volume edited by Rolf Tiedemann. See also Margaret Cohen's recent, useful essay, "Benjamin's Phantasmagoria: The *Arcades Project*," in David S. Ferris, ed., *The Cambridge Companion to Walter Benjamin* (Cambridge, UK: Cambridge University Press, 2004), pp. 199–220. Harry Levenstein, *Seductive Journey: American Tourists in France from Jefferson to the Jazz Age* (Chicago: University of Chicago Press, 1998), pp. 89–90, sums up the impact of the 1867 Exposition on Americans.

33. Christophe Charle develops at length the point about the lingering sense of trauma left by the 1871 defeat and the Commune in his account of Paris 1900. See his *Paris, fin de siècle (culture et politique)* (Paris: Seuil, 1998).

34. Bernard Marchand, *Les Ennemis de Paris: la haine de la grande ville des Lumières à nos jours* (Rennes: Presses universitaires de Rennes, 2009), esp. part three, chap. 9: "Les Critiques urbaphobes" and "Les grands mythes."

35. See Henri Loyrette, "La Tour Eiffel," in Pierre Nora, ed., *Les Lieux de mémoire*, III: *Les France* (Paris: Gallimard, 1992), 3: *De l'Archive à l'Emblème*, pp. 475–503, and Joseph Harriss, *The Tallest Tower: Eiffel and the Belle Époque* (Boston: Houghton Mifflin, 1975).

36. François Caron, "L'Embellie parisienne à la Belle Époque: l'invention d'un modèle de consommation," *Vingtième siècle* 47 (1995), pp. 42–57.

37. Notably, French historian Bernard Marchand gives top honors to Vienna in his history *Paris, histoire d'une ville, XIXe–XXe siècle* (Paris: Seuil, 1993), p. 220. On the brilliance of nineteenth-century Paris painters in social context, see Robert L. Herbert, *Impressionism: Art, Leisure, and Parisian Society* (New Haven, Conn.: Yale University Press, 1988), and T. J. Clark, *The Painting of Modern Life: Paris in the Art of Manet and his Followers* (New York: Knopf, 1985). On the decorative arts, see Debora L. Silverman, *Art Nouveau in Fin-de-Siècle France: Politics, Psychology, and Style* (Berkeley: University of California Press, 1989).

38. Theodore Child, *The Praise of Paris* (New York: Harper & Brothers, 1982), p. 52; Théodore Banville, *L'Âme de Paris, nouveaux souvenirs* (Paris: G. Charpentier, 1890), pp. 1–2: "Le phénomène essentiel et permanent de Paris, c'est que l'idée s'y boit avec l'air qu'on respire"; ". . . tous les êtres . . . savent tout sans avoir rien appris."

39. Victor Hugo's articles "Guerre aux démolisseurs!" from 1825 and 1832 were reprinted in his *Littérature et philosophie mêlées* (Furne et Cie, 1841). On Hugo and his influential "Old Paris" novel, *Notre-Dame de Paris* (1831), see Citron, *Poésie de Paris*, I: pp. 390–93. On preservation and writers more generally, see Choay, "Pensées sur la ville, arts de la ville," pp. 180–86. For a convenient entry into the work of twenty-eight leading scholars on modernizing Paris before Haussmann, see Karen Bowie, ed., *La Modernité avant Haussmann: formes de l'espace urbain à Paris, 1801–1853* (Paris: Éditions Recherches, 2001). Included are contributions by Nicholas Papayanis, Barrie Ratcliffe, Jeannene Przyblyski, David Van Zanten, Florence Bourillon, and others who have published fuller versions in their own books and articles elsewhere.

40. Pierre Pinon, *Atlas du Paris haussmannien: la ville en héritage du Second Empire à nos jours* (Paris: Parigramme, 2002), p. 176. See also Jordan, *Transforming Paris*, pp. 262–65; Louis Blanc, "Le Vieux Paris" (1867), in *Paris-Guide par les principaux écrivains et artistes de la France*, p. 18: "les villes ont une âme, qui est leur passé"; "et leur beauté matérielle n'a tout son prix que lorsqu'elle laisse subsister les traces visibles de cette autre beauté qui se compose de souvenirs."

41. John McCormick, *Popular Theatres of Nineteenth-Century France* (London: Routledge, 1993), pp. 206, 215, 218, 221; Roger Caillois, "Paris, mythe moderne," *La Nouvelle Revue française* 48, no. 284 (May 1937), pp. 682–99. On the popularity of crime and detective stories in the period, see Dominique Kalifa, *L'Encre et le sang: récits de crime et société à la Belle Époque* (Paris: Fayard, 1995).

42. Grisson, *Paris horrible*, pp. 1–4 (". . . brillant, pimpant, viveur et tapageur . . . ").

43. Molly Nesbit, *Atget's Seven Albums* (New Haven, Conn.: Yale University Press, 1992), pp. 62–66, 105–10; Ronnie L. Grad and Timothy A. Riggs, *Visions of City and Country: Prints and Photographs of Nineteenth-Century France* (Worcester, Mass.: Worcester Art Museum, 1982), pp. 128–32.

44. Naomi Schor, "Collecting Paris," in *The Culture of Collecting*, ed. John Elsner and Roger Cardinal (Cambridge, Mass.: Harvard University Press, 1994), pp. 252–74—on postcards as idealizing iconography.

45. Prominent among such popular works are Édouard Drumont's *Les Fêtes nationales* (1879), describing historic Paris festivities at their popular best (the same Drumont who later

whipped up the anti-Semitic, anti-Dreyfus crowds), Victor Fournel's *Le Vieux Paris* (1887) and Fournel's *Les Cris de Paris: types et physionomies d'autrefois* (1887), and illustrated history books by Albert Robida, such as *Paris de siècle en siècle* (1895).

46. See Elizabeth Emery, "Protecting the Past: Albert Robida and the *Vieux Paris* Exhibit at the 1900 World's Fair," *Journal of European Studies* 35, no. 1 (Mar. 2005), pp. 64–85.

47. David S. Barnes, *The Making of a Social Disease: Tuberculosis in Nineteenth-Century France* (Berkeley: University of California Press, 1995) and *The Great Stink of Paris and the Nineteenth-Century Struggle against Filth and Germs* (Baltimore: Johns Hopkins University Press, 2006).

48. Albert Callet, *L'Agonie du vieux Paris* (Paris: H. Daragon, Éditeur, 1911), pp. 8, 13–15. Callet quotes Cain: The "amoureux du Passé," Cain remarked (p. 8), were in a struggle "against the vandals, the fools [*sots*], the ignoramuses and the imbeciles who, with a tireless tenacity, keep tearing at our Paris."

49. Hervé Maneglier, *Paris impérial: la vie quotidienne sous le Second Empire* (Paris: Armand Colin, 1990), chaps. 8–10.

50. Alfred Delvau, *Les Plaisirs de Paris* (Paris: A. Faure, 1867), p. 3. Delvau also called Paris "the capital of pleasure" (chap. 12). A few years earlier, Richard Cortambert's book *Impressions d'un Japonais en France, suivies des impressions des Annamites en Europe* (Paris: Achille Faure, 1864) has the Japanese visitor exclaim: "Upon entering Paris, what strikes me especially was the air of sensual delight [*volupté*], the atmosphere of profane pleasures that one breathes with full lungs there" (p. 48); "Decidedly, Paris is truly the capital of pleasures" (p. 51).

51. Texier and Kaempfen, *Paris, capitale du monde*, pp. 9, 11: "Paris n'est-il pas la ville des plaisirs, le rendez-vous des désoeuvrés, le séjour privilégié des millionnaires?"

52. Camille Debans, *Les Plaisirs et les curiosités* (Paris: E. Kolb, 1889), pp. 5–6.

53. Maude Annesley, *My Parisian Year* (London: Mills & Boon, 1912), pp. 1–2, 32, 41, 253.

54. Captain Wray Sylvester, *The Nocturnal Pleasures of Paris, A Guide to the Gay City* (Paris: Byron Library, 1889), pp. 10, 11.

55. Delvau, *Plaisirs*, pp. 7–8.

56. Davis, *About Paris*, p. 47.

57. Sénateur XXX, "Spectacles à ne pas offrir aux étrangers," *La Revue des revues* 33 (15 April 1900), p. 148. Georges Montorgueil, preface of A.-P. Lannoy's *Les Plaisirs et la vie de Paris (Guide du Flâneur)* (Paris: L. Borel, 1900), p. ii.

58. Sylvester, *The Nocturnal Pleasures of Paris*, p. 11.

59. Maxime du Camp, *Paris* (Paris: Hachette, 1875), VI: pp. 332–33, 384.

60. On commercial entertainments of the late nineteenth century, see Charles Rearick, *Pleasures of the Belle Époque: Entertainment and Festivity in Turn-of-the-Century France* (New Haven, Conn.: Yale University Press, 1985), and Vanessa R. Schwartz, *Spectacular Realities: Early Mass Culture in Fin-de-Siècle Paris* (Berkeley: University of California Press, 1998).

61. Billy, *Paris vieux & neuf. La Rive droite*, pp. 241–42. Billy's phrase was "une pochade du génie français."

62. Élie Richard, *Le Guide des Grands Ducs* (Paris: Monde moderne, 1925), pp. 229–31: "Montmartre a fortement agi, depuis vingt-cinq ans, sur les imaginations françaises"; "The *braves gens* who want to save and relaunch 'l'esprit montmartrois' are not of the area [*pays*], nor from Paris, [and] often not from France"; "La gloire hôtellière, les méthodes épicières, les lancements touristiques hantent leurs projets."

63. Richard Whiteing, *The Life of Paris* (London: John Murray, 1900), pp. 209–10, 216, 219.

64. See, for example, the Baedeker Paris guides for 1900, p. 37, and 1904, p. 39.

65. Davis, *About Paris*, pp. 55–63. The Château Rouge was at 57 Rue Galande, in the back of a courtyard. The Père Lunette was around the corner on the Rue des Anglais. Grisson described the regulars of those establishments as drunks, prostitutes, scoundrels (*chenapans*). The two most famous dives were "assommoirs," the lowest order of cheap drinking place, filled with strong odors of "rancid grease, mildew, and a barracks-room emanation." See his *Paris horrible*, p. 144.

66. Davis, *About Paris*, pp. 55–56: "these are not the only abodes of poverty . . . and criminals in Paris . . . but they are the only places of such interest that the visitor sees."

67. Ibid., pp. 58, 60–62. Visits to the Paris morgue offered similar macabre thrills; see Schwartz, *Spectacular Realities*, chap. 2.

68. Sisley Huddleston, *Paris Salons, Cafés, Studios* (Philadelphia: J. B. Lippincott, 1928), p. 31.

69. Richard, *Le Guide des Grands Ducs*, pp. 92, 149, and Claude Dubois, *La Bastoche: bal-musette, plaisir et crime, 1750–1939* (Paris: Félin, 1997).

70. I examined an impressive collection of these publicity papers in the "Actualités" archives of the Bibliothèque historique de la Ville de Paris.

71. See Patrice Higonnet, *Paris, Capital of the World* (Cambridge, Mass.: Harvard University Press, 2002), chap. 5: "Negative Myths of the Parisienne," and Gay L. Gullickson, *Unruly Women of Paris: Images of the Commune* (Ithaca, N.Y.: Cornell University Press, 1996).

72. Paul Jarry, "Coins de palette, Croquis et paysages parisiens," *Bulletin de la Société Le Vieux Papier*, no. 1 (Jan. 1911), p. 5.

73. Lud.-Georges Hamon, "La Seine à Paris," *Le Mois littéraire et pittoresque* 8, no. 46 (Oct. 1902), p. 462.

74. Richard D. Mandell, *Paris 1900: The Great World's Fair* (Toronto: University of Toronto Press, 1967), p. 58; Lenard Berlanstein, *Daughters of Eve: A Cultural History of French Theater Women from the Old Regime to the Fin de siècle* (Cambridge, Mass.: Harvard University Press, 2001).

75. *Guide Armand Silvestre, de Paris et de ses environs et de l'Exposition de 1900* (Paris: Didier & Méricant, Éditeurs, 1900), pp. 8–10. On social and economic conditions conducive to prostitution, see Alain Corbin, *Les Filles de noce* (Paris: Flammarion, 1982), pp. 303–11. Studies of Parisiennes at work include Judith G. Coffin, *The Politics of Women's Work: The Paris Garment Trades, 1750–1915* (Princeton, N.J.: Princeton University Press, 1996), and Marilyn J. Boxer, "Women in Industrial Homework: The Flowermakers of Paris in the Belle Epoque," *French Historical Studies* 12, no. 3. (Spring, 1982), pp. 401–23.

76. Alain Corbin, "Paris-province," in *Les Lieux de mémoire*, III: *Les France*, 1: *Conflits et partages*, p. 808. See also Corbin's *Filles de noce*, part 2, on the decline of the licensed "maison close" and the rise of new forms of prostitution, such as the more comfortable, bourgeois-style "maisons de rendez-vous."

77. Charles Bernheimer, *Figures of Ill Repute: Representing Prostitution in Nineteenth-Century France* (Cambridge, Mass.: Harvard University Press, 1989). For positive stereotypes of the Parisiennes, see Paris-lover Georges Montorgueil's *La Parisienne peinte par elle-même* (Paris: L. Conquet, 1897), sketches of twenty types—from the family-centered *grande dame* and the religiously devout lady to the *fille* and *trottin*. All are portrayed sympathetically, but Montorgueil gives an especially warm treatment to the *filles de faubourgs*, whom he

considered the most Parisian of all (p. 108). On the "New Woman," see Mary Louise Roberts, *Disruptive Acts: The New Woman in Fin-de-Siècle France* (Chicago: University of Chicago Press, 2002), and Silverman, *Art Nouveau in Fin-de-Siècle France.*

78. The slang term "Paname" became widely popular during the First World War when soldiers on the Western Front and songwriters adopted it. On the origin of the word and its role as a successor to "Pantruche," see Claude Dubois, *La Bastoche*, pp. 130–32. The quarter of Belleville, as Gérard Jacquemet's excellent history presents it, seems to be a real-life model of Paname in many ways—tight-knit, largely working-class neighborhoods where residents (an exceptionally high proportion of them born in Paris) shared a vibrant street life, a distinctly "popular" accent, and a love of songs and singing: *Belleville au XIX siècle: du faubourg à la ville* (Paris: Éditions de L'École des Hautes Études en Sciences sociales, 1984). On the historical importance of neighborhoods and the imagined local community in Paris, see *Capital Cities at War: Paris, London, Berlin 1914–1919*, ed. J. M. Winter and Jean-Louis Robert (Cambridge, UK: Cambridge University Press, 1997), pp. 4–7. For excellent accounts of Parisian neighborhood life in the eighteenth century, see David Garrioch's *Neighborhood and Community in Paris, 1740–1790* (Cambridge, UK: Cambridge University Press, 1986) and *The Making of Revolutionary Paris* (Berkeley: University of California Press, 2002). For the first half of the nineteenth century, see Barrie M. Ratcliffe and Christine Piette, *Vivre la ville: les classes populaires à Paris (1ère moitié du XIXe siècle)* (Paris: La Boutique de l'Histoire, 2007), esp. chap. 8—on the quartier as a "point d'ancrage."

79. Tourists learned of the city's extraordinary density by reading the Baedeker guide (in the 1900 edition, *Paris et ses environs*, for example, see p. xxviii). On overcrowded lodging and dense building practices in the nineteenth century, see Ann-Louise Shapiro, *Housing the Poor of Paris, 1850–1902* (Madison: University of Wisconsin Press, 1985), esp. chap. 2: "Working-Class Housing in the Second Empire."

80. Maurice Grimaud, "La Circulation à Paris," Supplement à *Liaisons*, no. 150 (May 1968), p. 2. Grimaud, prefect of police, notes that 18,854 people were injured in traffic accidents in 1900 (and 229 killed), compared to only 11,417 injured in 1959.

81. W. Scott Haine, *The World of the Paris Café: Sociability among the French Working Class, 1789–1914* (Baltimore: Johns Hopkins University Press, 1996).

82. Clark, *The Painting of Modern Life*, chap. 4: "A Bar at the Folies-Bergère."

83. On the tradition of populist songs, in addition to Clark's "A Bar at the Folies-Bergère," see Jean-Louis Robert's "Paris enchanté: le peuple en chansons (1870–1990)," in *Paris le Peuple: XVIIIe–XXe siècle*, ed. Jean-Louis Robert and Danielle Tartakowsky (Paris: Publications de la Sorbonne, 1999), and "Folklore of the People's Paris," (chap. 4) in Charles Rearick, *The French in Love and War: Popular Culture in the Era of the World Wars* (New Haven, Conn.: Yale University Press, 1997). For a detailed account of workers' lives and economic difficulties—in many ways contrasting with the fictional Paname— see Lenard R. Berlanstein, *The Working People of Paris, 1871–1914* (Baltimore: Johns Hopkins University Press, 1984), and Nancy L. Green, *Ready-to-Wear and Ready-to-Work: A Century of Industry and Immigrants in Paris and New York* (Durham, N.C.: Duke University Press, 1997).

84. Jean Bastié, *Paris de 1945 à 2000* (Paris: Hachette, 2000), p. 101.

85. Gérard Noiriel's *Immigration, antisémitisme et racisme en France (XIXe–XXe siècle): discours publics, humiliations privées* (Paris: Fayard, 2007) gives the history of the hostility I refer to, though he does not discuss the notion of Paname or popular culture genres, such as song.

86. See Appendix 2 ("Landmark Paris Imagery") for more examples and details on the Paname myth across various genres.

87. The political history sketched here has been recounted in many more noteworthy books than can be cited here. Among them are: Yvan Combeau and Philippe Nivet, *Histoire politique de Paris au XXe siècle* (Paris: Presses universitaires de France, 2000)—on the conservative and nationalist Right gaining dominance in Paris politics; Philip G. Nord, *The Republican Moment: Struggles for Democracy in Nineteenth-century France* (Cambridge, Mass.: Harvard University Press, 1995); Maurice Agulhon, *Marianne au pouvoir: l'imagerie et la symbolique républicaine de 1880 à 1914* (Paris: Flammarion, 1989); Raymond Anthony Jonas, *France and the Cult of the Sacred Heart: An Epic Tale for Modern Times* (Berkeley: University of California Press, 2000).

88. See Charle, *Paris, fin de siècle*, and Giovanni Macchia, *Paris en ruines* (Paris: Flammarion, 1988; trans. from the Italian edition, 1985).

89. June Hargrove, "Les Statues de Paris," in *Les Lieux de mémoire*, II: *La Nation*, 2: *La Gloire* (1986), pp. 243–82; Agulhon, *Marianne au pouvoir*.

CHAPTER TWO

1. Pierre Darmon, *Vivre à Paris pendant la Grande Guerre* (Paris: Fayard, 2002), and *Capital Cities at War: Paris, London, Berlin 1914–1919*, ed. J. M. Winter and Jean-Louis Robert (Cambridge, UK: Cambridge University Press, 1997). On the "pleasure" sector during the war, see Charles Rearick, *The French in Love and War: Popular Culture in the Era of the World Wars* (New Haven, Conn.: Yale University Press, 1997), and Regina Sweeney, *Singing Our Way to Victory: French Cultural Politics and Music during the Great War* (Middletown, Conn.: Wesleyan University Press, 2001).

2. Jay Winter, *Sites of Memory, Sites of Mourning: The Great War in European Culture* (Cambridge, UK: Cambridge University Press, 1996), and Daniel J. Sherman, *The Construction of Memory in Interwar France* (Chicago: University of Chicago Press, 1999). These studies are both excellent as accounts of postwar memory and commemoration, though neither treats Paris at any length.

3. The fortifs were a key setting for "realist" songs—sad ballads about the poor and marginal people living on the edges of Paris. One such song was "Dans les fortifs" (lyrics by R. Champigny and F. L. Benech, music by Henri Piccolini) sung by Damia and others in the 1920s (the lyrics appear in *Paris qui chante*, 15 May 1922, pp. 8–9). Another sad, nostalgic tribute was "La Chanson des fortifs" (by G. Van Parys and M. Vaucaire, 1938), sung by Fréhel. Around the turn of the century, Aristide Bruant had celebrated the fortifs as a refuge for the homeless and a playground for many in his song "Pour les fortifs." See Guy Le Hallé, *Les Fortifications de Paris* (Paris: Horvath, 1986), pp. 256–57.

4. The Passage de l'Opéra was destroyed to make way for the completion of the Boulevard Haussmann. Louis Aragon, *Le Paysan de Paris* (Paris: Gallimard, 1926, 1953). See also Robin Walz, *Pulp Surrealism: Insolent Popular Culture in Early Twentieth-Century Paris* (Berkeley: University of California Press, 2000), chap. 1.

5. Élie Richard, *Paris qui meurt: Saint-Julien-le Pauvre, Le Roman de la Bièvre, La Cité et Notre-Dame* (Paris: Eugène Figuière, 1923), pp. 13–14, 15. The historian Jules Bertaut expressed the same mood in his *Le Boulevard* (Paris: Flammarion, 1924); see also his article about the demolition of the Passage de l'Opéra: "Les dernières victimes d'Haussmann," *Correspondant*, 25 Aug. 1925, pp. 610–21.

6. Michel Fleury, "Les Origines et le rôle de la Commission du Vieux Paris," *La Commission du Vieux Paris et le patrimoine de la ville (1898–1980)* (Paris: La Commission

du Vieux Paris, 1980), pp. 5, 6, 7. The members were city councilors, scholars, and administrators with a special interest in history.

7. Georges Pillement, *Paris poubelle* (Paris: J.J. Pauvert, 1974), pp. 9, 173, 202.

8. Albert Callet, *L'Agonie du vieux Paris* (Paris: H. Daragon, Éditeur, 1911), pp. 8, 10, 13. Callet portrayed the cause of the lovers of Paris as hopeless, a struggle carried on mostly for "honor," against the "vandals, fools [sots], ignoramuses, and imbeciles. . . ."

9. Michel Herbert, *La Chanson à Montmartre* (Paris: La Table Ronde, 1967), p. 404.

10. Francis Carco, "Montmartre," *Paris-Magazine*, 21 Oct. 1919, p. 322.

11. Francis Carco, "Montparnasse," *Paris-Magazine*, 25 Dec. 1919, p. 413.

12. Lucien Descaves, "Montmartre et ses amis," *Le Journal*, 28 Nov. 1929. Carco began writing his "souvenirs" with *De Montmartre au Quartier Latin* and *Mémoires d'une autre vie*, followed by *Montmartre à vingt ans* (1938). Other memoirs appearing in the 1920s and 1930s include Henri Fursy's *Souvenirs* (1928) and Dorgelès' *Quand j'étais montmartois* (1936).

13. Pierre Vitrac, "La Légende de Montmartre," *Les Nouveaux Temps*, 3 and 4 Jan. 1943: "La Butte représentait alors pour nous une sorte de village très lointain, où fleurissaient à foison, dans une bohème indispensable, les émotions et les rêves les plus intenses. Montmartre, c'était le cadre de la création, le sourire et les larmes de la jeunesse, mais d'une jeunesse qui (nous en doutions-nous, alors?) ne pouvait plus être la nôtre. Nous imaginions aisément que, le jour venu . . . nous arriverions au pied de la basilique du Sacré-Coeur, et que la vie commencerait. Nous avions lu les livres de souvenirs de Francis Carco."

14. "Où est-il donc?" lyrics by A. Decaye and Lucien Carol, music by Vincent Scotto (Fortin, 1926). Fréhel revived the song by singing it in a major 1936 movie, *Pépé le Moko*, starring Jean Gabin, directed by Julien Duvivier.

15. Richard, *Paris qui meurt*, p. 92.

16. The full title is *Guide des plaisirs à Paris. Paris le jour, Paris la nuit. Ce qu'il faut voir, Ce qu'il faut savoir, Comment on s'amuse, Où l'on s'amuse*, new rev. ed. (Paris, n.d. [circa 1926]), p. 5. Bruant was described as "the descendant of Villon." Le Boeuf sur le Toit (128 Rue Boissy-d'Anglas) was described as "one of the most chic bars of the quarter of la Madeleine, frequented especially by the most elegant young masters of avant-garde French literature" (p. 70). Among other glamorous newcomers listed was the new music hall the Empire (3 Avenue de Wagram).

17. Ibid., p. 105.

18. Sisley Huddleston, *Paris Salons, Cafés, Studios* (Philadelphia: J. B. Lippincott, 1928), p. 31.

19. *Guide des plaisirs à Paris*, p. 122.

20. Dudley Andrew and Steven Ungar, *Popular Front Paris and the Poetics of Culture* (Cambridge, Mass.: Harvard University Press, 2005), pp. 200–208.

21. *Guide des plaisirs à Paris*, p. 54 ("y menent un tapage joyeux").

22. Francis de Miromandre, *Dancings* (Paris: E. Flammarion, 1932, preface signed July 1927), pp. 17–18. "When Bolshevism reigns over the world, Maxim's will remain the supreme witness of the civilization of 1900," declared Miromandre. But he also noted that "youth has deserted" it.

23. Léon Werth, *Danse, Danseurs, Dancings* (Paris: F. Rieder et Cie, 1925), p. 92. "La tradition [of the quadrille] s'en est conservée au Moulin-Rouge et à Tabarin. Mais ce n'est point tradition vivante, c'est tradition morte. Peut-être la légende du *french cancan* agit-elle encore au-delà de l'Océan et au-delà de la Manche. Cependant, quand les danseuses du quadrille s'avancent en piste, soulevant du bout des doigts leurs jupes à volants, c'est

un spectacle mélancolique. Elles ressemblent à des fleurs séchées entre les feuillets d'un livre" (p. 111). The Moulin Rouge had only recently reopened (Dec. 1924) after a decade of closure due to a fire.

24. Albert Flament, "Soirs de Paris," *Conferencia*, no. 21 (20 Oct. 1932), p. 455. The operetta *La Veuve joyeuse* was based on a three-act comedy by Henri Meilhac. See Jacques Barbary de Langlade, *Maxim's: cent ans de vie parisienne* (Paris: Robert Laffont, 1990), p. 46. *La Dame de Chez Maxim*—a play (1899) by Georges Feydeau—was produced as movies titled *La Dame de Chez Maxim's* in 1933 and 1950. *Le Chasseur de Chez Maxim's* began as a play in 1923 and was made into movies in 1927, 1939, 1953, and 1976. *Le Merry Widow*, the operetta of 1905, was produced in movies in 1934 and 1952.

25. Jacques Pessis and Jacques Crépineau, *The Moulin Rouge* (New York: Saint Martin's, 1990), pp. 102–7; Dominique Jando, *Histoire mondiale du Music Hall* (Paris: Éditions universitaires, Jean-Pierre Delarge, 1979), p. 47.

26. G. Le Cardonnel, "Aristide Bruant," *Le Journal*, 12 Feb. 1925.

27. Robert de Saint Jean, "La Vie littéraire," *La Revue hebdomadaire*, no. 61 (23 May 1931), p. 490.

28. André Warnod, *Visages de Paris* (Paris: Firmin-Didot et Cie, 1930), p. 222. Warnod began by exclaiming simply: "L'avant-guerre!"

29. Ibid., p. 323. On early jazz in France, see Jeffrey H. Jackson, *Making Jazz French: Music and Modern Life in Interwar Paris* (Durham, N.C.: Duke University Press, 2003). On Blacks in postwar Paris, see Tyler Stovall, *Paris Noir: African Americans in the City of Light* (Boston: Mariner Books, 1998), and Brett A. Berliner, *Ambivalent Desire: The Exotic Black Other in Jazz-Age France* (Amherst: University of Massachusetts Press, 2002).

30. Warnod, *Visages de Paris*, p. 240.

31. Ralph Schor, *L'Opinion française et les étrangers, 1919–1939* (Paris: Publications de la Sorbonne, 1985) ; André Kaspi and Antoine Marès, ed., *Le Paris des étrangers depuis un siècle* (Paris: Imprimerie nationale, 1989), chap. 1.

32. *Atget photographe de Paris*, préface de Pierre Mac Orlan (Paris: Henri Jonquières, Éditeur, 1930), esp. pp. 12–21 of Mac Orlan's introduction.

33. Paul Valéry, "Fonction de Paris" (1927), in *Regards sur le monde actuel* (Paris: Stock, 1931), p. 154.

34. Warnod, *Visages de Paris*, pp. 224–26, 229, 235.

35. Ibid., pp. 224–26, 229.

36. Philippe Thiébaut, *Guimard: l'Art nouveau* (Paris: Gallimard, 1992), pp. 15–21, 30–34, 97–99.

37. Warnod, *Visages de Paris*, p. 221.

38. Louis Chéronnet was one of the most outspoken critics of the femininity of the 1900 style. See his *Découverte du monde: à Paris vers 1900* (Paris: Éditions des chroniques du jour, 1932). Robert Forrest Wilson, *Paris on Parade* (Indianapolis: Bobbs-Merrill, 1924, 1925), p. 1.

39. Morand's book *1900*, published in June 1931, went through 72 printings in the same year. A new edition was published in December 1933, and an enlarged, new edition with a new preface came out in November 1941.

40. Morand, *1900*, p. 209.

41. Artistide, *Aux Écoutes*, 16 May 1931. Robert de Saint Jean, "La Vie littéraire," *La Revue hebdomadaire*, 23 May 1931—on Paris not all beautiful.

42. Benjamin Crémieux, "*1900* par Paul Morand," *La Nouvelle Revue française* 37, no. 214 (1931), pp. 151–53. The reviewer also cited as an accomplishment of France, but not

Paris per se, the consolidation of France's colonial "domain"—a point most questionable from our current perspective.

43. Chéronnet, *Découverte du monde*, printed in May 1932.

44. Ibid., pp. 7, 22–23. The book is an album of old photographs by Nadar, Reutlinger, Branger, and Walery, among others. None of Atget's photos was included.

45. For these ideas about memory and history, I have drawn on Paul Ricoeur, *La Mémoire, l'histoire, l'oubli* (Paris: Seuil, 2000), esp. pp. 512–17.

46. Chéronnet, *Découverte du monde*, p. 11 n1. See also Pierre Mac Orlan's preface to the first album of Atget photographs published: *Atget photographe de Paris*, p. 1.

47. Léon-Paul Fargue, *Le Piéton de Paris* (Gallimard, 1939, reprint 1993), pp. 165–66, 168.

48. Ibid., pp. 170–83. On postwar women and their modern ways, see Mary Louise Roberts, *Civilization without Sexes: Reconstructing Gender in Postwar France, 1917–1927* (Chicago: University of Chicago Press, 1994).

49. Fargue, *Piéton de Paris*, pp. 169, 174.

50. Jeanne Landre, "Aristide Bruant et ses interprètes," *La Revue mondiale*, 1 Sept. 1929.

51. Anon., "1851 voyait naître Aristide Bruant," *La Lune*, 2 May 1951.

52. Bibliothèque de l'Arsenal, Ro 16.033, programs from the A.B.C. On themes of nostalgia and anti-modernist sentiment in interwar politics and art, see Romy Golan, *Modernity and Nostalgia: Art and Politics in France between the Wars* (New Haven, Conn.: Yale University Press, 1995).

53. Jean-Paul Coutisson, "Sous les toits de Paris," *Comoedia*, 30 April 1930.

54. Anon., "Un décorateur: Meerson," *Intransigeant*, 11 Feb. 1933.

55. Emmanuel Berl, *Marianne*, 26 Nov. 1932. Several years later, Marcel Carné's *Hôtel du Nord* (1938) focused on the same kind of little-people's Paris, practically untouched by twentieth-century travails.

56. Jean Valdois, "1900 vu par 1933," *Cinémagazine*, Feb. 1933, no pagination. The author also used the phrase "la belle époque" in passing. Among the other films set around 1900 were M. Ausonia's *Sous les ponts de Paris* (1925); *Le Chasseur de Chez Maxim's*, directed by N. Rimsky and R. Lion (1927); K. Anton's *Le Chasseur de Chez Maxim's* (1932); and *Crainquebille* (1933).

57. José Baldizzone, "Un siècle de Belle Époque," *Cahiers de la cinémathèque*, Mar. 1995, pp. 91–92. See also Christian Jouhaud, "La 'Belle Époque' et le cinéma," *Le Mouvement social*, no. 139 (April–June 1987), pp. 107–13.

58. On the successive official plans and the political dynamics frustrating implementation, see Rosemary Wakeman, "Nostalgic Modernism and the Invention of Paris in the Twentieth Century," *French Historical Studies* 27, no. 1 (Winter 2004), pp. 115–44.

59. Jean Giraudoux, *Pour une politique urbaine* (Paris: Arts et métiers graphiques, 1947), pp. 24–26; the article cited was written in 1930 and published in 1932.

60. On the worker suburbs (especially Bobigny) known as the "red belt," see Tyler Stovall, *The Rise of the Paris Red Belt* (Berkeley: University of California Press, 1990). Jean Bastié's *La Croissance de la banlieue parisienne* (Paris: Presses universitaires de France, 1964), a classic account still valuable, examines closely the suburbs to the south of the city.

61. M.-V. Vernier, *How to Enjoy Paris and the Smart Resorts, 1927–28* (Paris: International Publications, 1927–28), p. 13.

62. Gabriel Hanotaux, *Paris-Guide: le Guide de la vie à Paris* (Paris: Les Éditions "France-Amérique," 1926), p. ix.

63. Valéry, "Fonction de Paris," pp. 149–51.

64. Friedrich Sieburg, *Dieu est-il français?* (Paris: Grasset, 1930), pp. 129, 130.
65. Warnod, *Visages de Paris*, pp. 323, 349.
66. Vernier, *How to Enjoy Paris*, p. 18.
67. Ibid., p. 17.
68. Jean-Paul Sartre, "Paris Under the Occupation," trans. Lisa Lieberman, *Raritan*, 24, no. 3 (Winter 2005), pp. 143–47.
69. Bernard Marchand, *Paris, histoire d'une ville, XIXe–XXe siècle* (Paris: Seuil, 1993), pp. 260–67. Vichy ideological views (esp. denunciations of the cosmopolitan big city and unchecked financial speculation) come out in numerous chapters of *Destinée de Paris* (Paris: Les Éditions du Chêne, 1943), by such Paris historians as Bernard Champigneulle, Georges Pillement, Pierre Lavedan, and Marcel Raval. For the larger historical picture, see Philippe Burrin, *La France à l'heure allemande, 1940–1944* (Paris: Seuil, 1995). On the fate of the Saint-Gervais neighborhood, see Yankel Fijalkow, *La Construction des îlots insalubres, Paris 1850–1945* (Paris: L'Harmattan, 1998), pp. 153–59, 215–17. On the zone, see Jean-Louis Cohen and André Lortie, *Des Fortifs au périf: Paris, les seuils de la ville* (Paris: Picard, 1991), pp. 234–39.
70. Hervé Le Boterf, *La Vie parisienne sous l'Occupation, 1940–1944*, vol. II (Paris: France-Empire, 1975), pp. 113–18, 130, 135; Gilles Perrault, *Paris sous l'Occupation* (Paris: Belfond, 1987), pp. 110–12 (on Hitler), 114–18, 126–30.
71. Henri Michel, *Paris allemand* (Paris: Albin Michel, 1981), pp. 81, 88–89; Yvon Bizardel, "Les Statues parisiennes fondues sous l'Occupation (1940–1944)," *Gazette des Beaux-Arts* 83 (Mar. 1974), pp. 129–48.
72. Le Boterf, *La Vie parisienne* (Paris bei nacht), I: pp. 18–21; Michel, *Paris allemand*, pp. 233–36.
73. Gustave Fréjaville, "Théâtre des optimistes: à ta santé, Paris!" *Comoedia*, 29 Nov. 1941. In the revues at the Folies-Bergère too, tableaux of Paris 1900 were staples during the Occupation, as they had been in the decade before. Mentioned in press reviews (in *La Gerbe*, *Nouveaux Temps*, and *Comoedia*) were tableaux titled "the French Cancan," "La Rue de la Paix en 1890," "Le Fiacre de 1900," and the old standard catchall "La Parisienne à travers les âges." More generally, that venerable music hall's shows as a whole were touchstones of memory: the "enchantement [they produced] demeure le reflet d'une époque qui ne veut pas mourir," as an anonymous journalist remarked in the article "Edmonde Guy aux Folies-Bergère," *Nouveaux Temps*, 16 July 1943.
74. Anon., "Au Moulin de la Galette," *La Vie parisienne*, 23 April 1943, no pagination. *Comoedia*'s review took the same view that the pre-1914 epoch was undeservedly "slandered." On nostalgic entertainment, see also Le Boterf, *La Vie parisienne*, I: pp. 363, 382.
75. Léon-Paul Fargue, *Petit diagnostic de Paris* (Paris: Typographie de Jacques Haumont, 1955), pp. 8–9.
76. Among the books were Maurice De Waleffe, *Quand Paris était un paradis, mémoires 1900–1939* (Paris: Denoël, 1947), Jacques Chastenet, *La Belle Époque: la société sous M. Fallières* (Paris: Arthème Fayard, 1949), Maurice Testard, *Machine arrière: au joli temps de la belle époque* (Paris : Vigot Frères, 1949), Simon Arbellot, *J'ai vu mourir Le Boulevard* (Paris: Conquistador, 1950). Other movies include René Clair's *Silence est d'or* (1947), Max Ophuls' *Le Plaisir* (1951) and *Madame de ...* (1953), and *La Belle Otéro* (1954) by Richard Pottier. Sacha Guitry's *Si Paris nous était conté* (1956) put together all the then-familiar clichés.
77. Janet Flanner, *Paris Journal, 1944–1965*, ed. William Shawn (New York: Atheneum, 1965), pp. 5–8, 12 (Dec. 15, 1944 and Jan. 17, 1945). The tally of Parisians killed comes

from Antony Beevor and Artemis Cooper, *Paris after the Liberation, 1944–1949* (New York: Doubleday, 1994), p. 53 n.

78. Flanner, *Paris Journal*, pp. 24–26 (dated April 19) and pp. 26–28 (dated May 11).

79. Ibid., pp. 47, 51–52, 95 (articles from 1945–1948). Beevor and Cooper, *Paris after the Liberation*, pp. 164, 409–10. On the rent control law of 1948, see Jean Bastié, *Paris de 1945 à 2000* (Paris: Hachette, 2000), p. 324: the new law permitted rents to rise 27 percent in 1948, 94 percent in 1949, 36 percent in 1950, 20 percent in 1951, and 27 percent in 1952.

80. See the classic study of this willed forgetting and later "obsessive" remembering: Henry Rousso's *Le Syndrome de Vichy: 1944–198–*, translated by Arthur Goldhammer as *The Vichy Syndrome: History and Memory in France since 1944* (Cambridge, Mass.: Harvard University Press, 1991), esp. pp. 22–27. See also Gérard Namer, *Batailles pour la mémoire, la commémoration en France, 1944–1982* (Paris: S.P.A.G./Payrus, 1983).

81. On the contribution of movies, see the recent work of Vanessa R. Schwartz, *It's So French: Hollywood, Paris, and the Making of Cosmopolitan Film Culture* (Chicago: University of Chicago Press, 2007), chap. 1: "The Belle Epoque That Never Ended: Frenchness and the Can-Can Film of the 1950s." See also Christian Jouhaud, "La 'Belle Époque' et le cinéma," *Le Mouvement social*, no. 139 (April–June 1987), pp. 107–13.

82. Claude Charpentier, "Montmartre," *Sauvegarde de Paris* (Paris, 1963), no pagination; *France soir*, 11 Aug. 1955.

83. Thiébaut, *Guimard: l'Art nouveau*, pp. 110–11.

1. Clara E. Laughlin, *So You're Going to Paris!* (Boston: Houghton Mifflin, 1948), with an introduction, "Paris 1939–1947," by John L. Brown, p. v.

2. Janet Flanner, *Paris Journal, 1944–1965*, ed. William Shawn (New York: Atheneum, 1965), pp. 58–63, 82, 95; Tyler Stovall, *Paris Noir: African Americans in the City of Light* (Boston: Mariner Books, 1998), pp. 131–43; Herbert R. Lottman, *The Left Bank: Writers, Artists, and Politics from the Popular Front to the Cold War* (Boston: Houghton Mifflin, 1982), pp. 238, 240–45; Antony Beevor and Artemis Cooper, *Paris after the Liberation, 1944–1949* (New York: Doubleday, 1994), pp. 182–84, 394–399.

3. Roger Malher, "Aux-Folies-Bergère, Un merveilleux spectacle: 'C'est de la folie!'" *France au combat*, 11 April 1946. See also Serge Veber, "Oui, c'est de la folie!" *La Bataille*, 17 April 1946.

4. *Paris*, Syndicat d'Initiative (1948), pp. 3, 4, 6. Flanner, *Paris Journal*, pp. 82, 86, 91. On American tourists after the war, see Christopher Endy, *Cold War Holidays: American Tourism in France* (Chapel Hill: University of North Carolina Press, 2004). Richard Kuisel's *Seducing the French: The Dilemma of Americanization* (Berkeley: University of California Press, 1993) traces the larger history of Franco-American relations after the war.

5. Danièle Voldman, *La Reconstruction des villes françaises de 1940 à 1954: histoire d'une politique* (Paris: L'Harmattan, 1997); Bernard Marchand, *Paris, histoire d'une ville, XIXe-XXe siècle* (Paris: Seuil, 1993), pp. 277–81; Mehdi Lallaoui, *Du bidonville aux HLM* (Paris: Au nom de la mémoire, Diffusion Syros, 1993), pp. 44–46. The largest bidonville in the Paris region was Champigny, a shantytown of Portuguese (not North African) immigrant workers; the bidonville with the largest Algerian population was Nanterre's.

6. Le Corbusier's famous phrase for the modern city was "machine à habiter." See Virginie Picon-Lefebvre, *Paris—Ville moderne: Maine-Montparnasse et la Défense, 1950–1975* (Paris: Norma, 2003), pp. 209–10—on the machine metaphor in urbanist thinking back to Le Corbusier.

7. *Paris en question: une enquête du District de la Région de Paris* (Paris: Presses universitaires de France, 1965), pp. 15, 17. Lamour's remarks first appeared in his article, "L'Avenir de la région parisienne," *Revue politique et parlementaire*, no. 30–31 (Jan.–Feb. 1963), p. 32.

8. Alain Griotteray, Rapporteur général du Budget de la Ville de Paris, "Exigences du destin de Paris," in *Urbanisme, Revue française* 33, no. 84 (1964), p. 27.

9. *Paris en question*, p. 131.

10. Ibid., pp. 17, 131 (Lamour), 156 (Giroud). Lamour (p. 17) was one of many in the 1960s (and later) who evoked the depressing prospect of a "museum-city" and a mere "city of pleasures."

11. Pierre Dufau, *Pour la démolition de Paris* (Nancy: Berger-Levrault, 1967), p. 25.

12. Henry Bernard, *Paris majuscule* (Montrouge: Direction de l'Architecture, 1967), pp. 4, 19; Norma Evenson, *Paris: A Century of Change, 1878–1978* (New Haven, Conn.: Yale University Press, 1979), pp. 344–59—on the five new towns and the nine old centers that were redeveloped. The number of new towns was reduced from eight (envisaged in the early sixties) to five in 1969.

13. *Paris en question*, pp. 38–43.

14. Marchand, *Paris*, pp. 269–70.

15. Jean-Louis Cohen, "Menace sur Paris," in *Le Débat* (May–Aug. 1994) (a special issue entitled "Le Nouveau Paris"), pp. 57–59; Picon-Lefebvre, *Paris—Ville moderne*, pp. 42, 77, 104, 251–53, 261.

16. Hervé Martin, *Guide de l'architecture moderne à Paris, 1900–1990* (Paris: Alternatives, 1986), p. 277. Designed by architects Jean de Mailly and Jacques Depussé, the Tour Nobel offered 25,000 square meters of office space.

17. Evenson, *Paris: A Century of Change*, p. 187.

18. Martin, *Guide de l'architecture moderne à Paris*, p. 274. The Tour Fiat was forty-four stories high (180 meters). The Tour Manhattan, built to the north of the Tour Gan, did not intrude on the vista. The Tour Fiat was later renamed the Tour Framatome.

19. Interview in *Le Monde*, 17 Oct. 1972.

20. Evenson, *Paris: A Century of Change*, pp. 295–301; Michel Poisson, *Paris Buildings and Monuments* (New York: Harry N. Abrams, 1999), pp. 408–9. On the evolving profile of the La Défense towers, see Picon-Lefebvre, *Paris—Ville moderne*, pp. 182, 255–63. The Elf Tower (1985), notably, soared higher than any other, with a height of 187 meters (614 feet) and forty-eight stories. Originally planned for the 1970s, construction of the Elf Tower was delayed for years, and its design was changed to give it an ample façade in three units, allowing for more natural light with more office space toward the exterior.

21. Bernard, *Paris majuscule*, p. 30.

22. *Communication du M. le Préfet de la Seine au Conseil Municipal de Paris sur la Rénovation urbaine* (Paris: Imprimerie nationale, 1962), pp. 5–6. The *îlots insalubres* occupied only 258 hectares (with a population of 180,000), while the area to be renovated covered 1,500 hectares.

23. Evenson, *Paris: A Century of Change*, p. 194.

24. "Un Outrage aux sites parisiens: La Tour Maine-Montparnasse." Intervention de M. Frédéric-Dupont au Conseil Municipal de Paris, Séance du 29 novembre 1965, pp. 2, 5, 10–11.

25. On the fundamental elements of urbanist thinking, see Picon-Lefebvre, *Paris—Ville moderne*. Pompidou spoke the phrase about adapting to automobiles in a speech given on 18 November 1971, while visiting the new prefectures of the district of the

Parisian region on its tenth anniversary. *Le Monde* highlighted the words about autos as the title of a boxed article that appeared in the issue dated 20 November 1971: "Adapter Paris à l'automobile," *Le Monde*, p. 10. See also Mathieu Flonneau, "Georges Pompidou et l'automobile," *Vingtième siècle, revue d'histoire*, no. 61 (Jan.–Mar. 1999), pp. 30–43.

26. District de la Région de Paris, *Schéma Directeur d'aménagement et d'urbanisme de la région de Paris*, 1965, p. 203. On the cultural significance of the automobile in postwar France, see Kristen Ross, *Fast Cars, Clean Bodies: Decolonization and the Reordering of French Culture* (Cambridge, Mass.: MIT Press, 1995).

27. Evenson, *Paris: A Century of Change*, pp. 55, 58, 71; Jean Bastié, *Paris de 1945 à 2000* (Paris: Hachette, 2000), pp. 401, 405, 409.

28. The classic history is Henri Coing's *Rénovation urbaine et changement social: l'îlot no. 4 (Paris 13e)* (Paris: Les Éditions Ouvrières, 1966). On life in the quarter, see esp. pp. 5, 63–64. Coing writes that out of the 165,000 inhabitants of the arrondissement, 80,000 lived in a zone identified as Îlot no. 4 (p. 17).

29. Gilles-Antoine Langlois, *13e arrondissement: une ville dans Paris* (Paris: Délégation à l'action artistique de la Ville de Paris, 1993), pp. 160–61. In the thirteenth, the demolition of Îlot no. 4 began in 1956, the rest of the sector called Deux-Moulins (Îlot Châteaux-des-Rentiers and Îlot Choisy-Gare) in 1960, the Italie sector in 1966, Îlot no. 13 in 1955, and Îlot Bièvre in 1956. Some 6,200 inhabitants lived in the area renovated in the "operation Deux-Moulins," the area bordered by the Avenue de Choisy, the Rue de la Gare, Rue Edison, and Gentilly. About 1,400 of the inhabitants lived in furnished rooms. See Francis Godard, ed., *Enquête et analyse: la rénovation urbaine à Paris* (Paris: Mouton, 1973), pp. 13, 16. François Griffisch et al., Atelier parisien d'Urbanisme, *L'Évolution du parc immobilier de Paris 1954 à 1968: étude de 16 quartiers-types* (Paris: Atelier parisien d'urbanisme, APUR, 1969) reported that the number of new lodgings built by 1968 was about four times the number demolished (9,400 compared with 2,800), and the new floor space built was six times greater (532,000 square meters compared with 93,000). Pierre Lavedan, *Histoire de l'urbanisme à Paris* (Paris: Hachette, 1975), p. 538. See also Gérard Conte, *C'était hier ... Le XIIIe arrondissement* (Paris: L.M.–Le Point, 1992).

30. Godard, *Enquête et analyse*, pp. 16, 85.

31. To history-minded Parisians, the phrase recalled the brutal "conquest" of May 1871 when the conservative government based at Versailles sent in the army to retake Paris from the Communards. The phrase appeared in the 1959 planning document, for example, and in the 1962 Communication de M. le Préfet de la Seine, p. 6. See also Godard, *Enquête et analyse*; Maurice Doublet, Préfet de Paris, "Paris à l'heure des choix," *Seine et Paris* 46 (2e trimestre 1968), p. 46.

32. Bulldozing was also seen as "cleaning up" the "dirty," uncivilized parts of the city. But the "cleansing" trope, which Kristin Ross shows to have been a favorite of the French military trying to putting down rebellion in Algeria, should not be allowed to dissimulate the destructive, warlike character of the urbanist offensives. See Ross, *Fast Cars, Clean Bodies*; Lallaoui, *Du bidonville aux HLM*, pp. 47–53.

33. Louis Chevalier, *L'Assassinat de Paris* (Paris: Calmann-Lévy, 1977), pp. 243–59.

34. In addition to Morin's astute piece from the 1960s, see Richard Ivan Jobs, *Riding the New Wave: Youth and the Rejuvenation of France after the Second World War* (Stanford, Calif.: Stanford University Press, 2007).

35. Françoise Soulignac, *La Banlieue parisienne: cent cinquante ans de transformations* (Paris: La Documentation française, 1993), p. 36.

36. Evenson, *Paris: A Century of Change*, pp. 342–43. "Le Plan d'aménagement et d'organisation généale de la région parisienne" (PADOG) was officially adopted on August 6, 1960. The District de la région de Paris came into being by a law of August 2, 1961. See also Marchand, *Paris*, pp. 306–7.

37. André Chastel, "Du Paris de Haussmann au Paris d'aujourd'hui," *Paris: présent et avenir d'une capitale* (Paris: Institut Pédagogique Nationale, 1964), p. 17.

38. Pierre Bolle and Jean-Louis Quermonne, "Paris dans la France," *Table ronde* (29–30 April 1966); *Paris et sa région* (Paris: Association française de science politique, 1966), p. 2.

39. *Trésor de la langue française.*

40. Michel Carmona, *Le Grand Paris*, vol. I: *L'Evolution de l'idée d'aménagement de la Région parisienne* (Bagneux: L'imprimerie Girotypo, 1979), p. 654, citing a poll from 1976.

41. Michael Seidman, *The Imaginary Revolution: Parisian Students and Workers in 1968* (New York: Berghahn, 2004), and Kristin Ross, *May '68 and Its Afterlives* (Chicago: University of Chicago Press, 2002). Accounts by impassioned participants include Angelo Quattrocchi and Tom Nairn, *The Beginning of the End: France, May 1968* (London: Verso, 1998, first published in 1968) and Andrew Feenberg and Jim Freedman, *When Poetry Ruled the Streets: The French May Events of 1968* (Albany: State University of New York Press, 2001).

42. André Fermigier, "La mort de Paris II, Le secret d'un secret," *Le Nouvel Observateur*, 24 May 1967, reprinted in his book *La Bataille de Paris: des Halles à la Pyramide: chroniques d'urbanisme* (Paris: Gallimard, 1991), p. 46.

43. Fermigier, "La mort de Paris," *Le Nouvel Observateur*, 17 May 1967, reprinted in *La Bataille de Paris*, p. 38.

44. Chevalier, *L'Assassinat de Paris*, pp. 267–8. The transfer of the market from Les Halles was announced in January 1959, then announced anew in an official plan in the spring of 1960, then again in December 1961, and again in the fall of 1963.

45. Pierre-François Large, *Des Halles au Forum* (Paris: L'Harmattan, 1992), pp. 54, 55, 57, 58.

46. Jean-Pierre Babelon, Michel Fleury, and Jacques de Sacy, *Richesses d'art du quartier des Halles, maison par maison* (Paris: Arts et Métiers graphiques, Flammarion, 1967).

47. Large, *Des Halles au Forum*, p. 55.

48. Ibid., pp. 56–57. The quoted comments about a cultural revolution appeared in the *gauchist* periodical, *L'Idiot international*, 30 June–1 Sept. 1971.

49. Archives of the Paris Préfecture de Police, série F ("manifestations," Démolition des Halles). I have drawn on files not yet catalogued, which contain numerous police reports to the prefect on the dangers presented by the protests and the potential troublemaking by students and other youthful organizers, including "militants maoïstes" and the "Front de libération de la Jeunesse."

50. Bertrand Lemoine, *Les Halles de Paris* (Paris: l'Équerre, 1980), p. 219; Large, *Des Halles au Forum*, pp. 57–58.

51. Archives de Paris, Perotin, 101/77/1/45, Compte rendu de la Réunion présidée par M. Hely, Préfet, le lundi 28 juin 1971. The prefect's memos of June, July, and August are filled with confidential statements revealing the attitudes described in this paragraph.

52. André Fermigier, "Des Maisons qui avouent," *Le Nouvel Observateur*, 6 Sept. 1971, p. 42; Marcel Cornu, *La Conquête de Paris* (Paris : Mercure de France, 1972), p. 332. François Serrand, an association leader, expressed the same ideas in his book *Le Pari des Halles de Paris* (Paris: Aubin, 2001), p. 148.

53. Chevalier, *L'Assassinat de Paris*, pp. 235–39, 265, 266, 275 (Halles as Paris).

54. Louis Réau, *Histoire du vandalisme: les monuments détruits de l'art français* (Paris: Robert Laffont, 1994), p. 948. See also Georges Pillement, *Paris poubelle* (Paris: J.J. Pauvert, 1974), p. 18.

55. François Loyer, "Paris assassiné," *L'Oeil*, no. 191 (Nov. 1970); André Fermigier, "Les Assassins de Paris," *Le Nouvel Observateur*, 7 Aug. 1972; Norma Evenson, "The Assassination of the Halles," *Journal of the Society of Architectural Historians* 32, no. 4 (Dec. 1973), pp. 308–15.

56. Chevalier, *L'Assassinat de Paris*, p. 237.

57. André Fermigier, columnist for the *Le Nouvel Observateur*, was one of the most eloquent. On the new Paris, see, for example, his article "Des Maisons qui avouent," *Le Nouvel Observateur*, 6 Sept. 1971, in *La Bataille de Paris*, pp. 226–30.

58. Ionel Schein, *Pour Paris: anatomie d'une jungle* (Paris: Jacques Fréal, 1972), no pagination. See also Michel Ragon, *Les Erreurs monumentales* (Paris: Hachette, 1971).

59. Within the relatively low circular form of the Maison de Radio France was one tower seventy meters high (23 stories).

60. Schein, *Pour Paris*, no pagination.

61. Jacques Herbert, *Sauver les Halles, coeur de Paris* (Paris: Denoël, 1971), pp. 165–68. François Serrand's *Le Pari des Halles de Paris* makes a strong case for the impact of the associations.

62. François Chaslin, *Les Paris de François Mitterrand: histoire des grands projets architecturaux* (Paris: Gallimard, 1985), pp. 40–42.

63. Large, *Des Halles au Forum*, p. 61.

64. Ibid., p. 139.

65. A new *Plan d'occupation du sol* in 1974 laid the framework for a return to the capital's traditional forms and scale.

66. Fermigier, "La Chute de Paris?" *Le Monde*, 20 Aug. 1974.

67. Chaslin, *Les Paris de François Mitterrand*, p. 33.

68. Marchand, *Paris*, pp. 333–34. The three were the Albert report (1973), based on the views of foreign observers, the Hudson Institute's report (1974), which was the most optimistic about future growth, and the Beaujeu report (Nov. 1974).

69. Robert Bordaz, *Le Centre Pompidou: une nouvelle culture* (Paris: Ramsay, 1977), pp. 103–4.

70. "Paris, une idée de la ville, entretien avec Renzo Piano," in *Paris, ville internationale*, Dossier spécial of *Politique internationale*, no. 73 (Fall 1996), p. 49.

71. Large, *Des Halles*, p. 61; Anthony Sutcliffe, *Paris, An Architectural History* (New Haven, Conn.: Yale University Press, 1993), p. 179

72. Martin, *Guide de l'architecture moderne à Paris*, p. 271; Chaslin, *Les Paris de François Mitterrand*, p. 161: 100,000 square meters of office space were empty out of the total available 850,000 square meters.

73. Marie-Jeanne Dumont, in *Le Débat*, no. 80 (May–Aug. 1994), p. 31.

74. The architects were Claude Vasconi and Georges Pencréac'h. The latter had designed a commercial center for the *nouvelle ville* Cergy Pontoise. See Sutcliffe, *Paris, An Architectural History*, pp. 180–81.

75. Isabelle Nataf, "Les Halles chic et choc," *Paris villages*, no. 2 (1985), pp. 40–41. See also Guy Muller, "Les Halles aujourd'hui—Que reste-t-il," *Paris villages*, no. 2 (1985), p. 37.

76. Large, *Des Halles au Forum*, pp. 69–76.

CHAPTER FOUR

1. *Paris Île de France* (Paris: Office de Tourisme de Paris, Comité Régional de Tourisme d'Île de France, 1977), pp. 4, 22, 23, 31, 43–51.

2. *Les Parisiens aujourd'hui* (Paris: Institut français d'opinion publique, 1973), p. 139: "destruction de l'environnement; laideur des nouvelles constructions" were cited by 42 percent of the sample 2,512 residents interviewed. See also *Les Français et l'urbanisme* (Paris: Institut français d'opinion publique, 1974), the results of 2,291 interviews (À la demande de la direction de l'Aménagement foncier et de L'Urbanisme du Ministère de l'Équipement), a sampling of French opinion (not limited to Parisians).

3. Journalist André Fermigier and architectural historian François Loyer played major roles in bringing about the reevaluation of nineteenth century, beginning in 1973. André Fermigier, "Paris n'est plus Paris," *Le Monde*, 19 Sept. 1974, reprinted in Fermigier, "La mort de Paris II, Le secret d'un secret," *Le Nouvel Observateur*, 24 May 1967, reprinted in his book *La Bataille de Paris: des Halles à la Pyramide: chroniques d'urbanisme* (Paris: Gallimard, 1991), p. 304, "Les Paris du XIXe siècle, *Le Monde*, 20 Feb. 1975, reprinted in *La Bataille de Paris*, p. 311, and "L'histoire ne s'arrête pas en 1800," *Le Monde*, 21 Aug. 1974, reprinted in *La Bataille de Paris*, p. 295. Books, articles, and a major exhibit in the Hôtel de Sully in 1975 brought the fresh scholarly enthusiasms and findings to the public.

4. Michel Carmona, *Le Grand Paris*, vol. I: *L'Evolution de l'idée d'aménagement de la Région parisienne* (Bagneux: L'imprimerie Girotypo, 1979), pp. 152–59, 167–69.

5. On the POS of 1974 and 1977, see Anthony Sutcliffe, *Paris, An Architectural History* (New Haven, Conn.: Yale University Press, 1993), pp. 184–85.

6. On Portzamparc, see Simon Texier, *Paris contemporain: de Haussmann à nos jours, une capitale à l'ère des métropoles* (Paris: Parigramme, 2005), pp. 198–99.

7. Bernard Marchand, *Paris, histoire d'une ville, XIXe–XXe siècle* (Paris: Seuil, 1993), pp. 333–34. See also the report entitled *Place, vocation et avenir de Paris et de sa région* by Jacqueline Beaujeu-Garnier, a Sorbonne professor addressing the Comité consultatif économique et social de la Région parisienne, *Notes et études documentaires*, no. 4 (20 Dec. 1974).

8. Fermigier, "Les Assassins de Paris. Aucun régime n'a moins créé ni plus stupidement détruit que la Ve République," *Le Nouvel Observateur*, 7 Aug. 1972, p. 247, reprinted in *La Bataille de Paris*, pp. 249–51.

9. "Le Tourisme à Paris," *Paris projet*, no. 6 (1971), pp. 74–75. See also A. du Roy, *L'Express*, 24 May 1971, and Michel Ragon, *Les Erreurs monumentales* (Paris: Hachette, 1971), p. 70.

10. "Le Tourisme à Paris," pp. 74–75.

11. So much the better, opined *Le Monde*, dismissing the cancan as an outmoded national stereotype. Paul Chutkow, "Paris Is Still Kicking," *New York Times*, 3 Jan. 1988, section 10, p. 12.

12. On postmodernism as I have it summed up here, see Michel Maffesoli, *The Contemplation of the World: Figures of Community Style*, trans. Susan Emanuel (Minneapolis: University of Minnesota Press, 1996; original: 1993).

13. On the Nuit de la Fraternité, see Robert Sole, "Pari gagné pour SOS-Racisme," *Le Monde*, 18 June 1985.

14. Jean-Pierre Champit, "Une Ville éphemère," *Urbanismes & Architecture*, no. 239 (July–Aug. 1990), p. 81.

15. Jean-Pierre Rioux, "Resistances," in Jean-Pierre Rioux and Jean-François Sirinelli, eds., *La Culture de masse en France de la Belle Époque à aujourd'hui* (Paris: Fayard, 2002), pp. 277–82; David L. Looseley, *The Politics of Fun: Cultural Policy and Debate in Contemporary France* (Oxford: Berg Publishers, 1997); Jacques Rigaud, *La Culture pour vivre* (Paris: Gallimard, 1975)—on the need for cultural "animators" of participatory creative activities of all kinds for the entire population.

16. "Festivals, carnaval, parade, son et lumière, La Saison d'été à Paris," *La Croix*, 28 May 1977.

17. Marc Ambroise-Rendu, *Paris-Chirac: prestige d'une ville, ambition d'un homme* (Paris: Plon, 1987), pp. 324–27. See also Nicole Lesein, "La Culture sous le bonnet phrygien," *75-20 (le magazine du 20e arrondissment)*, no. 68 (Mar. 1984), p. 24.

18. "Les Ateliers de l'ADAC fêtent leur 10e anniversaire," *Ville de Paris*, no. 94 (Jan. 1988), p. 16.

19. François Barré, "Arts urbains pour espace social," *Urbanismes & Architecture*, no. 239 (July–Aug. 1990), p. 34. The institution now called the Centre international de création pour les arts de la rue was at first named Centre international de rencontres et de création pour les pratiques artistiques dans les lieux publics et les espaces libres.

20. Editorial by Jean Tiberi, *Paris le journal*, no. 97 (Sept. 1999), p. 5, and "Une politique culturelle ambitieuse," p. 6. The cultural budget rose from 109 million francs in 1977 to 810 million francs in 1988.

21. *À Paris* (Sept., Oct. 2002), no. 1, "À Paris, la plage," pp. 12–13, and "La Nuit est à vous!" pp. 50–51.

22. Marchand, *Paris*, pp. 319–20, 322. Both the net gain from Parisian births and from new residents moving in diminished between 1962 and 1968. Jean Bastié, *Paris de 1945 à 2000* (Paris: Hachette, 2000), pp. 81, 98.

23. Florence Haegel, "Le Maire de Paris en représentations," *Politix*, no. 21 (1993), p. 82.

24. Ibid., pp. 82–83.

25. "Paris capitale, mais aussi Paris aux cent villages," *Ville de Paris*, no. 1 (Oct. 1978). For good scholarly commentaries on the quartiers in the period, see "La vie des quartiers," Table ronde du CREPIF, *Cahiers du Centre de recherches et d'études sur Paris et l'Île-de-France* (CREPIF), no. 2 (Sept. 1983).

26. Florence Haegel, *Un Maire à Paris: mise en scène d'un nouveau rôle politique* (Paris: Presses de la Fondation nationale des sciences politiques, 1994), pp. 195–96.

27. Haegel, "Le Maire de Paris," p. 86.

28. Ibid., pp. 83–84.

29. On reworking the Place des Fêtes, see Jean-Louis Cohen and Bruno Fortier, *Paris: la ville et ses projets* (Paris: Babylone, Pavillon de l'Arsenal, 1992, Édition revue et augmentée), p. 262. On demolitions in the *grand ensemble* "les 4000," see the municipal magazine for La Courneuve, *Regards*, no. 282 (26 Feb.–11 Mar. 2009), "Le dimanche 23 fev. 1986," and no. 245b, "2001–2007: 6 ans d'actions communes"; see also Renouvel Gaëlle, "Faut-il détruire les barres?" *L'Express*, no. 2775, Sept. 2004. The process of redoing late twentieth-century works goes on today with major changes planned for Les Halles–the Forum and the garden.

30. Michelle Guillon and Isabelle Taboada-Leonetti, *Le Triangle de Choisy: un quartier chinois à Paris* (Paris: C.I.E.M.I. and L'Harmattan, 1986), p. 36.

31. See Michael Sibalis, "Urban Space and Homosexuality: The Example of the Marais, Paris's 'Gay Ghetto,'" *Urban Studies* 41, no. 9 (Aug. 2004), pp. 1739–58.

32. "Enquêter la vie associative," *Paris le journal*, no. 34 (15 Sept. 1993), pp.

9–11, 15. Associations in each arrondissement were linked to local government through consultative committees. In 1992 about 10 percent of the city's budget went to the associations. The municipality lent support also by providing a central clearing-house for associations in the Forum des Halles from December 1988 on, with meeting-and-exhibit rooms for groups and orientation for individuals. According to a public opinion poll in 1977, 52 percent of the French reported participating in associations; the percentage was only slightly lower for big city dwellers. The rate of participation in political and union organizations was lower than in non-political ones. Executives, industrialists, and members of the liberal professions were much more involved than workers. See SOFRES, *L'Opinion française en 1977* (Paris: Presses de la Fondation nationale des sciences politiques, 1978), pp. 169–70.

33. Hassan du Castel, "La Résistance des Parisiens aux projets immobiliers," *Le Monde diplomatique*, 26 June 1993, p. 26.

34. "Un Nouvel Urbanisme pour Paris," *Paris le journal*, no. 73 (15 Mar. 1996), pp. 4, 6.

35. Marc Gaillard, *Les Belles Heures des Champs-Élysées* (Amiens: Martelle, 1990), p. 208.

36. Florence Amalou, "Le Maire de Paris veut envoyer les chiens dans le caniveau," *Le Monde*, 1 Oct. 1999, p. 22. The workers were dealing with 24,000 kilometers of sidewalk.

37. "Habitat insalubre," *Paris le journal*, Dec. 1999, p. 48.

38. "La Lutte contre le bruit," *Paris le journal*, Dec. 1999, p. 48.

39. Patrick Clerc, "Bientôt la 'traque' pour les 2 millions de rats parisiens," *Ville de Paris*, no. 75 (April 1986), pp. 68–69.

40. *Ville de Paris*, no. 111 (July–Aug.), p. 15: La lettre du Maire, "Paris, capitale culturelle de l'Europe."

41. "Publiscope," no pagination, in *L'Express internationale*, no. 2027 (18 May 1990).

42. See Steven L. Kaplan, *Farewell, Revolution: Disputed Legacies, France 1789/1989* (Ithaca, N.Y.: Cornell University Press, 1995).

43. Marcel Roncayolo, "Une Géographie symbolique en devenir: entretien avec Marcel Roncayolo," *Le Débat* 80 (May–Aug. 1994), p. 4.

44. Nicolas Beau, *Paris, capitale arabe* (Paris: Seuil, 1995), p. 7: "Pour l'Orient, Paris a toujours été une capitale intellectuelle"; Michel Carmona [professor at the Université Paris IV-Sorbonne], "Le rayonnement de Paris," *Cahiers du Centre de recherches et d'études sur Paris et l'Île-de-France* (CREPIF), no. 9 (Dec. 1984), p. 200; *Télérama Paris*, no. 265 (14–20 Jan. 1998), p. v: "Puits de séances," "Images du monde, Paris, capitale mondiale du cinéma?" by Frédéric Chaleil. The city hall exhibit "Capitale du roller" took place in 2008.

45. François Chaslin, *Les Paris de François Mitterrand: histoire des grands projets architecturaux* (Paris: Gallimard, 1985), pp. 20–22; and, on the architectural dimension of the projects, Annette Fierro, *The Glass State: The Technology of the Spectacle, Paris 1981–1998* (Cambridge, Mass.: MIT Press, 2003).

46. Chaslin, *Les Paris de François Mitterrand*, pp. 34–35. Anthony Sutcliffe's *Paris, An Architectural History*, pp. 192–94, gives credit also to Jacques Chirac (both as mayor of Paris and as prime minister under Mitterrand in 1986–1988) for supporting Pei's project.

47. Chaslin, *Les Paris de François Mitterrand*, p. 59.

48. Ibid., pp. 67–72. Le Zénith was intended to be temporary, serving until a new hall of rock was built at the Porte de Bagnolet, but the abandonment of the latter (too expensive) made the temporary venue permanent.

49. Its opening, timed with an eye to the approaching presidential elections, was only partial and provisional that year.

50. Claude Dubois, *En parlant un peu de Paris*, vol. 1: *Les chroniques de Titi—octobre 1981–octobre 1990* (Paris: Jean-Paul Rocher, 2001), pp. 100–101: "La Prise de la Bastoche," Dubois's *Figaroscope* column of September 1989.

51. Julian Green, *Paris* (New York: Marion Boyars, 1991). The chapter entitled "A Secret City/Une Ville secrète" (p. 48) was first published in the *Oeuvres complètes* (Paris: Pléiade, 1972): "Paris est une ville dont on pourrait parler au pluriel, comme les Grecs parlaient d'Athènes, car il y a bien des Paris et celui des étrangers n'a que des rapports de surface avec le Paris des Parisiens."

52. Michel Pinçon and Monique Pinçon-Charlot, *Paris mosaïque* (Paris: Calmann-Lévy, 2001), pp. 43, 45. Foreigners made up 16 percent of the population in 1990, up from only 5 percent in 1954.

53. *Télérama hors série* (1997), Editorial, p. 6.

54. "Paris, ville contraste," *À Nous Paris! L'Hébdo du métro*, no. 14 (13–19 Sept. 1999), p. 1.

55. "Les Stars africains se font (ou se défont) à Paris," *Jeune Afrique Magazine*, no. 38 (June 1987), p. 11. For a full, well-researched account, see James A. Winders, *Paris Africain: Music and Migration since 1981* (New York: Palgrave Macmillan, 2006).

56. Michel Raffoul, "Dix ans de fêtes en noir et blanc," *Jeune Afrique*, no. 1429 (25 May 1986), p. 56.

57. Jean-François Pin, "Radios 'libres,'" *L'Express Paris*, no. 1856 (30 Jan. 1987), pp. 19–21. Eight stations jostled for the dial space between 92 and 93.

58. Stéphane Barret, "Radioscopie de la bande FM à Paris," *75-20 (le magazine du 20e arrondissement)*, no. 74 (Nov. 1984), pp. 26–29.

59. Marie-Elisabeth Jeannin, "Fréquence Paris plurielle, l'écho du monde ... et des banlieues," *Hommes & Migrations*, no. 1206 (Mar.–April 1997), pp. 121–22.

60. Guillon and Taboada-Leonetti, *Le Triangle de Choisy*, pp. 94–96; Anne Steiner, "Les cafés de Belleville," *Hommes & Migrations*, no. 1168 (Sept. 1993), pp. 23–25; Véronique Maurus, "La Goutte d'Or, ou l'anti-ghetto," *Le Monde*, 3 Sept. 1996 (anti-ghetto meaning here the optimistic view that the quarter has been renovated, and the population largely resettled there or nearby); Marc Ambroise-Rendu, "Paris La Goutte d'Or retrouve la fierté," *Le Monde*, 26 July 1993.

61. Marie-Hélène Bacqué and Sylvie Fol, "Mixité sociale et politiques urbaines," in Florence Haegel, Henri Rey, and Yves Sintomer, eds., *La Xénophobie en banlieue, effets et expressions* (Paris: L'Harmattan, 2000), pp. 58–59.

62. Michel Delberghe, "Fuite des classes moyennes, chômage à 25%: Clichy-sous-Bois, radiographie d'une ville pauvre," *Le Monde*, 6 Nov. 2005.

63. Haegel et al., *La Xénophobie en banlieue*, pp. 77, 85.

64. François Maspero, *Roissy Express: A Journey through the Paris Suburbs*, trans. Paul Jones (London: Verso, 1994), pp. 177–78. Writer/editor François Maspero with his photographer friend Anaïk Frantz followed the RER-B line in 1989 to explore the mostly working-class suburbs and then produced a fascinating travel journal and social study of what they encountered, town after town.

65. Françoise Soulignac, *La Banlieue parisienne: cent cinquante ans de transformations* (Paris: La Documentation française, 1993), p. 202 n34; Hervé Vieillard-Baron, *Les Banlieues françaises ou le ghetto impossible* (La Tour d'Aigues: L'Aube, 1994), pp. 111, 115–16.

66. Vieillard-Baron, *Les Banlieues françaises ou le ghetto impossible*, pp. 37–39 ; Haegel et al., *La Xénophobie en banlieue*.

67. Maspero, *Roissy Express*, p. 16, 172; Tricia Danielle Keaton, *Muslim Girls and*

the Other France: Race, Identity Politics, and Social Exclusion (Bloomington: Indiana University Press, 2006), pp. 33, 60, 87 (quoting the young man of African origin). Keaton, a young American scholar, carried out her ethnographic study in the mid-1990s in La Courtillières, a housing project in East Pantin, in the département Seine-Saint-Denis.

68. French law requires that communes of more than 50,000 inhabitants provide public housing (*logements sociaux*) at a rate of at least 20 percent of the total housing available. The Île-de-France overall meets that requirement, but Paris has fallen short for decades. The percentage of public housing available in Paris is about 14 percent. See Bastié, *Paris de 1945 à 2000*, p. 323. In 1999, for example, out of 1,322,540 dwellings, there were 153,020 *logements sociaux*—65,580 fewer than required by law. The same deficiency existed in 2004. Eric Le Mitouard, "HLM: Paris passe la vitesse supérieure," *Le Parisien*, 6 Oct. 2004. In 2004, 102,930 requests for public housing in Paris were made. The Mairie has been financing 3,500–4,000 new apartments a year. At that rate, Paris will reach the 20 percent mark in 2020. For recent details and explanations, see the Mairie's website: Paris.fr, and the online brochure: *Accès au logement social à Paris* (2005).

69. On the near-disappearance of the working class in Paris, see Bastié, *Paris de 1945 à 2000*, pp. 104–5.

70. Françoise Cachin, "Paris muséifié," *Le Débat* 80 (May 1994), pp. 298 (on the Louvre and Orsay), 302–3.

71. Andrew Lainsbury, *Once Upon an American Dream: The Story of Euro Disneyland* (Lawrence: University Press of Kansas, 2000).

72. For a detailed statistical report on retail trends over several recent years, see the Atelier parisien d'urbanisme, *Données sur le commerce parisien: la banque de données sur le commerce, résultats de la collecte de Juin 2003*.

73. A. F., "Les Hommes de la manche," *Télérama Paris*, no. 2494 (1–7 Nov. 1997). The largest group from abroad was from Latin America, and the next most numerous from Eastern Europe.

74. On demonstrations and their history since the late nineteenth century, see Danielle Tartakowsky, *Le Pouvoir est dans la rue: crises politiques et manifestations en France* (Paris: Aubier, 1998).

75. See the website of the Mairie de Paris (Paris.fr and "plaques commémoratives") for the latest details. In 2009, 1,060 of the city's commemorative plaques recalled events of the Second World War—out of a total of 1,300 for all events. Peter Carrier's *Holocaust Monuments and National Memory Cultures in France and Germany since 1989* (New York: Berghahn, 2005) gives the fuller history.

76. For an inventory of all the protected monuments of the twentieth century, see the Ministry of Culture's website: www.culture.gouv.fr/culture/inventai (bases Architecture et Patrimoine).

77. Michel Sarazin, "Sondage Urbanismes IPSOS, autoportrait dans tous les sens," *Urbanismes & Architecture, Paris capitale majuscule*, 231–32 (Oct.–Nov. 1989), Dossier: *Paris, Capitale majuscule*, pp. 28–30. Other surveys since the Second World War—discussed in Chapter 6—yielded similar responses.

78. David Harvey, *The Condition of Postmodernity* (Cambridge, Mass.: Blackwell, 1990), pp. 97–98, 117.

79. See M. Christine Boyer, *The City of Collective Memory* (Cambridge, Mass.: MIT Press, 1994) for a critical analysis of the postmodern city ("the city as radical artifice"). See pp. 10–11 for the line about the postmodern city as "patchwork" lacking coherence and harmony.

80. Bernard Marchand ends his history of Paris with a discussion of these competing options. See Marchand, *Paris*, p. 371: "La Place de Paris en France et dans le monde."

81. On "global cities" and Paris in particular, see Saskia Sassen's response to James W. White, "Old Wine, Cracked Bottle? Tokyo, Paris, and the Global City Hypothesis," *Urban Affairs Review* 33 (1998), pp. 451–77.

CHAPTER FIVE

1. *La Poésie de Paris dans la littérature française, de Rousseau à Baudelaire* (Paris: Les Éditions de Minuit, 1961), I: pp. 24, 36, 40.

2. Christophe Prochasson, *Paris 1900: essai d'histoire culturelle* (Paris: Calmann-Lévy, 1999), esp. chap. 2.

3. Valéry Larbaud, *Jaune Bleu Blanc*, in *Oeuvres de Valéry Larbaud* (Paris: Gallimard, 1958), pp. 779–81.

4. *Paris ses chansons: les 30 plus belles chansons sur Paris* (Paris: Paul Beuscher, 1995), pp. 10–13; "Paris je t'aime d'amour" (1930), lyrics by Battaille-Henri, music by Victor Schertzinger (p. 10: "Ô mon Paris, ville idéale"). For other hit songs rhapsodizing Paris, see Pierre Saka, *La Chanson française à travers ses succès* (Paris: Larousse, 1988), and *Paris, ses poètes, ses chansons*, preface by André Hardellet (Paris: Seghers, 1977). One particularly rich litany of clichés is "On ne Voit Ça qu'à Paris" (1934) from the film *La Crise Est Finie* (1934), lyrics by Jean Lenoir and Max Colpet.

5. E. B. Garey, O. O. Ellis, and R. V. D. Magoffin, *American Guide Book to France and Its Battlefields* (New York: Macmillan, 1920), pp. 31, 54, 57, 58, 62. The American guide went on to point out that the great city boasted several of the biggest structures in the world: the Eiffel Tower—the tallest monument; the Arc de Triomphe—"the largest triumphal arch" (162 feet high); and the Opéra—the largest theater. Up on the third platform of the Eiffel tower, the guide notes, "you will be nearly twice as high as you can get on any other monument in the world" (905 feet above the ground).

6. Germain Brice, *Description de la Ville de Paris et de tout ce qu'elle contient de plus remarquable*, 6th edition (Paris, 1713), pp. v, 17–18. In the fifth edition (1706) Brice used the phrase "la plus grande & la plus belle ville, dont on ait à présent connoissance."

7. Claire Hancock, *Paris et Londres au XIXe siècle: représentations dans les guides et récits de voyage* (Paris: CNRS Éditions, 2003).

8. Pierre-Paul Sagave, *1871 Berlin-Paris, capitale du Reich et capitale du monde, suivi de Paris-Berlin: à l'aube du troisième millénaire* (Paris: Albin Michel, 1995).

9. Lothar Müller, "The Beauty of the Metropolis: Toward an Aesthetic Urbanism in Turn-of-the-Century Berlin," in *Berlin: Culture and Metropolis*, ed. Charles W. Haxthausen and Heidrun Suhr (Minneapolis: University of Minnesota Press, 1990), pp. 38–41.

10. David Clay Large, *Berlin* (New York: Basic Books, 2000), p. 81.

11. Christophe Charle, *Paris, fin de siècle (culture et politique)* (Paris: Seuil, 1998), pp. 46–47. Charle uses quantitative measures of comparison, such as the number of foreign students studying in the two capitals and the proportion of artists born in each city displaying works in national exhibits around 1900.

12. On Vienna: Carl Schorske, *Fin-de-Siècle Vienna: Politics and Culture* (New York: Vintage Books, 1981)—one of my longtime favorites.

13. France Guérin-Pace, *Deux siècles de croissance urbaine: la population des villes françaises de 1831 à 1990* (Paris: Anthropos, 1993), p. 60.

14. Alain Corbin, "Paris-province," in Pierre Nora, ed., *Les Lieux de mémoire*, III: *Les France* (Paris: Gallimard, 1992), 1: *Conflits et partages*, pp. 776–823.

15. *Paris guide par les principaux écrivains et artistes de la France*, Première Partie (Paris: Librairie Internationale/A. Lacroix, Verboeckhoven et Cie, 1867), "Histoire de Paris," pp. 47–48: "la ville de Paris, en [p. 48] un mot, la reproduction exacte de chaque peuple pris en particulier, et en même temps élevé à sa dernière formule; si bien que, si chaque peuple avait à nommer la capitale de l'Europe, il mettrait le doigt sur Paris et dirait: La voilà!"

16. François Coppée, in *Les Capitales du monde* (Paris: Hachette, 1896), p. 22.

17. Victor Hugo, *Paris* (Paris, n.d.), vol. in *Oeuvres complètes de Victor Hugo*, p. 42 (from his Introduction), and pp. 115, 117 (from *Pendant l'exil*, published in 1875). The phrase "ville de lumière" appears in his essay "La Vision de Paris dans l'exil," p. 125.

18. *Regards sur le monde actuel* (Paris: Stock, 1931), "Fonction de Paris" (1927), pp. 145–54. See esp. pp. 148–51.

19. Albert Demangeon, *Paris, la ville et sa banlieue* (Paris: Bourrelier, 1933) p. 61.

20. J. F. Gravier, *Paris et le désert français* (Paris: Le Portulan, 1947), p. 195.

21. Jocelyne George, *Paris province: de la Révolution à la mondialisation* (Paris: Fayard, 1998), pp. 243, 255; Corbin, "Paris-province," pp. 776–823; Philippe Choffel, "Les Transformations des espaces urbains dans les années 90," *Regards sur l'actualité*, No. spécial 260 (April 2000), *La Ville en question* (Paris: La Documentation française, 2000), p. 19. For the demographic comparison with London, see Félix Damette and Jacques Scheibling, *La France, permanences et mutations* (Paris: Hachette, 1995), p. 125.

22. Jean Giraudoux, *Pour une politique urbaine* (Paris: Arts et Métiers graphiques, 1947), pp. 24–25—an article written in 1930 and first published in 1932. Giraudoux helped found a "Ligue urbaine" in 1928 to combat "vulgarity" and ugliness in modern urban life.

23. See *Urbanisme, revue française*, no. 55 (1957)—articles by Pierre Sudreau, Commissaire à la Construction et à l'Urbanisme pour la Région parisienne; landscape expert J. B. Perrin; and the journal's editor, Jean Royer.

24. Gravier, *Paris et le désert français*, p. 194.

25. Jacques Bonnet, *Les grandes métropoles mondiales* (Paris: Nathan, 1994), pp. 3, 6.

26. Serge Guilbaut, *How New York Stole the Idea of Modern Art* (Chicago: University of Chicago Press, 1983). See also the insightful commentary of Herman Lebovics, *Mona Lisa's Escort: André Malraux and the Invention of French Culture* (Ithaca, N.Y.: Cornell University Press, 1999), pp. 160–64.

27. *Place, vocation et avenir de Paris et de sa région*, Rapport présenté par Jacqueline Beaujeu-Garnier, au Comité consultatif économique et social de la Région parisienne, *Notes et Études documentaires*, no. 4 142–43 (20 Dec. 1974), p. 31.

28. Michel Carmona, "Le rayonnement de Paris," *Cahiers du Centre de recherches et d'études sur Paris et l'Île-de-France* (CREPIF), no. 9 (Dec. 1984), pp. 198–99.

29. Jean Montaldo, "Est-ce la mauvaise bouffe?" *Paris Match*, 15 Sept. 1973, pp. 3–5; "L'Explosion du rock," *Le Nouvel Observateur*, 31 Dec. 1979–Jan. 1980.

30. See the *Cahiers du CREPIF*, no. 26 (Mar. 1989), "Paris–Londres, L'Aménagement à l'heure de la compétition"—introduction by Jean Bastié and articles by Jean Robert, John Shepherd, and Anne-Marie Szalay. A fuller historical treatment is found in Youssef Cassis, *Capitals of Capital: A History of International Financial Centres, 1780–2005* (Cambridge, UK: Cambridge University Press, 2006).

31. Pierre Deshusses and Arnaud Leparmentier, "Berlin, hors le mur," *Le Monde*, 16 Mar. 2001.

32. *S.O.S. Paris Bulletin*, no. 16 (Dec. 1991), editorial, p. 1. S.O.S. Paris was organized in 1972, when Pompidou's urbanism was hitting its stride.

33. Yves Le Monnier et al., *Le Guide musardine du Paris sexy* (Paris: La Musardine, 2000), pp. 126, 130; Alphonse Boudard, *La Fermature: 15 avril 1946, la fin des maisons closes* (Paris: Robert Laffont, 1986).

34. Alfred Fierro, *Histoire et Dictionnaire de Paris* (Paris: Robert Laffont, 1996), p. 727. Tributes to the beauty of sites such as the Place de la Concorde were commonplace not only in travel guides, but also in sophisticated literary portrayals of the city—for example, André Billy's *Paris vieux & neuf. La Rive droite* (Paris: Eugène Rey, 1909), pp. 17, 49. For the interwar period, see Évelyne Cohen, *Paris dans l'imaginaire national de l'entre-deux-guerres* (Paris: Publications de la Sorbonne, 1999)—on opinions regarding the beautiful and the ugly.

35. Charles Péguy, "De la situation faite au parti intellectuel dans le monde moderne devant les accidents de la gloire temporelle," Premier cahier de la neuvième série (6 Oct. 1907), in *Charles Péguy, Oeuvres en prose, 1898–1908* (Paris: Gallimard, 1959), pp. 1167–78.

36. Jean Bastié, *Paris de 1945 à 2000* (Paris: Hachette, 2000), p. 713.

37. Bonnet, *Les grandes métropoles mondiales*, p. 144. For comparisons of the metropolitan areas, see Jacqueline Beaujeu-Garnier, *Paris: hasard ou prédestination? Une géographie de Paris* (Paris: Hachette, 1993).

38. Bonnet, *Les grandes métropoles mondiales*, p. 52.

39. *Paris en chiffres*, no. 5 (June–Aug. 1999), last page (no pag.) and no. 6 (Sept.–Nov. 1999), last page.

40. Bastié, *Paris de 1945 à 2000*, p. 21.

41. Ibid., p. 32.

42. The explanation of the 70 million figure does not come until much later in Bastié's book, on p. 183. See also "Paris séduit les touristes et Parisiens," *À Paris* [the municipality's magazine], no. 19 (June–July 2006), p. 13—with a reported 15.4 million checking into Parisian hotels (+14%) for a total of 33.7 million nights (+6.6%) in 2005.

43. *Paris en chiffres*, no. 4 (Mar.–May 1999), the (unnumbered) last page.

44. Bastié, *Paris de 1945 à 2000*, p. 707.

45. Ibid., pp. 31, 708, 712.

46. Ibid., pp. 25–26, 30. According to Bastié (p. 34), Greater Paris comes in fifth in the world for its gross domestic product—after Tokyo, New York, Los Angeles, and Osaka (Tokyo leads with 854 billion dollars). Paris with its total of 318 billion dollars is ahead of London (London's total is 267 billion). The "P.I.B. [gross domestic product] (in billions of dollars) comprises all forms of income (salaries, wages, pensions, etc.) rents and other real estate earnings, profits, and interest." A graphic in the concluding chapter (p. 708) shows with a large black sphere (representing forty firms) that "the headquarters of the largest world companies . . . are more numerous in Paris than in London."

47. For the historical perspective of decline, see, for example, recent histories (both valuable and well executed) by Patrice Higonnet, *Paris: Capital of the World* (Cambridge, Mass.: Harvard University Press, 2002), and (though less emphatic about decline) Colin Jones, *Paris: The Biography of a City* (New York: Viking, 2004). Alistair Horne's *Seven Ages of Paris* (New York: Vintage Books, 2004) does not treat the years since Charles de Gaulle, but his chapter on "la Belle Époque" presents that period before the First World War as the historical apogee for Paris.

48. *Mémoires du Baron Haussmann*, vol. II (Paris: Guy Durier, 1979, reprint of 1893 edition), p. 315, quoting Félix Narjoux, Architecte de la Ville, *Paris, Monuments élevés par la Ville, 1850 à 1880* (Paris, 1883). The line about the overall coherence of a beautiful city came from a member of the Chamber of Deputies (Chastenet) in a speech of 11 Nov.

1908, quoted in Pierre Pinon, *Paris, biographie d'une capitale* (Paris: Hazan, 1999), p. 260. Péguy, "Accidents de la gloire temporelle," p. 1174.

49. Léon Bopp, *Paris* (Paris: Gallimard, 1957), pp. 363–64.

50. See, for example, the *Plan directeur d'urbanisme de Paris, Rapport* (Paris, 1959), pp. 42–43, and François Moriconi-Ebrar, *De Babylone à Tokyo: les grandes agglomérations du monde* (Paris: Géophrys, 2000), p. 31.

51. Germain Brice, *Description nouvelle de la ville de Paris* (Paris, 1706, 5th edition), p. iv. Brice was more restrained in the first edition (1684), declaring Paris merely "one of the greatest and most beautiful cities of the world."

52. Julian Green, *Paris* (New York: Marion Boyars, 1991), p. 55.

53. Brassaï, *The Secret Paris of the 30's* (New York: Pantheon, 1976), p. 1, and Léo Larguière, *Les Îlots insalubres et glorieux de Paris* (Paris: Laurier Noir, 1946). On the successive editions of Willy Ronis's photos since 1954, see Françoise Morier, ed., *Belleville, Belleville: visages d'une planète* (Paris: Créaphis, 1994), p. 20. On some notable Parisians' affection for the homely banlieue, see Louis Cheronnet, *Extra-Muros* (Lithographies originales par Georges Annenkoff. Paris: René Hilsum, Au sans pareil, 1929), preface by Jules Romains—Nov. 1928.

54. Péguy, "Accidents de la gloire temporelle," p. 1166.

55. Henri Calet, *De ma lucarne, chroniques* (Paris: Gallimard, 2000). The passages cited above are from an article "Au courant du coeur," first published in 1952.

56. Cohen, *Paris dans l'imaginaire national*, p. 327. A very few banlieue spots were named, such as the riverbanks of the Marne at Champigny and Bonneuil.

57. Mondion, *Paris Complete: A New Alphabetical Guide for the Traveller in Paris* (Paris: Alphonse Taride, 1855), p. 51.

58. On Sacré-Coeur, see Raymond Jonas, *France and the Cult of the Sacred Heart: An Epic Tale for Modern Times* (Berkeley: University of California Press, 2000). On the Eiffel Tower and the famous protest of elites, see Loyrette, "La Tour Eiffel," in Pierre Nora, ed., *Les Lieux de mémoire*, III: *Les France* (Paris: Gallimard, 1992), 3: *De l'Archive à l'Emblème*, pp. 475–503.

59. Évelyne Cohen points out the contrast of attitudes toward the Eiffel Tower and the statues in a superb section titled "Le Beau et le laid" in *Paris dans l'imaginaire national*, pp. 208–29. For the numbers of statues erected (see her footnote 408 on p. 209), she cites a thesis by Jacques Lanfranchi.

60. *Le Véritable Conducteur parisien de Richard* (Paris, Édition de 1828, reissued by Les Éditions les yeux ouverts, 1970), p. 22.

61. Pierre Citron, *La Poésie de Paris dans la littérature française de Rousseau à Baudelaire* (Paris: Éditions de Minuit, 1961), II: 158–59.

62. Ibid., 254, 256–57.

63. M. H. Port, "Government and the Metropolitan Image: Ministers, Parliament and the Concept of a Capital City, 1840–1915," in *The Metropolis and Its Image: Constructing Identities for London, c. 1750–1950*, ed. Dana Arnold (Oxford: Blackwell, 1999), pp. 101, 113.

64. In Charles W. Haxthausen and Heidrun Suhr, ed., *Berlin: Culture and Metropolis* (Minneapolis: University of Minn. Press, 1990), see chap. 2: "The Beauty of the Metropolis: Toward an Aesthetic Urbanism in Turn-of-the-Century Berlin," by Lothar Müller, and chap. 3: "A New Beauty: Ernst Ludwig Kirchner's Images of Berlin," by Charles W. Haxthausen. On Hitler's views, see Alexandra Richie, *Faust's Metropolis: A History of Berlin* (New York: Carroll & Graf, 1999), pp. 469–70.

65. Friedrich Sieburg, *Dieu est-il français?* (Paris: Grasset, 1930), p. 127. On the poetic

tradition of human body imagery for Paris, see Citron, *La Poésie de Paris*, I: p. 29—on Eustache Deschamps (1340–1410); pp. 53, 54—Ronsard; p. 119—Mercier; on others, esp. the Romantics—II: pp. 40–46—and their images of Paris's head, arm, hands, heart, etc.

66. On this poetic tradition of Paris as a person, see Citron, *La Poésie de Paris*, II: p. 17. Among music-hall revues from the turn of the century were "Paris qui chante," "Paris qui danse," "Paris qui marche," "Paris qui passe," "Paris qui rit," "Paris qui roule," "Paris qui tourne," "Paris retroussé," "Paris roulant," "Paris s'amuse," "Paris s'éveille," "Paris s'expose," "Paris s'lave," and "Paris s'tord"—listed in the *Almanach des spectacles* (1902), Tables décennale, 1892–1901, p. 112. More famous were the grand-spectacle revues at the Casino de Paris from 1918 through the 1920s: notably, "Pari-ki-ri," "Paris qui danse," "Paris qui jazz," "Paris qui remue." In song, the personifying tradition went on in songs of Francis Lemarque ("Paris se regarde"), Léo Ferré, and Jacques Brel, to mention only a few.

67. On Paris as a woman, see Cohen, *Paris dans l'imaginaire national*, pp. 297–99, in addition to Citron, *La Poésie de Paris*, II. On Berlin and London, see Patrice Petro, "Perceptions of Difference: Woman as Spectator and Spectacle," in *Women in the Metropolis: Gender and Modernity in Weimar Culture*, ed. Katharina Von Ankum (Berkeley: University of California Press, 1977), pp. 41–43. On the prevalence of the feminine image of Paris in posters, see *Paris Posters* (Paris: Henri Veyrier, 1982), and the introduction by Réjane Bargiel-Harry, p. 7.

68. Karlheinz Stierle, *La Capitale des signes: Paris et son discours*, translated from German by Marianne Rocher-Jacquin (Paris: Maison des Sciences de l'Homme, 2001), pp. 329–30.

69. Charles Simond, *Paris de 1800 à 1900 d'après les estampes et les mémoires du temps*, vol. III: *1870–1900 Troisième République* (Paris: Plon, 1901), p. 9; Jules Romains, *Puissances de Paris* (Paris: La Nouvelle Revue française, 1919). See also his *La Vie unanime* (1908, 1926). Romains also depicted Parisian groups and gatherings of all sorts (audiences, crowds, passengers) as distinct collective beings, each with its own character and moods.

70. Louis Chevalier, *Les Parisiens*, Quatrième Partie: Unité des Parisiens (Paris: Hachette, 1985), pp. 299ff.

71. Adam Gopnik, *Paris to the Moon* (New York: Random House, 2000), p. 207.

72. Ibid., p. 206.

73. Hénard, quoted in Prochasson, *Paris 1900*, p. 41.

74. *S.O.S. Paris Bulletin*, no. 16 (Dec. 1991), editorial, p. 1. For another example, see the introduction to *Le Guide du routard: Paris 1994–95* (Paris: Hachette, 1994), with a banner featuring the "Villages of Paris" across the cover.

75. On recovering the vanished old Paris through one's imagination, see, for example, the introduction to the 1994 *Guide du routard*, p. 11, by Editor in Chief Pierre Jossé. See also Claude Dubois, *En parlant un peu de Paris*, vol. 1: *Les chroniques de Titi—octobre 1981–octobre 1990* (Paris: Jean-Paul Rocher, 2001), esp. the preface—on the importance of nostalgia and a call to cherish the memory of Paname.

76. Peter Ackroyd, *London, The Biography* (New York: Anchor Books, 2003), p. 743.

77. Jules Michelet, quoted in Citron, *Poésie de Paris*, II: p. 243.

78. Cassis, *Capitals of Capital*, p. 273.

CHAPTER SIX

1. The view of Paris-paradise surrounded by purgatory is the way "many Parisians saw the suburbs" in the late 1980s, wrote François Maspero in his book *Roissy Express: A Journey through the Paris Suburbs*, trans. Paul Jones (London: Verso, 1994).

2. Alain Schifres, *Les Parisiens* (Paris: Jean-Claude Lattès, 1990), pp. 84–85.

3. One stimulating recent literary study is Karlheinz Stierle's *La Capitale des signes: Paris et son discours*, translated from German by Marianne Rocher-Jacquin (Paris: Maison des Sciences de l'Homme, 2001). Other excellent studies are Priscilla Ferguson, *Paris as Revolution: Writing the 19th-Century City* (Berkeley: University of California Press, 1994), and Christopher Prendergast, *Paris and the Nineteenth Century* (Cambridge, Mass.: Blackwell, 1992).

4. Michel de Certeau, *L'Invention du quotidien*, vol. I: *Arts de faire* (Paris: Gallimard, 1990, new ed.), chap. 7, "Marches dans la ville," pp. 139–41. This book has been translated by Steven Rendall as *The Practice of Everyday Life* (Berkeley: University of California Press, 1984).

5. Vincent Lepot, "La Perception urbaine: un exemple, le Centre national d'Art de la Culture Georges-Pompidou et le quartier Beaubourg à Paris," in *La Grande ville, enjeu du XIXe siècle*, ed. Jacqueline Beaujeu-Garnier and Bernard Dézert (Paris: PUF, 1991), p. 384. Lepot interviewed merchants, residents, and passersby, and he found that of the recent residents two-thirds of the visitors (young or middle age for the most part) "like this type of form completely" and appreciate its originality.

6. Jean Tulard with Alfred Fierro, ed., *Almanach de Paris*, vol. 2 (Paris: Encyclopaedia Universalis, 1990), frontispiece. The ship, castle wall, and fleurs-de-lis together became the official symbol in the mid-nineteenth century. The slogan, *Fluctuat nec megitur*, also dates from that time.

7. On métro lines and stations in Parisian memory, see Alexandre Arnoux, *Paris, ma grand'ville* (Paris: Flammarion, 1949), p. 122. See also Marc Augé, *Un ethnologue dans le métro* (Paris: Hachette, 1986)—an extended meditation on the métro and memory, personal and societal. The point is well illustrated by a famous scene in the 1937 movie *Pépé le Moko*, in which Pépé (played by Jean Gabin), homesick for Paris, excitedly recalls the métro stations in a conversation with a visiting Parisienne.

8. Schifres, *Les Parisiens*, p. 17; Arnoux, *Paris, ma grand'ville*, pp. 103–4, 113, 121–23.

9. Alexandre Arnoux, *Paris en forme de coeur* (Paris: Fayard, 1954); Captain Wray Sylvester, *The Nocturnal Pleasures of Paris, A Guide to the Gay City* (Paris: Byron Library, 1889), pp. 138–39.

10. Louis Blanc, "Le Vieux Paris," *Paris-Guide par les principaux écrivains et artistes de la France* (Paris: Librairie Internationale, 1867), p. 18: "les villes ont une âme, qui est leur passé"; "et leur beauté matérielle n'a tout son prix que lorsqu'elle laisse subsister les traces visibles de cette autre beauté qui se compose de souvenirs,—souvenirs terribles ou pathétiques, qui amusement ou émeuvent, qui attristent ou consolent, mais donc chacun renferme un enseignement et sert à entretenir la flamme de l'esprit." Léon-Paul Fargue made similar observations in *La Flânerie à Paris* (Paris: Commissariat Général au Tourisme, 1946), p. 1: "C'est cette accumulation de siècles, de constructions, de rois, de débacles et de triomphes qui a doté Paris d'une âme réelle, d'une âme que l'on sent frissonner dans les creux sombres des arrondissements, comme des violons qui s'accordent dans le berceau d'un orchestre. . . . "

11. Arthur Conte, *Nostalgies françaises* (Paris: Plon, 1993), p. 11.

12. Ibid., p. 206. The poll was commissioned by *Figaro-Magazine*, and SOFRES carried it out, interviewing 700 people.

13. Henry Rousso, *The Vichy Syndrome: History and Memory in France since 1944* (Cambridge, Mass.: Harvard University Press, 1991).

14. On the "battle of Paris" during the Algerian War, see Pascal Blanchard, Éric Deroo,

Driss El Yazami, Pierre Fournié, and Gilles Manceron, *Le Paris arabe* (Paris: Éditions La Découverte, 2003), pp. 176, 241.

15. On the bicentennial, see Steven Kaplan, *Farewell, Revolution: Disputed Legacies, France 1789/1989* (Ithaca, N.Y.: Cornell University Press, 1995).

16. For many more examples and addresses, see Jacques Verroust, *Paris des connaisseurs: les boutiques qui font l'âme de Paris* (Paris: Flammarion, 2002).

17. "Paris, ville contraste," *A Nous Paris! L'Hébdo du métro*, no. 14 (13-19 Sept. 1999), p. 1.

18. *Télérama hors série*, 1998, *Un Été cosmopolite à Paris*, p. 3.

19. Basil Woon, *The Paris That's Not in the Guide Books* (New York: Robert M. McBride, 1931), pp. 3-4, 5.

20. Gérard Noiriel, *Immigration, antisémitisme et racisme en France, XIXe-XXe siècle: discours publics, humiliations privées* (Paris: Fayard, 2009), chaps. 4 and 6; Ralph Schor, *L'Opinion française et les étrangers, 1919-1939* (Paris: Publications de la Sorbonne, 1985).

21. Louis Chevalier, *Les Parisiens*, Quatrième Partie: Unité des Parisiens (Paris: Hachette, 1985). Part Four is on "collective existence" and section III (p. 379) is on the "Parisian personality." Chevalier's generalizing and subjective argument readily provokes skepticism among scholars, probably even more in the minds of those familiar with recent revisionist challenges to his account of the "dangerous classes" in his influential earlier book, *Classes laborieuses et classes dangereuses à Paris pendant la première moitié du XIXe siècle* (Paris: Plon, 1958), published in English as *Laboring Classes and Dangerous Classes in Paris during the First Half of the Nineteenth Century*, translated by Frank Jellinek (Princeton, N.J.: Princeton University Press, 1981). For that revisionist criticism, see Barrie Ratcliffe and Christine Piette, *Vivre la ville: les classes populaires à Paris (1ère moitié du XIXe siècle)* (Paris: La Boutique de l'Histoire, 2009). Here it is important to note that Chevalier's observations on population density and sociability patterns are not targeted by that revisionist work. For French scholars' views of Chevalier's *Les Parisiens* and recent studies following up his notion of a long-term Parisian spirit, see the "Avant-Propos" of *Être Parisien*, ed. Claude Gauvard and Jean-Louis Robert (Paris: Publications de la Sorbonne, 2004) and, in the same volume, Marie-Claude Blanc-Chaléard, "Hier à 'Saint-Antoine', aujourd'hui à Belleville: les étrangers et le creuset parisien depuis un siècle."

22. Chevalier, *Les Parisiens*, pp. 386-92.

23. Ibid., pp. 402-5.

24. Claude Dubois, *La Bastoche: bal-musette, plaisir et crime, 1750-1939* (Paris: Félin, 1997), pp. 131-32, 173.

25. Claude Dubois, "C'est loin, Montmartre? Rencontre. Entretien avec Louis Chevalier," *Le Monde*, 22 Sept. 1985, p. xii.

26. Julian Green, *Paris* (New York: Marion Boyars, 1991), pp. 48-50 (his essay titled "A Secret City/Une Ville secrète").

27. Jacques Carton, *Paris* (Paris: Arthaud, 1960), p. 28. The everyday character of the city that this lover of Paris identified was a "Parisian spirit" that was a matter of "the taste for beauty" pervading the myriad activities of daily life—"a kind of painstaking insouciance, of elegance even in routine [*occupations machinales*]," attributable to a history in which arts and artisans played a large role. "You can feel [that spirit] palpitate even in the air," but only by walking can you enter into an "intimate communion" with it.

28. Parisians know best that traffic part of their city's physiognomy too, and the majority reacts in a spirit of complaint, registered with city hall regularly. See, for example,

articles on complaints of noise and pollution, reported in the municipal magazine *À Paris*, June and July 2003.

29. Julien Gracq, *La Forme d'une ville* (Paris: Librairie José Corti, 1985), pp. 1–4; Jean-Paul Clébert, *Paris insolite* (Paris: Denoël, 1952), p. 14.

30. Stanley Milgram and Denise Jodelet, "Psychological Maps of Paris," in *Environmental Psychology: People and Their Physical Settings*, ed. Harold M. Proshansky, William Ittelson, and Leanne G. Rivlin (New York: Holt, Rinehart and Winston, 1976), p. 118.

31. Rodolphe Trouilleux, *Paris secret et insolite* (Paris: Parigramme, 2002), with photographs by Jacques Lebar. Andrew Hussey's *Paris: The Secret History* (New York: Bloomsbury USA, 2007) likewise stretches the word "secret."

32. Gracq, *La Forme d'une ville*, pp. 2–4.

33. *Brassaï, Paris by Night* (first published in 1933; reprinted in 1987 by Pantheon Books of New York), not paginated. The other collection of photographs discussed above is *Brassaï, The Secret Paris of the 30's* (New York: Pantheon Books, 1976), not paginated.

34. Clébert, *Paris insolite*, pp. 148, 161, 216, 245.

35. Jean Bastié, *Paris de 1945 à 2000* (Paris: Hachette, 2000), p. 184—statistics from 1997 and 1998.

36. Anne Le Cam, *Paris pour le pire* (Paris: Arléa, 2002), p. 7. Parisians' complaints about foul odors and filth go back seven centuries, David S. Barnes notes in his book *The Great Stink of Paris and the Nineteenth-Century Struggle against Filth and Germs* (Baltimore: Johns Hopkins University Press, 2006).

37. Francis Jourdain, *Né en 76* (Paris: Pavillon, 1951), pp. 89–90.

38. François Loyer, *Paris XIXe siècle, l'immeuble et la rue* (Paris: Hazan, 1994), pp. 268–70.

39. *Zurban Paris*, no. 94 (12–18 June 2002), pp. 16–21.

40. Michel Pinçon and Monique Pinçon-Charlot, *Paris mosaïque* (Paris: Calmann-Lévy, 2001), pp. 249, 252–53.

41. Thierry Jonquet, *Jours tranquilles à Belleville, récit* (Seuil, 2003), pp. 22–23; Anne Steiner, "Les Cafés de Belleville," *Hommes & Migrations*, no. 1168 (Sept. 1993), pp. 20–23, 26. "The quarter is in the end the place where one feels at home," concluded the sociologist who conducted the study. In the same issue is the study of the African workers in Belleville: "Les Résidents africains du Foyer Bisson Aiment Leur Quartier," by Patrick Jedynak, pp. 26–28. Thierry Fayt, *La Notion de village à Paris: Charonne, un espace humain* (Paris: L'Harmattan, 2000), pp. 10–11; Isabelle Nataf, "Les Halles chic et choc," *Paris Villages*, no. 2 (1985), p. 42.

42. One carefully observed study is David Lepoutre, *Coeur de Banlieue: codes, rites et langages* (Paris: Odile Jacob, 1997)—on adolescent social life and attitudes in the *grand ensemble* Quatre Mille (35 apartment buildings) in the northern suburb of La Courneuve. Like almost all the abundant literature on the disadvantaged suburbs, Dominique Schnapper's edited volume, *Exclusions au coeur de la Cité* (Paris: Anthropos, Ed. Economoica, 2001) stresses that the housing projects and their residents are not integrated into the life of the suburb or city.

43. Maspero, *Roissy Express*, pp. 172, 177, 266; Tricia Danielle Keaton, *Muslim Girls and the Other France: Race, Identity, Politics, and Social Exclusion* (Bloomington: Indiana University Press, 2006), pp. 33–35, 87, 89.

44. On the Creole identity, see David Beriss, *Black Skins, French Voices: Caribbean Ethnicity and Activism in Urban France* (Boulder, Colo.: Westview Press, 2004). On Africans in the banlieue: Christian Poiret, "Ségrégation, ethnicisation et politiques territorialisées:

les familles originaires d'Afrique noire en région parisienne," in *Immigration, vie politique et populisme en banlieue parisienne (fin XIXe–XXe siècles)*, ed. Jean-Paul Brunet (Paris: L'Harmattan, 1995); and Adil Jazouli, *Une Saison en banlieue: courants et prospectives dans les quartiers populaires* (Paris: Plon, 1995). On women's complex identities and cross-cultural go-betweens, see Catherine Wihtol de Wenden, "Contre quelques idées reçues sur l'immigration," *Les Annales de la recherche urbaine*, no. 49 (Dec. 1990), pp. 23–29, and Caitlin Killian, *North African Women in France: Gender, Culture, and Identity* (Stanford, Calif.: Stanford University Press, 2006). On comparative differences in the experiences of Black Africans, Maghrébins, Turks, and Asians, see Mirna Safi, "Le Processus d'intégration des immigrés en France: inégalités et segmentation," *Revue française de sociologie* 47–1 (Jan.–Mar. 2006) pp. 3–48. For a succinct historical overview, see Tyler Stovall, "From Red Belt to Black Belt: Race, Class, and Urban Marginality in Twentieth-Century Paris," in *The Color of Liberty: Histories of Race in France*, ed. Sue Peabody and Tyler Stovall, (Durham, N.C.: Duke University Press, 2003), pp. 351–69; Jacques Girault, ed., *Seine-Saint-Denis, chantiers et mémoires* (Paris: Autrement, collection France no. 16, 1998); and Marie-Claude Blanc-Chaléard, "Hier à 'Saint-Antoine', aujourd'hui à Belleville."

45. Jacques Perry, *Rue du Dragon: étude ethnologique d'une rue de St-Germain-des-Prés* (Paris: Éditions et Publications Premières, 1971), pp. 463, 470, 476.

46. Stéphane Jourdain, "Société, heureux parisiens," *Zurban*, no. 115 (6–12 Nov. 2002), p. 14, reporting on an ISEE survey.

47. Milgram and Jodelet, "Psychological Maps of Paris," pp. 119–24—on Parisians' favorite quarters, their choice for a last walk and a place to live. A survey by the Institut français d'opinion publique (1973) found the same preferences—for the eighth and sixteenth arrondissements, the Latin Quarter, and the first arrondissement (pp. 99–103). Parisians also made it clear that they considered as attractions (*attraits*) the stores and shops (43 percent) much more than monuments (16 percent)—p. 103, *Les Parisiens aujourd'hui* (1973), unpublished copy available through IAURIF (1A 11476), 15 Rue Falguière, Paris. See also "Paris, Une enquête psychosociale," *Sondages, Revue française de l'opinion publique*, no. 2 (1951), p. 24, also showing Parisians' fondness for the quays, the Latin Quarter, the Champs-Élysées, as well as Montmartre and the Grands Boulevards.

48. See Martin Pénet, "La Chanson de la Seine," *Sociétés et représentations: imaginaires parisiens*, special issue edited by Jean-Louis Robert and Myriam Tsikounas (CREDHESS, No. 17, Mar. 2004), pp. 51–66. The all-time hit that captures all these facets of the Seine's life in Paris is "Sous les ponts de Paris" (lyrics by Jean Rodor and music by Vincent Scotto), which dates from 1913.

49. *A Nous Paris! L'Hebdo du Métro*, no. 13 (6–12 Sept. 1999), p. 3, "Le Paris de ..." by Julian Champ (interview with Patrick Poivre d'Arvor); no. 14 (13–19 Sept. 1999), p. 7, "Le Paris de Patricia Kaas, Shopping et flânerie"; no. 6 (7–13 June 1999), p. 2, "Le Paris de Jacques Higelin (Paris populo, Paris de la fête)" by Julian Champ.

50. "Paris vu par Loràmt Deutsch," interview by Sandrine Pereira, *Zurban*, no. 115 (6 Nov. 2002), p. 6.

51. Louis Chevalier, *L'Assassinat de Paris* (Paris: Calmann-Lévy, 1977), pp. 272–75.

52. Jules Bertaut, *Les Belles Nuits de Paris* (Paris: Ernest Flammarion, 1927), pp. 36–38.

53. Louis Chevalier, *Histoires de la nuit parisienne* (Paris: Fayard, 1982), p. 25.

54. Joachim Schlör, *Nights in the Big City*, trans. Pierre Gottfried Imhof and Dafydd Rees Roberts (London: Reaktion Books, 1998), and Simone Delattre's masterful study of nocturnal Paris in the nineteenth century, *Les Douze Heures noires: la nuit à Paris au XIXe siècle* (Paris: A. Michel, 2000).

55. Alphonse Boudard, *La Nuit de Paris*, photos by Yves Manciet (Paris: Pierre Bordas, 1994), pp. 19, 89, 116.

56. "Paris la nuit," *À Paris* [the municipality's magazine], no. 19 (June–July 2006), p. 19. A good variety of essays on night in the contemporary city can be found in *Les Annales de la recherche urbaine*, no. 87 (Sept. 2000)—notably essays on Paris nights by Thierry Pacquot and sociologists Michel Pinçon and Monique Pinçon-Charlot.

57. *Télérama hors série: un été à Paris*, 1997, "Paris villages," "La Bastille perd la tête," pp. 6, 10.

58. A survey sampling opinions of 500 representative Parisians in 1989 did not ask about notions of Paris's soul, but it did ask respondents to cite an image representing the city, besides "Ville Lumière," which the questioners themselves named as the most obvious answer. The answers given were predominantly the well-established images and clichés: Paris as a woman, "la plus belle ville du monde," "le vieux Paris," Paname, along with some unflattering ones, such as "Paris poubelle." On the question of which touchable monument best represents Paris, no consensus or majority choice emerged. Highest percentage of answers (35 to 40 percent of responses each) were for Bastille, Notre-Dame, Arc de Triomphe, and Sacré-Coeur. Michel Sarazin, "Sondage Urbanismes IPSOS, autoportrait dans tous ses sens," *Urbanismes & Architecture, Paris capitale majuscule*, 231–232 (Oct.–Nov. 1989), Dossier: *Paris, Capitale majuscule*, pp. 28–30.

59. The proposals of the ten teams appeared together in a 38-page special issue of *Le Moniteur des Travaux publics et du Bâtiment*, titled *Grand Paris: les scénarios des dix architectes* (2009) and in a large exhibit at the Cité de l'architecture & du patrimoine from April to November 2009. A variety of probing reflections on the regional question can be found in special issue of *Esprit*, no. 348 (Oct. 2008), "Les Chantiers du Grand Paris."

CONCLUSION

1. Richard Le Gallienne, *From a Paris Garret* (New York: Ives Washburn, 1936), p. vii. Le Gallienne describes himself as one of the "innocents abroad"—that is, one "of those for whom to live in Paris is a form of romance, something like living in Baghdad or Samarkand."

2. Pam Cook, ed., *The Cinema Book* (New York: Pantheon, 1985), part 1, "History of the Cinema," by Annette Kuhn, p. 52: ". . . the central paradox of stardom: that stars are both ordinary and glamorous, . . . both a person and a commodity, both real and mythical, both public and intimate."

3. Michel Maffesoli, *The Contemplation of the World: Figures of Community Style*, trans. Susan Emanuel (Minneapolis: University of Minnesota Press, 1996; original: 1993), p. 32—on style as an aesthetic framework that encompasses a profusion of images.

4. Georges Montorgueil, preface to A.-P. de Lannoy, *Les Plaisirs de la vie de Paris (Guide du Flâneur)* (Paris: L. Borel, 1900), p. iii.

5. Paul Cohen-Portheim, *The Spirit of Paris* (London: B.T. Batsford, 1937), p. x. For the recent period, writers Adam Gopnik and Edmund White have given us particularly vivid accounts of the Parisian commonplace: Edmund White, *The Flâneur: A Stroll through the Paradoxes of Paris* (New York: Bloomsbury, 2001), and Adam Gopnik, *Paris to the Moon* (New York: Random House, 2000).

6. The *repas de quartier* have been held each year since 1998, organized by local associations with subsidies from the Région Île-de-France. On the old-fashioned riverside cafés, see Kali Argyriadis and Sara Le Menestrel, *Vive la Guinguette* (Paris: PUF, 2003).

7. Julian Green, *Paris* (New York: Marion Boyars, 1991), pp. 51, 53. Music-hall star

Mistinguett's song "Ça, c'est Paris" (1926) described typical Parisian women in amusing and flattering vignettes before concluding with a triumphant shout: "That, that's Paris!"

8. Green, *Paris*, pp. 10–3.

9. Michel de Certeau, *L'Invention du quotidien*, vol. I: *Arts de faire* (Paris: Gallimard, 1990, new ed.).

Selected Bibliography

For an extensive bibliography on all aspects of Paris history, see Philip Whalen's compilation at the website www.h-france.net/bibliogparis2005.html. Alfred Fierro's "guide to research and bibliography"—over 300 pages long—is also still extremely useful: see Alfred Fierro, *Histoire et dictionnaire de Paris* (Paris: R. Laffont, 1996). For works since 2005 (Whalen's end point) or before, one can search topics of interest in the databases *FRANCIS* and *Historical Abstracts*.

The works listed below are wide-scope or long-view studies and a few others that have been particularly important for my themes. They represent a very small sample of the valuable and informative works on Paris that I could add—or that can be found in the more extensive bibliographic sources listed above. The primary works and additional specialized studies used in this book are cited in the notes for each chapter.

The place of publication for works in French is Paris unless otherwise indicated.

THE CITY AS A WHOLE

Agulhon, Maurice. "Paris, la Traversée d'est en ouest," in *Les Lieux de mémoire*, Tome III, 3, pp. 869–909. Gallimard, 1988. Translated into English as *Realms of Memory*, ed. Pierre Nora and Lawrence Kritzman. Trans. Arthur Goldhammer. Vol. III: *Symbols*, pp. 523–52. New York: Columbia University Press, 1998.

Bancquart, Marie-Claire. *Images littéraires du Paris "fin-de-siècle."* Éditions de la Différence, 1979.

———. *Paris "Belle Époque" par ses écrivains*. A. Biro/Paris-Musées. 1997.

———. *Paris des surréalistes*. Seghers, 1972.

Barozzi, Jacques. *Littératures parisiennes*. Hervas, 1997.

Bastié, Jean. *Paris de 1945 à 2000*. Nouvelle Histoire de Paris. Hachette, 2000.

Charle, Christophe. *Paris, fin de siècle: culture et politique*. Seuil, 1998.

Citron, Pierre. *La Poésie de Paris dans la littérature française*. 2 vols. Éditions de Minuit, 1961.

Cohen, Évelyne. *Paris dans l'imaginaire national de l'entre-deux-guerres*. Publications de la Sorbonne, 1999.

Corbin, Alain. "Paris-Province," in *Realms of Memory*, ed. Pierre Nora, I: pp. 427–65. New York: Columbia University Press, 1996. The original is in *Les Lieux de mémoire*, Tome III: *Les France*, vol. I: *Conflits et partages*, pp. 776–823. Gallimard, 1992.

Favier, Jean. *Paris, Deux mille d'ans d'histoire*. Fayard, 1997.

Ferguson, Priscilla Parkhurst. *Paris as Revolution: Writing the Nineteenth-Century City*. Berkeley: University of California Press, 1994.

Fierro, Alfred. *Histoire et dictionnaire de Paris*. R. Laffont, 1996; trans. Jon Woronoff as *Historical Dictionary of Paris*. Lanham, Md.: Scarecrow Press, 1998.

Gaillard, Jeanne. *Paris, la ville, 1852–1870*. L'Harmattan, 1997; original 1977.

George, Joselyne. *Paris Province: de la Révolution à la mondialisation*. Fayard, 1998.

Harvey, David. *Paris, Capital of Modernity*. New York: Routledge, 2003.

Higonnet, Patrice. *Paris: Capital of the World*. Cambridge, Mass.: Harvard University Press, 2002.

Jones, Colin. *Paris: The Biography of a City.* New York: Viking, 2004.

Kok-Escalle, Marie-Christine, ed. *Paris: de l'image à la mémoire. Représentations artistiques, littéraires, socio-politiques.* Amsterdam: Rodopi, 1997.

Macchia, Giovanni. *Paris en ruines.* Trans. P. Bédarida. Flammarion, 1988.

Moret, Frédéric. "Images de Paris dans les guides touristiques en 1900." *Mouvement social* (July–Sept. 1992), pp. 79–98.

Murat, Laure, ed. *Paris des écrivains.* Chêne, 1996.

Noin, Daniel and Paul White. *Paris.* Chichester: John Wiley & Sons, 1997.

Pinon, Pierre. *Paris, biographie d'une capitale.* Hazan, 1999.

Prendergast, Christopher. *Paris and the Nineteenth Century.* Cambridge, Mass.: Blackwell, 1992.

Prochasson, Christophe. *Paris 1900: essai d'histoire culturelle.* Calmann-Lévy, 1999.

Rouleau, Bernard. *Paris, histoire d'un espace.* Seuil, 1997.

Stierle, Karlheinz. *La Capitale des signes: Paris et son discours.* Translated from German by Marianne Rocher-Jacquin. Maison des Sciences de l'Homme, 2001.

Sutcliffe, Anthony. *Paris, An Architectural History.* New Haven, Conn.: Yale University Press, 1993.

Wakeman, Rosemary. *The Heroic City: Paris, 1945–1958.* Chicago: University of Chicago Press, 2009.

Willms, Johannes. *Paris, Capital of Europe: From the Revolution to the Belle Époque.* New York: Homes & Meier, 1997.

PARISIAN PLACES AND THEMES

Buck-Morss, Susan. *The Dialectics of Seeing: Walter Benjamin and the Arcades Project.* Cambridge, Mass.: Harvard University Press, 1989.

Chevalier, Louis. *Montmartre du plaisir et du crime.* Robert Laffont, 1980.

———. *Les Parisiens.* Hachette, 1967.

———. *Les Ruines de Subure: Montmartre de 1939 aux années 80.* Robert Laffont, 1985.

Dubois, Claude. *Apaches, voyous et gonzes poilus: le milieu parisien du début du siècle aux années soixante.* Parigramme/CPL, 1996.

———. *La Bastoche: bal-musette, plaisir et crime (1750–1939).* Félin, 1997.

Faure, Alain, ed. *Les Premiers banlieusards: aux origines des banlieues de Paris, 1860–1940.* Grâne: Créaphis, 1991.

Fourcaut, Annie, Emmanuel Bellanger, and Mathieu Flonneau, eds. *Paris/Banlieues: conflits et solidarités: historiographie, anthologie, chronologie, 1788–2006.* Grâne: Créaphis, 2007.

Gérôme, Noëlle, Danielle Tartakowsky, and Claude Willard, eds. *La Banlieue en fête: de la marginalité urbaine à l'identité culturelle.* Saint-Denis: Presses universitaires de Vincennes, 1988.

Jacquemet, Gérard. *Belleville au XIX siècle: du faubourg à la ville.* Éditions de l'École des Hautes Études en Sciences sociales, 1984.

Jobs, Richard Ivan. *Riding the New Wave: Youth and the Rejuvenation of France after the Second World War.* Stanford, Calif.: Stanford University Press, 2007.

Kaspi, André and Antoine Marès, eds. *Le Paris des étrangers depuis un siècle.* Imprimerie nationale, 1989.

Kuisel, Richard. *Seducing the French: The Dilemma of Americanization.* Berkeley: University of California Press, 1993.

Levenstein, Harvey. *Seductive Journey: American Tourists in France from Jefferson to the Jazz Age*. Chicago: University of Chicago Press, 1998.

———. *We'll Always Have Paris: American Tourists in France since 1930*. Chicago: University of Chicago Press, 2004.

Lottman, Herbert. *La Rive gauche, du Front populaire à la guerre froide*. Seuil, 1981. *The Left Bank*. Chicago: University of Chicago Press, 1998.

Milza, Pierre and Antoine Marès, eds. *Le Paris des étrangers depuis 1945*. Publications de la Sorbonne, 1994.

Robert, Jean-Louis and Danielle Tartakowsky, eds. *Paris le peuple, XVIIIe–XXe siècle*. Publications de la Sorbonne, 1999.

Ross, Kristin. *Fast Cars, Clean Bodies: Decolonization and the Reordering of French Culture*. Cambridge, Mass.: MIT Press, 1995.

Rearick, Charles. *The French in Love and War: Popular Culture in the Era of the World Wars*. New Haven, Conn.: Yale University Press, 1997.

———. *Pleasures of the Belle Époque: Entertainment and Festivity in Turn-of-the-Century France*. New Haven, Conn.: Yale University Press, 1985.

Réda, Jacques. *Les Ruines de Paris*. Gallimard, 1993.

Rouleau, Bernard. *Villages et faubourgs de l'ancien Paris: histoire d'un espace urbain*. Seuil, 1985.

Schwartz, Vanessa R. *Spectacular Realities: Early Mass Culture in Fin-de-siècle Paris*. Berkeley: University of California Press, 1998.

Stovall, Tyler. *Paris Noir: African Americans in the City of Light*. Boston: Houghton Mifflin, 1996.

———. *The Rise of the Paris Red Belt*. Berkeley: University of California Press, 1990.

Winter, J. M. and Jean-Louis Robert, eds. *Capital Cities at War: Paris, London, Berlin 1914–1919*. Cambridge, UK: Cambridge University Press, 1997.

URBANISM AND ARCHITECTURAL HISTORY

Ambroise-Rendu, Marc. *Paris-Chirac: prestige d'une ville, ambition d'un homme*. Plon, 1987.

Chaslin, François. *Les Paris de François Mitterrand: histoire des grands projets d'architecture*. Gallimard, 1985.

Chevalier, Louis. *L'Assassinat de Paris*. Calmann-Lévy, 1977. Translated into English by David P. Jordan as *The Assassination of Paris*. Chicago: University of Chicago Press, 1994.

Cohen, Jean-Louis and André Lortie. *Des Fortifs au périf: Paris, les seuils de la ville*. Picard, 1991.

Coing, Henri. *Rénovation urbaine et changement social*. Les Éditions ouvrières, 1966.

Cornu, Marcel. *La Conquête de Paris*. Mercure de France, 1972.

Dufau, Pierre and Albert Laprade. *Pour ou contre la démolition de Paris*. Berger-Levrault, 1967.

Éveno, Claude and Pascale de Mezamat, eds. *Paris perdu: quarante ans de bouleversements de la ville*. Éditions Carré, 1991.

Evenson, Norma. *Paris: A Century of Change*. New Haven, Conn.: Yale University Press, 1979.

Fermigier, André. *La Bataille de Paris*. Gallimard, 1991.

Jordan, David P. *Transforming Paris: The Life and Labors of Baron Haussmann*. New York: Free Press, 1995.

Lavedan, Pierre. *Histoire de l'urbanisme à Paris*. Nouvelle Histoire de Paris. Hachette, 1975 (2nd ed., avec un complément bibliographique et un supplément 1974–1993 par Jean Bastié, 1993).

Loyer, François. *Paris Nineteenth Century: Architecture and Urbanism*. Trans. Charles Lynn Clark. New York: Abbeville, 1988. Original: *Paris XIXe siècle* (1987).

Picon-Lefebvre, Virginie. *Paris—Ville moderne: Maine-Montparnasse et la Défense, 1950–1975*. Norma, 2003.

Pillement, Georges. *Paris Poubelle*. Jean-Jacques Pauvert, 1974.

Pinkney, David H. *Napoleon III and the Rebuilding of Paris*. Princeton, N.J.: Princeton University Press, 1958.

Sutcliffe, Anthony. *The Autumn of Central Paris: The Defeat of Town Planning, 1850–1970*. London: E. Arnold, 1970.

Texier, Simon. *Paris contemporain: de Haussmann à nos jours, une capitale à l'ère des métropoles*. Parigramme, 2005.

Voldman, Danièle. *La Reconstruction des villes françaises de 1940 à 1954: histoire d'une politique*. L'Harmattan, 1997.

Index

Italicized page numbers refer to illustrations.

Algerians in Paris and suburbs,
102, 147, 148, 193
Americanization, 26, 92
Anti-semitism: 195; fin-de-siècle, 39, 41,
62, 65; circa 1930, 59; Second World
War, 71, 73; memory of Second World
War, 148, 153–154, 191–192, *192*;
contemporary, 148
Apache: dance, 123; delinquents, 32, 47, 66
Aragon, Louis, 48
Art: museums, 14, 172; Parisian creativity and
market, 19, 86, 121, 166, 167, 173
Art nouveau: Castel Béranger, 199; Guimard
métro entry, *45*, 49, 79, 80; Maxim's, 54,
215; "Modern style" scorned, 60–61, 62
Artists: Left Bank, 51, 83; for Les Halles, 106;
at Maxim's, 55, 56; Montmartre, 29, 30,
79
Associations, 110, 115, 134
Atget, Eugène, 25, 40, 59
Automobiles: circa 1900, 8, 19, 38; post-1945,
86, 92–93, 113, 121
Aymé, Marcel, 78, 79

Babylon, as metaphor for Paris, 6, 36, 41, 168
Bal Bullier, 30
Bals musettes (accordion dance halls), 32, 122,
144, 191
Baltard pavilions, 104, 106–107
Balzac, Honoré de, 86, 187, 194
Banlieue. See Suburbs
Bastié, Jean, 172–174
Baudelaire, Charles, 187, 212, 225
Beaubourg Center (Centre Pompidou): and
Les Halles pavilions, 106; planning
and construction, 110, 113–114; public
reception of, 120, 150, 179, 188, 202, 225
Beauty of Paris: in comparison, 168, 174–182,
176, 185; French writers on, 8, 9, 18,
70; Les Halles quarter, 105; and the
less attractive, 225; Louis Chevalier on,
211–212; monuments and vistas, 154,
178–180; "most beautiful city," 18, 169;
travelers and guidebooks on, 6, 7, 69, 227
Beauvoir, Simone de, 83
Belle Époque: memory of, 4, 44, *45*; period
label, 76; wax museum figures, 116
Belleville: artists in, 151; ethnic diversity,
146; and Paname, 37; anti-urbanist
mobilization, 134, 209; night, 212; as Old

Paris, 176, 204; Parc de, *181*, 204; urban
renewal, 97, 132, 204–206; young women
circa 1900, 35
Benjamin, Walter, 18
Bercy, 133, 134
Berlin: gendered image, 182; nineteenth
century, 161–162, 163; interwar years, 69,
165; twentieth century, 139, 157, 165, 167,
180–182
Bernhardt, Sarah, 57, 62
Bibliothèque nationale, 103; Bibliothèque
nationale de France, 140, 143, 217
Billy, André, 8, 9, 29
Blanc, Louis, 17, 21, 190
Bohemians, 29, 50, 51, 59
Bois de Boulogne, 75, 170, 176, 178, 212–213
Boudard, Alphonse, 214–215, 218
Boulevards. *See* Grands Boulevards and Streets
"Boulevard du crime," 26
Boulevard périphérique, 93, 220
Brassaï (Gyula Halász), 40, 176, 199–200
Brothels, 36. *See also* Prostitutes
Bruant, Aristide, 30, 32, 39, 53, 57, 58, 62, 66
Buffet, Eugénie, 39
Buttes-aux-Cailles, 52, 134

Cafés and bistros: 38, 52, 54, 80, 94,
104; contemporary, 152, 213, 217
Cafés-concerts, 38, 54, 60, 62, 74
Cain, Georges, 26
Canal Saint-Martin, 199, 204, 209, 209–210
Cancan, 33, 55, 58, 76 (movie *French Cancan*),
116, 122, 226
Capital (world center), 138, 164, 170
"Capital of the arts," 86
"Capital of the world": "Capital of the
civilized world," 7, 69; "cultural capital
of Europe," 138; "cultural capital of the
world," 105; post-1945 claim, 83, 138,
157; title of book (1867), 15, 16, 26
"Capital of pleasures": 2, 26–29, 44, 45, 128,
170, 186; "place of delights," 6. *See also*
Gaiety
Caran d'Ache (Emmanuel Poiré), 30, 55, 56
Carco, Francis, 50, 51, 67, 79, 198
Carné, Marcel, 40
Casque d'or, 134, 210; movie, 66, 76, 231, 233
Centrequatre, 151
Champs-Élysées, Avenue des: beauty, 133, 136,
169, 178, *179*; pre-1900, 17, 22, 62, 141;
post-1918, 55, 66; Second World War, 72,
72, 73; contemporary celebrations on, 216

Charpentier, Claude, 78,
Chat Noir, 30, 53
Chéret, Jules, 35, 56
Chéronnet, Louis, 63–64
Chevalier, Louis: 149; the city assassinated,
107–108, 188, 218; on love of Paris and
its beauty, 211–212; on night, 213; on
Parisians, 183, 186, 196, 197–198
Chevalier, Maurice, 39–40
Chirac, Jacques: as mayor, 115, 125, 126, 129,
134, 136, 138; as president, 143, 192
Cinema, 63, 139
Cinemas, 54, 122
City of Light. *See* "Ville Lumière"
Clair, René, 40, 67, 76
Claudius-Petit, Eugène, 87
Clébert, Jean-Paul, 200–201
Coing, Henri, 94
Commission du Vieux Paris, 48–49, 75
Commune of Paris (1871), 17–18;
commemoration, 154, *155*; Hôtel de
Ville in ruins, 42; memory of, 41; palace
destroyed, 178; *pétroleuses*, 34, 37;
strongholds of, 129, 132
Cosmopolitan Paris: architectural imports,
170; nineteenth century, 7, 17, 163;
contemporary suburbs, 148; contemporary
"world city," 193–194; late twentieth
century, 144–145, 152, 156, 173. *See also*
World city
Culture—state and city programs, 125–127,
130–131, 142–143, 150, 151

Dance halls, 30, 33, 38, 52, 53, 122
Davis, Richard Harding, 13, 31
De Gaulle, Charles, 85, 99, 104, 191
De-industrialization of Paris, 90–91, 113, 128,
149
Delanoë, Bertrand, 127, 193, 215
Delvau, Alfred, 26, 36
Demolition operations: nineteenth century, 11,
12, 21; twentieth century, 48, 94, 97, 98,
118 (Halles quarter), 204
Demonstrations, 152–153, *152*
Deutsch, Lorànt, 211
Disneyland Paris, 150–151, 217
District of the Region of Paris, 101
Dives (*assommoirs*), 31–32, 33, 53, 200
Dogs, 136–137
Doisneau, Robert, 40, 197
Dorgelès, Roland, 51
Drancy, 73, 192–193
Dreyfus affair, 39, 40, 60, 62, 65, 193
Drumont, Édouard, 25, 73
Dubois, Claude, 144, 149, 197, 218
du Camp, Maxim, 29

Eiffel Tower: lighting, 83, 212; protests against,

92, 93, 179; as symbol, 19, 41, 80, 188;
as tourist attraction, 19, 73 (Hitler's
visit), 114, 120, 202; view from, 180
Entertainments: late eighteenth century, 10
(vulgar); nineteenth century, 26–27, 29,
30, 34, 61; 1920s, 53; 1970s-90s, 119),
122; contemporary, 152, 173, 215
Exotica, 61, 194, 195
Exposition, colonial, 151
Exposition, international (1937), 151
Exposition universelle project for 1989, 139
Expositions universelles, world's fairs: 28; in
1855 and 1867, 14, 17; in 1878, 18; in
1889, 19, 25, 27; in 1900, 13, 25, 27, 35,
61, 76
Expressway. *See* Streets

Fargue, Léon-Paul, 64, 75
Fashion and haute couture, 35, 167, 173
Festivals, festivity: 125, 126, 130–131; Africa-
Fête, 145; Bastille Day, 131, 134; recent
creations, 153; in suburbs, 215
Fête de la Musique, 126
Fête de l'Humanité, 124–125
Feydeau, Georges, 56, 67
Fifth Republic, 85
First World War. *See* World War I
Flâneurs, 187, 199
Flanner, Janet, 76, 77
Folies-Bergère, 56–57, 83, 122, 200
Foreigners in Paris: 59, 67, 128–129, 133, 160;
in banlieue, 146–148; imaginings by, 226
Fortifs (fortifications), 46–47, 243n3
Forum des Halles, 111, 116–117
Fournel, Victor, 25
Franciliens, 102
Franco-Prussian War, 17
French Revolution: bicentennial 138, 193;
Paris's role, 14, 18 (centennial), 19
Front de Seine, 108, 109, 118

Gaiety, 27, 121–122, 139 (*joie de vivre*)
Gautier, Théophile, 14,
Gays, 124, 133, 200
Giraudoux, Jean, 69, 165
Giroud, Françoise, 86
Giscard d'Estaing, Valéry, 88, 110, 112, 114,
120, 132, 142
Global City. *See* World City
Goethe, Johann Wolfgang von, 158
Gopnik, Adam, 183, 184
Governance—prefect and Municipal Council,
40. *See also* Mayor
Grand Paris, le: 219
Grands Boulevards: decline, 47, *47*, 55, 122;
fashionable pleasure center, 22, 23, 28,
198; filth, 8; traffic, *169*; memory of, 60,
63, 74, 75, 76; 122; rehabilitation of, 136

Grand Dukes, 54. *See also* Tour of the Grand Dukes
Grands ensembles, 101, 118, 132
Gravier, Jean-François, 85, 165
Gréco, Juliette, 83
Green, Julian, 1, 144 ("Paris in the plural"), 176, 189, 225
Green spaces, 112, 115, 118, 120
Guidebooks: early, 176 (1706), 178–179 (1855); *Paris-Guide* (1867), 17, 21, 162–163; circa 1900, 7, 9, 16, 18, 20; focusing on "pleasures," 27, 28, 35, 189; 1920s, 52, 69–70; of 1948, 182; contemporary, 194, 227
Guimard, Hector, 45, 49, 60, 199

Halles, Les (central market): 38, 68, 76, 201, 212, 214; in 1960s, 90, 103–108, 212; garden, 112, 114; quarter, 118
Haussmann, Georges-Eugène, 11, 18, 20, 21, 29, 48, 174, 176
Heaven and Hell (*Ciel* and *Enfer*) theme cabarets, 53, 79
Hell, as metaphor for Paris, 1, 7; dives, 53
Hénard, Eugène, 184
Higelin, Jacques, 211
Historical societies: 22; Commission du Vieux Paris, 25
Hitler, Adolf, 181
Hôtel de Ville, 42
Hôtel du Nord, 134, 199, 209
Housing: first residential tower, 91; inadequacies before 1960s, 75, 86; postwar planning, 87; redeveloped areas, 96–98, 115, 118, 132, 140, 149, 257n68; suburbs, 73 (Drancy), 87, 101. *See also Grands ensembles*
Hugo, Victor: 17, 21, 22 (*Les Misérables*), 86, 187, 197; on Paris's historical identity, 13, 130, 163, 183; 196; statue, 74

Îlots insalubres, 25–26, 68, 86, 90, 113. *See also* "Slums"
Images of Paris: 1; and Grand Paris, 219; human, 182; woman, 2, 6; 262n66. *See also* Paradise; Hell
Imaginary and imaginaries, 3, 36, 38, 186–187, 222–223, 235n3
Immigrants and their progeny: postwar workers in suburbs, 84, 102; in late twentieth century Paris, 129, 132, 133, 144, 146; in late twentieth century suburbs, 144–145, 195, 206–207; contemporary identities and cultures, 146–149, 206–207; Moslem women, 207
Immigration: hostility to, 16, 124, 153, 195; museum of, 151

Jussieu, 90

Kubrick, Stanley, 89

La Courneuve, 84, 101, 132, 149
La Défense: 87, 88, 89, 112, 116, 118, 120; Grande Arche, 140
Land-use plans, 120
Lang, Jack, 125, 126, 140, 193
Latin Quarter, 75, 102, 133, 208, 213
La Villette: project for park and museum complex, 115, 141–143; park, 141, 143, 153, 202; science museum, 150, 202
Le Corbusier (Charles-Édouard Jeanneret), 87
Left Bank, 83, 209
Le Pen, Jean-Marie, 145, 153
Liberation: 76–77, 130; plaques and museum, 153–154
Lighting, 13, 28, 70, 85, 122
Literature, popular, 21
London: 9, 18, 87, 170; compared with Paris, 160, 161, 163, 165, 166, 167, 180, 182, 184, 185
Louvre: 73, 114, 141, 150, 178, 202; Pyramid, 225
Love in Paris, 65, 197–198
Love of Paris: Chevalier on, 211–212; contemporary love of a neighborhood and select areas, 203–204, 208, 218; historic sources, 8, 9, 21; twentieth century, 87, 99, 199, 211, 219
Lowlife: nineteenth century, 22; slumming and entertainment, 30, 31, 32, 53; twentieth century, 66, 200, 201, 215

Mac Orlan, Pierre, 51, 59, 64
Maison de la Radio, 120
Malraux, André, 99, 166
Marais, 70, 75, 105, 133, 141, 209, 210
Markets, street, 131
Marne-la-Vallée, 101
Marville, Charles, 11, 12, 23
Maspéro, François, 149
May 1968, events of, 102, 123
Mayor of Paris, 110, 115, 117, 127, 134
Maxim's: 4, 54–55, 167; in the arts, 56, 67, 215
Memory of lost Paris: 235n3; nineteenth century, 23, 25, 26; post-"Great War," 49, 50, 51, 54–55 (Maxim's), 57–58 (Montmartre); circa 1930, 63–66, 64, 67; 1970s, 108 (Les Halles); strongest memories (1985), 191
Ménilmontant, 37, 39
Mercier, Louis-Sébastien, 9, 164
Métro (the Métropolitain), 24, 74, 101, 220
Michel, Louise, 155
Michelet, Jules, 163, 180, 185
Midinettes, 35, 80
Mirande, Yves, 55
Mistinguett (Jeanne Bourgeois), 56, 79

Mitterrand, François: cultural programs, 126; *grand projects*, 123, 140–143; and Institut du monde arabe, 140; and Opéra Bastille, 140
Modernity, Paris as: nineteenth century, 10, 15, 18, 19, 40; twentieth century, 65, 85, 92, 170
Modernizing: criticized and deplored, 15, 16, 20, 121, 155; neighborhoods transformed, 94, *95*, 96; nineteenth century, 14, 15, 20; post-1945, 84, 85, 86, 90, 94; postwar urbanist mentalities, 98–99; in 1970s, 109–110, 112
Montaigne, Michel de, 9, 20, 86, 202
Montmartre: cabarets and chansonniers, 30, 195, 196; nineteenth-century entertainments and pleasures, 29–30, 32–34, 198; twentieth-century memory and defense of, 49–52, 57, 78; view from, 180; wine harvest festival, 126, *130*; working-class, 37; young women, 35
Montparnasse, 51, 91, 133
Montparnasse Tower: emergence, 90, 91–92, 108, 109, 179; post-Pompidou, 116, 120
Morand, Paul, 61, 64, 65, 67
Moulin de la Galette, 30, 33, 74
Moulin Rouge: early years: 32–34; 1920s-1950s, 55–56; post-1945, 76, 116; contemporary, 4, 122, 215, 227
Musée d'Orsay, 80, 150, 202. *See also* Orsay, Gare d'
Musée du Quai Branly, 151
Museum-city, 86, 138, 149–150, 172
Music halls, 54, 56–57, 65, 79, 122
Mystères de Paris (1842), 21

Nanterre, 84, 102
Napoleon III, 10, 18
Neighborhoods: cosmopolitan contemporary, 144 (Oberkampf), 146 ("Chinatown"), 146 (Goutte d'Or); destroyed, 94–95, 98, 122, 197; nineteenth-century "villages," 21, 37–38; postmodern, 155–156, 217; soul, 218; surviving, 129, 134, 184, 203, 204, 207–208. *See also* Belleville; Paname
New towns (*nouvelles villes*), 87, 101
New York City, 88, 166, 184
Night: nineteenth century, 28. 38; 1930s (Brassaï), 200; late twentieth century, 122, 123; contemporary, 212–216
Nogent-sur-Marne, 106
Notre-Dame: as emblem, 198; and modernizing projects, 90, 93, 99, 109; and tourism, 83, 120, 202; view from atop, 180
Nuit Blanche (sleepless night), 128, 215

Old Paris (*Vieux Paris*): inventorying and remembering, 25, 26; world's fair reproduction (1900), 25; nineteenth century, 2, *11*, 17, 20–24, 24; twentieth century, 44, 178, 214; 1920s, 53, 55; 1940s, 78 (old Montmartre); 1950s, 176 (Belleville-Ménilmontant); 1960s-1970s, 98, 107; late twentieth century, 135
Olympiades, 96, 97, 132–133
Opéra Bastille, 140, 143, 179
Orsay, Gare d', 107, 111. *See also* Musée d'Orsay

Paname: contemporary mementoes and vestiges of, 219, 224–225; decline and death of, 123, 128–129, 149, 186, 197; meanings and sources, 2, 37–40, 52, 242n78; memory of, 67, 78; urbanist disregard for, 112; Zairean slang term, 145
Paradise, as metaphor for Paris, 6, 158, 159, 186
Paris et le désert français, 85
Paris horrible (1882), 22
Paris-Plages, 127–128; *127*
Passages (arcades), 48
Péguy, Charles, 169–170, 175, 176, 183
Pei, I.M., 141
People of Paris, 20, 27 (gaiety), 29, 186, 196
Père Lachaise cemetery, 177
Photographers and photographs: Eugène Atget, 25, 59; Brassaï, 199–200; Chéronnet, Louis, album (1932), 63, 64; Manciet, Yves (1994), 214; Marville, Charles, 23–24
Piaf, Édith, 39
Picasso, Pablo, 56, 83, 105
Picturesque Paris, 21, 22, 24, 48, 86, 135, 187, 224
Place des Fêtes, 97, 131, 204, *205*, 205–206
Pleasures: contemporary, 215; gastronomic, 7, 14; 27, 119; sensual and sexual, 27–28, 168, 198, 212, 213; 1920s, 52–53, 57
Politics, 40–41, 65, 67, 70, 124, 152–153, 155
Pompidou, Georges: on automobiles and expressways, 92, 93, 109, *124*; modernizing Paris, 99, 110, 119; on towers, 88, 89; on world trade center at Les Halles, 90, 111–112. *See also* Beaubourg (Centre Pompidou)
The poor and poverty: pre-1900, 6, 7, 10, 22, 33, 38, 141; twentieth century, 47, 104, 144
Popular Front, 153
Popular literature and newspapers, 21–22
Population: total and density, 37, 100, 101, 160, 164, 171, 183; world ranking, 165–166
Populism: politics, 39, 115; popular song, 38; writers, 149
Pornography and erotic photographs, 7, 35
Postcards, 25, 35

Postmodern: cultural shift, 123, *124*, 153; critiques of, 155; urbanism, 131
Poulbot, Francisque, 51, 79
Prague, 168
Preservationists: 21, 23, 25, 48, 78; Les Halles, 104–105
Prévert, Jacques, 176
Prostitutes, 22, 35, 36, 39, 66
Provinces: Parisian attitudes toward, 159; Paris's influence on, 16; relationship to the capital, 156, 162, 164–165, 193

Quarter (*quartier*): 38, 129, 135, 203; meeting multiple needs, 208

Radio, 145–146
Rimbaud, Arthur, 18
Rambuteau, Préfect Claude-Philibert Barthelot, 20
Rats, 7, 107, 118, 137
Region or "le Grand Paris," 219
Renoir, Jean, 76
Representations, 1, 220–221, 235n3
RER (Regional Express Rail system), 101, 111, 116
Resistance (Second World War), 77, 153, 154
Restaurants and dining, 8, 14, 65, 119, 166–167 (decline)
Revolutions, 18, 40, 41
Romains, Jules, 183
Ronis, Willy, 40, 176
Rue Nationale, 95
Ruins, 18, 42, 106
Rungis, 103, 104

Sacré-Coeur: as emblem of Paris, 188; opponents of, 40; 50, *155*, 179; as tourist attraction, 73, 202
Saint-Denis, 69, 84, 87
Saint-Germain-des-Prés, 82
Salis, Rodolphe, 30
Sarcelles, 101
Sartre, Jean-Paul, 71, 82–83
Second Empire, 10, 16, 17, 19, 28, 49
Secret Paris, 198–202
Second World War. *See* World War II
Seine: beloved, 177–178, 208, 209; feminine, 34; and soul, 218; 266n48
Sewers, 15, 201
Sieburg, Friedrich, 70
"Slums": circa 1900, 7, 22; circa 1930, 68; post-1945 shantytowns (*bidonvilles*), 101, 102; contemporary, 137. *See also* Îlots insalubres
Slumming. *See* Tour of the Grand Dukes.
Sodom, Paris as, 28
Songs: celebrating Paris, 159, 173; circa 1900, 38, 39; post-1918, 47, 52, 58, 66

S.O.S. Paris, 184, 259n32
S.O.S.-Racisme, 124
Soul, of cities, 21
Soul, of Paris: generalized sense of, 190; particular places of, 193, *194*, 209, 218; use in debate about modernizing, 92, 99, 197, 218
Spirit (*esprit*): 196–197
Statues, 40, 41, 74, 178–180
Steinlen, Théophile Alexandre, 30, 58
Streets: automobile traffic circa 1900, 8, 38, *169*; Avenue de l'Opéra, *12*, *15*; expressways, 93, 101, 109, 112, 120, 123, *124*; filth and odors, 8, 9; new (ninteenth century), *15*, 16, 17, 26, 80; new (twentieth century), 50, 68, 203; old (pre-Haussmann), 21, 23, 24), 25, *33*, 80; Rue de Lappe, 32; vehicle traffic, 38, 74 (Occupation period), 92 (post-1945); vendors, artisans, and entertainers, 21, 37, 191. *See also* Grands Boulevards; *Boulevard périphérique*
Street furniture, 45
Suburbs (*banlieue*): 44, 49, 68–69, 73, 176–177 (beauty); alienation in, 147–149; Drancy, 73; *Grand Paris*/Greater Paris, 100, 146, 219–220, 221; 101; festivals, 216; late twentieth-century growth, 165, 171, 176, 189; social networks, 206; youth, 116–117, 197 (*loubard*). *See also* La Courneuve; New towns (*nouvelles villes*); Nogent; Saint-Denis
Sue, Eugène, 21, 53, 202
Surrealists, 226
Symbols of Paris, 188–189, *192*, 218, 263n6

Tabarin, 53, 55, 79
Techno Parade, 153
Tiberi, Jean, 134, 135
Toulouse-Lautrec, Henri de, 30, 40, 55, 57, 58, 66
Tour Albert, 90, *91*, 154
Tour of the Grand Dukes, 31, 32, 53, 54, 202
Tourism and tourists: nineteenth century, 15, 18 28, 29, 41; post-1945, 83; 1970s-1980s, 119, 121, 122; contemporary, 138, 168, 202, 217; 1999 statistics, 172–173. *See also* Travelers
Towers (*tours*): circa 1900, 7; interwar Montmartre, 49–50; post-1945, 87, 88–91, 108, 112, 116, 154. *See also* La Défense; Montparnasse Tower
Travelers and visitors: descriptions and praise of Paris, 6, 7, 8, 10; expectations, 14

Ugliness: Berlin, 162, 180; London, 180, 185; Paris, 7, 225
University and scholars, 6, 17, 138

Urbanists and urban planning: 1950s-1960s, 83, 87, 90, 93, 98, 99, 103, 187; 1970s, 113, 118; under Mitterrand, 140–142; regional planning (*le Grand Paris*), 165, 219–220. *See also* Urban renewal

Urban renewal: Second Empire, 10, 11, 20–21, 37; early twentieth century, 26; post-1945: 83, 90, 94, 96, 107 (Halles quarter), 206; post-Pompidou, 131; anti-urbanist reactions, 109–110, 118, 134, 204, 210

Utrillo, Maurice, 51, 67, 78

Valéry, Paul, 70, 163–164

Vandalism, 21, 49

Védrès, Nicole, 76

Vélodrome d'Hiver ("Vél' d'Hiv'"), 79, 191–192

Veuillot, Louis, 16

Viaduc des Arts, 143

Vichy regime and policies, 71, 86, 195

Vienna, 20, 69, 162, 163, 165

Vie parisienne, La (magazine), 35

Villages of Paris: nineteenth century, 37, 38, 49; twentieth century, 52, 78, 94–95, 120, 129 (mayor's program), 131; contemporary cosmopolitan, 144, 147

Village-like social relations, 204, 206, 207–208. *See also* Paname

Villas, 204, 208

Villemain Square and Garden, 134, *135*

Ville Lumière/City of Light: nineteenth-century origins, 10, 12, 13–14, 19, 20, 41, 161; twentieth century, 70, 82, 112, 121, 212; contemporary, 139, 151, 225. *See also* Lighting

Villon, François, 59, 130

Warnod, André, 51, 58–59

"Warts" and defects: pre-1900 filth, odors, foul air, 9, 10; twentieth century, 44, 70, 85, 86, 103 (at Les Halles), 113, 136, 137–138; recent complaints, 202–203; traffic and noise, 137, 138. *See also* Rats and Restaurants

Willette, Adolphe-Léon, 30, 51

Woman, Paris as, 9, 18 (*putain*), 34–37, 182, 186, 188

Women (*Parisiennes*): Second Empire, 16; late nineteenth century and Belle Époque, 35–38, *36*; twentieth-century descriptions, 196, 224; twentieth-century memory of, 61, 64–65, 80, 186

"World," as description of Paris, 1, 163

World city and global city: 156–157; rankings, 172, 174

Workers, 37, 94, 128, 132, 159

World War I (First World War), 44, 46, 47

World War II (Second World War): memory of, 154, 191, *192*, 257n75; Occupation, 71–82; statues destroyed, 180

World's Fairs. *See* Expositions universelles

Xenophobia, 16, 39, 59, 60, 67, 195

Youth: pre-1914 fun, 213; early 1960s, 99–100, 102; post-'68 culture, 123–124; concerts and sporting event venues, 216; contemporary *banlieues*, 116, 147; festivities, 153; night life, 213–214, 215, 217

Zénith, 143, 255n48

Zola, Émile, 22, 74, 187